Educational Planning

A Reappraisal

ORGANISATION FOR ECONOMIC CO-OPERATION AND DEVELOPMENT

Pursuant to article 1 of the Convention signed in Paris on 14th December, 1960, and which came into force on 30th September, 1961, the Organisation for Economic Co-operation and Development (OECD) shall promote policies designed:

- to achieve the highest sustainable economic growth and employment and a rising standard of living in Member countries, while maintaining financial stability, and thus to contribute to the development of the world economy;
- to contribute to sound economic expansion in Member as well as non-member countries in the process of economic development; and
- to contribute to the expansion of world trade on a multilateral, non-discriminatory basis in accordance with international obligations.

The Signatories of the Convention on the OECD are Austria, Belgium, Canada, Denmark, France, the Federal Republic of Germany, Greece, Iceland, Ireland, Italy, Luxembourg, the Netherlands, Norway, Portugal, Spain, Sweden, Switzerland, Turkey, the United Kingdom and the United States. The following countries acceded subsequently to this Convention (the dates are those on which the instruments of accession were deposited): Japan (28th April, 1964), Finland (28th January, 1969), Australia (7th June, 1971) and New Zealand (29th May, 1973).

The Socialist Federal Republic of Yugoslavia takes part in certain work of the OECD (agreement of 28th October, 1961).

Publié en français sous le titre:

LA PLANIFICATION
DE L'ENSEIGNEMENT
Vers une réévaluation

© OECD, 1983
Application for permission to reproduce or translate
all or part of this publication should be made to:
Director of Information, OECD
2, rue André-Pascal, 75775 PARIS CEDEX 16, France.

TABLE OF CONTENTS

Preface 7

Part One
THE EVOLUTION OF EDUCATIONAL
PLANNING CONCEPTS AND APPROACHES

Chapter 1

    AN OVERVIEW (C. Soumelis)..................... 12

      I. The Educational Planning Process and
         the Factors Affecting its Evolution 12
     II. Future Educational Policy Preoccupations
        and the Role of Educational Planning 27
  Annex. The Practice of Technocratic Educational
        Planning...................................... 44

Chapter 2

    EDUCATIONAL POLICY PLANNING AND EDUCATIONAL
    RESEARCH (K. Hüfner) 52

      I. The Evolution and Financing of
         Educational Research 52
     II. Educational Research : Different Types
        of Educational Research for Different
        Purposes of Educational Planning 56
    III. Educational Policy/Planning and
        Educational Research : Outline of an
        Analytical Framework 63
     IV. Conclusions and Outlook 69
    References 73

Chapter 3

    NEW FEATURES IN EDUCATIONAL PLANNING (K. Eide). 75

      I. Why Does Educational Planning Change ? .. 75

       II. Examining Process Qualities 79
      III. Field Testing 82
       IV. Action Research 84
        V. Partisan Counterfires 85
       VI. Dialectic Planning 87
      VII. Coping with the Environment 88
     VIII. Concluding Remarks 90

                        Part Two
            THE PRACTICE OF EDUCATIONAL PLANNING :
                     COUNTRY EXPERIENCE

Chapter 4

    EDUCATIONAL PLANNING IN COUNTRIES WITH
    FEDERAL SYSTEMS OF GOVERNMENT 94

    AUSTRALIA
       I. Introduction 94
      II. Organisation and Structure of Educational
          Planning 98
     III. Substantive Preoccupations and Areas of
          Concern 118
      IV. General Comment 129

    GERMANY
       I. Review of the Status and Perspectives of
          Educational Planning 131
      II. Issues of Main Concern in Federal Countries
          with Special Reference to Germany 151

Chapter 5

    EDUCATIONAL PLANNING IN COUNTRIES WITH UNIFIED
    SYSTEMS OF GOVERNMENT 158

    FRANCE
       I. Overview of Educational Planning in France.159
      II. The Integration of Educational Planning
          into the National Planning 186

    JAPAN
       I. Educational Progress in Post-War Japan 210
      II. Present State of the Education System
          and Educational Planning 213
     III. Educational Planning in the Overall
          National Development Planning 222
      IV. Future Tasks 224

    NORWAY
       I. Introduction 225
      II. An Overview of Educational Planning in
          Norway 227

                            4

        III. Organisation and Structure of
             Educational Planning 236
         IV. Some Areas of Special Concern 244

                        Part Three
               THE FUTURE OF EDUCATIONAL
                      POLICY/PLANNING

Chapter 6

    LONG-RANGE EDUCATIONAL POLICY PLANNING
    PERSPECTIVES IN OECD COUNTRIES : A REVIEW OF
    ISSUES AND POLICY PROPOSALS (J. Tinbergen
    and G. Psacharopoulos) 250

          I. Introduction 250
         II. From the Recent Past to the Near Future. 255
        III. The Demand for Education 258
         IV. The Supply of Educated Manpower 291
          V. Matching Supply and Demand 301
         VI. On Future Policies and Research 313
    Appendices 321

Chapter 7

    AN AGENDA FOR THE FUTURE : A FRAMEWORK FOR
    EDUCATIONAL POLICY PLANNING (G. Williams) 334

          I. The Background to Educational Planning
             in the 1980s 334
         II. Objectives and Priorities 340
        III. Attracting New Categories of Students .. 343
         IV. The Teaching Profession 346
          V. Buildings and Equipment 347
         VI. Finance 351
        VII. Planning Qualitative Change 354
       VIII. Problems of Uncertainty 356
         IX. A Final Recommendation 359
    References 360

Also available

PARTICIPATORY PLANNING IN EDUCATION (January 1975)
(91 74 08 1) ISBN 92-64-11259-6   390 pages   £5.40   US$13.50   F54.00

INTER-SECTORAL EDUCATIONAL PLANNING. "Document" Series (November 1977)
(91 77 06 1) ISBN 92-64-11698-2   308 pages   £7.30   US$15.00   F60.00

REVIEWS OF NATIONAL POLICIES FOR EDUCATION
(see OECD catalogue of publications)

INDIVIDUAL DEMAND FOR EDUCATION. Analytical Report (August 1978)
(91 78 03 1) ISBN 92-64-11803-9   120 pages   £3.40   US$7.00   F28.00

INDIVIDUAL DEMAND FOR EDUCATION. General Report and Case Studies: FRANCE, GERMANY, GREECE, UNITED KINGDOM. Bilingual (August 1979)
(91 79 03 3) ISBN 92-64-01922-7   386 pages   £9.30   US$19.00   F76.00

EDUCATION POLICIES IN PERSPECTIVE. An appraisal, by Maurice Kogan (December 1979)
(91 79 08 1) ISBN 92-64-12017-3   78 pages   £2.70   US$6.00   F24.00

Prices charged at the OECD Publications Office.

THE OECD CATALOGUE OF PUBLICATIONS and supplements will be sent free of charge on request addressed either to OECD Publications Office, 2, rue André-Pascal, 75775 PARIS CEDEX 16, or to the OECD Sales Agent in your country.

PREFACE

This book presents the results of the work carried out within the Secretariat and in Member countries in response to the decision of the OECD Education Committee for a reappraisal of educational planning. This reappraisal was deemed necessary in view of the general uncertainty which underlies any attempts to plan the development of educational systems in the years ahead. New problems are confronting these systems because of demographic and technological changes, contracting public budgets and competing new social needs for the scarce public resources, as well as the more general uncertainties which prevail about the future rate and pattern of social and economic development.

The reappraisal exercise had two main objectives :

1. to review how concepts, approaches and the actual practice of educational planning evolved during the past twenty years ; and
2. to identify new features of planning which could help educational authorities perceive and design future policies so as to cope better with prevailing uncertainties with regard to the development of education itself and of the broader socio-economic system.

A major problem for such policies is how to facilitate a new equilibrium between changing educational demand on the one hand and the responsive capacity of the education system on the other, and thereby make the most efficient use of scarce and in many cases insufficient financial resources.

The last twenty years were a period extremely rich in educational and broader social experiences, innovations, discussions and controversies. These took place against two entirely different backgrounds : the first half of the period was characterised by steady and unprecedented educational expansion accompanied by rapid economic growth and full employment ; the second has been marked by a grave economic crisis resulting in depressed labour markets which affected the demand for post-compulsory education, and in declining public budgets which affected the supply of education both quantitatively and qualitatively. In addition, the decline in birth rates has led to a diminution of enrolments at compulsory school level and to teacher surpluses in many countries.

An earlier attempt by OECD to evaluate the development of educational planning was made in 1970 as part of the Conference on Policies for Educational Growth. In that Conference the focus was primarily placed on the role that educational planning played in facilitating the expansion of education in OECD countries during the 1960s. The development of educational planning was particularly covered in three background reports (1).:

- <u>Educational Policies, Plans and Forecasts during the 1960s and 1970s</u> (Background Report No. 5).
- <u>Educational Planning Methods</u> (Background Report No. 8).
- <u>The Role of Analysis in Educational Planning</u> (Background Report No. 9).

More recently - and more limited in scope but very informative as to the role of educational planning in influencing national educational policies - was the analysis undertaken as part of the appraisal of the OECD experience with its Reviews of National Policies for Education (2).

The work done for the present reappraisal was undertaken jointly by the Secretariat and the participating Member countries with the help of outside experts.

Member countries were invited to submit national statements on the present state of educational planning, so as to allow matters of common interest to emerge and experiences to be shared. These statements were complemented by a synthesis report by the Secretariat and a number of expert contributions on long-range educational perspectives, new features in educational planning, and the relationships between politics, policy-making and planning.

This book has been divided into three thematic parts, in an attempt to give conceptual consistency to the large and varied number of contributions that were made to this activity. Part One, The Evolution of Educational Planning

---

1. <u>Conference on Policies for Educational Growth : The Development of Educational Planning</u>, Vol. VI, OECD, Paris, 1971.
2. M. Kogan, <u>Educational Policies in Perspective : An Appraisal of OECD Country Educational Policy Reviews</u>, OECD, Paris, 1979. See also : M. Webster, "Policy Planning for Education in OECD Member countries : Changing Perceptions and Emerging Concerns", Educational Policy Research Centre, Syracuse University Research Corporation, Syracuse, New York, 1970 (mimeo).

Concepts and Approaches, is made up of three chapters. The first chapter, An Overview, prepared by the Secretariat, attempts to :

a) identify the major factors which have affected the evolution of educational planning ;
b) assess the role that educational planning could play in the immediate and more distant future, assuming that the future socio-economic context will vary considerably from that of the past ; and
c) give technical information on how the so-called "technocratic" educational planning was practised.

The discussion has been influenced by, and is very much restricted to, the work done for the reappraisal activity.

Chapter Two, Educational Planning and Educational Research, by K. Hüfner, explains how much educational research had been neglected in the past and in turn discusses, on the basis of a model, possible communication links between planners and researchers. The application of such a model could facilitate communication between the two interlocutors, often operating in almost complete isolation from each other.

The third chapter, New Features in Educational Planning, by K. Eide, presents a number of features of educational planning which have tended to be neglected in the past and suggests several new approaches for educational planning.

Part Two, The Practice of Educational Planning : Country Experience, is made up of country contributions with two exceptions : the second part of the German case is based on K. Hüfner's initial paper : "Educational Planning in Federal Countries with special reference to Germany" and the second part of the French case is based on the initial paper by H. Tuchman on : "Educational Planning in the Context of Overall Socio-Economic Planning with special reference to France". The material is presented in two chapters : Chapter Four, Educational Planning in Countries with Federal Systems of Government, includes the cases of Australia and Germany ; Chapter Five, Educational Planning in Countries with Unified Systems of Government, includes France, Japan and Norway.

Part Three, Perspectives for Educational Planning, is made up of two chapters. Chapter Six, Long-range Educational Policy Planning Perspectives in OECD Countries : A Review of Issues and Policy Proposals, prepared by J. Tinbergen and G. Psacharopoulos, reviews a number of future crucial policy issues, suggests possible policy responses and outlines the role which educational planning can play in such responses. In Chapter Seven, An Agenda for the Future : A Framework for Educational Policy Planning, G. Williams presents a framework for educational policy planning as a guide to those responsible for such planning in individual countries.

Part One

THE EVOLUTION OF EDUCATIONAL PLANNING
CONCEPTS AND APPROACHES

Chapter 1

AN OVERVIEW

by
C. Soumelis
of the OECD Secretariat

I. THE EDUCATIONAL PLANNING PROCESS AND THE FACTORS AFFECTING ITS EVOLUTION

Educational planning as a process contributing to policy decision-making has always existed in one form or another. However, as an administrative function and a "scientific" specialisation, it is hardly more than twenty-five years old and in many OECD countries even younger. Yet, it has experienced a remarkable development, particularly during the 1960s, as is shown by the number of specialised units set up in both central and local educational administrations, and the amount of intellectual effort which has been invested in the subject.

The national statements for the reappraisal activity revealed both the wide differences among OECD countries as to the conception, practice and structure of educational planning and the degree of evolution of the educational planning process in each one of the Member countries during the last twenty years or so. This evolution has also been systematically documented in the OECD "Country Educational Policy and Planning Reviews".

Several factors have been cited as responsible for the development, evolution and structural differentiation of educational planning. Among them the following seem to be the most important and they are discussed briefly below :

- External and internal goals of the educational systems ;
- Pressures from acute conjunctural problems ;
- Changes in the overall socio-political thinking ;
- The diversified administrative structure of educational systems ;

- Structural shortcomings in the educational planning machinery ;
- The particular interests of those responsible for educational planning.

A. <u>External and Internal Goals of the Education System</u>

A distinction should be made from the outset between "external" and "internal" goals of educational systems. External goals indicate the system's obligation to respond to the educational needs of its environment. Internal goals pertain usually to what is happening within the system for its survival, growth or well-being. The distinction between these two categories of goals is helpful in that it underlines the great influence which internal goals, whether manifest or latent, exert on the system's behaviour and very often in a way which either constrains the attainment of external goals or provokes their modification.

1. <u>External Goals</u>

In addition to traditional external goals of educational systems such as the <u>development of the individual</u>, the <u>promotion of knowledge</u>, etc., three major goals have received special attention from the late 1950s and throughout the 1960s, namely : <u>meeting the manpower needs of the economy, ensuring equal educational opportunities to all citizens and enhancing efficiency</u>. The first goal received high priority because national authorities had felt that without a sufficient number of well qualified personnel the objective of economic growth would have been seriously compromised. The second goal derives from the political obligation of Western democracies to offer equal opportunities to all their citizens, and the assumption that this could be met through the broad democratisation of educational opportunity. The third goal, efficiency, was introduced as a guarantee that the attainment of the other two goals, both of which assumed a continuous growth of education systems, would be pursued under conditions of economic efficiency.

The pursuit of these three external goals undoubtedly conditioned educational planning and gave rise to the three classical approaches to it ; namely : the "manpower", the "social demand" and the "rate-of-return" approaches, all well documented in the relevant literature (1). The "rate-of-return" approach, which takes into account the increased employment benefits stemming from every additional year of study over the employment life span of an individual, was

---

1. For a rapid review and evaluation of all three see : <u>Conference on Policies for Educational Growth : The Development of Educational Planning</u> : Vol. VI, OECD, Paris, 1971, pp. 69-138.

rarely used for public educational decisions (2). It was the other two approaches which mainly dominated educational planning, particularly during the 1960s.

The implementation of these approaches led to the notion of "technocratic" educational planning (3), as contrasted to the "political" or "conflictual" mode of planning (4). These two models were seen as the two extremes of a spectrum of possible modes of educational planning.

The technocratic model implies a clear distinction between the "policy-maker", or a policy-making group, and the "planner" or the planning team. The policy maker establishes a series of broad strategic objectives, such as "meeting national needs for qualified manpower", "equality of educational opportunity", etc., while the planner's role is to express these strategic objectives in operational terms and devise means of encouraging the educational system as a whole, or parts of it, to move towards the selected policy objectives. This distinction between the policy-maker and the planner, which derives from the inherent dual nature of planning the political and technical is still valid in many national administrations and is still advocated by several specialists (5). The question which was often raised, though it very seldom received an answer, relates to how the policy maker decides and sets these policy objectives.

The "political" model, on the other hand, denies the existence of any easily recognisable group of policy makers which sets strategic objectives. Instead, policies are made on the basis of a series of tactical decisions that emerge from the interplay of a universe of pressure groups of which no one is powerful enough to be able to impose its views on the others. The role of the planner, according to this approach, is not to build precise and detailed "plans" of how to meet particular policy objectives : such attempts are doomed to failure because they are certain to conflict with objectives of one or more pressure groups and some of the proposed means may be opposed, at any particular time, by one or more of the interested groups. Instead, the role

---

2. See for example : C. Soumelis, "Do Rates-of-Return Matter for Public and Private Educational Decisions ?", in Higher Education Vol. X, May 1981.
3. See Annex for a brief presentation of the practice of technocratic educational planning.
4. G. Williams, "Educational Planning, Past, Present and Future", OECD, Paris, 1978 (mimeographed).
5. "Towards a reappraisal of Educational Planning : Summary Record of the Discussions and Main Conclusions" of the Meeting of National Representatives and Experts, held at the OECD Headquarters, Paris, on 12-14 May, 1980, OECD, Paris, 1980 (mimeographed).

of the planner must be the tactical one of mediating between the different interests involved. It is the planner who has to be well informed about the nature and strength of conflicting pressures in order to establish a policy which will be the result of the various tactical pressures. Of necessity, the conflictual model denies the prospective function of educational planning and focuses only on short-term policies particularly linked to the annual allocation of resources through the budget.

Neither of these two extremes of the planning spectrum has ever been followed in its pure form, and for several good reasons. Even in the most administratively centralised western countries policies are not set on the basis of the political power of only one group. On the other hand, in the more pluralistic democracies, governments in power are normally the strongest single pressure group and they are responsible for interpreting and synthesising the demands of the various pressure groups. There has undoubtedly been a continuous change in the perception and practice of educational planning "from the quantitative technology of planning towards interactive, consultative and participative deliberation ; from convergent planning in which authoritative allocation can be decided towards multi-value assessments which will hold open a larger number of options" (6). But this does not mean that there is at present any clearcut idea as to where exactly the golden mean lies between these two ends and the discussions in meetings did not reveal any. The final form of the style of educational planning largely depends on the political process in operation in each country. In fact, as discussed below, it was the evolution of political thinking as it moved towards increased pluralism which has influenced the development of the political function of educational planning in the OECD countries.

During the 1960s an important shift took place, particularly in the more developed OECD countries, from the manpower objective to that of meeting the manifest social demand for education. The basic assumption underlying this shift was the belief that the satisfaction of social demand would have helped automatically to meet the manpower needs of the economy, leaving the distributive function to the labour market mechanisms. It was also assumed that the more complex external goal of equality of opportunity would be better attained by satisfying social demand, which in practice led to measures for the continuous expansion of all parts of education systems which was registered during the 1960s. It should be noted that educational systems have intelligently managed to attain external goals through growth which is one of the fundamental internal goals of

---

6. M. Kogan, "The Relationship Between Education Policy, Planning and Politics", OECD, Paris, 1980 (mimeographed) p. 1.

any system. However, the attainment of the growth objective did not lead, necessarily, to the attainment of the two external policy objectives. This was made evident at the OECD Conference on "Policies for Educational Growth" in 1970 (7).

Studies undertaken in the United States (Coleman Report), The United Kingdom (the Plowden Report), Sweden, France, Greece and elsewhere have clearly shown that school performance is greatly influenced by the social class from which pupils originate. In view of the organisation of educational systems and the practices followed by them, the satisfaction of social demand through an autonomous growth proved to be anti-egalitarian biased, in spite of its initial intuitive appeal to those who have claimed that educational opportunity should be as widespread and democratic as possible.

The fast growth of educational systems did not help the attainment of the economic growth objective either. From a manpower planning viewpoint, such uncontrolled growth resulted either in the over-production of certain types of educational output or in shortages of other specialities. One of the papers (8) prepared for the Reappraisal activity attempted to explain this observed mismatch between educational supply, which grew autonomously, and the demand for qualified manpower. It was argued that despite manpower forecasting efforts, wherever they took place, there was an almost complete breakdown of relevant information flow from the labour market to the individuals in the educational system to enable them to take appropriate decisions. This lack of effective labour market feedbacks resulted very often in a cobweb dynamic situation in the job market, particularly for college graduates, who seem to be influenced when deciding about further education by such labour market signals as salaries, unemployment, etc. The situation whereby education and the labour market are linked over time by cobweb cycles has been extensively documented in the United States. The author argues, therefore, that given this fact we cannot reject the hypothesis that a similar situation applies to other OECD countries. He maintains in turn that, unless some stabilising action is taken via educational planning, periods of graduate unemployment or vacancies for qualified personnel should succeed one another (9). It is thus evident that the efficiency" objective is not met. On the contrary, the observed mismatches and the wastefulness of resources which accompanied educational growth during the sixties gave rise to an accountability problem which became more obvious in

---

7. <u>Conference on Policies for Educational Growth</u> : <u>Educational Policies</u>, OECD, <u>op. cit.</u>, pp. 9-65.
8. G. Psacharopoulos, "Educational Planning and the Labour Market", OECD, Paris, 1978 (mimeographed).
9. <u>Ibid.</u>, p. 16.

the late sixties and early seventies, i.e. some years before the onset of the first economic crisis.

2. Internal Goals

Like all social systems the education system also pursues goals which have to do with its survival, growth and well-being. Because of the importance that educational systems attach to the implementation of these goals, even when this has to be done at the expense of external goals, there are many who think that educational planning was used by education systems for achieving maximum organisational consistency during their expansion period rather than for facilitating change, which is seen often as a threat to the system. To modify this attitude proposals were made for profound changes in the concept and practice of educational planning in order to upset the organisational balance reached in the past and facilitate changes in required directions (10).

Organisational and planning theory has attempted to explain this almost inherent conflict between external and internal systems goals with reference to the existing separation of the administration (administrative decision-making sub-system) from its executive supra-structure, responsible for policy-making. This separation, together with the permanent structure of the administration on the one hand and the less permanent structure of the executive sub-system of national administrations, facilitate the inherent tendency which social systems have to increase their autonomy vis-a-vis their supra-systems in order to pursue their internal goals. In such a situation, planning, having itself a permanent structure, associates itself more with the administrative sub-system than the executive policy-making one. This makes for a "slow, silent and almost invisible encroachment by administrative outlooks of the executive (policy-making), resulting in the patient erosion of what "can" be done by what "will" be done, which, in the natural course of institutional activity, is hard to distinguish from what "is being done" (11).

B. Changes in the Overall Socio-Political Thinking

Undoubtedly, changes which have occurred during the last twenty years in socio-political thinking in most of the OECD countries have influenced the evolution of educational planning, given the direct relationship which exists between the various political processes and the mode of

---

10. See Chapter 3 of this volume.
11. Ozbekhan, "Towards a General Theory of Planning" in E. Jantsch, Perspective of Planning, OECD, Paris, 1969, p. 139.

planning practice. Kogan argues, in fact, that the model of the majoritarian representative leadership, which allows a majority of citizens to determine political leadership and which in turn makes policies and decisions on behalf of the entire society, fits well with the centralised, quantitative and authoritative planning which prevailed in the early 1960s and was promulgated by the OECD. On the other hand political pluralism, and more so populism, both of which seek to maximise, although to a different degree, the direct decision-making capacity of the electorate thus limiting the discretion of "decision-makers", fit more with the notion of "participatory planning". Such planning attempts to appreciate the wishes of individuals or groups who are affected by certain decisions and therefore emphasises in practice such devices as public participative methods, social attitude surveys, cost benefit analyses, etc. (12).

The onset of the participatory educational planning movement was facilitated by the gradual political move, which took place in most of the OECD countries under the pressure of powerful political forces, from authoritative majoritarian government to practical, political pluralism. For the education systems, the turning point towards political pluralism coincides approximately with the 1968 events when university students as a pressure group demanded forcefully to be heard, arguing that government decisions did not reflect their educational aspirations and needs. It was the beginning of a sort of pluralistic era for the educational systems of many OECD countries. However, one could easily observe today that pluralism has not progressed much and does not seem to be a well accepted and established political process. OECD countries with long tradition in central administrative practices are still under the influence of traditional majoritarian leadership directly affecting educational systems and hence educational planning, despite an increasing demand for expanding pluralism. On the other hand, in countries with well-established decentralised educational systems, pluralism at the local level is more visible. Educational planning at the local level is becoming increasingly participatory, facilitating the expression of people's wishes or explicitly taking account of them in the formulation of decisions. At the macro level, however, where overall national policies are set, ultimate educational decisions are taken either by Parliaments or by Governments. At this level, participatory planning becomes problematic and educational planning has on the whole retained its technocratic nature. In many instances, however, even at that level, educational planning has begun to devise structures which could allow it to enlarge its scope by enriching its information base either through direct consultations and/or by surveying the needs and interests of all social elements involved.

---

12. M. Kogan, op. cit., p. 5.

In France, for example, as the French national report indicated, the mode of planning has moved, in the Commissariat du Plan, from a formal rigid plan for national action to an indicative one which provides general directives about desired national orientations and allows for continuous adaptation and change in response to new information. In addition, a political dimension was gradually introduced, balancing the previously extremely technical nature of the planning process. This was achieved through various consultative committees which serve as instruments for implementing the principle of participation at the national macro level. More particularly, the Commission for educational matters in the Commissariat du Plan, which was initially composed entirely of civil servants, now consists of representatives of all the social groups having an interest in education (13).

The argument for participatory planning was based on three main premises and objectives :

a) the broadening of the power structure of policy-making, to improve the capacity of decision centres to respond more effectively to the educational needs and aspirations of the interest groups involved ;
b) the enrichment of the information base for effective policy-making so as to ensure that all those concerned could effectively express their views, values and objectives ;
c) the educative value which participation in policy-making has for the individuals, various groups and the system as a whole.

At an earlier OECD meeting (14), there was a quasi-unanimous predisposition to avoid any sharp distinction between participatory planning and participatory decision-making. This was the first attempt to integrate planning functionally into the policy-making process or at least not to separate them as is the case with technocratic planning. There was, however, no consensus as to whether or not planning should be integrated into policy-making and to what degree. The inter-relationship problem between planning and policy-making became one of the major issues in reappraising educational planning. The issue is of extreme importance for the future role of educational planning, for most of the ineffectiveness of educational planning in influencing educational policies could be explained on the basis of the existing functional and structural separation of planning from policy-making. Since the outcome of the policy-making process is the end result of the interplay between normative political thinking and consequential policy analysis, the separation of policy-

---

13. See Chapter 5 below, p. 158.
14. <u>Participatory Planning in Education</u>, OECD, Paris, 1974.

making (political) from planning (technical) is rather arbitrary. Structural separation, however, might take place because of the need to increase efficiency through the principle of the division of labour.

Whilst Kogan keeps "politics", "policy-making" and "planning" separate, acknowledging, however, their strong interrelationship and overlapping, participatory planning, which has been seen as ".. neither an alternative nor a separate form of planning but ... a necessary element in any national planning for larger, complex systems of education" integrates planning to policy-making (15). The logic of this seems to lie simply in the fact that "preference functions" of large social systems, like education, cannot possibly be set in the absence of all those concerned, or if some groups feel they are being manipulated by others. Involving more people in the planning process does not necessarily imply that policies become more intuitive or political and the search for acceptable solutions less technical. On the contrary, participatory planning, which attempts the attainment of multi-value, multi-objective functions demands much more careful analysis of all factors involved, taking explicitly into account existing conflicts.

Thus, participatory planning, whether at the local or central levels, should not be seen as a power struggle among those involved in the setting of policies. It should rather be seen as a "technical" process whereby systematic and thorough policy analysis is taking place enabling conflicting views to be more clearly thought out, not necessarily to be reconciled, and accounting both for the actual demands of the participating groups and the future needs of society. The most powerful criticism against educational participatory planning is exactly the one which argues that there is a fear that those involved in the process will attempt to maximise their short-term benefits at the expense of the benefits of future generations. This attitude is particularly risky for educational policies with long-lasting effects. On the other hand, technocratic planning, which is very low in its participative intentions, seems to place more emphasis on the long term, thus neglecting the present as well as the qualitative aspects of education, concentrating almost exclusively on the quantitative ones.

These differences between "technocratic" and "participatory" planning create a real dilemma for those concerned with the practice of educational planning as to how much participation and how much technical quantitative analysis should be introduced in the actual educational planning process. There is, of course, no consensus among specialists

---

15. E. von Moltke, "The Collegiate System of the State University of New York/Buffalo", in *Participatory Planning in Education*, *op. cit.*, p. 217.

and practitioners alike about any particular model but there is general agreement that, if the technical aspects which technocratic planning provides are removed from the policy-making process, one is left only with pressure groups, and this may lead to an oligopolistic rather than a perfect competition decision-making situation.

This observation automatically raises the organisational issue in relation to the participation of various groups in the planning process. This is essentially a political problem whose solution can only be sought in accordance with the overall political traditions prevailing in each national setting. It seems, however, opportune to remind ourselves of the function of planning. According to Kogan, "planning in any of its modes and guises moves the process from the broader political system into government and somewhat nearer convergence and the closure of positions. Information is systematised and structured so that technical appraisals, facts and collations of different subjective valuations are brought together into some kind of logical hierarchy, or financial or social costing. In systems theory language, planning is part of the process of interest reduction. In that respect it may be high or low on its participative intentions, according to taste and fashion, but because it is involved in interest reduction it puts a high premium on convergence or at least in creating some kind of order out of eclecticism ; even when it eschews "hard techniques" it must use some technological and quantified approaches in its tasks. The recent acceptance that planning might be a process through which decisions are validated because of participation of many groups does not affect its role as serving decision-making. In principle, planning carries no authority but is seen as one means by which the impacts on the political system, of the main client groups and dependent institutions, are reconciled with the technical framework of demography, budget making and, increasingly, other institutional factors" (16).

The above, evidently, presents a rather conventional function of planning with, perhaps, an important difference : it does not seek consistency and optimal solutions but "convergence" which reflects compromises and which could be achieved at various political environments, although it shows a preference for convergence through increased political validation with a view to helping in the realisation of politically sound policies. It also provides some ideas about what organisational arrangements might be appropriate.

---

16. M. Kogan, op. cit., pp. 3-4.

C. The Diversified Administrative Structure of Educational Systems

All educational systems are structured horizontally in "sub-systems" according to the type of education they offer. Each of these sub-systems is in turn structured vertically in two, three or more administrative levels, namely : the school or other educational institution, the local, central and, where applicable, federal administrative levels. Decisions affecting the behaviour of the educational sub-systems are taken at each of these levels, each one of these being endowed with a different degree of decision-making authority. Planning, seen as a function of decision-making, is directly linked to these decision-making structures and the techniques and means employed are therefore a function of the complexity, uncertainty of the time horizon, and the size of the school population affected by each type of decision. It is evident that as one moves from the central down to the school unit the decisions become decreasingly complex and uncertain and affect fewer pupils.

In administratively centralised educational systems, as for example in France, where the most important educational policy-decisions are taken at the central (national) administrative level on behalf of the whole system, educational planning is performed either in the Ministry of Education or in the central planning unit (the "Commissariat au Plan").

In administratively decentralised systems, where the local education authorities are responsible for a large range of important decisions, educational planning is performed at both the central and the local levels. The English report makes this very clear by indicating that whilst the function of educational planning remains the same at both levels, its objectives clearly differ. According to the report, the role of planning at the central level (the DES) "... is to assist the Secretary of State in formulating, deciding and promulgating policy at national level, aimed at giving guidance to the educational providers on the direction and speed of educational development, and on significant national trends and priorities that need to be taken into account in planning and making provisions" (17). At the local level, on the other hand, the objective of educational planning is to help local authorities plan the provision for their areas "having regard both to national policies and to local circumstances" (18).

---

17. "Reappraisal of Educational Planning : Country Report : England", OECD, Paris, 1980 (mimeographed), p. 1.
18. Ibid., p. 2.

The Norwegian report (19) states that the planning function is carried out by a number of units of public administration, often not specifically designed as "planning units", located at various administrative levels where educational planning might take place, namely, central government, local level (country school boards, community councils) and the school level itself (parents, teachers, pupils). The report makes it clear that the tasks of educational planning at each of these levels varies considerably according to the types of decision to be taken by the authorities involved. In Norway a vertical interdependence was gradually installed among these various levels as a result of the evolution of educational planning which followed the decentralisation of the educational system. The role of central planning in Norway is to develop a strategy on the basis of the overall development in pupil numbers and flows, the supply of teachers and other educational resources and the institutional cost structure, as it relates to the type and size of institutions. On that basis it sets minimum standards and develops policy frameworks according to which regional and local authorities act. However, local authorities, if they so wish, can exceed these standards but totally on their own financial responsibility. Such a model seems to incorporate enough flexibility for integrating central with local decisions without the former subordinating the latter.

In Federal countries, such as Canada, Germany, Australia and the United States, a third administrative level is superimposed on the previous two. The degree of constitutional responsibility of the federal administrative level in educational matters became a decisive factor in determining the role of educational planning at the federal level. Because Federal Ministries of Education (when they exist) have no or very little authority in state educational policies, they have developed, in almost all cases, a triple objective : to co-ordinate, to the extent that this is possible, state educational policies ; to undertake nation-wide educational programmes complementing state programmes ; and to assist financially state educational programmes, when needed.

Educational planning work to help attain these three objectives has varied according to the emphasis placed on each of them. The responsibility for the implementation on the first objective, for example, was vested, in most cases, in national councils, by type of education, such as the Educational Council (_Bildungsrat_), the Standing Conference of Ministers of Education (_Ständige Konferenz_), and the Academic Council (_Wissenschaftstrat_) in Germany. In Australia, the co-ordinative role of the Commonwealth is undertaken through the Australian Education Council, which comprises

---

19. See below.

the state and Commonwealth Ministers of Education, the Conference of Directors-General of Education and the meetings of TAFE Directors (20). The Australian Constitution permits the Commonwealth to provide financial assistance to the states thus allowing it to become indirectly involved in state educational matters. This Commonwealth state relationship is taken care of by the Schools' Commission and the Tertiary Education Commission, which advise the Commonwealth on the allocation of Commonwealth funds to the states.

It has been observed (21) that Federal official or semi-official agencies with educational policy interests but little administrative or executive power have tended to concentrate their efforts on analytical studies, including forecasts. For example, before the United States Office of Education became a major spender of Federal Government funds, it was largely an agency concerned with research and forecasting. Similar examples could be quoted for other countries. Political sensitivities around such tactics are not difficult to understand as federal agencies may be tempted by this means to increase their influence on policies despite the fact that their direct authority is limited.

D. The particular interests of those responsible for educational planning

The evolution of educational planning was also affected by the professional, academic or political interests of those involved in educational planning whether in educational administrations or universities. In the absence of any broadly accepted theory, or even conceptual framework, educational planning had to sustain consecutively the intellectual influence of a large number of academic disciplines, such as economics, sociology, education, mathematics, operational research, systems and social systems engineering, management, public administration, etc. This shows the multidisciplinary nature of educational planning and the political authority carried by each one of these disciplines during the last twenty years. At first economists, then later sociologists as well, seem to have had most influence on the theory of educational planning, whilst operation-researchers and systems analysts have influenced more the techniques of technocratic planning and in particular the treatment of quantitative information. On the other hand, educationists and political science theorists, late comers to the field, contributed to a shift in educational planning from quantitative to qualitative dimensions and from authoritative/technocratic to participatory/conflictual characteristics (22).

---

20. For more details, see Chapter 4. A below, p. 94.
21. OECD, Conference on Policies for Educational Growth, Vol. VI, op. cit., p. 43.
22. For a more thorough discussion, see K. Eide, "Educational Planning in Perspective", OECD, Paris, 1978 (mimeo).

E. **Structural Shortcomings in the Educational Planning Machinery**

The evolution of educational planning has also been influenced by its structural arrangements within educational administrations, both at the national and at the local levels. With the ever-increasing importance of the planning function for the policy and decision making process in the sixties, special structures were developed to accommodate it. These structures have since evolved continuously as a function both of the importance given to planning at a particular time and of the shortcomings planning had experienced in the past, particularly due to the initial administrative set-ups which very often had restrained the operational effectiveness of the planning function by hindering communication between planning and policy making. On the other hand, the changes which have occurred in the perception of educational planning have directly affected its organisation. However, this was not always the case, because of the inertia which administrative structures show toward change. This was made evident in two specific cases :

i) in countries where a kind of administrative decentralisation began at the end of the sixties and the early seventies and
ii) where the notion of "participatory planning" gained ground.

In both cases old educational planning structures, which grew considerably and gained administrative power, showed a robust tendency to resist change. In most of the OECD countries this was the case with the various educational planning offices within the central administrative machineries which performed the planning function following consistently the technocratic model, having as their main job the preparation of some kind of educational plan or White Paper.

This behaviour hindered, on the one hand, the decentralisation of the planning function and, on the other, the adoption and the setting in operation of participatory planning structures despite attempts made in this direction by changing the composition of policy committees or through consultations and opinion surveys.

In Norway an interesting development gradually took place during the last twenty years as the result of a deliberate effort on the part of the authorities concerned to move educational planning from an exclusive function of the central administration only to one encompassing all those involved in educational policy at all administrative levels. This development, of what seems at present to be a well integrated administrative structure, was made possible through the establishment of strong vertical and horizontal communication links.

From the country reports two general structural models emerged, clearly affecting educational planning : the first prevails in countries with traditional centralised administrations, the second applies to countries with decentralised educational systems. There is, however, ample evidence that two opposite developments are in operation in these countries which may gradually push the two initial model structures towards greater convergence. In fact, in the first group of countries, there is a clear movement towards decentralisation which slowly, but steadily, is gaining ground ; in the second group of countries the movement is toward increased co-ordination of local policies within a national (or federal) policy framework. The content of these two movements seems to depend on the degree of coherence that can be achieved among the various administrative levels and parts of the education system through communication links. Educational planning will both affect and be affected by this development.

F. Pressures from Acute Conjunctural Problems

Past experience shows that educational planning became fashionable whenever the education system had to face particularly pressing problems. This seems to be the case at present, as discussed below. This observation justifies the description often given to the behaviour of educational planning as being more reactive to problems rather than active and anticipatory, i.e. endeavouring, as it should, to anticipate problems and develop strategies to shape and control them. The persistence in the past of such short-sightedness, has very often eliminated from planning its anticipatory function and turned it into a mere administrative short-term problem-solving activity. This development has been facilitated, if not encouraged, by the fact that political receptivity has in the main been short-term, thus obliging planning to take care mainly of short-term matters, usually at the operational level, to facilitate the annual budgetary process. Without denying the necessity for operational planning, professional planners argue that, despite existing political realities, there is always need for strategic long-term planning as a basis for broader public discussion, with a view to enhancing communication between various groups in society and clarifying policy issues. This viewpoint, which is taken up in the discussion below concerning the future role of educational planning, provides a useful basis for reappraising educational planning practices in that it provides a political justification for long-term planning as well as a realistic link between short-medium and long-term educational planning.

II. FUTURE EDUCATIONAL POLICY PREOCCUPATIONS AND THE ROLE OF EDUCATIONAL PLANNING

A. The Present and Future Educational Policy Context

The context of future educational policy development differs, in some instances drastically, from that of the past.

As was seen earlier, the basic characteristics of the 1960s were :

- a high degree of optimism as to the potential of education to contribute to both economic growth and social equity ;
- a continuously growing economy which made it possible for governments to finance an ever-increasing social demand for education leading to the extraordinary growth of education systems in all OECD countries.

The context of the late 1970s has been different. It is characterised by :

- increasing doubt as to the potential of education per se to help attain the socio-economic objectives and particularly the objective of equality of opportunity, given the persistence of social, economic and educational inequalities ;
- an economic system which has suffered two consecutive crises, with rapid decrease in economic activity and consequently a serious unemployment problem, with substantial loss of public financing capability ;
- because of the economic crisis social priorities have changed, with education losing its previously privileged social rank.

The 1980s began as a direct continuation of the late 1970s, showing further accentuation of the above trends, so that at present the following characteristics can be observed in the majority of OECD countries :

- low economic activity ;
- high unemployment rates and particularly youth unemployment ;
- high levels of inflation ;
- changing attitudes towards the value and role of education for society and for the individual, resulting in low political priority for education ;
- drastically contracting public budgets ;
- rapid technological changes in some economic sectors ;
- profound demographic changes resulting in decreasing school population and faster-growing population at the retirement age ;
- growing demand for different kinds of education from new population groups.

Little change is expected in many of these trends during the 1980s. However, the new technological changes are not expected to inflict their full impact before the end of the decade and certainly not earlier than the middle of the 1980s. This indicates that OECD countries will remain for quite a long period in a situation of high uncertainty. Final directions will largely depend on normative choices, to the extent that these can be made during the transition period. The need for such normative choices, based on the definition of socially acceptable policies, is increasingly felt in OECD societies in view of the fact that, given the inherent inertia of social systems, desirable future directions cannot be achieved if past trends are allowed to dominate policy formation. There are at least three preconditions to effecting any change : the necessary political will ; increased understanding of the kind of society that people wish to see develop and to which a new educational philosophy can be turned ; and a "technocratic" appreciation of what the desired changes imply, including an estimation of the resources, of all kinds, required to attain the new policy objectives within a "reasonable" time period, the duration of which will depend on national conditions.

B. Educational Policy Preoccupations and the Role of Educational Planning

Country Reports and expert papers alike indicated clearly that in almost all OECD countries educational systems, although with varying degrees of intensity, are facing serious problems calling for technical analysis to assess, and as far as possible control, both short- and longer-term consequences. As the English report states, "planning interest in both quality and resources is likely to continue undiminished" (23).

In view of the fact that the time dimension varies according to the type of problem at hand the discussion below is pursued under two dimensions : <u>short-medium</u> and <u>long</u> term.

The main educational policy/planning preoccupations which emerged from the country reports relate to or arise from the following issues : the demographic problem, with its immediate and future implications for the size of the educational system, the teaching profession and the labour market ; persisting high rates of unemployment, particularly among youth ; changing social demand for education ; changing demand, quantitatively and qualitatively, for qualified manpower ; and persisting slow economic growth with its restrictive effects on public budgets. These problems, which are closely interrelated, are discussed under two headings :

---

23. Country Report : England, <u>op. cit.</u>, p. 57.

- redeployment of educational resources ;
- education and the labour market.

1. Redeployment of Educational Resources

Most of the OECD countries since the late 1960s/early 1970s have been experiencing a fall in birth-rates which in turn has affected school enrolments. School systems in countries like the United States, the United Kingdom, France, Germany and New Zealand, have already witnessed serious reductions in their populations. For example, primary education in Germany between 1972 and 1980 lost 1 341 000 pupils, which corresponds to a 32 per cent reduction (24). The corresponding reduction in Belgium was 14 per cent between 1970-77 ; in the United Kingdom between 1972-78, 9.5 per cent ; in Italy for the same period, 8.9 per cent ; and in France between 1970-77, approximately 6 per cent (25). Other countries have entered this phase later ; this is the case, for example, of the Netherlands, whose primary education suffered a reduction of 24 per cent between 1975-79 while a further reduction of approximately 20 per cent is expected to take place between 1979 and 1985 (26).

The decline in the number of births will make its impact felt on the different parts of the education system at different times. This would mean that as the number of students declines in one level of education it increases in other levels. On the other hand, recent social policies in most of the OECD countries are designed to reverse the demographic trend and help increase the birth rate. To the extent that these policies are successful, this will mean that the number of children entering school will increase. This has already happened in some countries, as for example in England and Wales where the number of births reached its lowest level in 1977 and has shown a recovery, although modest, since 1978.

In view of the fluctuating nature of demographic trends educational policy makers and planners are faced with a two-fold problem : the more immediate one of how to deal with contracting school systems (with all its direct repercussions, particularly on the teaching profession) ; and a longer-term one, in which contraction may be succeeded by expansion but which, however, will not affect all school levels uniformly.

---

24. Bundesminister für Bildung und Wissenschaft, Grund- und Struktur Daten ; 1981-82, Bonn, 1981, p. 24.
25. Eurostat : Education and Training 1970-71, 1977-78 Luxembourg, 1980, p. 158.
26. S.C.P. Office : Social and Cultural Report 1980, Rijswijk, the Netherlands, 1981, p. 110.

The short-medium term problem is further complicated by the fact that this situation is seen by public financing authorities as an opportunity for making savings by proportionately reducing public educational expenditure. On the other hand, educational authorities generally take the view that reduced school population provides an opportunity for ameliorating the quality of education through a number of measures, among which the following were proposed in the various country reports :

- reducing excessive competition in schools ;
- putting more resources into the education of disadvantaged groups, particularly the handicapped ;
- improving the teacher-pupil ratio ;
- increasing training opportunities ;
- developing systematic provision of in-service training and study leave for teachers ;
- bringing all buildings up to required standards ;
- increasing the provision of equipment ;
- strengthening various educational support services.

The prerequisite for attaining these objectives is that educational public authorities succeed in maintaining the level of required funds. There is ample evidence, however, that this is not always the case. Already, some governments have decided to make significant cuts in their educational spending. In the United Kingdom, for example, it was decided that public educational spending would decrease to over 9 per cent for the period 1978-79 to 1983-84 (27).

The prime issue, therefore, as it was stated in several country reports, is the level at which governments will be prepared to trade off a reduction in the level of services for qualitative improvements. Evidently, the trade-off point in each country will be a function of the degree of political pressure put on governments, stemming particularly from teachers' and parents' associations and the value which political authorities will put on education for the continuous development of their societies.

Three financing approaches are possible in the short run. The continuation of the past incremental approach, though at a reduced rate ; a zero-growth educational budget ; and a negative growth educational budget. Among these, the most probable seem to be the last two ; because, as stated in the English Report, "for most of the 1980s at least there are not likely to be major new increases in the total scale of provision ; the resource prospect is one of redeployment and better use within roughly constant or even declining total volume". (28) None of the country reports

---

27. The Times Educational Supplement, 4 April, 1980, p. 1 (see also English Report, op. cit., p. 23).
28. Ibid., p. 4.

have indicated an opposite trend. A zero-growth educational budget under fluctuating school population will necessitate a redeployment of public resources inside the education system with some of its parts receiving more and others less. A negative-growth educational budget, which implies a redeployment of public resources among the social sectors and away from the education system, will mean that, over and above the internal redeployment of resources, all parts of the education system will be relatively losing resources.

Under these conditions, the role of educational planning at both central and local levels will be multifold. In the first instance, it would be necessary to disentangle the problem and identify its various components for a better appreciation of both its short-medium and longer-term implications. In the second place, it will be necessary to make a quantitative estimation of the immediate effect of the demographic changes on the school population and on that basis to calculate the necessary resources in teaching personnel, finance and school buildings by educational sub-system. Alternative solutions could be generated on the basis of various assumptions about the magnitude of such ratios, as for example the teacher/pupil ratio, with a view to providing a feedback to policy-makers so as to arrive at the "best" trade-off point. In addition, the socio-economic effect on small communities of the need to close down schools, as is already the case in several OECD countries, needs to be carefully considered and the cost involved in moving the children of these communities to bigger ones should be calculated ; it may well be that this type of cost may offset the direct savings from the closure of schools.

However, the most important and politically delicate role that educational planning has to perform at present relates, firstly, to the long-term consequences of the demographic factor, and, secondly, to those emanating from the short-medium term application of the "redeployment" approach. In view of this type of possible secondary effect, policy-makers may well be advised to base their actual decisions not exclusively on the short-medium term feedback but also to take into account its long-term effects. More precisely, educational planning has to trace through the educational system the demographic wave at least up to the end of higher education. The uncertainty involved in such an exercise pertains to the behaviour of the birth rate during this period. If the birth rate increases, as seems to be the case in several OECD countries, it is certain that the parts of the education system which are losing students today will be gaining them tomorrow. The question here relates to whether actually contracting systems would have enough flexibility to augment their capacity rapidly, particularly in view of the time required to train new teachers. A possible consequence of the prolongation of recent practices to cut back on staff by reducing the intake of teacher colleges could be a gradual ageing of the teaching profession and a massive retirement at the time when the school population will start again to grow. It is apparent that if actual policies are drawn solely on the basis of the actual decline of the school population and the pressure of current public financial stringency, they will have a seriously destructive effect on the longer-term capacity of education systems.

In view of this dilemma, educational planning may be called upon to analyse the consequences of possible alternative educational financing systems. For example, in countries where the ideal of a generalised public system has to be safeguarded at all costs, increased participation of local authorities in the financing of education may need to be seriously considered, particularly in those countries where such contributions are small or nil. Still another solution might lie in the modification of existing educational financing systems with a view to increasing the direct contribution of the "consumer", at least for certain types of education, as discussed by Tinbergen and Psacharopoulos in Chapter 6.

2. Education and the Labour Market

Study of the relationship between education and the labour market has been a permanent feature of the agenda of national educational planning. During the 1960s the need was to produce enough qualified manpower to help sustain and accelerate economic growth. By and large, the system worked well, in spite of sectoral mismatches which, however, in an expansive situation was rooted out by the substitution mechanism. The situation is now different. The recent economic recession, with all its negative effects on employment, particularly among the young ; the rapid technological changes occurring in some industries which are bound to affect both qualitatively and quantitatively the composition and size of labour markets ; the need for structural adjustments to raise the competitiveness of the economic system ; and the ever-growing demand from several social groups, such as married women, to enter the labour market at a time when it is contracting, create a new context which make the education-labour market relationships highly uncertain and very problematical from both an economic and a social viewpoint.

It is thus not surprising that most of the country reports paid particular attention to this kind of relationship. The OECD itself has, over the years, paid special attention to the analysis of the issues of youth unemployment, transition from school to work, vocational education and training and developments in higher education, all of which are emphasised in the national reports. On the basis of these it is possible to identify a set of issues in the education-labour market relationship with short- medium- or long-term implications for public policy to

which educational planning could make a contribution.
These are :

- youth unemployment ;
- transition from school to work, together with
  related curriculum implications ;
- raising labour productivity through education and
  training ;
- labour market information on manpower demand and
  the functioning of the labour market system ;
- assessment and appreciation of the impact of the
  anticipated technological changes on the labour
  market.

This set of issues evidently calls for, on the one hand, "a more comprehensive planning so that appropriate balance and range of measures might be developed" (29) and on the other, long-term educational planning on the basis of the likely evolution of the demand for different levels of manpower qualifications, as the German Report urges.

While traditional forms of manpower forecasting are generally rejected, a gradual, although hesitant, return to manpower planning emerges from several of the country reports. The German Report, for example, states that "long-term forecasting of the demand for labour must be improved, with the emphasis of research being laid on establishing what qualifications in particular guarantee the broadest possible employability and a high degree of flexibility in working life" (30). The French report, underlining the importance of qualified manpower for the country's economic growth, says : "(France's) single national resource lies in the quality and training of her women and men. This means that the future of our country depends largely on the efficiency of our educational system, its capacity to adapt to the new world and its insertion power into a changing society and economy". The report, however, is rather critical of the way "labour" has been treated in the macro-economic model of the VIII Plan for the manpower projections. The model establishes a relationship between the increase in the quality of labour and the increase of production costs. In other words, an increase in manpower qualifications is directly translated into an increase in wages and salaries, i.e. increase of production costs, regardless of productivity gains.

Manpower planning problems are referred to in the Australian Report, but it remains uncertain as to whether manpower forecasting should continue or not. The Williams Committee, for example, although aligned to previous reports (the Martin Committee in 1965 and the Universities Commission in 1972) which had accepted that social demand

---

29. See below Chapter 4-A, p. 94.
30. See below Chapter 4-B, p. 131.

for places should determine the numbers in universities, suggesting at the same time the unreliability of past manpower forecasting, "nevertheless recommended that the Tertiary Education Commission should continue to undertake and publish forecasts in the fields of medicine, dentistry and veterinary science and to undertake forecasts of social demand" (31). The question which, according to the report, was left unanswered by the Committee was "whether forecasts, and presumably a manpower planning approach, should extend beyond the three fields it specified" (32). The Report, however, did make the point "that if manpower considerations are to play a larger part in educational planning, improved information will be required on the workings of the labour market" (33). On this need for information which is discussed below there is general concern in the country reports. The English report, for example, refers to some concrete local experiments which attempt to bring the schools (pupils) closer to industries for a direct exchange of information (34).

The adaptation of the curriculum, at all educational levels, to changing employment needs is another major educational planning preoccupation raised in the country reports. A number of them point to the increasing evidence that school-leavers are experiencing difficulties either in obtaining jobs or in keeping their jobs because of inadequate preparation. The English report refers to the public debate initiated in 1976 which "was made against a background of public disquiet and critical comment that the schools were failing to equip their pupils adequately for the changing demands of adult life, at a time when some school-leavers were experiencing difficulty in obtaining jobs. Criticism was aimed at standards of achievement, acquisition of basic skills, and the relevance of the curriculum" (35). Despite the well-rooted belief in educational circles that "schools do not cause youth unemployment and they are, by themselves, not able to remedy it" (36), the positive role of the curriculum in increasing the employability of young people is generally acknowledged.

It emerges clearly from the above discussion that educational planning efforts in the analysis of the education - labour market relationship will be particularly directed towards two areas :

> i) increasing and managing the information flow from the labour market to the potential students to facilitate their educational decisions, leaving

---

31. See below, p. 120.
32. See below, p. 120.
33. See below, p. 121.
34. See Country Report : England, <u>op. cit.</u>, p. 47.
35. <u>Ibid.</u>, p. 32.
36. See below, p. 121.

to the labour market the allocative function to balance up demand and supply ;
ii) curriculum changes, at all educational levels, in response to changing employment needs, with emphasis on the need for such curricula to be as broadly based as possible so as to increase the adaptive capacity of the individuals in the light of changing job functions.

With regard to manpower planning, apart from specific sectors such as medicine, teaching, etc., where the supply is by and large publicly determined, the effort is likely to focus on analyses of the probable long-term development of the labour market and the expected changes in the educational attainment of the labour force in view of the desired increase in productivity, envisaged technological changes and changes expected in the composition of the production system, particularly the fast growth of the service sector, as it is argued by Tinbergen and Psacharopoulos below.

C. The Information Basis for Educational Planning

Since planning is par excellence an information-based activity, it is not surprising to see wide interest shown in almost all the country reports in various types of information. Interest focuses on the following categories of information :

- the value that society places on education ;
- pupils' attitude towards education and work ;
- education research output both for curriculum development and policy-making ;
- the functioning and performance of the education system ;
- the functioning and future development of the labour market ;
- the probable effect of micro-processors on educational technology ;
- the probable development of the economy.

In their reports, countries underline the need for both more information where it is lacking and better or "proper" information. According to the British report, for example, "proper, for authorities' decisions, means information that is easily assimilated, directly relevant to the problem of management, comparable with other sets of data, and sufficiently up-to-date" (37). An additional need would be for effective dissemination of information from the centre downward to the localities and from local authorities upwards. The New Zealand report suggests that

---

37. Country Report : England, op. cit., p. 39.

through the necessary information and its effective flow, education could be made the subject of public comment, as distinct from being politicised.

The above seven categories of information fall under two main groups : information for __management__ and information for __planning__ purposes. Information for planning could in turn be divided into two sub-groups : information for __adaptation__ (short-term) and information for __change__ (longer term). The collection and processing of information for management and adaptation should be fast and amenable to immediate dissemination and application. Information for planning for change, on the other hand, emanating as it does from educational research and long-term socio-economic analysis, will involve longer delays ; if such delays, however, become inordinately protracted, there is a risk that the results would be already obsolete. Tinbergen and Psacharopoulos argue that thanks to the silicon chip and the "mini-type" tracer studies they propose, such research delays could be shortened so that research results could be more useful to policy makers.

A more challenging task for educational planning, and perhaps a new one, would be the organisation and management of operationally effective information systems, designed in particular to provide links between what is happening both in the labour market and the educational system. Such systems could be particularly useful in building up advance warning mechanisms that would facilitate better understanding of individual demand for education. (38)

D. __Functional and Structural Differentiation on Educational Planning__

The discussion in several of the country papers referred explicitly to the need to identify specialised planning functions for specific tasks at various levels of the policy/decision-making process. It has been suggested, for example, that planning should assist in : identifying the problems ; establishing objectives ; making choices ; assessing the success of the programmes ; etc. The Canadian report, on the other hand, describes the planning functions as consisting of : policy development, preparation of programme plans, programme development, programme implementation, programme approval and allocation and programme evaluation. (39) Hüfner, in Chapter 2 below, sees planning as a multi-phase and multi-level process consisting of three closely interlinked phases/activities ;

---

38. On the characteristics of such a system see : K. Harnqvist, __Individual Demand for Education__, OECD, Paris, 1978, Vol. I.
39. "Reappraisal of Educational Planning : Country Report, Canada", OECD, Paris, 1980 (mimeographed) pp. 9-10.

programming, implementation and evaluation. These are performed at three functional levels of planning, and take account of the time dimension, namely :

a) strategic educational policy/planning : establishment of long-range goals by making strategic choices ;
b) programme educational policy/programming : establishment of interim objectives ;
c) operational educational policy/planning : achievement of short-range targets within given time-cost performance requirements.

Thus, planning practitioners and theoreticians alike appreciate the practical and conceptual reality that planning practices differ according to decision-making level - i.e. type of decision - and the activity performed. For example, under this schema, the forecasting activity pursued consistently by planning units could be seen as a programming activity at the strategic level ; whilst the preparation of the annual budget is a programming activity at the operational level - hence the need for treating explicitly and separately the various functional and structural dimensions of planning.

1. Functional Differentiation

A functional differentiation of educational planning similar to that of Hüfner was presented in an earlier OECD publication. (40) It is outlined below as one possible model for an operational conceptualisation of educational planning. Four conceptual decision-making sub-systems are considered, namely : the normative, strategic, operational and administrative. (41) These sub-systems, which do not necessarily imply any structural hierarchy, represent four classes of decisions, conceptually integrated, each one of which presupposes certain planning activities. We could, therefore, distinguish four corresponding planning sub-systems or levels. Each of the four classes of decisions is characterised by a different degree of generality, ranging from the most general normative decisions to the least general administrative decisions. The basic process which takes place at each of the four decision-making levels is therefore a continuous reduction of the degrees

---

40. Decision-Making in Educational Systems : The Experience in three OECD Countries, OECD, Paris, 1977.
41. Others have also proposed multi-level concepts using somewhat different terminology : Policy, Strategic, administrative levels (see articles of Beer, Forrester, Ansoff, Brandenburg in Jantsch (Ed.) Perspective of Planning, OECD, Paris, 1969. Beer decomposes the administrative level in two tiers, one for the control of action and the other for the action itself.

of freedom incorporated in the decisions of the superior level as one moves from normative to strategic to operational to administrative decisions. This shows the high degree of interdependence which exists among those four decision-making sub-systems, as well as the constraining effect that the preceding decision has upon the next one.

This functional breakdown of the "deciding process" does not imply corresponding structural arrangements, for all four classes of decisions could be taken by one and the same structure. This is the case, for example, with small and simple social systems. (42) In large and complex social systems such as the education system it may happen, as in fact does happen in most cases, for reasons of division of labour, that each one of the four classes of decisions is carried out by different structural components. Whether there should be a structural differentiation corresponding to the four conceptual classes of decisions is a practical question to be resolved independently in each national setting. However, the content of each class of decision and the corresponding function of planning could be, to some extent, specified.

In a general way, normative decisions have to do with what should be done ; strategic decisions with what could (when and how) be done ; operational decisions with what will (when and how) be done ; and administrative decisions with what is being done.

a) Normative Planning

Normative educational decisions pertain

i) to the setting of a general educational philosophy compatible with society's values and its current and future needs ; and
ii) to the selection of a set of policy objectives and behaviour norms and the values implied by them, to facilitate the implementation of the system's objectives.

Since the philosophy of the education system and its behaviour norms are developed and set as the "wills" of the system, they are constrained only by :

a) the overall socio-political value system ;
b) the education system's "survival" and "well-being" objectives ; and
c) the educational needs of society at large.

---

42. One may consider the individual as the smallest social system. The individual, however, becomes an element of bigger social systems.

Technological, financial and other resource type of constraints are not taken into account at this level. They are certainly taken into account at the strategic level when alternative courses of action for meeting policy-objectives are considered, and thus, together with an assessment of the capacity of the system to attain the objectives set within a desired time horizon, serve as feed-back into the decision-making process.

The planning techniques employed at this level could vary from simple authoritative personal value judgements to the application of sociological surveying and other techniques such as Delphi, technological forecasting, etc. Their role is to help policy-makers arrive at :

i) a representative appreciation of people's values, attitudes towards education and their educational needs ;
ii) at a well thought-out assessment of future societal developments.

Normative planning could be either authorative when one authority, whether political, administrative or even academic, engages itself in the planning activity on behalf of all those concerned, or participatory, when all those involved in and/or affected by educational developments directly participate in the setting of policy objectives and the formulation of society's educational objective.

Examples of such planning are not very frequent. At the international level the OECD Policy Conference on Economic Growth and Investment in Education, held in Washington D.C. in October, 1961, could be considered as normative planning in that it promulgated on behalf of the participating Member countries an educational philosophy which affected national educational policies and reforms in many OECD countries during the 1960s. A recent example at national level could be taken from the Danish Educational Planning and Policy in a Social Context at the End of the 20th Century : U-90 report. As stated in the report itself, the U-90 is a framework rather than a plan taking a long-term perspective and covering all sectors of the Danish educational system, seeking to relate educational development to the changing social and economic context. The planning work was undertaken, on behalf of the Ministry of Education, by the Central Council of Education, a body which exercises neither political nor executive powers, and the U-90 report was meant to serve as a basis for a general debate in the country on the future development of Danish education. Consequently, it contains practically all the elements on which the formulation of a national educational policy could be based. In this sense, it reflects the broader objective of the Danish political authorities, to establish through the Danish Council of Education an open-ended normative educational planning process where all concerned could participate before decisions on specific educational policies for the future could be taken. The participatory elements in this process are exemplified by the fact that the Council which was charged with the preparation of the report "is a body in which many different political views are represented ... (and) ... there are representatives of the largest and most influential professional and industrial bodies, and individuals having different knowledge about and experience in educational matters, and each with his personal engagement in the problems under discussion" (43) ; in addition, since the report was meant for public debate, this allowed views which had not been considered in the preparation of the report to be heard. (44)

b) <u>Strategic Planning</u>

The attainment of the educational policy objectives incorporated in the adopted educational philosophy requires policy decisions with regard to its specific components. This decision-making phase corresponds from a planning viewpoint to what is often called "programme" or "strategic" planning.

Strategic planning has two functions : <u>search and selection</u>. It searches for the identification of possible programmes and, on the basis of certain criteria, selects among them those which appear to make up the "best" strategy. Programme identification and programme selection, particularly for long-term policies, are complicated activities requiring the selection and analysis of a great amount of information on the system's actual performance and capacity, society's present and future educational needs, the future development of the economy, labour market and technology and, of course, the financing capacity of the educational system.

Strategic planning, if done effectively, ensures the <u>external stability</u> of educational systems through proper appreciation of and responses to the educational needs and aspirations of the various parts of the society ; otherwise, a relative isolation of the educational system from its environment may occur, as has been the case in many countries in the past. In the changed socio-economic context which now prevails, strategic planning in education must cease to rely primarily on enrolment and/or manpower forecasts for estimating future educational needs. Alternative hypotheses will need to be developed based on a wider variety of factors, such as technological development, value changes, etc., and not merely those which

---

43. U-90, page 8.
44. <u>Reviews of National Policies for Education :
Denmark</u>, OECD, Paris, 1980.

derive from an extrapolation of past developments. It would also need to develop the requisite flexibility so as to absorb environmental and internal disturbances during the implementation period and perhaps be endowed with appropriate control authority so as to influence programme implementation.

c) Operational Planning

Operational planning is concerned with what <u>will</u> in fact be done in the immediate future. Operational decisions pertain, therefore, to the short/medium term, depending on the nature of the plans to be implemented, whilst the time horizon of strategic planning may be extended beyond the medium term. More precisely, the role of operational planning consists of identifying and selecting specific projects with a view to implementing selected programmes. The project design follows programme specifications which become one of the basic inputs flowing into operational planning. Other inputs to be considered in project design are immediate resource constraints, existing capacity, etc. With regard to resource inputs there is a fundamental difference between strategic and operational planning : at the strategic level resources are treated as variable, in the sense that the education system has the means to modify its resources in the long run ; at the operational level, however, resources are treated as fixed and in practice are directly related to the annual budget. In the absence of coherent programme planning, operational planning is left only with the information on last year's budget, which becomes the basic information in project preparation leading usually to incremental budget decisions. This procedure, known as "incremental budgeting", which is in current practice in almost all countries, does not allow any significant degree of freedom for long-term educational policy making.

d) Administrative level

Administrative decisions pertain to what <u>is being</u> done. More precisely, major administrative responsibilities include : operating and maintaining the system, implementing new projects, and evaluating the system's performance. The corresponding "planning functions" are difficult to disentangle. The most obvious function at this level is, of course, <u>control</u> rather than planning. However, some "planning" in the broad sense of the term also takes place. There is occasionally need for "interpreting", for example, control specifications (e.g. laws), or "appreciating" the system's needs as well as those of its clients with a view to proposing changes, additions or omissions.

It is interesting to note that as one moves from the normative downwards to the administrative level, the importance of planning gradually diminishes, whilst the importance of control grows. That explains why occasionally both researchers and practitioners restrict planning to the upper three levels and sometimes even to the first two. However, if one accepts that planning is a function of decision-making, one is bound to see its presence at all decision-making levels. What changes is the time-horizon, the mode and the techniques employed.

2. Structural Differentiation

The above differentiation of decision-making and consequently of planning in four functional levels does not necessarily imply a corresponding structural hierarchy. This was made evident with reference to very small systems, such as for example the individual, the family, the small enterprise, etc. However, as the system grows it shows a tendency, for efficiency reasons, to develop a differentiated structure corresponding usually to types of decisions or subjects to be taken care of. The educational systems in almost all countries have over time developed horizontal and vertical structural differentiation, i.e. by type of education and by level of decision-making. The vertical structure is of more interest from an educational planning viewpoint since it corresponds to the types of decisions discussed earlier. What type of decision is each structure responsible for ? To answer this question one has to know the degree of administrative "_autonomy_" enjoyed by the structures. Autonomy is defined in this respect in relation to the ability of a system to take and change at its will any one of the above four classes of decisions ; the more decisions it can take and change the more autonomous the system is. For example, a local educational authority of an administratively decentralised educational system enjoys greater autonomy than a "local authority" in a centralised educational system. Similarly, a private school enjoys greater autonomy than a public one.

Study of the actual relative autonomy of each educational structure would lead to better appreciation of its decision-making and consequently planning responsibility. For example, a school unit within public educational systems does not have to engage in normative or strategic, or even operational, planning ; this is the responsibility of its superior administrative structures. However, in the case of the Yugoslav public educational system or of private systems, where schools are relatively self-managed, schools have to rely on themselves for things which involve them in decisions which could be of an operational or even strategic type. As educational systems are divided into smaller and smaller, but autonomous units, their decisions, whether strategic or operational, tend to become simplified, less well-prepared and more narrow in scope, relying solely on the information processing capacity of one or two individuals and on extremely limited information inputs, emanating usually from their close environment. This brings us back to the need for broader information systems for decisions at any level, if such decisions are not to enhance the isolation of the educational system or its constituent parts.

Annex

THE PRACTICE OF TECHNOCRATIC EDUCATIONAL PLANNING

A. Introduction

Given the two major policy objectives, i.e. <u>social equality</u> and <u>economic growth</u>, educational planning had developed a variety of specific techniques to help the educational system foresee its future growth. Its aim was to accommodate the social demand and satisfy manpower requirements for promoting and sustaining economic growth. The application of these techniques led in practice to what may be called "technocratic" planning. From this point of view, it is worth mentioning the considerable progress which has been made in the development of the technical and statistical bases for educational planning, something contemporary criticism of early technocratic educational planning tends to ignore. (1)

Two major developments should be emphasised :

i) the development of a variety of sophisticated mathematical models to facilitate, among other things, the forecasting of school enrolments and manpower demand ;
ii) the improvement, and in many cases the setting, of the foundations of educational statistics.

Educational planning, in its early years, had to operate with a very poor statistical system. This was repeatedly stated whenever serious planning work had to be done. It was generally felt that statistics of education were inadequate in coverage, precision and analytical value in comparison with most other social and economic statistics.

This was a serious obstacle at the national level to the assessment and analysis of educational developments. The situation was worse when it was a question of

---

1. G. Williams, "Educational Planning, Past, Present and Future", OECD, Paris, 1978 (mimeographed) p. 6.

investigating interdependencies of economic and educational developments with a view to making long-term forecasts. (2) On that point, it is worth recalling that two of the pioneers of educational planning at that time, John Vaisey and Friedrich Edding, undertook what were essentially data-gathering exercises in areas that are considered commonplace to-day. (3)

The OECD and other international organisations, particularly UNESCO, played a considerable role in the development of educational statistics ; the effort is being continued. Three fundamental OECD works are worth mentioning :

a) Methods and Statistical Needs for Educational Planning, which presents, in a systematic way, the basic statistics needed for applying any one of the various approaches of the so-called technocratic educational planning, published by the OECD in 1967 ;
b) the classical work by R. Stone, Demographic Accounting and Model Building, OECD, 1971, which presents a fully fledged demographic accounting system designed to bridge the work in mathematical modelling and data systems ; and
c) a series of volumes, in which the educational systems of Member countries have been converted to a standardised classification scheme to allow for inter-country comparisons, published by the OECD under the general title, Classification of Educational Systems.

To this should be added the work on educational performance indicators which was undertaken either independently (4) or within the general OECD programme on "social indicators".

Significant effort was invested in the development of mathematical models for educational planning. This was undertaken simultaneously by national educational administrations and/or national planning boards, the academic community and international organisations. In this respect, the role of OECD, both in supporting and undertaking developmental work itself, was also very considerable. The mathematical models developed at that period fall into three major categories :

---

2. For the problematic statistical basis of the late 1950s see : I. Svennilson et al., Targets for Education in 1970, OECD, Paris, 1962.
3. G. Williams, op. cit., p. 6.
4. Indicators of Performance of Educational Systems, OECD, Paris, 1974.

i) models exclusively for the education sector ;
ii) models exclusively for the manpower sector, and
iii) models relating the education sector to other social sectors. (5)

In addition to models falling in one of these three categories, there exists a large number of various other types of mathematical models designed to tackle a variety of specific educational problems. (6)

B. <u>Models Exclusively for the Education Sector</u>

These models have as their main objective to calculate the evolution of some basic variables pertaining to the education system per se.

Three basic models are in use : (a) models of flows of students within the educational system based on the following identity : (7)

$$n_t + r_t + v_t = g_t + d_t + r_{t+1} + m_t$$

where : n_t : is the number of new students in a particular grade coming from the previous grade ;
r_t : is the number of repeaters ;
v_t : is the number of students who have left the education system and are re-entering it now (these are like new students) ;
g_t : is the number of students successfully finishing the grade ("graduates") at the end of the school year ;
d_t : is the number of drop-outs during the school year ;
m_t : is the number of student deaths during the school year ;
r_{t+1} : is the number of repeaters at the end of the school year ;
t : is the time of reference (corresponding to a particular school year).

---

5. For various classification systems of mathematical models see : <u>Mathematical Models for the Education Sector : A Survey</u>, OECD, Paris, 1973. For an introduction to various types of mathematical models for educational planning see : H. Correa, "A Survey of Mathematical Models in Educational Planning", in <u>Mathematical Models in Educational Planning</u>, OECD, Paris, 1967.
6. For a survey with relevant discussion of a large number of mathematical models for educational planning in various OECD countries see : <u>Mathematical Models for the Education Sector : A Survey</u>, <u>op. cit.</u>, plus Appendix.
7. H. Correa, <u>op. cit.</u>, p. 26.

46

(b) models for calculating teacher demand on the basis of the number of students in each grade ; (c) cost models for calculating the total amount of financial resources needed.

Student flow-models are of two types. The simplest one is based explicitly on population figures and observed enrolment ratios. The second one considers population figures at the first year of the education system in order to calculate new entrants ; after that it is based on transition coefficients from each grade to the next throughout the education system. Flow models of this type have been used by national educational authorities for forecasting the evolution of the flows of students and constitute the technical basis of the social demand approach to educational planning. (8)

A time-step computer-based simulation model (SOM) developed by the OECD Secretariat attempted to link together the above three models i.e. the student flow model, the teacher supply model and the cost model. (9) After being slightly modified SOM has been used by the Planning Services Division, Education Department, Victoria, Australia. (10)

C. Models Exclusively for the Manpower Sector

These are models which help in forecasting the manpower requirements of the economy. These "manpower requirements" are used in turn as targets for planning the educational supply of various types of graduates at various educational levels.

Several such models have been employed in the past. (11)

a) Regression models correlating the number of employees in a particular occupation with total employment, production, total population, national income, productivity, or some other variables ;

---

8. See for example : P. Armitage and C. Smith, "The Development of Computable Models of the British Educational System and their Possible Uses" in OECD, Mathematical Models, op. cit.
9. "SOM : A Simulation Option Model for the Education System", OECD/CERI, Paris, 1970.
10. Education Department, Simulation Option Model : Project Report 1978, Victoria, Australia, 1978.
11. See for example : H. Goldstein, "Methods of Forecasting Demand for and Supply of Scientists and Engineers", OEEC, Paris, 1958 (mimeo) for a description and evaluation of methods utilised in a number of European countries. See also Forecasting Manpower Needs for the Age of Science, OEEC, Paris, 1960 and H. Parnes, Forecasting Educational Needs for Economic and Social Development, OECD, Paris, 1962.

    b) models extrapolating past trends in the growth of an occupation ; and
    c) models estimating anticipated supply of particular types of personnel on the basis of present stocks, anticipated educational supply, and anticipated losses due to death, retirement and withdrawal from the labour market.

D. Models Relating the Education Sector to other Social Sectors

These models attempt to link the education system simultaneously with other sectors, primarily the economic and manpower ones.

Two categories of such models have been developed :

    a) multi-equation econometric planning models, with or without linear programming properties, which attempt to link the various levels of the education system to the economic production system ; (12) and
    b) input-output type of models which attempt to link simultaneously the education sector, in the form of a student flow-matrix, to the economic production sector, in the form of an activity input-output matrix, and the labour market, including teachers, in the form of an occupational flow-matrix. (13)

It may not be an exaggeration to say that all OECD countries which engaged, in the early 1960s, in some form of educational planning followed the "technocratic" model. So much was this practice generalised that educational planning was made almost synonymous with technocratic planning. To the extent that this observation is true it may explain why criticism launched in the late sixties against this planning approach (which will always be valid for the same purpose) on many occasions was seen as criticism against educational planning itself.

As mentioned above, national educational planning units had been set up with a view to facilitating the implementation of well established policy objectives, namely social equality and economic growth. Their mandates, therefore, were well prescribed and their role had thus been limited to interpreting in quantitative terms the educational resource implications for attaining these objectives.

---

    12. See for example : Econometric Models of Education : Some Applications, OECD, Paris, 1965.
    13. P. Levasseur, "A Study of Inter-Relationships between Education, Manpower and Economy", in Socio-Economic Planning Science, Vol. 2, 1969, pp. 269-295.

Meeting the "equality" objective was interpreted as encouraging social demand for all types of education and satisfying it through a continuously growing educational system. From an educational planning viewpoint this implied the following operation : (14)

- Appreciation of the relative state of the education system at a particular time ;
- Forecasting of population growth ;
- Forecasting of pupil enrolments ;
- Estimation of resources namely, teaching, personnel, school buildings and financing.

On the other hand, meeting the economic growth objective implied estimating the manpower requirements for attaining desired growth targets on the basis of two assumptions : a given macro-production function and a desired productivity growth. This involved the following educational planning operations :

- Forecasting manpower requirement on the basis of expressed economic growth targets ;
- Translating manpower forecasts into educational supply with specific educational qualifications.

The above planning operations were facilitated with the use of mathematical models and the computer.

It is evident that the two main educational policy objectives mentioned above are not necessarily compatible. Their relative priority will in any case vary from country to country, depending on each country's stage of development. In practice, within the OECD area the relatively less economically developed countries put their efforts into manpower planning whereas the group of more developed countries followed a social demand approach.

The first group of countries participated in the well-known OECD programme the Mediterranean Regional Project (MRP) whilst the countries of the second group cooperated within the Educational Investment and Planning (EIP) programme. Both programmes developed rich experiences in terms of both methodological/analytical work and of concrete national planning situations. (15)

---

14. For a comprehensive country report on these operations, see <u>Investment in Education : Ireland</u>, OECD, Paris, 1966.
15. These have been documented in the following OECD publications : (a) <u>MRP Country Reports</u> (Greece, Italy, Portugal, Spain, Turkey and Yugoslavia) ; (b) <u>Investment in Education, Ireland</u>, Paris, 1966 ; <u>Educational Policy and Planning : Country Reports</u> (Sweden, 1967 ; Netherlands, 1967 ; Austria, 1968).

E. Efficiency Considerations

In addition to the above macro-planning operations, technocratic educational planning dealt with two other problems ; the efficiency (external and internal) of the educational system itself, with a view to increasing its "productivity" ; and the preparation of the annual budget. The efficiency consideration, which was either forgotten during the years of economic euphoria or never actively pursued, gave rise to two particular notions of efficiency :

i) the relative efficiency, or economic profitability, of the investment in education as compared to the profitability of the same amount of investment in other sectors of the economy ; and
ii) the "systems productivity" or its internal efficiency.

The first notion of efficiency resulted in the so-called "rate-of-return" approach to educational planning, which, contrary to the social demand approach, takes into account the employment benefits carried for every additional year of education and compares it to the implied costs, whether to the individual and/or the society, for obtaining this additional year of education. The final product from this comparison is a rate of return which indicates the degree to which the additional year of education is profitable. It is evident that the basic assumption underlying this approach is the existence of a direct relationship between income and level of education.

The second notion of efficiency, which has been confused with the economic concept of efficiency (productivity), has been used to evaluate the performance of a particular education system. It assumes that the most efficient education system is the one whose output (number of graduates) is equal to its input (number of first year entrance) at any period of time. In other words, the output/input ratio equals 1, measured in numbers of students.

F. Preparation of Annual Budgets

The preparation of the annual budget for the education sector followed the incremental approach which in most of the cases was applied to each level of education separately. This was, for example, the case in England and Wales between the mid-1950s and 1960s when all White Papers during this period dealt only with individual sectors of the education service and, as a result, did not measure competing claims on resources. (16)

---

16. Reviews of National Policies for Education : England and Wales, OECD, Paris, 1975, p. 11.

Several attempts were made to implement a Programme Budget system in a few countries, as for example the United States, the United Kingdom, etc. The results were not those desired, for the incrementalistic attitude remained unchanged at least at the overall public budget level and for parliamentary bargaining. However, it is worth following the developments in the United Kingdom for installing a sort of Planning Programming Budgeting System (PPBS) which was initiated in 1961 when the Report of the Plowden Committee on the management and control of public expenditure was accepted by the Government at that time. (17) This effort was reinforced in 1964 when the Government at that time "was concerned to plan national resources in greater detail than at any time since the early 1950s and to try to relate its own policies, particularly for the social services, to the likely growth of the economy". (18) Two additional developments took place :

i) the adoption in 1970 of the Programme Analysis and Review (PAR) system, as a means of defining objectives, establishing alternative ways of achieving given aims and analysing the results of expenditure of resources so that valid comparisons with costs could be made" (19) ; and

ii) the development of the Department's programme budget based on a rolling three-year programme which was prepared on the basis of the PAR results and compiled by annual submissions from Departments to the Treasury.

More particularly, the programme budget "has been designed to show the determinants of education expenditure - how much is needed merely to maintain standards in the face of population increase, how much arises from growth in the numbers choosing to participate in education, how much is needed to accomplish planned improvements in the system". (20) The PAR machinery was modified in 1976 and the three-year rolling programme replaced by an annual stock-taking submitted to Ministers collectively so that they might direct the shape of the Programme. (21) This meant the return to annual incremental budgeting procedures, which is the budgeting practice par excellence in all OECD countries.

---

17. Ibid., p. 11.
18. Ibid.
19. Ibid., p. 12. See also : Country Report : England, op. cit., pp. 95-97.
20. Ibid., p. 13.
21. Country Report, England, op. cit., p. 97.

Chapter 2

EDUCATIONAL POLICY PLANNING AND EDUCATIONAL RESEARCH

by
K. Hüfner

I. THE EVOLUTION AND FINANCING OF EDUCATIONAL RESEARCH

After a long honeymoon which began in the 1950s and went on into the early 1970s there has been increasing public criticism of the functions and structures of education. Ambitious programmes for educational research and development (ER&D) have been appearing since the mid-1960s, but nevertheless frustrations run high today and expectations have been unfulfilled. Why was ER&D not more useful ? Have expectations of the educational decision-making systems been too high, or was it educational policy/planning that failed ? These are the questions that must be raised today.

Even in the United States with its relatively large and sophisticated commitment to ER&D, initial optimism was soon accompanied by rising scepticism on the part of educational policymakers. In 1966, F. Keppel wrote : "Two antithetical factors - a distaste for innovation on the one hand, and an exaggerated craving for fashionable ideas, on the other - have disrupted and reduced the effectiveness of modern educational research and form. By the 1960s, however, the nation seemed to have made a new start on an old problem. In most of the educational acts of the Congress there were provisions for research, either as major thrust of the programme or as an integral part of its operations. Even more important was the realisation that education would have to change the scale of its thinking on how to bring about the revolution in its practices the future demanded" (Keppel, 1966, 119)*. About 10 years later, a committee which reviewed the operation of the U.S. National Institute of Education commented as follows :

---
*See References page 73.

> " i) social science research generally is only slowly developing the sophistication that allows it the luxury of predictable results ;
> ii) the problems of bringing about and measuring changes in human learning and behaviour are vastly more complex than those of technological change and are cut across by difficulties of cultural tradition, linguistic style, and emotional factors that simply do not exist to the same degree when one is dealing with things rather than people ; and
> iii) the need for improvement in the results of education is so clear and so great that all interested parties (legislators, educational policymakers, teachers and parents) develop an initial enthusiasm for education R&D only to have its halting and limited results seem at best unsatisfactory and at worst inexcusable".
> (U.S. National Institute of Education, 1975 : 65-66).

In Canada, for many years, the Ontario Institute for Studies in Education, OISE, "was a frequent whipping boy upon which the public and the press vented their rage ; educational R&D institutions in other provinces and countries have undergone the same experience..." (Churchill, 1975 : 49).

S.S. Dunn demonstrates that despite the growth of ER&D in Australia, "the major educational policy decisions are only marginally influenced by research and development. Very often the decision is made and selective research data are used to legitimize the decision. Alternatively, evaluations are carried out with the data selectively gathered to justify the policy". He also points out "that research and development projects cannot provide answers to value questions, and educational policies are often basically value decisions. Research can in a democracy provide data on public opinion and can provide information on which the public can develop informed opinions. Research in the politics and political economy of education is an underdeveloped field in Australia" (Dunn, 1979 : 23).

The Ministry of Education in the Netherlands suggested that one of the main courses which prevented ER&D from having a larger impact upon educational policies was a "credibility gap" which has arisen as a result of unfulfilled expectation from the social sciences.

In Germany, a dramatic increase of ER&D activities occurred between 1963 and 1972 ; the number of ER&D institutions rose from 7 in 1963 to 25 in 1972, and the expenditure in this field rose from 6.14 to 63.26 million Deutschmarks during that period (Edding/Hüfner, 1975). This expansion in ER&D was almost parallel to the expansion of the German educational system itself. However, both systems developed their own dynamics independently of each other. It was for this reason that in 1974 the Education Commission of the German Education Council published its recommendation on "Aspects of Planning Educational Research" in the hope that it may serve three purposes :

- within the research community : as orientation for all scientific disciplines which participate or intend to participate in educational research ;
- within the educational administrations and research foundations : as orientation for new research strategies within the different fields of educational research ;
- and - last but not least - as a useful instrument for the promotion and evaluation of research projects in this domain (Deutscher Bildungsrat, 1974).

Since then the Education Council has ceased to operate, the administrative agreement on its establishment having expired in 1975. This agreement was not renewed, mainly because of increasing political polarisation on educational issues. Germany has since been without a moderating link between ER&D on the one side and educational policy/planning on the other.

The lack of such a link in most of the OECD countries has hindered the good relationship between ER&D and educational policy/planning. For this reason we intend to concentrate here on the general problems of this relationship in functional and structural terms :

According to S. Churchill, in order for an educational renewal system to exist, three elements must be present :

i) a political decision-making structure based on free public discussion and criticism with effective means of controlling the responsibility of political leaders : a democracy, in short, with appropriate levels of control ;
ii) an efficient executive structure, obedient to political control, the whole system of people and resources stretching from the classroom teacher to the highest administrative official ;
iii) a responsive structure for conceiving new solutions to problems, evaluating their effectiveness, and supporting their implementation, i.e. an educational R&D system, broadly defined (Churchill, 1975 : 50).

It should be stressed that in order to find appropriate solutions for educational problems, educational policy/planning must take into account the third component. This implies making changes in the relationships between these structures as well as within each of them. We will be concentrating on two problems in this area :

a) the ER&D system, its present state and necessary future, and
   b) the relationship between educational policy/planning and educational research.

But before doing so, one other issue should be mentioned which arose in the debate several times, namely the volume of ER&D expenditure.

There has been growing concern as to whether the funds spent on ER&D are well spent. Apart from legitimate questions about how decisions are made to spend the research money, there is also the question of whether enough money is spent on ER&D. If we use the proportion of total educational expenditures which is devoted to ER&D as an indicator we can compare it with expenditure on other social activities in a given country, as well as with the ER&D efforts of other countries. This indicator is, of course, only a first step towards raising the question of whether there are enough funds available to spend in a rational way.

Compared to the huge expansion of student bodies, teaching staff, institutions and the overall spending on education during the 1960s and early 1970s, the funds allocated for ER&D have been and have remained relatively small. Although the rates of increase in ER&D outlays were quite remarkable it must be kept in mind that those expenditures did not, even by the broadest possible definition, reach the minimum target of 2 per cent of the education budget in a given country as proclaimed by René Maheu, former Director-General of UNESCO. Even in the United States, the ER&D system received relatively little federal money compared to R&D expenditures in other areas of social activity : in 1971, the United States spent almost 4.7 per cent of the total health budget for health R&D, 1.5 per cent for agriculture R&D, but less than 0.4 per cent for ER&D in education (Malmquist/Grundin, 1975 : 15; see also Tyler, 1976 : 51).

In 1972 OECD reported that "the proportion of the education budget devoted to R&D never exceeds 0.5 per cent and very often represents less than 0.1 per cent" (OECD, 1972 : 31 ; quoted after Malmquist/Grundin, 1975 : 104).

In 1974, an OECD survey concluded as follows : "Educational R&D expenditures remain very low in European OECD Member countries. In most of them they represent less than 0.1 per cent of total educational expenditure (compared to 0.5 per cent in the United States, the only corresponding country in Europe being Sweden, with roughly the same figure). Given the general dissatisfaction with current educational structures, however, it might be asked whether it is not in the end more expensive not to finance the scientific contribution to educational change than to finance it in bolder and more resolute terms" (OECD, 1974 : 35-36).

The present tendency to cut these already low budgets is in sharp contrast to the proposals being made in the middle 1970s. These recommended an increase in the share of ER&D to between 1 and 5 per cent of total educational expenditure as proposed in the United States. By referring to these proposals we do not want to ignore the fact that general agreement has never been reached as to what proportion of total national expenditure should be devoted to ER&D activities. It is, of course, difficult to determine what the "optimal" or "minimal" proportion should be. Nevertheless it should be emphasised again that national ER&D budgets in OECD countries have been extremely low as compared to R&D budgets for other social activities and to industrial R&D budgets which, in the United States for example, vary from 5 to 30 per cent.

II. EDUCATIONAL RESEARCH : DIFFERENT TYPES OF EDUCATIONAL RESEARCH FOR DIFFERENT PURPOSES OF EDUCATIONAL PLANNING

Educational research can be defined both broadly and quite narrowly. Narrowly, it is the relationship between science, especially pedagogics, and the educational system. By this definition it has always existed but with the development of the social sciences it has become an interdisciplinary science of instrumental importance to the planning of education. For this reason we will use the broader definition according to which all scientific disciplines can contribute to educational research, as indicated, by names such as pedagogical psychology, sociology of education, economics of education, educational administration science, etc.

This notion has been explicitly recognised in Germany when in 1963 the "Max-Planck Institut für Bildungsforschung" was founded. In Switzerland, the term "Bildungsforschung"/"Recherche en éducation" was used in 1975 for the same reasons (Gretler, 1980 : 19-25).

Educational research has been growing over the past 50 years, increasing its range of scientific disciplines and widening its perception of problem areas. Whereas the early educational research programmes were conducted by philosophers, historians, and psychologists, those disciplines are now accompanied by anthropology, economics, sociology, political science, biological sciences, etc. Educational research is not only expanding in the number of scientific disciplines it uses, but is also becoming increasingly complex in its concepts of institutions and processes. This statement of Tyler (1965) is a good example : "the school is no longer thought of simply as a place where teachers and children assemble for classes ; the work of sociologists, anthropologists, and social psychologists has given the school meaning as a social institution in which traditions develop, aspirations are encouraged or dampened, communication is facilitated or distorted, activities are given direction and differential rewards, and students sense expectations which may greatly influence their own educational efforts. Hence the school as a social institution has become a relevant part of the map of education, and the variables involved are seen as potential factors influencing learning and teaching."

He concludes that the field of educational research requires much more sophisticated inquiry today than was deemed necessary in earlier years.

Today, the functions of educational research are manifold. They are no longer restricted to the question of what and how to teach, and therefore, of how to organise educational establishments. They include the production of important information for planning educational activities ; the evaluation of programmes, procedures and materials for results and cost in time, effort, and money, providing criticism, innovation, and stimulation for change in education ; and - last but not least - developing a more adequate and valid theory about educational processes and institutions. Although educational research is still at the beginning of its scientific development, some attempt should be made to classify its component parts.

The dichotomy of basic/conclusions oriented vs. applied/decision oriented educational research is well known and does not require much further explanation here. Controversies arise, however, if educational research is defined so narrowly that applied research is excluded. An example of this occurred in Kerlinger's Presidential address to the AERA Annual Meeting in 1977 when he argued as follows : "In this address, I will defend the following three propositions. One, there is little direct connection between research and educational practice. Two, bodies of research aimed at theoretical understanding of psychological, sociological, and other behavioural scientific phenomena of possible relevance to educational thinking and practice may have beneficial though indirect effects on educational practice. A corollary is that basic research is more important than applied research in its potential effect on education. And three, two major obstacles to research influencing educational practice in the long term are the programmatic-practice notion that research should pay off and that it should be relevant to contemporary social and educational problems" (Kerlinger, 1977 : 5). Seen from a narrow definition, of equating educational research to basic research, Kerlinger's statement is correct. But his position is as extreme as the position of those who claim that there is no such thing as basic research in education because education, being a practical activity, means that all true educational research is applied. In fact, however, a continuum exists within which basic research and applied research form two extremes.

It should be stressed here that there are important relationships between basic and applied educational research when issues of financing and organising ER&D arise. The Dutch Ministry of Education clearly recognised this in saying that one of the main obstacles to larger impact of ER&D in the classroom was "... the paradox of the accent on practical research at the expense of so-called irrelevant theoretical research, which in part endangers the formulation and testing of hypotheses and the ability of research to generalise in the long term and thereby also endangers the quality and significance of that same practical research" (Council of Europe, 1978 : 3). We will return to this problem later on.

The Dutch statement implies that those engaged in basic/fundamental research have more freedom of choice. The institutions in which those researchers are working are not expected to undertake research to which educational policy-making institutions attach conditions in terms of anticipated output. In that sense basic/fundamental research is "free research". However, policy-making institutions are the "big spenders" ; they are subsidizing educational research in all forms and in many different places. Therefore, they also express - whether good or bad - certain expectations vis-à-vis institutions mainly engaged in basic research. The Ministry of Education of the Netherlands view of a balanced system of educational research and policy/planning is not always shared.

In this connection it should also be mentioned that the term "applied" might be misleading, because the distinction between basic and applied research is often difficult to make. Of course, the expectation of applied research is that its outcome will be immediately applicable. Basic research, on the other hand, is not expected to have applicable results, at least in the short or medium term. In the long run it might, via certain "translations", very well be applicable, as Kerlinger would maintain. Thus the major differences between basic and applied research apart from the degree of freedom of choice - seems to be the time allowed for productivity. Applied research, no matter how "bound" it is, asks for results within a relatively short time. Therefore it is very often in danger of violating certain scientific standards in terms of methodology, interpretations of results, etc.

Both basic and applied research in education can be undertaken as

    a) macro or micro research, and
    b) internally oriented or externally oriented research. If we combine these types of object oriented research we have four classification possibilities :

Figure 1

LEVEL AND ORIENTATION OF EDUCATIONAL RESEARCH

Orientation \ Level	Micro	Macro
Internally	11	21
Externally	12	22

Internally-oriented micro research might refer, for example, to teacher-student relationships at the institutional level but also to the pedagogical and psychological dimensions of educational planning groups at the national level. Internally oriented macro research, on the other hand, refers to the education system of a country as a whole and can - depending upon the degree of disaggregation - include several levels.

In the 1960s and 1970s there was general agreement that ER&D requires interdisciplinary efforts. The Galtung classification has four types of research activity for which the term "interdisciplinary collaboration" is being used :

"a) research conducted within a common institutional framework by research workers trained in different disciplines, each working in his own discipline, but influenced by occasional contacts with colleagues ;
b) a common research programme divided into sub-programmes each based on a special discipline, the findings typically presented in separate chapters or volumes of a joint research report ;
c) a programme undertaken by an inter-disciplinary research team, working together and preparing joint reports ;
d) a situation in which the individual research worker has trained himself in more than one discipline, representing in himself interdisciplinary competence". (Quoted from Eide, 1971).

Type (c) has many factors working against it. The career expectations of young researchers together with institutional arrangements in higher education and discipline-oriented recruitment combine to make a climate that is normally unfavourable to interdisciplinary work.

There are at least five different institutional settings in which ER&D takes place :

- universities and teacher colleges
- independent research institutes
- administrative departments of education, at different levels
- consulting firms
- international (governmental and non-governmental) organisations.

Research institutes, universities and other structures of higher education are the "classical" institutions of educational research, but certain limitations should be taken into account. In Germany, for example, universities show a keen research interest in almost everything on or off the planet, but nevertheless their research on matters such as higher education is strikingly neglected. Financially independent research institutes are rare ; independent educational research institutes are even more rare. Very often, the dependence on governmental institutions is too direct to allow for basic research. Foundations, either private or public sector "buffer institutions", might be a very helpful way to ensure the necessary "freedom of choice."

Research groups directly linked to departments of educational administration have the advantage of direct access to the data base of the "object system" but they also face certain dangers which cannot be overlooked. The first is that "top" administration might ask them for all kinds of "quick research" services such as those normally provided by consulting firms to deal with immediate problems. Secondly, being close to the "object system" with its built-in administrative inflexibility does not allow such research groups to think in terms of innovative alternatives.

International organisations seldom undertake educational research themselves. Their most important function is to identify new ideas and transfer them by organising meetings and publishing comparative data. In planning education and educational research their job is normally to take the "most advanced country case" as an example for the use of other Member countries.

An "optimal solution" for ER&D evidently would not imply one type of educational research activity undertaken in one specific type of organisation. Before developing an overall system within which educational research can fulfill its function as a "reflexive mechanism", the relationship between educational policy/planning and educational research must be analysed.

There are 3 functional levels to be considered here : ER&D, educational policy/planning (EPP) and actual educational practice. These three levels are determined by different external conditions, interests and working situations.

The level of ER&D is determined by, *inter alia*, the following factors :

- the social organisation of science
- the division of labour and specialisation in science
- manpower capacities and professional orientations
- formal training courses and career patterns
- the value system and criteria of scientific work.

The criteria of scientific work at the ER&D level are basically the measurement of performance, the selection of research topics, etc. However, educational research cannot offer a comprehensive theory of educational processes and institutions, since it combines so many different disciplines, and so the application of scientific criteria is rather difficult. This particularly applies to interdisciplinary research, which is not based upon the continuing research tradition of most of the mono-disciplines. At the ER&D level research takes place either in institutions of higher education or in specialised institutes outside the universities.

The level of educational policy/planning is determined by, inter alia, the following factors :

- the interrelationships between the education and the employment system ;
- the competition for financial resources among the education sector and other public sectors ;
- the overall conditions of Western political democracies, especially the short-run election cycles.

Educational policy/planning agencies have a keen interest in ER&D results which can be used for different educational planning activities. One way to secure an information and communication flow of this sort is to establish ER&D centres within the educational administrations of the planning agencies of a country. As mentioned above, the flexibility of ER&D activities can be increased by such means as those, but at the same time their degree of scientific autonomy will be decreased.

The level of educational practice is determined by, *inter alia*, the following factors :

- the network of administrative regulations ;
- the specific organisational features of educational institutions ;
- the organisation of teaching and learning processes ;
- the needs and interests of teachers, students and parents.

First of all, it should be mentioned that ER&D is connected to educational practice since it is a science which does intend among other things, to solve practical problems. Furthermore, the findings of ER&D ask for testing under the conditions of normal educational practice. In this sense, educational practice is a testing mechanism for scientific ER&D. But educational research activities at the educational practice level also involve activities at the institutional level such as curriculum development, consultancy on curriculum implementation, and teacher training activities.

Looking at the various types and levels of ER&D, it becomes obvious that ER&D has different organisational structure and time requirements from those of educational policy/planning in administrative systems. ER&D with its broad range of activities tends to be a lengthy process which often does not produce the short-term results expected by the educational policy/planning system. As we know from the experiences in many countries over the past 15-20 years, their natural differences have led to conflicts between the "two separate worlds" and to the search for better solutions. In the Netherlands, the Educational Research Institute (SVO) does not itself undertake research, but acts as a national agency for the financing, promotion, and supervision of ER&D. It has developed a strategy, which is still in the experimental phase, of long-term research programming for the planning and co-ordination of ER&D projects (Council of Europe, 1978:4). Switzerland has made a comprehensive inventory of organisations and personnel in educational research (Gretler, A., 1979) and introduced a permanent data collection system for ER&D projects (Centre suisse de coordination pour la recherche en matière d'éducation, 1978). In Great Britain, an ad hoc group was set up in 1978 to give advice on research priorities. It represents local educational authorities, researchers, Her Majesty's Inspectorate and the Department of Education and Science (DES). Now the DES is taking a greater initiative in stimulating ER&D in identifying policy priorities. In Germany the Education Commission made some concrete proposals which should be mentioned here (Deutscher Bildungsrat, 1974). Referring to the three functional levels outlined above, the Commission suggested a structure for co-operation within and between these levels. At the ER&D level they propose a common approach to research planning by developing "research chains". At the educational policy/planning level a regular exchange of information and experience is recommended, together with consistency in educational data collection. Finally, at the level of educational practice, they suggest, in addition to close cooperation between regional centres, the establishment of a problem-oriented documentation centre of curriculum research and development. These examples differ in direction but all indicate the necessity for a comprehensive review of the relationships between ER&D and educational policy/planning. We will address ourselves to these problems from a general analytical viewpoint in section III.

III. EDUCATIONAL POLICY/PLANNING AND EDUCATIONAL RESEARCH : OUTLINE OF AN ANALYTICAL FRAMEWORK

Whenever the relationship between educational policy/planning and ER&D is discussed the first question is how ER&D is utilised by educational policy/planning. If we put this question to an educational planner or administrator, the answer will vary according to their images of

a) the functional relationships between educational policy/planning and educational research ; and
b) the functions and structures of educational research itself.

If we want to answer this question scientifically, we need a theory, or at least an analytical framework, which will allow us to make a historical analysis of the educational policy in a given country during a given time period. The answer will most probably differ depending upon the country and the time period in question.

We have to develop over-all planning mechanisms which link the planning and organisation of ER&D on the one side with the planning and organisation of educational policy/planning on the other.

Before developing an analytical framework which demonstrates this relationship, let us use the scheme suggested by Churchman and Schainblatt to classify some of the issues involved. Our problem is to identify the activities and arrangements which permit the most promising and efficient relationships between educational policy/planning and ER&D.

Churchman and Schainblatt indicate four positions which we can adapt for our purposes :

Figure 2

The Educational researcher \ The educational planner	Understands the educational researcher	Does not understand the educational researcher
Understands the educational planner	"mutual understanding"	"persuasion"
Does not understand the educational planner	"communication"	"separate function"

By this analysis there are four ways to classify the relationship : "separate function", "communication", "persuasion" and "mutual understanding".

The "separate function" position applies when the educational researcher's responsibility is to analyse a particular problem and present a formal solution to the educational planner, who either accepts it or rejects it. It is the planner's responsibility to decide whether to accept the recommendations but, no matter what criteria he uses, he cannot be said to understand the researcher, because a mere acceptance or rejection does not imply "understanding". A need for any such interaction is precluded in this model.

The "communication" position is that the educational planner understands the educational researcher but not vice-versa. Once the educational planner understands the educational researcher's efforts and his procedure, "communication" appears to be a straightforward process for him.

The "persuasion" position has a somewhat different image of the educational planner. It means that it might not be possible to educate the educational planner to be more of an educational researcher. Even if this can be done the first step still consists in breaking down his "innate" resistance to new ideas and research procedures. In order to "sell" the educational research to the educational planner the educational researcher has to know him well enough to be able to influence his attitudes and behaviour.

A common characteristic of all three positions is that they hold the educational planner to be responsible for a possibly inefficient relationship. The fourth position, which is supposed to overcome the shortcomings of the other three, is that of "mutual understanding", which implies not only an "appreciation" of each other but an intensive interaction which would substantially affect the activities of both the educational planner and researcher. "Mutual understanding" implies, first of all, that the educational planner and the educational researcher are familiar with each other's tasks and organisation, their similarities and dissimilarities.

Educational planning consists of three closely interlinked phases or activities : programming, implementation and evaluation. It is a continuous process of learning and revision in which the evaluation activity of the "first round" becomes - at least partially - the basis of the programming activity of the "second round" (Hüfner, 1978).

By introducing "planning levels" as an additional structural dimension of the educational planning process, we can analyse the relationships between the various elements of the educational planning process at different administrative levels. The complexity of the system is expressed by the different relationships between sub-systems. The interrelationships between the three phases of the educational planning process over time have to be specified by level. In a planning set-up, global planning strategies (= programming at the national level) have to be translated into programmes at a "lower" level. This process involves the specification of global goals with respect to time, space and subject. The result at each level will consist of decision premises which function as "constraints" at a lower level.

These "planning levels" are, as indicated above, administrative and not functional. However, the number of levels does not yet answer the question of whether the educational policy/planning set-up of a given country is decentralised. In order to answer questions of centralisation and decentralisation, level-specific indicators for the type and number of constraints have to be analysed.

Finally, a functional differentiation of educational policy/planning has to be introduced which takes into account the time dimension. Generally speaking, there are three different functional levels to be distinguished :

a) strategic educational policy/planning : establishment of long-range goals by making strategic choices ;
b) programme educational policy/planning : establishment of interim objectives ; in other words : incremental progress towards accomplishing long-range goals ; and
c) operational educational policy/planning, achievement of short-range targets within given time-cost performance requirements.

All three technical activities in educational planning, namely programming, implementation and evaluation are necessary at all three functional levels of educational planning. If we combine these two dimensions of educational planning, nine different information requirements can be identified, as shown in Figure 3.

Figure 3

TWO-DIMENSIONAL TAXONOMY FOR EPP
INFORMATION REQUIREMENTS

	Programming	Implementation	Evaluation
Strategic EPP			
Programme EPP			
Operational EPP			

The complexity of the educational policy/planning system increases the need for communication and exchange of information. Different types of information are necessary for the combination of different functional and technical aspects of educational policy/planning. Besides "routine" information, new "innovative" information must be sought. Educational research outputs play a major role in educational policy/planning inputs in both cases. However, the mutual understanding concept as outlined above implies that ER&D fulfills other functions as well. New approaches must be tested and made generally applicable.

The preceding paragraphs show that the elaboration of a "mutual understanding" model between educational policy/planning and ER&D is more complicated than originally anticipated. Having looked into the problems of basic research at the ER&D level and those of applied research at the level of educational practice, educational policy research seems to us the most promising type of ER&D at the educational policy/planning level. According to Etzioni "Policy research is concerned with mapping alternative approaches and with specifying potential differences in the intention, effect and cost of various programmes. It differs from applied research in much the same way that strategy differs from tactics : it is more encompassing, longer-run in its perspectives, and more concerned with goals of the unit for which it is undertaken, that is, it is more critical" (Etzioni, 1971:8) ; he furthermore argues that "policy research differs from basic research as strategy differs from theory. It is much less abstract, much more closely tied to particular actions to be undertaken or avoided. While basic research aims chiefly to uncover truth, policy research seeks to aid in the solution of fundamental problems and in the advancement of major problems" (Etzioni, 1971:12). In other words, educational policy research is solution-oriented and interdisciplinary by nature ; it is a schedule-oriented, intermediary discipline.

These programmatic statements have, of course, to be tested by their actual impact. van de Vall and Bolas studied three independent samples from 40 social policy research projects in the following three domains of policy-making in the Netherlands :

1. industrial and labour relations ;
2. regional and urban planning ;
3. social welfare and public health.

They attempted to analyse and evaluate the structural features of social research utilisation as well as the main functions of social policy research in organisational decisionmaking. They concluded that "inter-organisational dependence, the operation of a committee, the researcher's active participation in detecting and reformulating the research problem constitute an optimal structure for social policy research" (van de Vall/Bolas, 1980/81:9). The authors specify three functions of the utilisation of social research results :

   a) the cognitive,
   b) the communicative, and
   c) the diagnostic (*).

They found that publishing research results for the general public relates positively to policy impact, and using different feedback strategies besides the submission of a report is accompanied by higher rates of policy impact. Finally, comparing external with internal research in social policy formation, they concluded that a project's impact upon organisational decisionmaking is greater when it deals more with the organisational aspect of social policy research. Although no corresponding studies on education are as yet available, it can be assumed that similar results will be obtained.

Finally, the information/communication issue should be further elaborated. In order to guarantee the institutionalised cooperation of educational research institutes at different functional levels, the following recommendations have been made : the exchange of information, multilateral consulting and task specific cooperation with regard to educational reforms. In Germany, for example, the Education Commission proposed the foundation of a central information and documentation unit for educational research. They found the present information and communication base to be insufficient for three reasons :

   a) in technical terms, because the ER&D system has no comprehensive information system about the research in progress and planned in the different institutions at the three functional levels ;
   b) in institutional terms, because the different institutions collect information which might be relevant for planning educational research in the absence of an over-all system of information collection and processing ;
   c) in functional terms, because the present information base serves only limited information demands (e.g. science : internally oriented exchange of information via scientific publications).

This criticism clearly indicates that the mere institutionalisation of a data bank would be insufficient. It is a necessary but not sufficient condition which does help the information storage and diffusion process, especially at the ER&D level (see, for example, the ERIC in the United States and the EUDISED of the Council of Europe). However, the large demand for information, which is related

---

* For a different approach, see Weiss (1979).

to an improvement of the information base in educational research, can only be satisfied if the collected material is transformed into different forms of publications. For the United States, in 1975, an analysis of citation patterns was undertaken to measure the impact of basic research on educational literature. Figure 4 shows the flow of information among the following three categories of periodicals :

1. basic research journals in the social sciences,
2. educational research journals, and
3. educational magazines written for practitioners (Kiesler/Turner, 1977:89-109).

It is interesting to note that basic research literature has an influence on education literature. Kiesler/Turner argued that "even ignoring the fact that the basic research literature is smaller and publishes relatively few education-relevant articles, we find that education research journals are equally likely to cite basic research journals as they are to cite work published in other educational periodicals. We also find that education-relevant articles in the basic research journals do draw on education literature, although less frequently than on basic research literature. Finally, the citation pattern of education magazines suggests that there is some direct translation at basic research findings into the world of the practitioner". (Kiesler/Turner, 1977:99).

Earlier we described the rapid expansion of ER&D in the 1960s and early 1970s. This growth concentrated upon two types of ER&D :

1. applied research on the educational policy/planning problems of state administrations ;
2. research on the development, diffusion and application of material structures and processes for the educational practice of different institutions.

Neither type is basic research, and the second is much more cost-intensive than the first.

The amount of basic educational research – that is, research not tied to the immediate practical applicability of its findings, has gone down dramatically in many countries. Since we know that applied research depends very much upon the results of basic research, self-reflexive, financially independent mechanisms are necessary to guarantee the further development of educational research at the first functional level mentioned above.

Figure 4 **PATTERN OF CITATION IN THE EDUCATION LITERATURE, UNITED STATES, 1975**

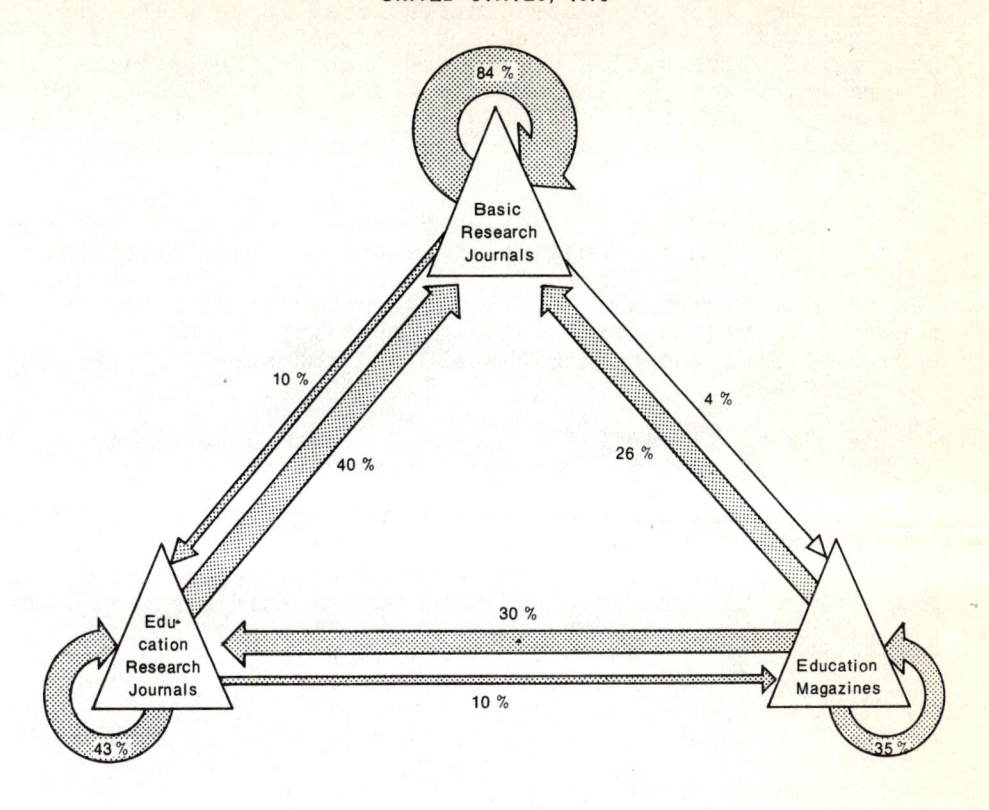

IV. CONCLUSIONS AND OUTLOOK

Experience in the ER&D sector reveals the need for an improvement in the relationship between the "two worlds". In the following paragraphs, these possibilities and limitations are described, some of the major problems summarised and an agenda for further research is suggested.

In the United States, the concept of ER&D has been derived from the non-academic world, primarily industry, agriculture and technology. As Keppel put it in 1966 : "... the act of financing research, in itself, is no panacea for the educational problems of the future. Equally important in a decentralised system is to stimulate a willingness to test the results of research, to put into practice the best of tested innovations. To this end, research and demonstration centers were established in 1964 at several universities across the country. New regional laboratories were on the drawing boards in 1965, designed to serve education much as the agricultural experiment centers long served and stimulated the development of agriculture".

"A network that linked every stage from basic research to product, from the original idea to education practice, had to be forged". "Essential are close ties with the educational system at all levels, co-ordination with state departments of education, and the availability of research personnel from the academic world and industry" (Keppel, 1966:123-125).

Applying a scientific model of research utilisation to the educational realm seems to have been the biggest mistake : "The methods have unduly copied designs from the natural sciences and have often been inappropriate for the problems under consideration (Busch, 1976:2). As ER&D developed it became clear that the product of educational research rarely provides the kind of scientific generalisations which the EPP system asked for. It became obvious that ER&D cannot produce brilliant technical solutions to pressing problems of EPP. ER&D can affect EPP, but it is and will be a slow, non-specific process, not a linear interaction which can be neatly expressed in a simple model.

In many countries, the 1960s were the times of "easy-research money", and rapid growth in the ER&D sector. During this time, many researchers from the social sciences engaged themselves in ER&D. ER&D budgets jumped up too quickly and did not allow for the necessary solid development of quality and expertise. This field still is, as one mentioned earlier, at the beginning of its overall scientific development, and it still has difficulty in applying strict scientific criteria. At the same time, it should be stressed again that the overall resources available to ER&D have been and remain insufficient. Dramatic increases which led to certain "expansion illnesses" could be obtained for the 1960s but the level of ER&D financing is still extremely low compared to the ER&D levels for other social activities. At present the pendulum has swung from EPP euphoria and ER&D optimism to heavy cuts in public budgets and laissez-faire policies for the education sector. This is a result of general economic problems like stagflation and unemployment but it also reflects the fact that education is no longer at the peak of the "policy attention cycle" as it happened to be in the 1960s.

This leads us to some observations about the policy system of which EPP is a relatively small, and uninfluential part. The existence of "political cycles" of alternating periods of public concern and neglect with regard to educational issues, cannot be ignored. EPP is confronted with major financial problems in education and ER&D. As mentioned above, there are many conflicts between the "two cultures" and the gap can only be bridged by continuously renewed attempts at mutual understanding. Time is often a very limited resource in the EPP process which often - especially in the case of political cycles - leads to frustrating situations for the educational researcher. Often the EPP system does not wait until the research results become available ; sometime it might even happen that the reported results are simply ignored because the policy attention for specific educational matters has already gone.

Another issue which should be taken into account is the normative aspect of the interaction between ER&D and EPP. There are three obstacles which complicate the relationship between the two systems. First, there are built-in conflicts in the educational policy-making process. Policies are the outcome of political compromises which lead to solutions which do not correspond to the original problem. Second, the educational reality is too complex to be described in terms of a few easily manipulated variables. The ER&D system tends to "increase complexity", whereas the main task of the EPP system is to "decrease complexity". Third, the knowledge produced by ER&D presupposes a consistent theoretical framework for interpretation, but the social sciences in pluralistic societies offer competing theoretical approaches which require the financial support of different educational research strategies.

This analysis calls for a rethinking of the functional relationships between ER&D and EPP. In Section III a first attempt has been made to delineate the relevant issues. This approach seems to be more promising than the analysis of single concrete, but isolated and non-transferable cases in which ER&D results have led to major breakthrough in EPP. The history of individual cases certainly offers some existing insights, but it can be assumed that in most cases many misunderstandings and compromises have led to decisions that are far removed from the original findings of ER&D and of EPP. Finally, there will be no case where the special value of the ER&D contribution can be assessed correctly.

In the past, ER&D suffered from completely false expectations. There were and are no clear pay-off relationships, the application of linear models failed. Husén described the potential contribution of ER&D to EPP as a "percolating process", others stress the "enlightenment function" of ER&D which has a "trickling down effect" over time. The value of specific research results cannot be quantified. ER&D helps to clarify specific EPP problems and increases awareness of follow-up problem policies.

To sum up, ER&D can and should help the EPP system to think about educational issues ; to formulate the problems involved, and to gain new ideas and perspectives on educational developments. All this experience should not prevent us from improving the functions and structural relationships within and between the two systems. However, the ER&D system cannot and should not be transformed into an EPP system and the reverse is equally unthinkable. On the contrary, there are strong arguments in favour of maintaining the tensions between the two systems as necessary and built-in checks and balances (Levin, 1978:165-166).

Finally, there are some research issues which would help to clarify the present relationship between ER&D and EPP. For example, there are no national studies on educational policy research of the type which has been discussed (see pages 66-67) (cf. van de Vall/Bolas, 1980/81). Further, similar studies like those made by Kiesler/Turner for the United States (see page 68) should be undertaken for other states. In addition, there should be more work on the economics of ER&D : new information is needed on the level of ER&D expenditure as a proportion of national educational expenditure. This will involve the creation of a commonly held definition of ER&D expenditure. The cycles of ER&D financing should be studied in detail, especially as they relate to overall "policy attention", demographic and economic cycles and educational finance cycles. Last but not least, national studies showing the "trickling down effect" of ER&D are recommended.

REFERENCES

Bush R.N. Educational Research and Development : The Next Decade. Stanford Center for Research and Development in Teaching, Stanford, June 1976, 35 p.

Centre suisse de coordination pour la recherche en matière d'éducation. Enquête permanente sur la recherche et le développement éducationnels en Suisse. Index cumulatif. December 1978.

Churchill S. "Restructuring Educational R&D in Ontario", in Interchange, Vol. 6, 1, 1975, pp. 49-64.

Churchman C.W. & Schainblatt A.H. "The Researcher and the Manager : A Dialectic of Implementation", in Management Science, Vol. II, 4, February 1965, pp. B-69-B-87.

Council of Europe. Educational Research Policy in European Countries. 1978 Survey. Report submitted by the Ministry of Netherlands. Council of Europe, Strasbourg, 22 November 1978 (DECS/Rech(78)82).

Deutscher Bildungsrat, Empfehlungen der Bildungskommission. Aspekte für die Planung der Bildungsforschung. Klett, Stuttgart, 1974.

Dunn S.S. "The Research Contribution to Policy : A Researcher's Overview". In Shellard, J.S. (Ed.), Educational Research for Policymaking in Australia. Hawthorn, Victoria, Australian Council for Educational Research, 1979, pp. 18-26.

Edding F. & Hüfner K. "Probleme der Organisation und Finanzierung der Bildungsforschung in der Bundesrepublik Deutschland", in Roth, H., and Friedrich, D., Bildungsforschung. Probleme - Perspektiven - Prioritäten. Part 2 (Vol. 5). Stuttgart, Klett Verlag, 1975, pp. 419-453.

Eide K. "Educational Research Policy", OECD, Paris, 1971 (mimeo).

Etzioni A. "Policy Research", in American Sociologist, Vol. 6, 1971, pp. 8-12.

Gretler A. "La recherche éducationnelle en Suisse", in Revue française de pédagogie, No. 47, April-May-June 1979, pp. 109-122.

Gretler A. "Bildungsforschung heute", in <u>Bulletin der Schweizerischen Gesellschaft für Bildungsforschung</u>, Vol. 13, 31 (May 1980), pp. 19-25.

Hüfner K. "Educational Planning in Federal Countries with Special Reference to the Federal Republic of Germany", OECD, Paris, 1978.

Husén T. "Policy Implications of the IEA Findings and Some of their Repercussions on National Debates on Educational Policy", in <u>Studies in Educational Evaluation</u>, Vol. 3, 2, Summer 1977, pp. 129-141.

Keppel F. <u>The Necessary Revolution in American Education</u>, Harper & Row, New York, 1966, 201 pp.

Kerlinger F.N. "The Influence of Research on Education Practice", in <u>Educational Researcher</u>, Vol. 6, 8, September 1977, pp. 5-11.

Kiesler S.B. & Turner Ch. F. (Eds.) <u>Fundamental Research and the Process of Education</u>. NIE, Washington, D.C., 1977.

Levin H.M. "Why isn't Educational Research more Useful ?", in <u>Prospects</u>, Vol. 3, 2, 1978, pp. 157-166.

Malmquist E. & Grundin H.U. <u>Educational Research in Europe Today and Tomorrow</u>. CWK Gleerup, Lund, 1975.

OECD. "Survey of Educational Research and Development". OECD, Paris, November 1972 (mimeo).

OECD. <u>Research & Development in Education : A Survey</u>, OECD, Paris, 1974.

Tyler R.W. "The Field of Educational Research", In Guba, E., and Elam, S. (Eds.), <u>The Training and Nurture of Educational Researchers</u>. Sixth Annual Phi Delta Kappa Symposium on Educational Research. Phi Delta Kappa, Bloomington, Ind., 1965, pp. 1-12.

Tyler R.W. (Ed.). <u>Prospects for Research and Development in Education</u>. McCutchen, Berkeley, Calif., 1976.

US National Institute of Education. <u>R&D Funding Policies of the National Institute of Education : Review and Recommendations</u>. Washington, D.C., 1965.

van de Vall M. & Bolas Ch. "Utilizing Social Policy Research for Solving Social Problems. An Empirical Analysis of Structure and Function", (22 p.) in the <u>Journal of Applied Behavioral Science</u>, 1980/81.

Weiss C.H. "The Many Meanings of Research Utilisation", in <u>Public Administration Review</u>, September/October 1979, pp. 426-431.

Chapter 3

NEW FEATURES IN EDUCATIONAL PLANNING

by
K. Eide

I. WHY DOES EDUCATIONAL PLANNING CHANGE ?

In another context, we have postulated the following changes in the theory and practice of educational planning in recent years (1) :

- A widening of the scope beyond purely educational matters.
- A broadening of the conceptual framework to include elements from a variety of research disciplines.
- A profound change in the conception of planning as an administrative function.

Such changes, noticeable in a wide range of countries, are highly interrelated, and may have a common cause. It could be simply that as a political/administrative function, educational planning has become more mature, and better adapted to the reality in which it operates. While planning practitioners have come to master their tasks better, planning theorists may finally have recognised some of the experience gained from practice.

In addition to this, changes may have occurred in the political and administrative context in which educational planning operates. Such changes may again be related to a more general change in the climate surrounding educational activities and policymaking.

Some elements of general organisation theory may be helpful in this context. An organisation living in a static environment, with stable requirement from the outside and clearly defined boundaries to its responsibilities, is

---

1. "Educational planning in Norway" in Educational Planning, Vol. IV, 1976.

probably best served by an organisational structure corresponding to the bureaucratic hierarchies so well described by Max Weber.

However, an organisation trying to survive, or even expand, in a very turbulent environment, with rapidly changing and contradictory external requirements and diffuse boundaries as to its actual responsibilities, will have to develop a quite different internal structure. The number of hierarchical levels will have to be reduced, horizontal communication will have to be emphasized, decision-making must be much more decentralised, and overlapping responsibilities accepted. Such internal structural changes primarily aim at greater adaptability and learning capacity in the organisation as a whole. In addition, the organisation must develop its capacity to influence its environment, in order to bring it under a reasonable degree of control, or at least to achieve a certain level of predictability in its behaviour.

Organisational structures and forms of planning usually show close correspondence, unless planning is used as an instrument to change the established organisational structure, in a process of dialectic policymaking. In the ideal type of bureaucratic hierarchical organisations, planning can be undertaken on the assumption that there exists one consistent set of objectives governing the organisation's activities. The prime planning task will then be to programme the organisation's activities to obtain maximum consistency with the given objectives, and to see that the various parts of the organisation actually behave accordingly. Within such an organisation, the planning function could be described as a search for optimal solutions and the consequent consistency control.

In a very turbulent environment, however, planning functions must, by necessity, develop quite different features. The planners must accept that within the organisation, many different sets of objectives are operating, and the actual decisions made will reflect compromises. The search for "optimal" solutions thus becomes rather meaningless. Instead, planners must identify the range of solutions that might be acceptable to a sufficiently large part of the organisation to become actual policy. Consistency control ceases to be a prime planning function ; instead planners must identify emerging problems and conflicts and help the organisations to face them, without offering a "right" solution. As planning will have to be done in all the operational units, a central planning agency must primarily assist such units in their planning ; it cannot do the planning for them. And an essential planning function will be to identify new developments in the environment, and possibly also devise strategies for changing the external milieu of the organisation. Instead of consistency control, the essential planning function consists of enhancing the learning capacity of the organisation as a whole.

Seen in this perspective, the proposed changes in educational theory and practice become more easily understandable. Increased concern for developments beyond education, a wider conceptual framework, as well as different ways of performing the planning function are responses to an educational system existing in a much more turbulent and changing environment.

But has such a change in the environment of education really occurred ? The answer must clearly be in the affirmative.

An essential element in this development is the change in a few decades from being information-poor to information-affluent societies. The traditional predominance of the school in the provision of information and knowledge, particularly to the young, has completely broken down. As an institution providing access to information, the school has become redundant. It is striving to become instead an essential instrument for the preparation of young people - and grown-ups too - for the selection of appropriate information. Not surprisingly, the school as an institution going through this dramatic transition suffers attacks and distrust, both from the outside and from many of its own members.

The rest of society is as strongly affected. Are we preparing the majority of youngsters for jobs bound to disappear in a decade or two ? Are we relating schools to local environments which will be out of existence, at least in their present form, in less than a generation ? Already today, 10-15 per cent of the adult population - and among them many youngsters - are rejected by the economy as useless. If, as it seems, this percentage will increase to 20 or 25 per cent, will the school have to begin training students for lifelong unemployment ? Most of the jobs threatened by "rationalisation" are held by females today. What kind of life will the school train the girls for ? Finally, perhaps half of all work efforts in our societies are unpaid. Will the school go on neglecting this essential part of work life ? Or shall we assume that such unpaid work functions will continue to be professionalised and institutionalised ?

From the point of view of education, this is truly a turbulent environment. It may seem that such external developments threaten even a minimum level of functioning of educational activities in our societies. It is inevitable that a large social system such as education will have to attempt at least to moderate some of this turbulence, simply as a matter of survival.

The obvious break-down of the notion of a consistent set of internal objectives for educational activities adds to the planner's troubles. Theories and models taken from single scientific disciplines are obviously inadequate as a basis for understanding and manipulating this situation. The planners will need a stock of theories taken from different disciplines, if they are to have a chance of coping with their tasks.

But those tasks have changed. Initially, planning was thought of as an instrument for helping the top of the organisational hierarchy to control the rest of the organisation, but this position has proved untenable. Other groups within, or even outside, the organisation may claim the services of planners. In such a situation, the search for "optimal" solutions and consistency becomes meaningless.

The peculiarities in the development of educational planning can hardly be fully explained in this way. Probably, the form in which central planning was initially introduced - in education as in other fields - must also be seen as an instrument in a power game. At least partly, it can be understood as an attempt to shift the control over to new groups. This is particularly clear in the case of such planning approaches as "management by objectives", "programme budgeting" and "accountability". But as the political climate around and within education changes, planning has to adapt to the needs of many groups.

Organisational changes are slow, often too slow, to adapt to new organisational needs. Just as the forms of planning initially introduced were partly aimed at changing traditional power balances within the organisational system, new forms of planning may be used to compensate for organisational inertia and to speed up change. Planning modes are not passive reflections of the environment ; they can be instruments for deliberately changing policy. This is true for planning in education as well as in other fields, where similar changes in the planning functions are emerging.

In what way do such changes in the planning function manifest themselves ? They must necessarily become visible in the form of a change in the concrete tasks of the planners. There is no doubt that a variety of such new tasks are emerging. The main purpose of this paper is to call attention to a few examples of such new features in educational planning. They should be seen as illustrations of the main thesis of this paper, that the planning function is undergoing a profound change. Other illustrations, perhaps even more significant, might have been presented. The aim of this paper is only to focus on a few types of new tasks, which seem to be compatible with the general developments indicated above.

The examples chosen may conveniently be labelled as follows :

- Examination of process qualities
- Field testing

- Action research
- Partisan counterfires
- Dialectic planning
- Coping with the environment

Nothing very dramatic hides behind those labels, as will be revealed as they are dealt with in turn. They may, however, represent interesting additions to the tool kits of the educational planner, often replacing worn-out traditional tools.

II. EXAMINING PROCESS QUALITIES

Traditionally, planning in a specific field focuses on the delivery of input from other sectors, and the delivery of output to other sectors. Relationships between input and output are assumed to be purely technical, a matter for specific expertise in that field.

Planning advice based on such assumptions must necessarily be misleading, as it ignores essential elements of the whole operation. It is fairly obvious to those involved in education, as well as to those responsible for policies in the field, that educational performance cannot be measured solely by output indicators. The way in which educational input is turned into output is in itself an essential factor in performance evaluation. For all activities in which the provision of services is an important element, process qualities must necessarily be taken into account in an evaluation of the activity. This is particularly true for education, where the processes in question take an exceptionally long time. Most people today spend, in fact, between 1/5 and 1/6 of their life-time in educational processes. It is simply ridiculous to assume that what happens to them in all that time is irrelevant, except for the final outcome.

Thus educational planners have had to approach the tricky issue of process qualities, in order to somehow fit those phenomena into their planning models. We can, of course, find a number of quantitative measures that could be used as proxies for process qualities. Yet, it is indisputable that the most relevant evidence is to be found among those directly involved in the process, in their ways of experiencing it. Researchers and others studying the system from the outside somehow become second rate experts on process qualities, as compared to those directly experiencing them. This may be the reason why full recognition of the importance of process qualities meets with so much resistance, particularly among various experts. An outstanding example is the emphasis in work on social indicators upon "output indicators", in spite of the consequent loss of relevance and usefulness in policy terms.

An example of this is the tendency in several countries to organise education according to the traditional principles of industrial organisation. Schools are assumed to benefit from economies of scale, to allow for a wide variety of specialised expertise within the school. Each group of experts specialises in a specific aspect of the pupil, his progress in a certain subject, his reading ability, his mental health, his physical health, his speaking difficulties, his social background, etc. At the same time, in a true supermarket manner, the pupils are invited to choose among a wide variety of options, not only in terms of subject but also in terms of the level at which the subject is taught. The teaching itself is to a great extent preprogrammed, but individualised according to a running diagnosis of the individual pupil. The term "delivery of services" is appropriately applied to such an educational process.

The consequence seems to be a huge educational institution, largely isolated from the population it serves, and struggling with a wide range of compartmentalised expertise, viewing each child from their own specific professional angle. Internal communication tends to break down, anyone attempting to care for the pupil as a whole human being ending regularly at the bottom of the professional hierarchy. As to the pupils, they shuttle from one department to another, seeing perhaps 20 grown-ups and 200 fellow pupils in the course of a week, but not belonging anywhere.

In the long run, serious planners cannot avoid the question of how such an educational setting is experienced by those directly involved : the teachers, as those delivering more or less preprogrammed services, and the pupils who have such services directed at them. Comparisons will have to be made with process qualities involved in quite different organisational arrangements for school-based education.

In examining such aspects of the educational process, planners may still use researchers and other experts to report on how the process is being experienced. Their preferences may be mapped, and their actual reactions measured. Such information complicates, of course, the planner's judgment. It is no longer a simple matter to calculate optimal solutions, as one has to accept several actors in the field, probably with widely differing preferences. Unless the planner explicitly or implicitly weighs the preferences of the different parties involved, planning problems have no nice and neat answers.

At the same time, collecting research-based information on the preferences of those involved may to many planners seem a rather indirect way of approaching the problem. Much more reliable evidence on individual preferences, and on collective preferences emerging from compromises between individuals, would be available if those involved could make decisions themselves. We would then get a much more profound insight into how process qualities are really felt by them, and what kind of operational compromises they are able to agree upon.

In other words, the logical consequence of recognising process qualities as important elements in planning for future developments of a system, is to move from the stage of questionnaire-based data-collecting to practical experiments in changing power structures towards more influence for those directly involved.

In practice, this means that a part of the planning function is transferred to the operational level and to those directly involved in the educational process. Developing the organisational arrangements most appropriate for the kind of power balance aimed at, may still be a task for the central planners. But the actual shape of the educational process will to a great extent be beyond his field of competence. He will also have to accept major trade-offs between process qualities and final products, without being in a position to insist that this is "irrational" or "inefficient". Yet, if the planner is willing to give up the out-dated ambition of defining "optimal" solutions, he may still be able to assist policymakers at all levels in their weighing of the different pros and cons.

In this context, an essential planning task may be to analyse the existing power structure, and the consequences of changes in this structure. To what extent is the power structure internal to the school determined by external regulations ? What are the incentives governing decisions taken at that level ? Will formal decentralisation of decision-making transfer power to other forces outside the school, at the central or local level, and which would these forces be ? How can the clients of the system - the local community, the parents and the pupils themselves - be put into a position of having a genuine influence on what is being offered by the school ? How does formal arrangement for parental influence compare with influence by local authorities reflecting the political structure in the schools environment ? How does such influence affect the chances of genuine partnership in decision-making for the pupils ?

Who has a say in educational matters is primarily a political question. The actual decisions emerging from a given formal power structure is to some extent an open question. There is no "right" answer to be found by the planner. But analysing how organisational arrangements can be developed to allow for a genuine reflection of the experience of process qualities is a challenging planning task.

III. FIELD TESTING

The approaches indicated above as consequences of genuine interest in process qualities may have a more general applicability. Much traditional planning is based on the more or less explicit assumption that activities can be described and monitored in terms of production functions. The specific "technical" coefficients linking policy instruments to objectives are to be provided by specialised researchers. The planner's task is to tie together all partial information available on the system as a whole and to turn this into a model for simulation and monitoring.

In complex systems, such as education, research rarely offers clear-cut answers to questions about how a change in factor x will influence factor y. Some empirical answers may, of course, be found, but they are usually based on research models with a very low degree of autonomy. Changes in variables outside the model may easily change all the observed interrelationships within the model.

Experiments with careful control over all relevant variables have, in fact, rarely added much to our understanding of the functioning of educational institutions and systems. Our insight into such systems owes much more to a wide variety of less controlled experiments, in which a wide range of factors have been changed. The fact that in such cases we cannot attribute changes in dependent variables to changes in specific independent variables, does not prevent such experiments from offering new insight into the complex interrelationships characterising educational phenomena. It is, in fact, the broad spectrum of such experiments, and more or less accidental change processes, which has built up most of our present knowledge of education, thus forming also the basis for realistic planning activities.

If, as educational planners, we still insist upon thinking in terms of production functions, the kind of evidence emerging from such experiments is difficult to utilise.

However, if we stop defining our tasks as a search for optimal solutions, and turn to the far more realistic task of identifying a variety of groups of factors satisfying a more or less wide range of requirements, experiments of this type become an essential planning tool.

Normally we will find that a certain change leads to improvements in a number of dimensions, while in some other dimensions the changed situation may be regarded as neutral or even as less satisfactory. Judgement as to what alternative is "best" will depend on the values attached to the different objectives ; there is no "objective" answer to be provided by the planner.

Far more important than searching for such answers is the gradual exploration of the field of acceptable solutions. Most people, including most policy makers, grossly underrate the range of alternatives for satisfying a given number of basic requirements. Strongly deviating school experiments are thus more important as illustrations of the range of possible acceptable solutions than as prototypes for a new system. They demonstrate that the range of choice is often much wider than we tend to think, and that within this range we may satisfy certain objectives much better than before, without seriously endangering other objectives.

Educational research is not part of educational planning, but it forms an important basis for such activities. However, the organisation or initiation of more or less controlled change experiments, and the careful follow-up of locally generated changes, is possibly an even more important source of planning-relevant insight. This kind of data provides the planners with possibilities for sorting out a wide variety of options for political choice, and for analysing possible consequences of different options.

Seen as a process over time, such an interplay between change activities and planning could form the backbone of major reform activities. As a planning approach, it offers more chances of adaptation to reality, as well as for general acceptance of reform ideas, than the traditional preparation of "a plan" for subsequent "implementation". When the possibility for such alternative planning approaches exists, it may even be asked whether planners should be at all concerned with the preparation of plans in the traditional form.

Major recent educational reforms in the Scandinavian countries may serve as examples here. Vaguely defined initial ideas have been tested out in alternative forms for up to a decade before reforms have been generalised. This experimental learning process has not only led to new understanding about how reform ideas can be effectively put into practice, but also about possible weaknesses in the reform ideas themselves. The final outcome cannot be tested against initial reform plans in terms of "success" or "failure" as, in the process, ideas have changed about what "success" means in this context.

There has certainly been a tendency to oversell Scandinavian reform activities as an example of scientifically-based, pre-planned change processes. In retrospect, it is easy to see that most of the reforms can, in fact, be described as vast, collective learning processes, in which the main inputs were practical experience at the operational level, and widespread reactions to those experiences, rather than scientific findings.

In such field testing of promising new directions, educational planners can have a major role to play. They should be well placed to identify possible new openings for desirable change, often in the form of locally initiated experiments. They should have the means to provide a general framework within which experiments can have a fair chance of surviving, and they should be able to offer professional support to those directly involved. Furthermore, planners have an essential task of bringing together the insight gained from a variety of field experiments, interpreting and evaluating this material, and drawing more generalised conclusions from it. They should also be capable of identifying problems arising within such experiments, and of examining ways of overcoming them.

The extent to which educational planners can find such useful roles to play in educational reform processes may be decisive for the future definition of educational planning as a political/administrative function.

IV. ACTION RESEARCH

More or less controlled field experiments may be initiated from the outside, or they may emerge from within an institution. One may, however, move even further away from the traditional pattern of experimental changes, with follow-up studies of the extent to which the changes were "successful". If the feeling exists, inside or outside the institution, that some aspects of the institution's operations do not function adequately, change processes could be initiated without any pre-definition of targets.

This form of action research presupposes a fairly wide agreement on certain weak points in an institution's operations, and at least some vague notions as to the desirable direction of possible changes. The external research component of such projects often consists of a diagnosis of the present situation, trying to identify potential agreement on such weak points and change directions. What changes should be undertaken is largely a matter for the institution itself to decide. It does not normally follow from the analysis of outside researchers. The latter, however, assist in clarifying the results of initial change processes, in staging an internal assessment of those processes, and in the development of further change strategies.

The outcome of such a change process is not clearly defined in advance, and may come as a surprise both to the people primarily involved in it and to the researchers associated with the project. The responsibility for the final results must clearly lie with the practitioners themselves, while a genuinely catalytic function of researchers implies that they do not attempt to monitor the change processes in terms of their own objectives. At first sight, such change processes seem to offer little scope for planners. This would be true, if planners stuck to their traditional role of advising on how to move from a given situation to a predefined, more desirable one. There is, however, an essential planning function hidden in the specific elements of malfunctioning within systems and institutions. There may also be an essential planning function associated with the identification of "unstable" points within existing systems, which could be strategic variables for change. We shall return to this point below.

Furthermore, as mentioned above, important planning tasks may be related to the creation of a system of borderline factors permitting the change processes to occur. They may possibly also prevent specific vested interests from running away with the whole show.

Equally important, however, is the role of planning in providing information helping the actors in the change process to understand their situation and the various options open to them. This kind of information will often relate to the interdependency between the specific innovating agency and its environment. In principle, this planning task is no different from the regular provision of background information for decision making at any level within organisations. However, in a genuine action research context, there is no room for the planner's ideas about optimal solutions or manipulatory monitoring operations.

In summing up, it is essential to underline the changed role of the planner in this context. Studying changes emerging from action research processes is not only a means by which planners can gain increased insight. It also turns upside-down the traditional notion that planners are there to assist a small number of decision-makers in monitoring a large number of passive human elements. The elements have become actors and decision-makers, and they have no use for special planning efforts unless the planners serve their purposes. Both theory and practice in planning should be able to cope with such a challenge. Traditional theory and practice cannot.

V. PARTISAN COUNTERFIRES

This rather dramatic label covers some relatively common phenomena, although they are often disregarded in more traditional planning theory. In most systems, a wide range of decisions are taken by local or institutional authorities at lower levels. On such decisions, policy-makers and planners at more central levels have few possibilities of direct intervention. There are scores of good arguments for decentralised decision-making within such huge systems as education. On the other hand, decentralised decision-making reduces the ability of the system to defend itself against strong external pressure-groups. Small, semi-autonomous decision-making centres may easily fall prey to such pressure-groups, maintaining nationwide, centralised power. Teacher unions, religious and political organisations are possible examples.

What often happens is that central authorities, while not intervening with actual decisions taken at the local level, still try to influence the local power-structure involved in making such decisions. This kind of strategy implies building up the strength of certain local parties in order to achieve a proper power balance as seen from the centre. There is, of course, no objective point of balance in such a case ; what is sought is a local power-structure able to generate decisions not too different from those wanted by central authorities.

The formal power-structure may, for instance, leave a series of important decisions to local bodies representing teachers, pupils and parents. If, in practice, this arrangement functions as an alliance between teachers and parents against the pupils, depriving the latter of even their traditional possibility of playing off school and parental authority against each other, some redressing of the power situation may be necessary. Counterfires may take many forms, from strengthening the countrywide organisations of students, reducing the negative sanctions towards students available to the teachers, such as marks and examinations, removing certain decisions from the tripartite bodies and leaving them to students alone, etc.

Correspondingly, devolution of decision-making power to local levels may lead to greater institutional power, leaving local political bodies more or less out of the picture. This could be redressed through stronger local representation in institutional steering bodies, or by cutting many of the direct links between the institutions and central agencies, forcing the institutions to fight for their interests with local authorities without help from the centre. Another version, not uncommon in many countries, is the development of parental influence in ways which in fact strengthen social inequality. There is firm evidence of parental influence regularly being biased towards wealthy and well educated parents with successful children in school. In many cases, politically elected bodies will be more balanced in social terms, as the weaker groups have had more chance of building up their collective strength in a broader political context. Shifting local influence from parental representatives to local political bodies may thus in many cases redress an imbalance in power terms between different social groups.

These are some examples of what we have termed "partisan counterfires". It is basically a question of political strategy leaving, however, a wide scope for planning activities. The substance of such planning work is the study of power structures, and more in real than in formal terms, the consequences for such structures of possible changes in formal terms, and a search for legal, financial, organisational and informative arrangements which can influence power structures at various levels in desired directions. Such forms of educational planning are presented here as a typical top-to-bottom approach within a hierarchy. It should be mentioned, however, that similar approaches can be developed for local planning in an attempt to influence higher decision-making levels.

VI. DIALECTIC PLANNING

Dialectic planning represents the antithesis to the notion of consistency which is a characteristic feature of traditional planning. Conventional planning theory sees maximum consistency in actions all through an organisation, and at different times, as the "raison d'être" of planning. The starting point for dialectic planning is completely different. It takes off from the assumption that most organisations and systems have reached a form of balance, based on the relative power of the various actors involved. Changing important parameters within the system will to many of the actors seem like a threat to their interests, more than as a chance to improve their position. Changes have substantial costs, and resistance to change among most actors will be considerable.

In order to change a system of this nature, one will have to identify parameters where the present situation seems to represent a potential imbalance in the sense that strong actors can be made interested in, or at least willing to accept, some changes. Furthermore, the parameters in question must be "strategic variables", which means that the changes cannot easily be isolated from the rest of the system. As all systems have extensive capabilities of immunising changes in specific variables, one has to search for parameters with unavoidable repercussions in essential parts of the whole system. In other words, the aim is to create imbalances that spread through the system as a whole.

Such a deliberate creation of inconsistencies, disturbing the balance in more and more parts of the system, is not unusual as a political strategy. Politicians are, however, far ahead of most planners in this respect. Planners still mostly tend to think that changes happen in jumps from one balanced and consistent situation to another. However, practical experience provides rather overwhelming evidence that this is rarely the way things happen, and that policies based on such assumptions have little chance of success.

A typical example is the apparently logical assumption that a major reform in a school system must be preceded by retraining of the teachers. In practice, however, no-one has ever managed to retrain teachers for an educational system not yet in existence. The only way of doing it seems to be to introduce the reform, and then to assist the teachers in their gradual adaptation to it. In the same way, few countries have managed to change simultaneously the totality of their educational system. Fairly regularly, certain parts of the system are subject to reforms, creating major imbalance between those parts and others. This in turn gradually creates a situation in which new parts of the system are ripe for reform. The essential point here is to start a reform movement at a point within the system where changes cannot be isolated and made less damaging to the system as a whole. A fair guess would be that, in terms of levels, primary education is probably the most strategic part in this respect, although this may differ from country to country.

Thus, dialectic planning aims at the deliberate creation of imbalances, inconsistencies and contradictions in systems, in such a way as to promote gradual changes in desired directions within the system as a whole. The planning part of such an operation involves diagnosis of the system and identification of its strategic parameters, as well as analysis of repercussions to be expected through interventions on such strategic dimensions. As a planning approach, it may seem rather manipulatory, but it is probably not more so than most conventional approaches. To a surprising degree, the strategy involved in this kind of planning may be spelt out. Making it explicit may even increase the chances of success, provided, of course, that sufficient political strength can be mobilised to carry the changes through.

VII. COPING WITH THE ENVIRONMENT

In a turbulent environment, educational planning cannot restrict itself to the passive role of predicting external developments, and suggesting possible adaptations to such developments within education. Policy makers dealing with education cannot avoid adopting a position in relation to such external development, which may threaten the proper functioning of the whole educational system. In the same way, educational planners are gradually forced to analyse essential societal developments far beyond education.

Such new tasks in sectorial planning follow from the increasing recognition of intersectorial interdependence in public policy. Policy makers and planners in other sectors will increasingly have to form opinions about education policy in order to deal with their own problems, and educational planners have to do the same.

The simple notion that the contribution of education to the national economy can be measured as an input into a total production function for society, has lost its credibility. The same has happened to the idea that education can be linked to the economy through a simple transformation of educational degrees and diplomas into occupational functions. The interplay between education and the economy is far more complex, and its essential features are likely to escape such mechanistic interaction models.

Essential in this respect is the choice of technology in the various sectors of economy, and its far-reaching repercussions, not only for employment, work organisation and skill requirements, but also for learning potentials within the economy itself. Those responsible for educational policy cannot just passively observe the changes following from technological choice, they must be actively engaged in order to safeguard the essential societal interests which they represent.

Correspondingly, the general development of communication and information functions in our societies has profound implications for the general learning milieu, not only within educational institutions, but also in society at large. Educational authorities and educational planners must have an important stake in the development of a consistent public policy in this field.

Education is an essential part of general cultural policies, and is also strongly influenced by policies that go beyond education. The interplay between general cultural policy, and the development of educational institutions should be an important concern for educational planners, in view of its significance for the development of a society's general learning potential.

Research policy has important implications for major parts of the educational system. In a sense, education may be seen as the most important agent for the development and dissemination of research. On the other hand, a major part of our research efforts may primarily be seen as part of a general learning function, adding more to generalised understanding of phenomena than to the extension of the frontiers of science. It is essential that educational planners should be concerned with the educational aspects of research policy.

The family and the local environment are still essential learning milieus in our societies, and their ways of functioning are closely interrelated to those of the school. General tendencies towards a weakening of those external learning milieus will not only have strong repercussions within the educational system, but may have grave consequences for the total learning capabilities in society as a whole. Education has too long reacted passively to such external developments, accepting roles for educational institutions which probably could be better performed elsewhere. Educational planners cannot in the long run continue to neglect such external factors.

Social policy calls more and more upon the educational system to assist in its increasingly difficult tasks, often beyond any reasonable expectations. Educational policy makers and planners must see social policy partly as an extension of their own responsibilities, and they must actively include such external factors in their own planning.

When moving into policy areas beyond education, educational planners can hardly expect to compete with planning experts in those fields. They have, however, specific contributions to make, based on their responsibility for and insight into education and learning functions penetrating all sectors in society. An educational policy restricting itself to the running of purely educational institutions has few chances of coping with today's realities. Only when education and learning are seen as a total societal function, in interplay with a wide range of other essential functions, can such policies gain a fair chance of meeting emerging needs. It may seem like a superhuman task for educational planners to assist in the development of such policies, but the future fate of educational planning will largely be determined by its ability to meet such a challenge.

VIII. CONCLUDING REMARKS

In this paper we have indicated certain new features in educational planning. They are not peculiar to the field of education, but may be found in some form or other in many sectors where planning is applied. They may be more frequent in areas where the development of planning is more recent, and less entrenched in traditional planning theory.

All the examples mentioned have a common background in the breakdown of the notion of planning as purely a matter of programming organisational behaviour in order to maximise its internal consistency. It is fairly well recognised by now that within most organisations, a variety of goal structures are in operation and do influence actual decisions. Organisational behaviour is therefore the end result of compromises between all those goal structures. It cannot be expected to favour particular goals without affecting others. This makes the planner's search for "optimal" solutions rather meaningless and raises grave doubts about the value of consistency per se.

Planning gradually has to adapt itself to serving at the same time a variety of clients with deviating goal structures. There is only one way of doing this properly, namely to define planning as a pedagogical function, aiming at the stimulation of learning within the organisation as a whole. It happens, not quite accidentally, that the recognition of a multiplicity of goal structures within organisations coincides with a tendency towards more turbulent environments for most institutions in our societies. Forms of organisation and planning well suited for static activities fall short of coping with constantly shifting external requirements, demands and pressures. Organisations with a fair amount of decentralised decision-making, more horizontal organisation structures, and maximal learning ability, seem better adapted to survival and success in this kind of environment. The new features in planning are simply a sometimes rather delayed response to this development.

The consequences for planning in theory and practice are, however, fundamental. Not only have most traditional planning techniques become obsolete, and quite new techniques have to be developed, but the substance of planning itself is profoundly changed, as well as the professional skill requirements for planners. Their functional role within organisations has to be drastically redefined. The above-mentioned examples of attempts to cope with this new situation must be seen as illustrations. However, they may also be seen as pointing towards elements of a new planning theory, not only more compatible with actual planning practice, but capable of enriching and guiding this practice.

Part Two

THE PRACTICE OF EDUCATIONAL PLANNING :
COUNTRY EXPERIENCE

Chapter 4

EDUCATIONAL PLANNING IN COUNTRIES WITH FEDERAL SYSTEMS OF GOVERNMENT

A. AUSTRALIA

This report has been prepared by the Education Planning Group in the Australian Department of Education as a contribution to the activity of the OECD Education Committee "Towards a Reappraisal of Educational Planning". The report follows the guidelines suggested by OECD for country reports. References are given in the report to various sources where further information may be obtained on developments relevant to educational planning in Australia.

I. INTRODUCTION

The organisation and structure of educational planning in Australia needs to be viewed in the context of the evolution of State and Commonwealth roles in the provision of education. The changing relationships of the Australian federal system have affected profoundly the ways in which educational planning is undertaken in Australia and the substantive planning preoccupations of State and Commonwealth agencies.

There is no formal machinery within the Australian federal system for overall educational planning apart from sectoral planning related to the Commissions which advise the Commonwealth Government on funding allocations in the areas of school and tertiary education respectively. In this context, the web of relationships, both formal and informal, that associate State and Commonwealth agencies assume importance. Educational planning in Australia is a matter of complex relationships involving various State and Commonwealth agencies as well as research and other interested groups. The relationships have also changed considerably in the past twenty years as the Commonwealth has assumed a larger role in the funding of education, particularly of higher education. Through its funding role the influence of the Commonwealth Government on the setting of educational priorities has also grown.

In constitutional terms education is primarily a responsibility of the States. The six Australian States and the Commonwealth territories each have their own administrative structure for education (1). While this is the formal constitutional position, the Commonwealth provides financial assistance to all sectors of education in the States and has additionally a direct responsibility for financial assistance to students, for funding research and for providing education in the Commonwealth territories.

As the Commonwealth Government has become significantly involved in funding all aspects of education, its influence on educational priorities and planning has grown. However, the extent of this influence varies between the levels and sectors of education in accordance with the extent of Commonwealth funding involvement in each sector. The influence of the Commonwealth is greatest in the area of higher education where the Commonwealth now has full funding responsibility ; it is less in the case of schools and technical and further education where the major funding is provided by the States with the Commonwealth's role that of "topping up" State provision.

In appraising educational planning in Australia, it is also necessary to note that there is a significant non-government school sector in Australia. The Commonwealth Government's Schools Commission provides partial financial support for non-government schools, which also obtain financial support from the States. There is further comment in a later section of this report on this aspect of educational planning in Australia.

In view of the significance of the pattern of funding Australian education for the organisation and concerns of educational planning, a brief review of recent developments follows.

Funding of the Australian Education System

Prior to the Second World War, the Commonwealth had little involvement in the funding of education in the Australian States and its responsibilities were restricted to the Territories. Since 1945 Commonwealth involvement in

---

1. Following the granting of self-government to the Northern Territory on 1 July 1978, moves were initiated to transfer responsibility for education in the Northern Territory to the Northern Territory Government. This transfer was effectively completed by 1 July 1979.

the funding of education has grown, in part as a consequence of the disparity of financial resources between the Commonwealth and the States with the Commonwealth Government's assumption of full control over income tax in 1942.

To assist the States in areas of particular need, the Commonwealth has made grants to the States for specific purposes, including education, under section 96 of the Constitution. Certain of the conditions attached to education grants have, at times, been a source of conflict with the States.

The intrusion of the Commonwealth into the funding of education has been an incremental process, but with a significant increase of involvement in the early nineteen-seventies. Support for universities began in the 1940s with a major expansion from 1957. The system of colleges of advanced education was set up and supported from 1965. The Commonwealth began assistance to secondary schools, both government and non-government, with programs aimed at up-grading science laboratories and facilities (1964) and libraries (1969). Per capita grants for recurrent expenditure to non-government schools began in 1970. Commonwealth involvement in the schools area culminated in the establishment of the Schools Commission in 1973.

Prior to 1 January 1974 the Commonwealth and State Governments shared the funding of higher education on an agreed formula basis. Since that date the Commonwealth Government has assumed full responsibility for the funding of universities and colleges of advanced education. Tuition fees in tertiary education have been abolished. Commonwealth funds are provided on the advice of the Tertiary Education Commission. This body was set up in 1977 as an amalgamation of the former Universities Commission, Commission on Advanced Education, and Commission on Technical and Further Education.

The respective Commonwealth and State Government expenditure on education by sector for 1976-77 is set out in the table below.

Because the Commission system of funding education is one of the most distinctive factors of educational planning in Australia further comment is provided below on the role of the Schools Commission and the Tertiary Education Commission. The Commissions have an influence on formal and informal relationships between the Commonwealth and the States and an appreciation of their role and influence is central to an understanding of educational planning in Australia.

The relationships are also influenced by contacts that occur through the Australian Education Council, the Conference of Directors-General of Education and the

COMMONWEALTH AND STATE EXPENDITURE
ON EDUCATION BY SECTOR : 1976-77

In Aus. $ m.

	Commonwealth	States	Total	States % total
Schools	725.2	2 458.3	3 183.5	77.2
TAFE	109.2	272.9	382.0	71.4
University	642.3	-	642.2	-
Advanced Education	465.6	-	465.6	-
Other*	219.5	247.6	467.1	53.0
Total	2 161.8	2 978.8	5 140.6	57.9

* Other expenditure includes student assistance of $ 298.4 m and the remainder is expenditure on research, curriculum development and administration.

meetings of TAFE Directors and the Chairman of co-ordinating boards in higher education. The Australian Education Council comprises the State and Commonwealth Ministers of Education, and comment on its role is given below.

This introductory section has dealt briefly with some of the structural factors that influence educational planning in Australia. Further background information on the Australian education system as it existed in early 1976 is given in the Australian Background Report for the OECD education review of Australia (2). There is a good deal of information on post-secondary education in Australia in the report of a recent Commonwealth inquiry into education and training (3). The reports of the Schools Commission provide information on education at the school level and the reports of the former Universities Commission, Advanced Education Commission, and TAFE Commission may be consulted for the tertiary sectors (4).

---

2. Education Policy and Planning : Transition from School to Work or Further Study in Australia, OECD, Paris, 1976.
3. Education, Training and Employment : Report of the Committee of Inquiry into Education and Training, Canberra, 1979.
4. The 5th and 6th Reports of the Universities Commission, in particular, contain a good deal of information on the approach to planning in the university sector. 5th Report (1972), 6th Report (1975).

II. ORGANISATION AND STRUCTURE OF EDUCATIONAL PLANNING

In describing the organisation and structure of educational planning in Australia, it is convenient to outline separately the arrangements existing at Commonwealth and State levels. This approach has been followed in this report but it should be borne in mind that there is a good deal of interaction between Commonwealth and State agencies, and the separate description of Commonwealth and State arrangements does not convey the reality of Commonwealth/State educational relations. In addition to governmental contacts, interaction through agencies such as the Schools Commission and Tertiary Education Commission and a variety of other arrangements such as working parties and committees and a range of informal contacts there is an inter-play of Commonwealth/State educational relations through the Australian Education Council which associates the Commonwealth and State education ministers. The account that follows attempts to indicate something of these various dimensions of Commonwealth/State relations that influence the organisation and structure of educational planning in Australia.

1. Education Planning at the Commonwealth Level

Perhaps the most distinctive feature of educational planning in Australia is the use of education Commissions by the Commonwealth to advise on the allocation of Commonwealth funds to the States for education and relative matters within the sectors of education they cover. The two statutory authorities that perform this function are the Schools Commission and Tertiary Education Commission. The nature of their roles influences the ways in which educational planning is undertaken in Australia both at Commonwealth and State levels. Accounts follow on the role of each of these agencies. In addition to these Commissions, educational planning at the Commonwealth level involves the Commonwealth Department of Education and an outline is given of the way in which educational planning is organised in that Department.

Schools Commission

The establishment of the Schools Commission by the Commonwealth Government in 1973 was a culmination of growing support by the Commonwealth for education at the level of schools. This was in a context where the constitutional responsibility for the provision of educational services lay with State Governments.

During the 1960s educational services in Australia had come under increasing strain due to expanding population and changing social and individual expectations. In addition, particular difficulties faced by some States in overcoming problems such as the education of socially and economically disadvantaged children and children in isolated areas could only be alleviated by the injection of large amounts of additional funds. Further, the issue of government funding to alleviate grossly inadequate conditions of schooling in poor non-government schools had become a pressing political and social issue.

Commonwealth interest in educational provision at school level was expressed first by grants for a building program for science laboratories, and the introduction of a senior secondary scholarship scheme (1964), and subsequently by a secondary school libraries program (in 1969). In the 1970s, in addition to an evolving and expanding assistance to students, the Commonwealth has assumed a major role in funding education, largely through payments channelled through the Schools Commission since its establishment in 1973.

The main mechanism for the Commonwealth's involvement in education activity in the States has been section 96 of the Constitution, which permits the Commonwealth to offer grants to the States under terms and conditions determined by the Commonwealth Parliament, and section 51 of the Constitution (the social services provision), which under sub-section xxiiiA permits the Commonwealth to provide benefits to students and thus affords considerable scope for direct Federal Government participation in education.

The Schools Commission was preceded by the Interim Committee for the Australian Schools Commission. This Interim Committee reported to the Commonwealth Government in May 1973 in a report entitled <u>Schools in Australia</u> (known as the "Karmel Report") and the major recommendations of this report were accepted by the Government. Subsequently, late in 1973 the Schools Commission was established and legislation was passed to authorise the expenditure of approximately $ 750 million for 1974 and 1975. Since 1973 the Commission has continued to advise the Commonwealth government on the needs of schools, and since 1975 annual appropriations have been authorised by legislation after an initial two year program (1974-75) funds have been provided annually by legislation.

Functions

Broadly the functions of the Commission laid down in the <u>Schools Commission Act</u> are :

    a) to recommend to the Minister for Education, after consulting with interested parties, what Commonwealth Government funds should be made available

to schools and school systems throughout the country to ensure acceptable standards, and what conditions should attach to these funds ;
b) to enquire into and report upon any aspect of primary and secondary education, either at the request of the Minister or on the Commission's own initiative.

In making its recommendations the Commission is required to consider the need for improving the quality of existing school provision and to promote increased and equal educational opportunities. Factors which are to be taken into account by the Commission include :

- the primary obligations of governments to provide and maintain government school systems that are of the highest standard and are open without fees or religious tests to all children ;
- the prior right of parents to choose government or non-government schooling for their children ;
- the educational needs of handicapped children and young persons ;
- the needs of disadvantaged schools and of students in all schools who are disadvantaged in their education for social, economic, ethnic, geographical or other reasons ;
- the need to encourage diversity and innovation in schooling ;
- the desirability of providing special opportunities for students of demonstrated ability ;
- the economic use of resources ;
- the need to stimulate public interest in and support for improvements in education.

Public participation is ensured by the Minister's obligation to cause each Commission report to be laid before each House of the Parliament. This provision ensures that the Commission can give public advice and that there can be public debate as the background to the taking of decisions by the Government on that advice.

Membership and Meetings

The Schools Commission is essentially an advisory body. It provides advice to the Commonwealth Government on matters relating to the funding of schools, and related matters as indicated above. When the Government has taken decisions following consideration of the advice of the Commission, it is involved in the administration of programs which emerge from Government action. Like the Tertiary Education Commission, the Commission operates within guidelines from the Government which indicates the level of funds available and other policy directives which the Commission is required to take account of in making its proposals.

The Commission consists of three full-time and nine part-time Commissioners. The full-time members may be appointed for terms up to seven years, while the part-time members may be appointed for terms up to three years and they may be reappointed. Under the Schools Commission Act, the Minister is not bound to appoint any particular person because of a State or interest group or professional affiliation. The present full-time members were appointed when the Commission was established. They come from planning, administrative and economic backgrounds in education. The part-time members come from all States and their affiliations relate to both Government and non-governmental schools, to teaching, administrative, teacher and parent organisation roles. Most major interest group concerns are discernable within the range of members appointed. The general mode of working is to proceed by consensus on any matters which involve policy development. Proposals for financial grants not involving policy issues are frequently resolved simply by majority votes.

Program Administration

In respect to the detailed administration of programs, the Commission operates on a decentralised basis. For Government schools, money is advanced to States which set up their own internal distribution and management arrangements for Government systems. For some specific purpose programs, by agreement between the Commission and the States, committees with particular patterns of membership are established by the States to supervise implementation of the program.

In the case of non-government schools, program administration is also decentralised by establishment of Planning and Finance Committees in each State for General Recurrent and Capital Grants funding and through committees within Catholic systems for specific purpose programs applicable to those systems.

For the one small program, administered by the Commission itself, amounting to 0.8 per cent of the total funds, that is the Special Projects Program, there are Innovations Committees in each State which make recommendations to a National Innovations Committee and thence to the Commission itself.

The Commission's objectives are implemented not only through the substantial financial contribution which it makes towards improving the basic levels of resources through the two major general purpose programs (the General Recurrent Grants Program and the Capital Grants Program) it also operates five specific purpose programs as well as undertaking studies, commissioning research and publications and sponsors change by deploying consultants to stimulate activities in particular educational fields.

The specific purpose programs direct expenditure towards promoting particular initiatives while the activities, of the consultants, the research studies and the publications are intended to help create a climate of receptivity to new ideas and to encourage institutional change.

Organisation and Funding Mechanisms

The Schools Commission allocates funds to government schools and Catholic systems through their central authorities, and to non-government schools which are not groups in systems individually, according to their differential needs. Some of the programs encourage joint activity and sharing of resources for both government and non-government schools, and are distributed on a joint basis. The programs through which funds are distributed are :

- the 'general' programs :
  . General Recurrent Grants Program
  . Capital Grants Program

- and the 'specific purpose' programs :
  . Disadvantaged Schools Program
  . Services and Development Program
  . Special Education Program
  . Special Projects Program
  . Migrant and Multicultural Education Program.

Effectiveness of the Commission

Funds which are distributed under the programs to central authorities are expended largely at their discretion. The Schools Commission is thus, to a considerable extent, dependent on goodwill and common purpose in achieving its objectives. In allocations to individual non-government schools, and to systemic schools in the case of some Programs, the Schools Commission is able to be more precise and prescriptive in allotting funds for specific purposes.

An issue of particular concern at the present is the question of balance in funding across the government and non-government school sectors at a time when Commonwealth contributions for schools are limited because of economic and budgetary considerations. This issue has considerable implications for the development of educational patterns and administrative and funding strategies.

The Commission's effectiveness is dependent on its maintaining a realistic relationship with its Government as well as with its "clients". While the Commission is independent in the advice it offers, and does not always achieve total acceptance by the Government of its recommendations, it is seen as a fair mediator in allocation of resources.

The policy of the present Liberal-Country Party Government is that the States should receive sufficient general purpose revenues to permit them to define their own priorities. The Government has re-affirmed at recent meetings of the Australian Education Council that it will continue to make contributions from its own Budget to the general expenditure programs of both government and non-government schools and also continue with special purpose programs.

Tertiary Education Commission

The Tertiary Education Commission was set up in 1977 through the amalgamation of the three commissions that advised the Commonwealth Government on the allocation of funds to post-secondary education. Its establishment has been paralleled by the setting up of similar coordinating bodies in four of the States. These developments have marked an increased concern with coordination in the planning and administration of post-secondary education. The paragraphs that follow outline developments that led to the setting up of the Tertiary Education Commission.

The Universities Commission was established in 1959 on the recommendation of the Murray Committee to advise the Australian Government on the financial needs of universities having regard to "the balanced development of universities so that their resources can be used to the greatest possible advantage of Australia". The establishment of the Commission inaugurated Commonwealth funding of universities on a "shared-funding" basis with the States.

Development of the advanced education sector resulted from the recommendations of the Committee on the Future of Tertiary Education in Australia (The Martin Committee) which in 1964 identified a need for a greater diversity of tertiary institutions. To advise the Australian Government on the provision of financial assistance for colleges of advanced education, the Commonwealth Advisory Committee on Advanced Education was established in 1965. In 1971 the Commission on Advanced Education was set up as a statutory body to carry on the work by the Commonwealth on a "shared-funding" basis until 1974. Advanced education has evolved as a sector of higher education that is vocationally oriented, tertiary in character but flexible in its emphasis and oriented towards teaching at the undergraduate rather than post-graduate level.

A third Commonwealth Commission in the post-secondary areas followed the Report of the Committee on Technical and Further Education (the Kangan Report) in 1974. The

Kangan Report represented the first comprehensive survey of needs and resources in TAFE. Its Report led to significant Commonwealth funding of technical and further education provided on the advice of the Australian Committee on Technical and Further Education which in 1975 became the Commission on Technical and Further Education.

However, Commonwealth support for technical and further education has been provided on a different basis from universities and advanced education where "shared-funding" existed prior to 1973. Since 1973 the Commonwealth has had total responsibility for the funding of universities and colleges of advanced education. With technical and further education, the major part of funding is provided by the States with the Commonwealth providing "topping-up" funding. The Australian Education Council has considered changes in the respective funding responsibilities of the Commonwealth and the States, for these three sectors as well as for schools, but there are no indications that changes are likely to occur in the foreseeable future.

It was against the background of development and diversification of Australian post-secondary education that the Commonwealth Government decided to amalgamate its three post-secondary commissions into the Tertiary Education Commission. Under its Act the Commission is required to perform its functions with the object of promoting :

a) the balanced and coordinated development of tertiary education in Australia ; and
b) the diversifying of opportunities for tertiary education.

The former separate Commissions have been replaced by three Councils within the structure of the Commission which are concerned with each of the sectors of tertiary education. The Chairman of each of the Councils (Universities, Advanced Education, TAFE) is a full-time member of the Commission. In addition to the Chairmen of the Councils, the Commission has a full-time Chairman and five part-time Commissioners. The Councils provide advice to the Commission on matters within their sectors of education and the reports of the Councils are included in the triennal reports of the Commission to the Government which provide funding recommendations.

This arrangement is intended to allow full recognition of the distinctive characteristics and needs of each of the sectors of tertiary education, which can be articulated through the Councils, while providing for coordination through the Commission. A feature of the arrangement set up in 1977 was the decision to include technical and further education within the scope of the Tertiary Education Commission. The decision reflected the increasing priority that Commonwealth Governments have given to technical and further education since the Kangan Report in 1974.

Since its establishment, the Tertiary Education Commission has operated within "guidelines" procedures which the Commonwealth Government has introduced. Under this policy, the Government issues "guidelines" to the Tertiary Education Commission and Schools Commission which indicate the level of funds available and other policy directives which the Commissions are required to take account of in making their proposals. The sequence of events involved in the "guidelines" and consultative procedures, in the case of the Tertiary Education Commission, is shown below.

Prior to 1976, the Commissions operated within a framework of triennial planning and funding. In 1976 a modified system of "rolling triennia" was introduced which provided Government with the advantage of more control over its annual budget, but which reduced the advantages to institutions of firm triennial programs. More recently the Commonwealth has re-introduced fixed triennial funding for recurrent grants but not for capital grants.

The Committee of Inquiry into Education and Training gave major consideration to the planning and administration of post-secondary education in the Australian Federal system. This involved consideration of the respective roles of the Commonwealth and the States including the role of the Tertiary Education Commission. It concluded that the specification of national interests does not give a precise guide to the distribution of responsibilities between the Commonwealth and States for educational planning and administration, hence it regarded cooperation and consultation as the essential ingredients of an effective Federal system.

In this context of cooperation and consultation, the Williams Committee suggested that the Tertiary Education Commission had five functions to perform in triennial planning. This statement of arrangements for triennial planning has been modified to take account of the Commonwealth"s "guidelines policy" and these received the support of the Australian Education Council at a special meeting in June 1979. The modified statement of Tertiary Education Commission functions reads as follows :

1. The TEC initiate with appropriate State authorities and universities the preparation by them of comprehensive plans for each forthcoming triennium.
2. These comprehensive triennial plans would be the subject of detailed consultation by the relevant Councils of the TEC with their State counterparts and may be modified in the process of these consultations.
3. On the basis of these triennial plans, the TEC would formulate a comprehensive proposal. This might be in the form of State by State chapters with an overview and would comprise Volume 1 of the TEC Triennial Report.

4. Volume 1 would be the subject of consultation between the Commonwealth Minister and State Ministers.
5. Following this consultation, the Commonwealth Ministers would prepare proposals and recommendations for consideration by his Government.
6. Following decisions by the Commonwealth Government, the TEC, after consultation with State authorities, would make any adjustments to the triennial plans that might be necessary in the light of the financial provision determined by the Commonwealth Government.
7. The revised plans would constitute Volume 2 of the TEC Triennial Report and form the basis for the preparation of the States Grants (Tertiary Education Assistance) legislation.

The Williams Report also recommended that the structure of the Tertiary Education Commission should be reviewed by the Commonwealth Government during 1980. However, the States did not press for an early review of the structure of the Tertiary Education Commission at the June 1979 meeting of the Australian Education Council, and it will be for the Commonwealth Government to decide when, and if, the structure of the Tertiary Education Commission should be reviewed. The Australian Education Council did decide, however, that the present planning and consultative arrangements should be reviewed after 1981 after the completion of the planning cycle for the 1982-84 triennium.

The planning and consultative arrangements endorsed by the Australian Education Council in June 1979 reflect the accumulation of experience over some years in arrangements for triennial planning of higher education. In particular, they reflect the experience of the earliest of the Commonwealth's advisory Commissions, the Universities Commission.

The use of the Commission system of triennial planning has been within a framework set by major government inquiries. The Murray Report of 1957, the Martin Reports of 1964 and 1965, the Kangan Report of 1974, and more recently the Williams Report of 1979 have set this framework. Within this framework, the procedures developed by the Universities Commission have been extended and modified as the later Commissions were established. These have involved the careful collection and analysis of information, systematic processes of consultation with institutions, State authorities, and other relevant parties. General and specific issues relevant to the development of the system have been identified in the course of these processes of consultation and data collection, and a number of special inquiries have been conducted on major issues. These special inquiries have covered such subjects as the expansion of medical education, tertiary education in Sydney, Melbourne and Albury-Wodonga, nurse education, open tertiary education and postgraduate education for management. The establishment of the Tertiary Education System represents the culmination of some years of experience of triennial planning of tertiary education and the desire to further these planning procedures in more coordinated ways across the sectors of tertiary education.

Commenwealth Department of Education

The Commonwealth Department of Education and Science was set up in 1966 as a consequence of increased Commonwealth involvement in education. It replaced an earlier body, the Commonwealth Office of Education, which had been established in 1945.

There have been a number of changes since the Department was established. In 1972 the education and science components of the Department were divided into separate departments. Various statutory and non-statutory agencies have been created within the education portfolio. These included by July 1979 the following bodies : Tertiary Education Commission, Schools Commission, Curriculum Development Centre, the Education Research and Development Committee, the National Aboriginal Education Committee, the Commonwealth Teaching Service, and the Australian Capital Territory Schools Authority. All of these separate agencies report direct to the Minister for Education on matters relating to their specific charter. The Department, on the other hand, is expected to have a wider knowledge of relevant Government policies over the broad spectrum. The Minister needs to be able to look to his Department to provide advice overall, including consideration of priorities. The close liaison which the Department maintains with other central departments, such as Finance and Prime Minister and Cabinet, is important in this respect. Because of this knowledge, the Department has a responsibility to present options and an analysis of their implications for the Government, and it is in a position to comment independently from a general policy viewpoint on the advice received from these agencies.

The policy and planning roles of the Department of Education need to be viewed in this context. The Department provides the Minister for Education with advice on general educational policy, on planning and funding issues, and the coordination of national education programs. In addition to these policy and planning functions, the Department administers programs of student assistance and programs in such fields as international education, Aboriginal and migrant education, and language teaching.

In 1975, the organisation of the Department was reviewed and a number of deficiencies were identified in the structure of the Department. These included an inability to respond adequately to ad hoc demands, a need for better contingency and long-range planning, a need to integrate new functions more adequately, and a requirement for greater flexibility in the use of staff resources.

Following this review, the Department was re-organised with the creation of two new bodies to undertake policy/management and planning functions. These bodies were :

a) a Management Group ; and
b) an Education Planning Group.

The Management Group comprises the most senior officers of the Department. It is chaired by the Secretary of the Department and meets regularly each week to consider the major policy and management issues facing the Department.

In its policy and planning functions, the Management Group is assisted by the Education Planning Group (EPG). This Group was created by amalgamating the former Policy, Planning and Review, and Research Branches of the Department. The EPG is regarded as a flexible pool of resources that can be used according to changing needs and priorities. One objective is to create a closer interaction between the policy, planning, and research functions of the Department. The management of the Group is based on a collegiate concept of management with the five senior officers of the Group meeting to allocate tasks and resources and take other management decisions.

The Education Planning Group has not been operating sufficiently long to enable the effectiveness of this approach to be assessed. Most of the resources of the Group tend to be allocated to short-term policy issues frequently involving the provision of advice to the Minister. Little by way of longer-range educational planning has yet been attempted although the Group has undertaken several special projects as a means of relating current policy concerns to longer-term policy and planning issues. These have involved multicultural education and early childhood education. Current work is on projects dealing with the relationships between education and the labour market, and a review of the role of the Department in the language teaching area. A special unit has recently been established in the Group to bring together its work in the area of school to work transition.

A further means of relating policy and planning issues is provided by the involvement of the EPG in follow-up of reports of inquiries in education, and in the preparation of submissions to Government inquiries in education and related fields. A recent example has been provided by the involvement of a project team within the Group in follow-up on the Report of the Committee of Inquiry into Education and Training (the Williams Report). A major inquiry such as this provides the opportunity to integrate a number of policy interests of the EPG within a broader policy and planning framework.

2. Educational Planning in the States

Perhaps the most distinctive feature of educational planning in the States in the past fifteen years has been the development of coordinating authorities at the post-secondary level in response to the development and diversification of tertiary education. A strong stimulus to this development was provided by the creation in 1965 of advanced education as a distinct sector of education to provide for a range of additional activities in institutions complementary to the universities. Following the Kangan Report of 1974, technical and further education (TAFE) was recognised as a distinct sector of post-secondary education. The development of State coordination authorities in most States was a response to the need to plan and administer a larger and more diversified system of post-secondary education.

These developments were generally distinct from the role of State Education Departments in planning and administering school systems in the States. However, the overall pattern has varied between the States, and technical and further education is administered in most States by the State Education Department although it is recognised by the Commonwealth as a section of tertiary education for funding purposes. Two States (South Australia and New South Wales) have separate departments to administer the TAFE sector.

The sections of this report that follow deal separately with educational planning in the States at the tertiary level and in State Education Departments.

Post-secondary Educational Planning

Advanced education grew rapidly in the decade following the Martin Report. An important influence was the inclusion of teacher training institutions within the advanced education sector for funding purposes. Following this period of rapid growth, the changed economic and social context of education existing by the middle of the nineteen-seventies focused attention in most States on issues relating to coordination and rationalisation of post-secondary provision. A feature of the past five years has been a series of inquiries conducted in most States which have examined coordination and rationalisation issues (5).

---

5. The inquiries were : Committee on Post-secondary Education in Western Australia (the Partridge Committee, 1976), Committee of Inquiry into Post-secondary Education in South Australia (the Anderson Committee, 1978), Committee of Inquiry on Post-secondary Education in Victoria (the Partridge Committee), Committee on Post-secondary Education in Tas. (Karmel Committee, 1976), Ministerial Working Party on Tertiary Education in Tasmania (the Kearney Report, 1978).

These inquiries have generally led to the establishment of coordinating authorities to plan and administer post-secondary education in the States.

The following are some of the main developments in the States during this period.

Western Australia

The Western Australian Post-secondary Education Commission commenced operating in December 1976. It has fifteen members and reports to the Minister. The task of the Commission is the promotion, development and coordination of post-secondary education throughout the State. It fulfils this task by providing advice on a wide range of matters to the institutions concerned, the State Government and the Commonwealth Tertiary Education Commission. Recent investigations by the Commission have resulted in one teachers' college being phased out, a federation of tertiary facilities being formed in a country region and the upgrading of the status of the Technical and Education Directorate within the Western Australian Department of Education.

South Australia

The Tertiary Education Authority of South Australia was established in July 1979 as a statutory coordinating body for the post-secondary sector. The five-person Authority reports to the Minister for Education, and its principal function is to advise him on matters pertaining to post-secondary education. It also has a responsibility to advise individual institutions and the Tertiary Education Commission. It is expected that its work will lead to a more rational planning and development of post-secondary education relating to the administration of colleges of advanced education, the accreditation of tertiary courses leading to a formal award, the merger of a number of colleges of advanced education and the reduction of intake into pre-service teacher education courses.

Victoria

In May 1978 the Victorian Parliament established the Victorian Post-Secondary Education Commission. Two authorities, the Victorian Institute of Colleges (responsible for advanced education) and the State College of Victoria (responsible for teacher education) continue to exist so far but are to be abolished, whilst the Department of Education retains responsibility for technical and further education. The Commission has two full-time and six part-time members and it reports to the State Minister of Education. Its function is to advise on the planning, organisation, administration and coordination of post-secondary education in Victoria ; this includes advising the Victorian Minister and the Commonwealth Tertiary Education Commission on funding, courses and establishment of new institutions.

Queensland

A Joint Advisory Committee for Post-Secondary Education in Queensland was set up in late 1976 to explore ways of ensuring effective cooperation and coordination in the present and future operation of post-secondary education in Queensland. The Committee is an advisory body to the Minister and comprises the Chairman of the Board of Advanced Education, the Director-General of Education and the Vice-Chancellors of Queensland's three universities.

Tasmania

The Tertiary Education Commission of Tasmania was established in January 1979 as a non-statutory body. The Commission comprises a chairman and deputy chairman, appointed by the Minister, ex officio the Vice-Chancellor of the University of Tasmania, the Principal of the Tasmanian College of Advanced Education and the Director of Further Education. The Government decided that the technical and further education system, which would be regarded as part of the tertiary sector, would continue to be administered by the Department of Education, but agreed to establish a State Council for Further Education.

New South Wales

The New South Wales Higher Education Board was set up in 1976 ; it replaced the three existing bodies dealing with the post-secondary sector. The Board's functions include :

- the development of existing and the establishment of new higher educational institutions ;
- the establishment of new programs of study for the purpose of rationalisation and avoidance of unnecessary duplication of resources.

The Board reports to the New South Wales Minister for Education ; it has three full-time and ten part-time members. The Board liaises with the Councils of the Commonwealth Tertiary Education Commission on the development and financial needs of post-secondary education in the State. Recent recommendations considered by the Board have included proposals to close one college of advanced education and to amalgamate others. These are at present under consideration by the Government.

In June 1979 the New South Wales Minister for Education announced that a single Education Commission for public education would be established as a statutory body. The Higher Education Board will retain its functions and its direct access to the Minister. A representative of the Board, nominated by the Minister, will be appointed to the thirteen-person Commission.

The responsibilities of these coordinating bodies differ somewhat between the States, including the matter of responsibility in relation to technical and further education. As pointed out above, responsibility for technical and further education is retained in most States by State Education Departments. The Committee of Inquiry into Education and Training (the Williams Report) pointed to problems of coordinating certain areas of advanced education and technical and further education, and drew to the attention of the Governments of New South Wales and Queensland the need to make provision for administrative coordination of middle-level activities in TAFE and colleges of advanced education.

The Williams Committee also recommended that the Australian Education Council appoint a special Standing Committee on Post-secondary Education consisting of the Chairman of the Commonwealth's Tertiary Education Commission and the Chairman of the State post-secondary authorities. When the Australian Education Council considered this recommendation at a special meeting in June 1979, it decided not to support this proposal. Instead, it was agreed that the Chairman of the Tertiary Education Commission should convene regular consultative meetings involving State post-secondary authorities. Relations between the Tertiary Education Commission and State post-secondary authorities have become a significant aspect of the planning and post-secondary education in Australia.

State Education Departments

In preparing this national report, the Commonwealth Department of Education invited comments from State Education Departments on the main topics covered by the OECD guidelines. The responses from the States indicated that there has been a reappraisal of the role of educational planning in most State Education Departments in recent years.

This reappraisal has been associated with developments such as the following :

a) decentralisation of administrative responsibility to regions within the State ;
b) the assigning of planning responsibility to operational and policy units with a central planning unit providing planning services to these units ;

c) an increased level of concern with efficiency and effectiveness in resource use ;
d) the need to assess changes in the social and economic context of schools, as for example produced by high levels of youth unemployment, demographic changes, and a more diversified ethnic composition in the Australian population, and to meet demands for an increasingly diverse range of educational services ;
e) more use of participative and consultative processes involving parents, teachers and community groups.

A number of States in their responses mentioned the influence of the trend to devolution of administrative responsibility to regions within the State and to the level of the individual school. With this development of greater devolution of authority, planning within central offices of State Education Departments has become less preoccupied with detailed planning and more prepared to utilise the skills of professional and educational planners. Regional offices are generally expected to undertake planning functions within their areas of responsibility.

A second general trend reported was for planning responsibilities to be assigned to operational and policy units with planning units providing a service function for these units. There has been a good deal of concern in the State Educational Departments to establish planning as an aspect of policy formulation and to integrate policy and planning functions.

Various methods have been used to integrate policy and planning functions, but the general trend may be elaborated by the procedures followed in New South Wales and South Australia. In the case of New South Wales, educational planning changed significantly during the period 1971 to 1976. There was a shift during this period from a mainly manpower approach through a social demand approach with a growing range of involvement and with more comprehensive and explicit planning and policy statements. This led to the explicit recognition that planning occurred continuously at all levels in the education system and in all functional areas.

It was also recognised that planning was an integral part of management, policy formulation and decision-making, and that the coordination of planning was a major responsibility of the most senior officials in the Department. Accordingly, the previously existing Division of Planning, which had a research orientation, was restructured in its functions and in its service role to become the Division of Planning Services. These changes were based on a clear rejection of the view that it is appropriate to have a separate planning division which would have the sole carriage of "planning" or of "evaluation of the system".

This approach led to a Policy and Planning Group and a Policy Support Unit being established in 1977 to serve as ongoing central coordinating, planning, policy development and review agencies within the Department. The function of Policy Planning Groups at the Regional Levels has been foreshadowed and some have been established.

An element in these developments has been the production of a Corporate Plan for the Department of Education. The Corporate Plan is the major source of advice to the Government and it is regularly updated. The Plan is expressed in qualitative and quantitative terms. It establishes objectives for a ten-year period with firmer aims for a three-year period. It includes manpower and enrolment projections, priorities and costed initiatives which may be introduced. While it reflects an incremental approach to planning, there is considerable concern with maintaining flexibility and the possibility of changing emphases and directions. The Plan therefore contains contingency strategies.

Attempts have been made to relate this Corporate Plan to plans submitted by other Government agencies for other social and economic sectors. This has been done through the machinery of the Premier's Department and Treasury.

The approach taken in South Australia has some similarities with the New South Wales approach. However, until recently planning within the Education Department was influenced by the existence of an umbrella planning unit covering all education sectors, the South Australian Council for Educational Planning and Research. This agency has now ceased its activities so that it is now clearly recognised that initiatives for planning lie within the Education Department.

As in New South Wales, planning is an aspect of the activities of all operational units. A Planning Section exists within the Directorate of Research and Planning. Its activities have concentrated on projections of numbers of students, teachers and schools, and there has been only limited formalised coordinated planning.

The lack of focus for the coordination of planning has led to two complementary developments :

a) the development of a Policy Planning Document as a declaration of the main initiatives for policy development for a two-year period ; and
b) the establishment of a Policy Review Unit to coordinate corporate planning and policy development.

The Policy Planning Document has been prepared as an exercise in setting organisational directions, policies and priorities. This Document was developed through a process that involved the preparation of a summary of trends as a scene setting document. This led to the identification of a set of issues to be addressed in the plan.

The coordinating group for the plan then addressed each issue by selecting a set of alternative policy responses to the issue. These alternatives were then discussed by working groups at a conference of senior officials which led to the selection of preferred options.

The preferred options and the rationale supporting their solution were then consolidated into a draft plan which was circulated widely for reactions. The bodies consulted included teacher organisations, parent organisations and other State Government bodies. A final form of the plan was then prepared on the basis of bodies. A final form of the plan was then prepared on the basis of these consultations. The current plan will be reviewed at the end of the two-year planning period in a rolling planning process.

The Policy Review Unit in the Department will be concerned with broad policy planning, the identification of areas for policy development and monitoring the implementation of policy. It will absorb the Policy Planning Document and become responsible for establishing rolling planning procedures. It will be concerned with the development of policy "green" papers as draft policy positions to be circulated widely for reactions and policy "white" papers which document the settled policy positions. While planning and policy development will be carried out, in most cases, within operational units, the Policy Review Unit will provide the coordination, monitoring, and evaluation of the planning process. It will be responsible for medium- and long-term planning initiatives. The procedures for educational planning in the New South Wales and South Australian Education Department have been outlined to illustrate certain trends in the approach to education planning in State Education Departments in Australia. The general trends towards administrative devolution, the close linking of planning functions with policy formulation and review and broader participating and consultative processes may also be found in the other States.

3. Commonwealth/State Relations in Educational Planning

As pointed out above, there is no overall planning agency in Australia that associates the Commonwealth and the States in planning activities. Rather, there is a web of relationships involving various Commonwealth and State agencies. The relations vary according to the level and sector of education. The Tertiary Education Commission and the Schools Commission exercise roles of some significance through their funding activities, and provide both vehicles for Commonwealth influence and channels for consultations and cooperation between the States and the Commonwealth.

Commonwealth/State educational relations are also influenced by the activities of agencies such as the Curriculum Development Centre and the Education Research and Development Committee. In addition to these bodies, the Australian Education Council, the Conference of Director-General of Education and meetings of TAFE Directors, provide channels for consultation between the States and with the Commonwealth. The Australian Education Council comprises the State and Commonwealth Ministers for Education and it provides a vehicle of consultation between State and Commonwealth Governments in education. Comments follow on the role of the Council.

Australian Education Council

The first meeting of the Council was called in 1936 on the initiative of the New South Wales Minister for Education. The Commonwealth Minister for Education became a member of the Council in 1972. From July 1979, the membership of the Council comprises the six State Ministers for Education, the Commonwealth Minister and the Northern Territory Minister for Education. The increasing activity of the Council as a form of consultation between the Australian Government on education matters led to the establishment in 1978 of a permanent secretariat to service the Council.

A Standing Committee of senior officials assists the Council in its activities. Until recently it comprised the Permanent Heads of the State and Commonwealth Departments of Education and, in addition, in the two States where more than one Department administers educational services, the Directors of Technical Education have attended Council meetings. Membership of the Standing Committee has now been extended and diversified and it is now representative of all sectors of education.

The constitution of the Council refers to the following functions :

- The provision of a basis of continuous consultation on education among the governments represented.
- The promotion of the development of education in Australia.
- Arranging the mutual exchange of information regarding education in Australia and abroad.
- The maintenance of high standards of education through cooperation.
- The promotion and adoption where desirable of consistent policies on educational problems.
- Consideration of the effects of educational policy on community development and national welfare.
- Examination of the educational provisions necessary for the development of the individual.

- Consideration of the educational provisions necessary to ensure the continuity of an adequate supply of qualified manpower for industry, commerce and the professions.

The proceedings of the Council and its Standing Committee are confidential. Meetings are usually held three times in two years with Chairmanship of the Council rotating and each State acting in turn as host. Being a voluntary body without statutory authority, the Council cannot bind its members to implement decisions agreed on.

A major purpose of the Council over the years has been to influence the level and nature of Commonwealth funding for education. The Council has generally reflected the preference of the States for specific purpose education grants from the Commonwealth to the States to be made available as block grants rather than earmarked for particular programs.

In the 1950s Commonwealth funds were sought for school buildings, particularly where Commonwealth housing developments related to defence establishments, immigrant hostels, engineering works and the like had led to a sudden increase in the number of school children in a particular area.

The publication in 1957 of the Murray Committee Report on Australian Universities and in 1964 of the Martin Committee Report, which recommended the development of new types of tertiary institutions in Australia, led the Council to approach the Commonwealth Government for financial assistance to teacher training, technical education, primary and secondary education and assistance to senior school students.

A survey made of needs in Australian schools was undertaken on the initiative of the Council, which at that time comprised only State Education Ministers, and a statement was presented at the 1960 Council meeting and revised for presentation at the 1963 meeting. The statements were then presented to State Premiers who discussed them at Premiers' Conferences (6). The survey pointed to the needs of Australian schools in such matters as an adequate supply

---

6. The Premiers' Conference is a meeting of the political heads, the Premiers, of each of the six States and the Australian Prime Minister. It is a consultative process. The chief item at the regular Conferences has, since 1942, been the size and distribution of Federal reimbursement grants under the Uniform Taxation Scheme. The Conference is convened at least once a year.

of trained teachers, school buildings and equipment and other supplies. This request for special financial assistance for schools was not met by the Commonwealth Government.

In 1970 the Council updated the survey, showing a shortfall of over $ 1 444 million required for schools over the next five years. The Commonwealth took the position that it was not willing to extend its program of special purpose education grants but argued that general purpose financial assistance grants and support of the States loans program was adequate to meet priority demands in education.

The Council has set up working parties and committees from time to time to investigate particular questions. Working parties in recent years have included the following :

- Working Party on Pre-school Education
- Working Party on National Collections of Educational Statistics
- Working Party on Transition from School to Work or Further Study
- Working Party on Commonwealth/State Coordination of Post-secondary Education
- Working Party on Education and Employment
- Working Party on Relationships between the Schools Commission and the State Education Departments
- National Study of School Building Costs
- Research Study of Staffing and Resource for Government Schools in Australia and New Zealand.

These working parties indicate something of the range of subjects that have been considered by the Council in recent years. While the Council cannot be regarded as a planning agency, its role as a forum for the discussion of policy issues involving the States and Commonwealth forms part of the context of educational planning in the Australian Federal system. There has been a trend for the Council to exercise a more significant role as a national consultative body in recent years, in particular since the Commonwealth Minister became a member of the Council in 1972, and it is likely that the Council could in the future have greater significance in overall educational planning in Australia.

III. SUBSTANTIVE PREOCCUPATIONS AND AREAS OF CONCERN

The substantive preoccupations and areas of concern vary according to the particular responsibilities of Australian education authorities. At the Commonwealth level preoccupations and areas of concern can, in part, be identified by the terms of reference of inquiries established by the Commonwealth in recent years. A recent report, that of the Committee of Inquiry into Education and Training (the Williams Committee) indicates a number of these concerns.

The Williams Committee was set up by the Commonwealth Government in September 1976 to review a range of matters relating to the provision of education and training. The Committee reported in February 1979. Its terms of reference included a number of subjects relating to the provision of education facilities and services including the magnitude of the provision, the pattern of institutions and objectives, access and re-entry. The other part of the terms of reference of the Committee related to the relationship between the education system and the labour market. A number of specific questions, including youth unemployment and the use of manpower forecasts, were included in this part of the terms of reference.

At the time this report was prepared, the Commonwealth Government had not announced its decisions on the recommmendations of the Williams Report. A special meeting of the Australian Education Council was held on 29-30 June 1979 to enable the State and Commonwealth Ministers of Education to consult on the proposals of the Report. The Report provides detailed information and analysis of a number of substantive preoccupations of Australian educational planning.

1. Education and the Labour Market

The inclusion of the relationship between the education system and the labour market in the terms of reference of the Williams Committee illustrates the development of increased concern with this subject in Australia. Previous national inquiries in education established by the Commonwealth Government had not been given the task of examining this subject.

Educational planning at the post-secondary level in Australia has, in the main, been concerned with the development of education in response to social demand criteria. Manpower considerations have on the whole played a minor part except in a few specialised fields such as medicine, dentistry, and veterinary science.

When the Universities Commission was set up following the Murray Report it undertook a certain amount of manpower analyses in expensive, specialised fields such as medicine. Special public inquiries were set up by the Commission from time to time to investigate manpower requirements in particular fields and development in some faculties has been influenced by the outcomes of these inquiries. Manpower forecasts have generally proved unreliable, and planning undertaken on the basis of forecasts has not prevented surpluses developing in these fields.

In 1965 the Committee on the Future of Tertiary Education in Australia (the Martin Committee) considered the role of manpower forecasts in planning tertiary education. The Committee was sceptical of the reliability of manpower forecasts and declined to recommend a policy of restricting the entry of students into various courses in tertiary education on the basis of forecasts of future needs. The Committee took the view that conflicts between students aspirations and community needs should be allowed to be resolved by the operation of supply and demand in the market. Its general position, like that of the Murray Committee, was that a university education should be available to all students with the interest and intellectual capacity to profit from it.

The Universities Commission, in general, followed the approach of the Murray and Martin Committees. In its Fifth Report in 1972 the Commission referred to two extreme positions - the one that places should be provided for all qualified persons who want a university education, the other that places ought to be provided in relation to the needs of the community for qualified manpower. The Commission rejected the second approach. It judged that social demand for places should determine the number of universities, subject to two restrictions :

a) that the qualifications for entry should be pitched at a level that give marginal students something like a 50/50 chance of graduating ; and
b) that pressures to increase the number of places should not prejudice the quality of teaching, scholarship and research spreading finances too thinly.

The Williams Committee in its report took the same basic approach as the Martin Committee and Universities Commission. It suggested the unreliability of past manpower forecasting, but nevertheless recommended that the Tertiary Education Commission should continue to undertake and publish forecasts in the fields of medicine, dentistry and veterinary science and to undertake forecasts of social demand. One question left unanswered by the Committee was whether forecasts, and presumably a manpower planning approach, should extend beyond the three fields it specified. While the Committee discussed manpower forecasting in the field of engineering, it did not take a position on whether courses should be provided in this field in response to assumed manpower requirements.

The Committee also recommended that the Australian Education Council should maintain and publish forecasts of teacher supply and demand. However, the general approach of the Committee was that educational opportunities, except in the few fields it specified should not be limited on the basis of forecast manpower requirements. The Committee also noted that the concept of imbalance between supply and demand is not free from ambiguity and is sometimes used to justify restrictive practices. The Committee recommended periodic inquiries into this concept.

One problem identified by the Williams Committee, and by another Government Committee that examined structural adjustments in Australian manufacturing industry, is a deficiency in the information available on the workings of the labour market. The Williams Committee recommended an intensified research effort to overcome the most serious of these deficiencies. It also recommended the establishment of a Centre for Youth Studies that would provide a focus for research on the entry of young people into the labour market. These recommendations are currently being considered by the relevant Government departments. The Williams Report makes the point clearly that if manpower considerations are to play a larger part in educational planning, improved information will be required on the workings of the labour market.

The current interest in the relationship between the education system and the labour market has been stimulated by high levels of youth unemployment in Australia. The incidence of unemployment is greatest for the 15-19 age group in the labour force. There was a sharp increase in the percentage unemployed of the 15-19 age group from just under six per cent in August 1974 to 15 per cent in February 1975 and then to a peak of 21 per cent in February 1975 and then to a peak of 21 per cent in February 1978 at a time when the percentage unemployment among the whole force rose just over 2.4 per cent to a peak of 7.4 per cent in February 1978. Between 1974 and 1977 youth unemployment fluctuated between 2.8 and 3.1 times the general level of unemployment. There are indications over a larger period of a relative increase in the ratio of youth to overall unemployment.

The Williams Committee concluded from its analysis of youth unemployment that the rough similarity of the ratios of increase in the percentage unemployment of various groups in the labour market pointed to the more general factors which caused the recession and which sustained it.

The Committee therefore took the position that schools do not cause youth unemployment and they are, by themselves, not able to remedy it. The Committee also concluded that there is not a single problem of youth unemployment and there is not a single or simple solution. Nevertheless, the Committee recommended a range of measures that it believed would contribute to enhancing the employability of young people.

These proposals included measures to improve the teaching of basic skills in schools, an extension of transition services and programs, further special courses for unemployed young people in technical colleges, and a wider range of pre-employment and linking programs involving technical colleges. The Committee also recommended the establishment of a special Centre for Youth Studies. The terms of reference of the Committee precluded it from considering the role of job creation schemes.

One issue raised by the Williams Committee that is likely to require further consideration is how education and labour market training schemes should be related in more comprehensive planning so that an appropriate range and balance of measures might be developed. This issue arose from the Committee's consideration of the role of the Special Youth Employment Training Program (SYETP), a training scheme that has been providing training for about 80 000 young people per annum. The Committee recommended that SYETP be considered as part of a range of education and training programs and that the range of programs and the balance between them be appraised by a joint committee of the National Training Council and the Technical and Further Education Council of the Tertiary Education Commission.

The proposals of the Williams Committee were discussed with the States at a special meeting of the Australian Education Council held on 29-30 June 1979. This was a preliminary discussion of the Report and it may be expected that it will require continuing consultation between the Commonwealth and the States on some aspects.

One aspect of education and employment relationships that has received a good deal of attention in Australia in recent years is the transition from education to work. This was the subject of our OECD review of Australian education carried out in 1976. The review identified a number of issues that required further consideration. These include the problem of the early school leaver who entered employment with limited qualifications and skills, and the adequacy of guidance and counselling services.

The Australian Education Council considered the report of the OECD examiners early in 1977 and decided to set up a Commonwealth/State Working Party on the Transition from School to Work or Further Study. Labour authorities were invited to participate in the work of this Working Party. The Working Party has to date reported twice to the Australian Education Council. At a meeting in 1978 the Council decided to set up a further Working Party on Education and Employment to review the state of transition services and programs. This Working Party reported to the June 1979 special meeting of the Council convened to consider the Williams Report. The Council in response decided to set up a committee to stimulate action in the area of school to work transition.

This account of recent Australian experience with education and labour market relationship demonstrates an increased awareness of issues involved in this subject. Most attention has, to date, focused on the matter of transition from school to work and a feature has been the role that the Australian Education Council has played in promoting the investigation of this question. More recently, the Williams Report has opened up for consideration by education and manpower authorities, at both State and Commonwealth levels, a broader range of issues involved in these relationships. It is too soon as yet to suggest what the outcomes of this consideration may be. It is likely that one matter that will require consideration is how collaboration should be promoted between education and manpower authorities in a range of issues relating to education and manpower planning.

2. Teacher Supply and Demand

The forecasting of teacher supply and demand has become an issue of concern in educational planning in Australia in view of evidence of an emerging teacher surplus. This subject has been of concern both to the States and also to the Commonwealth because it is responsible for the funding of teacher training in colleges of advanced education and universities. There has been collaboration through the Australian Education Council in the study of this question. The Williams Report has observed that one of the most striking features of the current estimates of excess supply is that awareness of a potentially serious imbalance emerged so recently. In 1975 the Universities Commission drew attention to the possibility of employment difficulties in teacher training in "the relatively near future". In response to the evidence of emerging teacher surplus in several school systems, the Australian Education Council in February 1976 set up a working party on teacher supply and demand. This comprised representatives of the Commonwealth, State education authorities, and Catholic education authorities.

The report of this working party was released in February 1978. Its conclusions were broadly similar to those of earlier studies made by Commonwealth authorities, viz, that on current trends there were likely to be substantially more locally trained teachers available in the period up to 1985 than government and non-government schools could employ, at both the primary and secondary levels. This report was prepared on a cooperative basis by the States and Commonwealth. State Education Departments provided information on existing teacher numbers, on wastage rates and on demand for teachers over the projection period. State Boards of Advanced Education provided estimates of the numbers of future graduates from pre-service teacher training courses from both universities and colleges of advanced education.

When the Australian Education Council considered the report, it decided not to continue this working party. However, the Williams Committee recommended that the Australian Education Council should assume the responsibility for maintaining and publishing forecasts of teacher supply and demand in Australian schools. It recommended that the forecasts should be presented in such a manner that the sensitivity of the forecasts to policy variable such as class size and average hours of teaching could be assessed.

The demographic context in which this exercise was carried out is one in which projections have shown increasing primary enrolments until 1979 followed by a substantial decline through to 1985 (which would be below 1977 levels) and then a steady but slow increase in enrolments up to 2000. Projections of secondary enrolments show a decline until 1980 followed by a period of moderate growth to a level in 1985 about 6 per cent higher than in 1977. There would then be a further decline to around 1993 followed by a steady increase to 2000 which would restore the 1985 level.

There have been criticisms of the report of the Australian Education Council working party which has centred around :

a) the accumulation of the surplus from one year to the next ; and
b) the estimates of supply from "other sources".

Both the Williams Report, and another Commonwealth report which has considered manpower planning in Australia, have agreed that better quality information is needed on the operations of the labour market as a basis for educational planning and manpower policy. It is likely that this subject will receive attention in the context of the follow-up on these reports.

3. <u>Planning Concerns for State Education Departments</u>

State Education Departments in their responses to the Commonwealth Department of Education indicated the following substantive preoccupations and areas of concern :

New South Wales	identifying needs in reconciling conflicting objectives and of meeting new demands through evaluation of existing programs, by redeployment of resources and by re-orientation of professional activities ; devolution of decision making responsibility in education.
Victoria	literacy and numeracy ; transition from school to work ; community expectations ;

	promotion of choice and diversity within and between schools ; school/community relations ; specific school staffing problems.
Queensland	public concern about accountability ; issues of accreditation and assessment - the composition and functions of the Board of Secondary School Studies, school level assessment, curriculum development, reporting student performance ; appropriate responses to pressures for change, educational responses to restrictions on funding.
South Australia	resource deployment in education ; education and labour market ; devolution in decision making responsibility in education, strategies for equality of educational opportunity - Aboriginal education, multicultural education ; disadvantaged schools projects, long-range educational perspectives.
Western Australia	teacher supply and demand, examination of the potential interest in specialised secondary schools, procedures for forecasting changes in school enrolments, general policy interests include the provision of educational resources in rural education, the maximisation of parental choice of school, the utilisation of schools' facilities in areas of declining enrolments, the reorganisation of the Department's administration and the collection of resources to regions.
Tasmania	planning issues related to reports of committees of inquiry - Secondary Education in Tasmania, Tertiary Education in Tasmania, Primary Education, the Future of District Schools, Tasmanian Education : Next Decade (TEND Report), Further Education in Tasmania ; careers education and youth unemployment issues.

It will be seen that these concerns cover a broad spectrum of issues although some concerns are common to a number of States. These include resource deployment in a changed economic and social context, school/community relations, and school staffing issues. Teacher education is currently being investigated by a national committee of inquiry, which is expected to report towards the middle of 1980, and all States have instituted State inquiries in parallel to the national inquiry.

Collaboration between the States and the Commonwealth in the examination of specific issues is sometimes arranged through the Australian Education Council and the Conference of Directors-General of Education. A recent example has been a study of Staffing and Resources for Government Schools which the AEC has commissioned the Australian Council for Educational Research (ACER) to undertake. Direction of this project is undertaken by a steering committee appointed by the AEC, and all States are represented on a project reference committee. New Zealand is also cooperating in this study.

Most educational planning in State Education Departments is concerned with short-term policy responses to issues of the type indicated in the lists given above. State Education Departments have generally given less attention to longer-term issues. However, there are indications in the reports from State Education Departments that some departments are now devoting more attention to longer-term issues.

4. <u>Links Between Educational Planning and Educational Research and Development</u>

Educational research and development in Australia has grown considerably from a narrow base over the past decade. Even so, the size of the total educational research and development effort remains small when compared with some other OECD countries and educationalists in Australia continue to rely heavily on research conducted abroad. After a period of rapid growth in the early nineteen-seventies, the research and development effort has stabilised in more recent years under the impact of restrictions on government expenditure. This stabilisation of R&D expenditure has highlighted the question as to whether educational R&D in Australia is unduly fragmented and in need of more rationalisation and coordination of effort.

This diffusion of the national R&D effort is in part a characteristic of the Australian Federal system. Pluralism in research funding sources is generally regarded as a desirable approach to research funding although there has been increased discussion in recent years of whether more attention should be given to the setting of national research priorities. Funding bodies such as the Education Research and Development Committee have set up groups to advise on research priorities.

In addition to this issue, there are a number of questions relating to the role of research in policy development and planning. The Australian experience has generally been that research including evaluation is more likely to provide legitimacy for policies and programs, or to improve their efficiency, rather than lead to reforms.

It is true that some major changes may have been influenced by research which had an influence on professional and community values, but even when this happens the key decisions are political. One example of this was provided in the setting up of the Schools Commission and the development of its programs. The creation of this body, which has had a major impact on changes in primary and secondary education in Australia over the last seven years, was decided by the Government of the time in the light of its education policy relating to determining and meeting the needs of schools. Nevertheless, the development of the programs of the Commission in such areas as disadvantaged schools drew heavily on Australian and overseas research relating to educational disadvantage.

Similarly, curriculum development in Australia, which gained considerable impetus during the nineteen-seventies, has been strongly influenced by major curriculum initiatives in the United States and United Kingdom, and by research findings on the outcomes of these initiatives.

Research and development is increasingly becoming recognised as an activity which is most effective when it evolves from practitioners instead of being imposed on education systems in a bureaucratic "top-down" manner. A prime example of this in Australia is provided by the Schools Commission's Innovations Program, which gives the opportunity to teachers, parents and the community generally to develop initiatives.

One of the most characteristic ways in which research is linked to educational planning in Australia is through the work of national educational committees of inquiry. Both State and Commonwealth Governments have made considerable use of committees of inquiry to examine particular policy and planning issues. It has been common for these inquiries to commission research studies and to draw upon these studies in forming their conclusions and recommendations. The Committee of Inquiry into Education and Training commissioned several research studies, and the current National Inquiry into Teacher Education has also commissioned several research studies. Similarly, submissions to these committees of inquiry frequently draw on research findings and so draw these findings into broader policy and planning discussions.

An aspect of this trend in Australia has been for parliamentary committees of inquiry to focus attention on the state of research knowledge in particular fields of education under consideration. An example of this influence was the conducting by the Australian Council for Educational Research in 1975 of the first Australia-wide survey into literacy and numeracy in schools as a result of an initiative taken by the House of Representatives Select Committee on Specific Learning Difficulties. While the results of the survey were generally comparable with similar countries, the survey revealed certain deficiencies that education policy makers have sought to redress. One consequence is that the Australian Education Council is currently considering a proposal for a comprehensive program of action directed at improving the teaching of basic skills in schools and involving the development of diagnostic tests and the national monitoring of literacy and numeracy.

While committees of inquiry often provide vehicles for research studies to influence policy making, it is still not uncommon for major education initiatives, such as the development of open-plan schools, to take place without the backing of research findings. Research "after the event" has on occasions caused public concern at decision-making without adequate prior research and consultation.

This experience may have influenced the approach taken by the recent Committee of Inquiry into Education and Training in its report. The Williams Report advocates development of the education system through a process of evolutionary adjustments. This would be based on continuing monitoring and review of the system. The monitoring and exchange of experience on various promising innovations is advocated by the Report.

There is comment in this paper on the concern of Australian education departments to relate educational research, policy and planning more closely. Developments in several State education departments and in the Commonwealth Department of Education have been outlined. In the Commonwealth Department of Education, an Education Planning Group has been set up which amalgamates the former policy, planning and research branches of the department. There is a deliberate policy in the Group to mix policy, planning and research personnel in allocating staff to project teams. In State education departments it was fairly common for research to be linked with guidance in units staffed by psychologists ; now it is common to link the research function with the planning division.

Overall, the past decade has been marked by the establishment of a number of agencies either with research and development missions such as the Education Research and Development Committee, or which have a fairly substantial research and development orientation in developing their programs such as the Curriculum Development Centre and the Schools Commission. Closely related to the trend to relate policy and planning functions more closely, is a fairly general concern to link research more closely with policy and planning. While it is difficult to assess overall what the outcomes have been, there would seem to be a greater awareness of the role of research in policy development and planning than was the case at the start of the nineteen-seventies. The question remains as to how best to link educational research to policy making and planning at all levels of the education system.

5. Teacher Education

The tendency for committees of inquiry to play a significant role in educational planning in Australia may be further illustrated in the field of teacher education. The Commonwealth Government set up in 1978 a National Inquiry into Teacher Education. All the States and Territories are cooperating in this inquiry, and four States have set up their own inquiries in parallel to the National Inquiry.

The Committee of Inquiry reported towards the middle of 1980. The orientation of the Inquiry was toward qualitative aspects of teacher education rather than quantitative. The Committee has been asked to report on present methods and procedures in teacher education and to make recommendations on any changes which might assist in achieving improved teaching and learning in Australian schools and pre-schools, both Government and non-Government. The Committee took note of the differences which exist in educational policies, organisation and practices in the States and Territories. It has been asked to state its assumptions about the objectives of education in Australia for the next 25 years and the education, experience and competencies required of teachers at various career stages to fulfil the roles perceived for them. The Committee took also account of the report of the Williams Committee.

In carrying out its inquiry the Committee had regard to a number of issues related to the selection of teachers, pre-service programs, in-service education and development of teachers, and the roles, relationships and responsibilities of various educational institutions in pre-service and in-service teacher education and re-entry programs. In addition to these issues, other issues referred to the Inquiry include the relationships between institutions engaged in teacher education, professional bodies, employing authorities and the wider community.

The report of this Inquiry will be of value for educational planning at various levels in Australia. The findings of the Inquiry should be relevant to the planning activities of Commonwealth agencies, State Education Departments, State post-secondary coordinating authorities and individual institutions.

IV. GENERAL COMMENT

The description of the organisation and structure of the Australian system of educational planning given in this paper points to some of the main features of the system. Educational planning in Australia is profoundly influenced by the Australian Federal system. The forms of educational planning have reflected changing Commonwealth and State roles in education. The respective Commonwealth and State roles vary between the levels and sectors of education in accordance with the extent of financial responsibility.

There is no comprehensive educational planning in Australia covering all levels and sectors. Complex relationships involving Commonwealth and State agencies are a characteristic of the system. While there is still an absence of comprehensive planning, both at State and Commonwealth levels, there have been moves towards more integrated planning and administration in post-secondary education. This trend has been marked by the establishment of the Tertiary Education Commission by the Commonwealth and the setting up of post-secondary coordinating authorities in four of the States following State inquiries.

There have also been some moves towards a more comprehensive approach in relating the education and training systems, as for example, in the terms of reference of the Williams Committee. However, the results are to date limited, and education and training tend, on the whole, to be separately planned. The follow-up on the Williams Committee Report may provide an indication whether there will be any move towards more integrated planning of education and training.

In the complex web of relationships involving State and Commonwealth agencies, the Australian Education Council is tending to assume a more significant role as a forum for consultation between the Commonwealth and the States. Working parties set up by the Council have provided useful means of joint Commonwealth/State investigation of issues.

There are various indications of some reappraisal of educational planning in Australia since the early nineteen-seventies. This reappraisal has included attempts in a number of education departments at both State and Commonwealth level to relate planning more closely to policy formulation and review, an increased concern with coordination and rationalisation in resource use in the education system, greater use of participatory and consultative mechanisms, and an increased level of Commonwealth/State cooperation in education. New administrative mechanisms have developed at both the Commonwealth and State level during this period with broad coordinating mandates covering two or more sectors of post-secondary education in an attempt to promote increased efficiency in resource use.

The Australian approach to educational planning may be illustrated by the roles of agencies such as the Tertiary Education Commission and Schools Commission. This paper has pointed out how the system of triennial planning through the commissions has evolved, and has indicated characteristic features of this approach. These have included the careful collection and analysis of information, extensive consultative procedures, and the carrying out of special inquiries where major issues have been identified. This approach needs to be viewed in the context of the Australian Federal system involving the interplay of political processes and Commonwealth/State relations.

B. GERMANY

I. REVIEW OF THE STATUS AND PERSPECTIVES OF EDUCATIONAL PLANNING (7)

1. <u>Introductory remarks concerning the distribution of responsibilities for education and educational planning in Germany</u>

In the Länder of the Federal Republic of Germany, the organisation and instruments of educational planning have been built up since the beginning of the sixties. It was not until the beginning of the seventies, however, that systematic and comprehensive educational planning came into existence at the Federal level. To understand its functioning, tasks, organisation and approach, one must be acquainted with the distribution of responsibilities in the areas of education and educational planning. In addition, the Basic Law provides for various constitutional rights, such as the right to the free choice of educational institutions and of one's occupation and the right of the parents to educate their own children ; these rights provide both orientation and limits to the planning of education.

Germany is a State with a federative structure. In the field of education the legislative, administrative and financial competencies are assigned mostly to the Länder. According to the Constitution, the Basic Law, the Federation is responsible only for those tasks which have expressly been assigned to it while the Länder have a kind of "general competence" for government tasks. In the education system, this phenomenon is described as the "Kulturhoheit" of the Länder.

The educational responsibility of the Federation, which is partly a responsibility shared with the Länder,

---

7. This Part is taken from the German National Report, (OECD, Paris, 1979, mimeographed).

was extended in 1969 in the process of extensive constitutional amendments (the so-called "reform of the financial system"). It now covers the following areas :

- The in-the-firm training (non-school) part of vocational education including vocational further education ;
- Framework legislation for higher education ;
- Participation in the building and extension of universities as a co-operative task of the Federation and the Länder (financing : 50 per cent by the Federation and 50 per cent by the Länder) ;
- Promotion of scientific research (shared with the Länder) ;
- Regulation of educational grants for pupils and students (financed two-thirds by the Federation and one-third by the Länder) and of vocational training grants ;
- Civil service legislation including legislation governing teacher, including university teacher, pay.

According to this distribution of competencies all other educational responsibilities - in particular the whole school system and its financing, including teacher training and employment - lie with the Länder. Therefore it was important that the Federation and the Länder in 1969 also agreed on a constitutional basis for joint educational planning : they can co-operate on the basis of agreements in educational planning and in the promotion of institutions and projects of scientific research of supraregional significance.

On this basis, the Federation and the Länder are able to harmonize their concepts of educational reform and educational planning. On the basis of a joint analysis of problems and tasks they can establish supraregional goals and agree on the necessary measures and funds required for their implementation. Furthermore, it is possible in this way to incorporate educational planning in Germany's overall policy, i.e. to co-ordinate it with economic, labour market and social policies as well as regional policy. The heads of Government of the Federation and the Länder explicitly required educational planners to take into consideration this wider scope of policies and to co-ordinate their financing proposals with the financial planning of the Federation and the Länder.

An important part of educational services is provided by institutions other than government agencies, that is to say by industry and by the so-called "freie Träger" ("independent sponsors") (i.e. associations, churches, trade unions, chambers, political parties). The independent sponsors supply a large part of educational services in the elementary sector (kindergartens) and in the further education sector - usually with financial support from the governments. In-the-firm training under the dual system, which is highly developed in Germany, is overwhelmingly provided by industry. Around 60 per cent of each age group receive training within a combined in-the-firm training/school system, as a rule after passing through secondary level I (75 per cent of those leaving general school at that level engage in this type of training). However, a growing number of those with a higher education entrance qualification also choose this kind of training after leaving secondary level II. Owing to the special importance of the training services provided by industry and due to the few possibilities of government to control the number of training places offered in this sector, special instruments of planning and financing which now constitute an essential and at present particularly significant part of educational planning in the Federal Republic were created in 1976 under the Training Places Promotion Act.

2. Organisation and activities to-date of the joint educational planning of the Federation and the Länder

On the basis of the constitutional amendments of 1969, the Bund-Länder-Commission for Educational Planning was set up under an administrative agreement in 1970. In 1975, this Commission was given additional tasks by a skeleton agreement between the Federal and Länder Governments on joint research promotion. It is now called "Bund-Länder-Commission for Educational Planning and Research Promotion" (abbreviated BLK).

Tasks of the BLK

The first and most important task of the Commission was to draw up a joint long-term outline plan for the co-ordinated development of the whole education system. In addition, it has to prepare medium-term planning stages and programmes for the implementation of urgent measures, to draw up a joint educational budget and to co-ordinate and evaluate the promotion of model experiments for innovations in education. The plans adopted are regularly reviewed by the Commission and necessary modifications proposed (updating).

Membership of the BLK and decision-taking procedure

When dealing with educational planning tasks, the Commission is composed of seven representatives of the Federal Government and of one representative of each of the eleven Länder. The following departments of the Federal Government are represented : the Office of the Federal Chancellor, the Federal Ministry of Finance, the Federal Ministry of the Interior, the Federal Ministry for Labour and Social Affairs, the Federal Ministry for Youth, Family

Affairs and Health, the Federal Ministry of Economics, the Federal Ministry for Research and Technology and the Federal Ministry of Education and Science, which bears central responsibility on behalf of the Federal Government. The Länder are de facto represented by the Ministers and Senators of Education while the Ministers of Finance of the Länder are deputy members as a rule. Representatives of the Science Council, of the local authorities' central associations and of the Federal Institute for Vocational Research take part in the meetings of the Commission in an advisory capacity while the Secretary-General of the Conference of the Länder Ministers of Education takes part as a permanent guest.

The Commission meets at ministerial level. It is supported by the work of four committees, which are composed of high-ranking officials, i.e. the committees for "Educational Planning", "Educational Budget", "Innovations in Education" and "Research Promotion". Any planning activity carried on by these bodies of Ministers of their representatives is also a step of policy-forming and eventually leads to decisions. Such a planning procedure embedded in the framework and process of politics occasionally gives rise to certain inconsistencies - because compromises have to be made - or inevitably leaves some questions open. On the other hand, it guarantees a relevant and realistic approach and prevents a technocratic procedure lacking in political responsibility.

This aspect is emphasized even more by the fact that the Commission submits its recommendations to the Heads of the Federal and Länder Governments for deliberation and decision-taking. A decision requires the consent of at least nine of the twelve heads of Government. However, it binds only those who have consented to it.

The variety of membership of the Commission and of its tasks as well as the procedure by which decisions are taken reflects the fact that the Bund-Länder-Commission for Educational Planning is a _government_ commission. This is what distinguishes it from the _Conferences of Länder Ministers_, such as the Permanent Conference of Länder Ministers of Education and Cultural Affairs (_KMK_). Even after the setting up of the BLK, the KMK has remained the body in which the Education Ministers of the eleven Länder bring about "self-co-ordination", a task necessary in a federative State, and in which they, in particular, secure a minimum of uniformity and comparability of the education system. For this purpose, the KMK has adopted a large number of agreements and recommendations. Furthermore, it does important work with regard to the provision of the quantitative bases of educational planning. In 1975, it set up a "Commission for Statistics Forecasts and Educational Economics (Data Commission)" in order to bring together these activities.

The General Plan for Education 1973-1985

The first General Plan for Education for the Federal Republic of Germany was adopted by the BLK in 1973. When it was submitted to the Heads of Government, the Bund-Länder-Commission expressed its view that the General Plan for Education was but the beginning of joint educational planning. Yet it is the first planning effort which comprises all sectors of the education system nationwide for the period up to 1985. Planners were able to build on the preparatory work done by mixed scientific/public advisory bodies (Science Council, Education Council), which had presented extensive preliminary considerations regarding urgent structural reforms and the quantitative extensions required as well as the necessary improvement of the material and personnel equipment of the education system.

On the basis of the existing capacities and the educational facilities available on the one hand and the expected future demand for education and training on the other, the General Plan for Education for the first time evolved quantified goals for the Federal Republic as a whole with regard to the number of places required and the need for personnel, space and material equipment for each of the planning years 1975, 1980, 1985. In addition, it established guidelines and stated necessary measures for further structural reforms of the education system including pilot experiments, which seemed necessary before any final decisions could be taken. The educational budget defined the financial framework for the implementation of the planned measures on the basis of economic and financial policy data and assumptions as well as on the basis of partially alternative calculations of the cost-effects of the planned measures.

Relationships with other types of planning (sectoral and regional/local plans)

It has already been pointed out that the General Plan for Education is a joint long-term outline plan. The assignment of the joint planning task to the Federation and the Länder under the constitution has not altered the legislative and administrative competencies in the education sector. Therefore the realisation, the putting into practice of the agreed goals, lies with those responsible for it under the constitution, i.e. mostly the Länder.

The plans adopted by the Bund-Länder-Commission represent political declarations of intent and commitments on the part of the supreme executive authorities of the Federal and Länder Governments and, as overall goals, they provide the yardstick for sectoral, regional and local material and financial planning. Under this "umbrella", there is a planning structure which may appear extremely complicated to the uninformed observer.

On the one hand, regional outline plans and local detailed plans, as well as their execution, and the provision of funds with budgets and financial plans, are the responsibility of the State and local levels involved. (For example, regional school development plans are the responsibility of the Länder, local development plans that of the administrative districts and municipalities ; the building or expansion of universities is the responsibility of the Federal and Länder Governments as a supraregional task and that of the Länder as a regional task). On the other hand, the structure and process of planning, decision-taking and implementation correspond to the sectors or levels of the education system (kindergarten and school development plans, university extension plans, planning for sufficient vocational training places and further education facilities). Taken together, it is a very complex planning system consisting of a large number of planning and decision-taking bodies (above all the parliaments) and agencies in charge of implementation which try to combine necessary central guidelines with local flexibility. That of course means a mutual and simultaneous planning process instead of a one-way-oriented, hierarchical one. Thus, for example, the school development plans of the Länder and of the local authorities are oriented to supraregional standards and the university extension plans to the capacities considered necessary on the national level. But at the same time, the local authorities, industry, the independent sponsors and associations, just like the Länder and the Federation, introduce their experiences and their goals into the joint planning process. This purpose is served - in addition to regular public discussion - not only by permanent contacts in joint bodies such as the BLK, the KMK, the planning committee for university building, but also by hearings organised by the Bund-Länder-Commission before adoption of their plans. Such a hearing of all those responsible for education and of all those affected by it is also planned to be held with regard to the new envisaged updating of the General Plan for Education 1979/80 with a time horizon of 1990.

Further BLK planning instruments

The Bund-Länder-Commission for Educational Planning has at its disposal further instruments with which to influence the realisation of established educational policy goals beyond the outline plan, and, if necessary, fix new priorities which may become necessary. First, it prepares medium-term phased plans, which can either cover the education system as a whole (such as the cost and financing plan 1975-1978) or concentrate on priorities (such as the medium-term phased plan for priority areas of vocational education 1975).

In 1976, the BLK adopted a programme for the implementation of urgent measures aimed at reducing employment risks for young people; the programme was intended as a special effort to cope with the needs for education and training of the age-groups with a high birth-rate. With such phased plans and programmes, the Federal and Länder Governments can give concrete shape to their planning intentions and agree on more detailed goals and measures, including their financing.

Updating of the General Plan for Education

At present, the Bund-Länder-Commission is updating the General Plan for Education itself. Its task here is to compare the actual development of the education system with the goals established in 1973, to review these goals and the priorities fixed at that time and finally to extend the planning horizon to the year 1990. One of the major aims is to make allowance for the greatly decreasing birth-rates and for the changed general conditions of the labour market (cf. Section 5. "Priorities for the eighties").

3. Evaluation of the results of educational planning at the Federal and Länder levels

Joint educational planning has greatly contributed to the expansion and modernisation of the German education system. Educational opportunities would probably in any case have been extended as age-groups grew larger and innovations were put into practice. But especially in the expansion phase it was important that the Federal and Länder Governments co-ordinated their actions and reached agreement on the aims and the pace of expansion as well as on structural changes. Admittedly certain reservations must be made here regarding their ability to bring about a consensus and thus regarding the success of joint educational planning. Nevertheless the discussion around federal educational planning and its financing, which began with great intensity at the time of the constitutional changes of 1969, has made it possible to ensure the availability of the resources required for the expansion and improvements of the education system. There were setbacks in the form of disputes about the educational budget and about the budgetary and financial plans of the Federal, Länder and local Governments, which in fact have to appropriate the funds. But the steep rise of expenditure on education from DM. 27.6 billion in 1970 to DM. 64.2 billion in 1978 shows that educational policy was on the whole successful in competing for gradually scarcer resources. An important reason for this success is that educational policy was the only public sector presenting a long-term programme based on sound estimates of demand to prove its material requirements. To the extent that there was a lack of staff and space at the regional and local levels, reference was made to the standards fixed by the General Plan for Education.

The desired staff ratios had been partially reached in the first basic planning year for primary and secondary levels in general schools, and they had been improved for elementary education. In some cases, however, they had not been reached, as in vocational schools, where there is still a shortage of qualified teaching staff. Of course, the "educational streams" sometimes took a different course than had been expected. Educational planning assumes a so-called structure rate model and estimates the distribution of 100 per cent of one age-group among the various educational courses. These "participation rates" were in some cases confirmed by what actually happened but in others they either exceeded or fell short of the original forecasts.

Here it is necessary to make a general remark on the guidelines which are the basis of German educational planning : they are first and foremost marked by the citizen's right to the free choice of training and occupation, a right embodied in the constitution. In addition, it is a goal of educational policy to keep the young individual's educational options open as long as possible and to ensure the greatest possible measure of transfer possibilities between the various sectors of the education system.

Educational planning should not aim to constrain or narrowly direct the educational career of pupils and trainees. On the contrary, it should provide a great variety of educational opportunities in accordance with anticipated demands, thus leaving room for the realisation of individual educational goals instead of preventing such realisation by unnecessary restriction of admission. If bottlenecks are expected, educational planners must respond quickly and with the greatest possible flexibility to supplement scarce education and training capacities. This has been practised successfully in the past years in response to an imminent shortage of vocational training places and to the widely applied numerus clausus at the universities since 1974.

The greatest possible opening of educational institutions in compliance with the educational aspirations and needs expressed does not of course mean that educational planning may neglect the requirements of the labour market, i.e. the opportunities and risks of subsequent employment. Information and orientation as well as educational opportunities which provide widely utilisable qualifications and flexibility are, however, given preference over the instrument of direct control. This strategy is advisable also because it is hardly possible, in a changing and largely market-oriented economy, to forecast the medium-term, let alone the long-term, demand for labour when it is broken down by occupational specialisation and levels of qualification. This is true for all except a few selected public sectors, such as teachers. The co-ordination of the employment and education systems has become even more difficult since 1974 when full employment ceased to be the norm. This problem will be dealt with in more detail in connection with the future priority areas of German educational planning.

On the basis of financial support for pilot experiments, jointly provided by the Federation and the Länder, the BLK has considerably encouraged innovation within the education system. Priority areas to date have been the further development of elementary education (both in terms of curricula and organisation), the experimental operation of comprehensive schools, improvements in the three-tier school system including greater possibility of transfer, new developments in the upper grades of secondary schools, teacher training, especially further training, the use of media at school, greater encouragement and support for handicapped people, the introduction of a basic vocational education year of various types as well as models for higher education.

In future, models for a better integration of foreign children in education and training will represent a new priority area. In view of the complexity of innovative efforts in the education system it is important that the BLK carries out summary evaluations of the jointly supported model experiments.

The joint educational planning efforts were less successful in their attempt to provide a common framework for the structural reforms going on in the Länder. Even when the General Plan for Education was adopted in 1973, there were minority votes by a group of Länder concerning two major issues of organisation. These dissenting opinions made it necessary when making a decision on the planning body. Such issues were :

- Integration of the first two secondary level I grades into a so-called orientation cycle for the purpose of keeping open the pupil's educational career options a little longer. While one group of Länder and the Federation were in favour of an organisation of this orientation cycle which was independent of the type of school, another group of Länder took the view that it must also be possible to assign the orientation cycle to the various types of schools at the secondary level I (compulsory general school, intermediate school, grammar school) while securing curricular co-ordination and transfer possibilities.
- While one group of Länder and the Federation maintained that the aims and principles set up for the secondary level I implied the organisational form of an integrated comprehensive school, another group of Länder thought the time was not yet ripe for it, and advocated a retention of the three-tier school system while the evaluation of experience

gained in the model experimental programme with various types of comprehensive schools had not been concluded.

In the course of the updating of the first General Plan for Education, which is still underway, the issue of the pros and cons of adopting the comprehensive school as the standard school in the country was again the centre of attention. The above-mentioned groups of Länder continue to take differing views on the introduction of comprehensive schooling throughout the country. However, it appears that a consensus can be reached to the extent that all Länder will eliminate the time limit (originally 1981) on the nationwide recognition of the examinations passed at comprehensive schools. Negotiations on what the curricular conditions of such recognition should be are still going on within the KMK.

A successful arrangement would not mean uniformity of school policy among the Länder, but it would ensure the mutual recognition of equivalent examinations and thus the minimum of transparency, mobility and equality of opportunity required in a federative State. Such a minimum consensus about the particularly important political issue of comprehensive schools might help to speed up the general efforts to bring about comparability and equivalence of examinations among the Länder, the possibility of transfer from one Land to another and the co-ordination of school and shop-training elements of the dual training system. This goal is served not only by joint educational planning by the Federation and the Länder but also by the activities of the Conference of the Länder Ministers of Education and Cultural Affairs, which were intensified in response to the Federal Government's report on the structural problems of the federative education system.

4. Sectoral planning in education

It has already been pointed out that, under the "umbrella" of joint outline planning by the Federation and the Länder, sectoral planning is carried out at different levels of government. These sectoral planning activities concentrate on problem analysis, the definition of goals, decisions on measures to be taken and the provision of funds for specific sub-sectors of the education system. For the school sector there are the land legislation and the school development plans of the Länder (framework) and of the responsible local government authorities. For the planning of education in the elementary sector there are mainly local bodies at the level of districts or municipalities including independent institutions. In some Länder an outline plan is adopted at Land level too, which provides the criteria for local planning on the basis of the requirements linked with the financial grants awarded by the Land. By way of example, two sectoral planning activities which are carried out at the supraregional level will be described below. One is a sector in which the Federation and the Länder co-operate on a joint task stipulated by the constitution (building and/or extension of universities). The other example is a planning task performed jointly by government and industry (vocational education in the dual system).

a) Planning of the building and the expansion of universities including university clinics

For the purpose of expanding important infrastructure areas, the instrument of the so-called joint tasks was created in 1969 by means of a change of the constitution. To assist the Länder, the Federation was given the right to participate in the planning and financing of university construction, the improvement of the regional economic structure and the improvement of the agrarian structure as well as coastal protection. The law on the joint tasks of "university construction and extension" (University Construction Act) provided the basis for the setting up of a joint Federal and Länder planning committee. Its members are the Federal Minister for Education and Science, who is chairman, the Federal Minister of Finance and one minister of each of the eleven Länder. The Science Council, an advisory body composed of scientists and experts from the Federation and the Länder, participates in the drawing up of the outline plan. The projects for the outline plan, including relevant documents, are submitted to the Science Council by the Land concerned. The council's recommendations form the basis for the deliberations of the planning committee.

The planning committee presents the outline plan to the governments of the Federation and the Länder. The governments incorporate in their draft budgets the amounts required for the implementation of the outline plan in the coming year, the budgets are then decided on by the parliaments. Since 1969 the Federal and Länder Governments have each paid half of the costs of building and extending universities. The implementation of the outline plan, however, is the responsibility of the Länder.

The joint planning and investment effort made by the Federation and the Länder in the last 10 years has brought about a major quantitative expansion and the modernisation of the German higher education sector. Between 1970 and 1978, the number of study places (on the basis of so-called floor space standards) increased from 470 000 (1971) to 737 000 (1978). The long-term construction goal is 850 000 study places. This construction volume is almost reached in the 9th outline plan until 1983, which has just been adopted. The floor space assigned is so calculated that - in view of the exceptional situation created by the age-groups with a high birth-rate - it can accommodate the expected number of at least 1 million students for a period of transition.

Since the inception of joint outline plans, the Federation and the Länder have jointly invested approximately DM. 22.3 billion in university construction (up to and including 1978). This considerable joint effort and the rapid expansion of the higher education sector show that the joint task of university construction has stood the test. Yet there is criticism of this planning instrument and procedure : it points out that such joint planning by the executive authorities leaves the parliaments hardly any scope for modifications of the planning result and therefore for using their right to approve the annual budget. The planning level shared by the Federation and the Länder is occasionally described as "grey zone" owing to the lack of control and opportunity for revision.

In favour of retaining the joint task it should be pointed out that the need for modernising the German universities will continue to exist in the long term. Furthermore, since the student body is highly mobile, it makes sense to coordinate structural extensions for higher education at the federal level.

b) <u>Planning of vocational education in the dual system</u>

With regard to the legislation governing vocational education in the dual system, the Federal Government is responsible for the in-the-firm training part and the Länder for the school part. The Federal Vocational Education Act 1969 is the legal basis for vocational education outside schools and for vocational further education.

The in-the-firm training part of vocational education is provided by industry, trade, commerce and agriculture, as well as by the independent professions. Besides the representatives of the Federal and Länder Governments, the employees' representatives also have a say in the Federal Institute for Vocational Education which - as an institution directly responsible to the Federal Government and having legal capacity - has been entrusted with essential functions concerning the preparation of vocational education policy.

In the middle-seventies it became apparent that the age groups leaving school from 1977 onwards would meet with an insufficient supply of training places. The most important task was to bring about a consensus between Government, industry and the trade unions that there should be training places for all those young people who wanted them. There were disputes over the most suitable way to reach this goal.

After intensive political discussion, the Law to promote the provision of training places (Training Places Promotion Act) was passed in 1976. Its most important elements are a systematic planning procedure, the procurement of an improved planning basis and a mechanism for interfirm financial adjustment as an instrument with which to secure sufficient training capacities.

The Federal Minister for Education and Science was required to keep track of the regional and sectoral development of the supply of training places and the demand for them and to report on the situation to the Federal Government by 1st March of every year in the so-called "Vocational Education Report", which is to describe the expected development in the years to come. If - in relation to the demand for training places - the availability of a balanced supply of training places seems uncertain, the report is required to make suggestions as to how the expected deficit can be eliminated.

In addition, the legal basis for the assessment of the situation for obtaining the data required was created. This includes information on the number of new training contracts concluded every year and the number of training places which remained vacant, broken down by occupations, in which formal training is provided, as well as by the number of previous years' candidates not yet placed. The demand for the year to come is estimated on the basis of the number of school leavers, surveys of students' demand behaviour in earlier years and of young people's training aspirations.

With the Training Places Promotion Act, the task to ensure a sufficient supply of training places was embodied in legislation. The stock-taking and forecast which the law requires to be made every year clarify the size of the training challenges to be tackled and the problems still awaiting solution. It obliges all those involved to take part in a public discussion on how the remaining problems can be solved on the basis of facts. This discussion begins in the course of the drawing up of the Vocational Education Report, above all in the chief committee of the Federal Institute for Vocational Research, in which all concerned, including industry and the employees' representatives, take part.

The plans which have been drawn up annually since 1977 and the resultant efforts made by government and industry have brought about a major expansion of the supply of training places. The number of new training contracts rose to 602 000 in the training year 1978/79 (as compared to 462 000 in 1975). The Federal and Länder Governments have also contributed to an increase in training capacities. This has been done by increasing the number of training places in the civil service itself, increasing full-time vocational school opportunities and promoting inter-firm training activities which supplement training in small firms. Both sectors of investment have been co-funded by the Federal Government in the years in which the training places situation has been particularly tight. Most of the Länder have, in addition, initiated programmes to subsidise more industrial training places which benefit directly those groups which are in particular need of encouragement (the handicapped, foreigners etc.). Finally, in co-operation with the labour administration, they have greatly expanded preparatory courses for training and work for young people belonging to such groups.

The joint efforts of all those participating have helped to make it unnecessary so far to appeal to the financing provisions of the Training Places Promotion Act. To date, the prevailing opinion has been that there is no need to invoke the above Act, which provides for a compulsory vocational training contribution to be levied from industry and to be apportioned to those firms providing training, as long as a sufficient supply of training places for young people can be ensured in other ways.

5. Priorities of educational planning tasks for the 1980s

The following statements cannot provide more than a rough outline of the main problems and tasks confronting educational planning for the 1980s. Two reservations must be made right from the outset : firstly, it is a statement made on the basis of today's situation ; even longer-term planning cannot prevent unforeseen problems from arising or secondary problems from suddenly gaining primary importance as a result of actual developments and public discussion. Secondly, fixing educational priorities is the responsibility of the bodies in charge of planning, whose decisions are not always predictable.

Thus, the work on the updating of the General Plan for Education with a planning horizon until 1990 is still underway, as was mentioned above. Without anticipating the final decisions of the BLK and other planning bodies, it can be said that the following problems and tasks will be central to educational planning efforts :

a) Full vocational training for all young people

The need to ensure sufficient educational opportunities, both in quantity and quality, for the age groups with a high birth-rate has largely absorbed educational planning capacities and the resources available. This has been the case despite a controversial general discussion on the development of the German educational structures in the 1960s and 1970s.

The goal of vocational qualification for the greatest possible number of young people has increasingly been pursued and realised in Germany. The task of creating a sufficient supply of training and study places for the larger age groups will continue to enjoy priority until about 1983 at secondary level II and during the whole of the 1980s in the higher education sector. And this is so not only for educational policy reasons : the development of the labour market and of unemployment has shown that if further vocational training is provided for all young people it will greatly relieve the labour market for those age groups and provide tne young people themselves with far better initial opportunities for their subsequent transition to work.

Therefore, the plans and other measures outlined above are continued with emphasis on the sector of vocational education, the aim being in particular to bring about improvements for those groups which are underprivileged and for those regions with particularly few opportunities. The weaker regions are strengthened above all by means of a systematic extension of vocational full-time schooling and inter-firm training places. These are both co-funded temporarily by the Federal Government by means of special programmes. The provision of training places according to regions by the Länder is also a great help.

In the higher education sector, the goal is to enable universities to meet the demand for study places for first-year students whose number will probably increase considerably from the early to the mid-eighties. In November 1977 the Heads of the Federal and Länder Governments took a decision of principle concerning the opening up of the universities, according to which additional admission restrictions are to be avoided and existing ones removed gradually. This will require an exhaustive and flexible utilisation of existing training capacities as well as of those under construction or planned. In addition, special excess-load measures need to be envisaged. Since 1978, the Länder have submitted annually updated reports on the type and scope of these special measures.

b) <u>Securing and improving the quality of educational supply</u>

In the elementary sector, at the primary level and at secondary level I, a quantitative relief as a result of shrinking age groups is already making itself felt. Around 1983/84 it will reach secondary level II, also.

For educational planning in Germany, the basic demographic factors have changed markedly : the annual number of births has fallen by approximately 40 per cent between the mid-sixties and the early seventies and has since been stabilized at this level. This development offers a great opportunity for the education system : excessive competition in school and the shortage of training opportunities can be reduced. It will become increasingly possible to give attention and support to individual pupils and trainees in accordance with the individual's talents, inclinations and aptitudes.

A prerequisite, however, is that educational policy succeeds in keeping up the level of the required funds (staff, rooms, equipment) and, where necessary, obtaining additional funds.

A major aim of educational planning must be to secure adequate funding, in competition with other policy areas for generally scarce funds. Of course the demands must not be exorbitant, and it would be impossible to make a case for a growth of educational expenditure like that of the sixties and seventies. It must, however, be made clear that now we have a chance of realising planning standards which are in keeping with the actual demand, thus creating the conditions for successful work at the educational institutions in the interest of the individual pupil.

More teachers will have to be provided for vocational schools. The downward demographic trend necessitates special arrangements for securing enough kindergartens and schools locally for the future as well as the present. In those areas particularly affected by the decline in the birth rate, kindergartens and schools will have to be continued even if they are underoccupied by normal standards. Calculation of the number of personnel required will have to take this factor into account. In addition, however, teacher training and in particular further training for teachers have to guarantee that teachers can be employed as flexibly as possible because this is the only way to cope with the changing demands for staff caused by major demographic fluctuations.

The quantitative relief of the education system also makes it possible to think afresh about the aims of learning and the curricula. There is wide discussion in Germany at present about what young people should learn and in what form they should learn it in order to be prepared for work, family, leisure and in general for life in our society. The aim of "securing the fulfilment of the pedagogical task" will be given more central attention also in the updated version of the General Plan for Education. Emphasis will be placed on a well-balanced encouragement of intellectual, creative, social and practical skills and on the development of a readiness for lifelong learning.

c) <u>Special support for groups hitherto underprivileged in their educational opportunities</u>

The general expansion of the education system has also brought about greater equality of opportunities. Thus, the prospects of working class children and of girls to participate in further education courses and in higher education have been increased considerably.

The large-scale expansion of the education system and the quantitative relief to be expected are reason enough to give greater attention to those groups which, despite generally improved educational opportunities, still do not participate sufficiently in education and training or have lately come to be in need of special encouragement.

The participation rate of <u>girls</u> in vocational education is still far below the rate which would correspond to their share of the population ; while their share in the number of those young people without training contracts is far higher than those of boys. Also, the training opportunities for girls in the dual system are concentrated on a very small range of occupations.

The Vocational Education Report makes a separate analysis of this development and suggests special efforts to enlarge and improve the vocational training opportunities for girls. Some examples are : increased participation of girls in vocational training in the public sector, promotion of additional training places for girls in some Länder, a joint pilot experimental programme of the Federal Government and industry for the increased training of girls in crafts/technical occupations, drawing the attention of girls, parents and industrial firms to the fact that such training is possible and promising.

The education and training of the <u>children of foreign workers</u> will feature as a special planning task in the forthcoming updated version of the General Plan for Education. In 1977, approximately 690 000 foreign children between 6 and 18 years of age lived in Germany. The proportion of births of foreigners has meanwhile risen to approximately 15 per cent of all births and indicates the future average participation rate of foreign children in the number of school children. In some residential districts, this percentage is already higher.

The educational participation of foreign children has to date been much lower than that of German children. Some of them do not comply with the compulsory schooling requirements (up to age 18). The purpose of educational planning measures here is to enable foreigners, too, to be integrated in the German education system, which is a prerequisite for taking school-leaving examinations. At the same time, the option for these children to return to their home country must be kept open (for example by instruction also in their mother tongue). Success in school-leaving examinations has a decisive influence on the prospects of receiving vocational training. In order to provide greater encouragement to foreign children, both the teacher/pupil ratio and the equipment should be improved for those regular classes in which the number of foreign children exceeds a certain percentage.

The third group which is considered to be in need of special assistance is the group of <u>children with learning impairments or handicaps</u>. It is assumed that, in principle, these children should as far as possible be taught together with other children in regular institutions. This requires improved measures to prevent, or recognise at an early stage, handicaps and to provide systematic encouragement for these children. The updated version of the General Plan for Education, however, will also develop goals and make provision for special educational institutions which will nevertheless be required for some children with learning impairments and handicaps.

d) <u>Improved co-ordination between education and employment</u>

The changes in the employment situation since the 1974 recession have made the transition from school to work much more difficult for many young people, compared with the period when there was full employment or even overemployment. In the coming years, the situation will be made more difficult by the fact that the number of those leaving the education system and looking for first employment will increase considerably. These are the reasons why the updated General Plan for Education will devote a separate section to the changes in the relationship between the education and employment systems.

As it was pointed out above, educational planners cannot take their decisions exclusively on assumptions concerning developments in the labour market, which is partly characterised by major long-term incertainties. However, educational planning will have to make its contribution to making the transition from school to work easier for all young people. It can help to reduce the discrepancy between their qualifications and the requirements of the labour market. These goals are to be realised by the following measures :

- Reduction of the number of young people leaving compulsory general school without a final examination. Failure to acquire this qualification has often been an insurmountable obstacle for pupils wishing to transfer to vocational training.
- Systematic introduction of a tenth year of education with a vocational orientation preparing pupils for working life and including the basic vocational education year.
- Broad-based vocational basic education to permit individuals to master subsequent changes at the place of work and to be able to influence such changes also.

- Consistent extension of general and vocational further education.
- Trial and extension of so-called double-qualification courses in secondary level II, which lead to both a university entrance qualification and a first vocational qualification, thus enabling the holder to embark on an occupation immediately.
- Broad-based basic vocational education in all study courses, increased practical orientation, and improved study counselling.

The updated General Plan for Education, however, will also state the prerequisites to be fulfilled by the employment system if co-ordination is to be successful. These include investments securing old jobs and creating new ones ; re-designing jobs and improving work organisation so as to bring about the best possible utilisation of the increased qualification potential ; revision of the rigid civil service law in the public sector, which so far has made entry to this sector of the employment system exclusively conditional upon formal qualifications acquired in the education system, but hardly at all upon experience and achievements during one's working life. Finally, the possibilities of long-term forecasting of the demand for labour must be improved, with the emphasis in research being laid on establishing what qualifications in particular guarantee the broadest possible employability and a high degree of flexibility in working life.

e) Extension of the further education sector

Since the development of the labour market is subject to changes which are hard to forecast on a long-term basis, initial training must - as the OECD pointed out a long time ago - be supplemented by further education opportunities. In addition to vocational further education, general further education will also gain significance : firstly because, in the long range, working hours will probably be further reduced and leisure hours will increase, thus increasing the possibilities for further education ; secondly, because orientation in an increasingly complex world also demands that education for family, society and leisure activities be further developed.

The system of further education in Germany is difficult to plan because responsibilities for it are spread over a wide variety of institutions and organisations, a factor which, on the other hand, makes for a variety of opportunities. Utilisation of these opportunities will largely depend on whether and when educational leave can be extended to all those in employment.

Table 1

FEDERAL REPUBLIC OF GERMANY
THE DISTRIBUTION OF COMPETENCE IN THE FIELD OF EDUCATIONAL PLANNING

Part of the Educational System \ Level	Bund (Federation)	Länder (Regional)	Gemeinden (Local authorities)
Elementary education :	Innovative pilot projects (BLK)	Planning and financing guidelines provided by the Kindergarten Acts and partly by outline planning Innovative pilot projects (BLK)	Planning of youth services, Forecasting educational needs, Co-operation with autonomous bodies providing elementary education
Primary education : Lower secondary education : Higher secondary education :	Innovative pilot projects (BLK) Annual report on vocational education Forecasting of manpower needs and qualification research	School development planning Innovative pilot projects (BLK) Programmes to secure the supply of vocational training places	Local school development planning
Tertiary education :	Modernisation of existing and construction of new facilities (together with the Länder), Innovative pilot projects (BLK), Forecasting of manpower needs (labour market) and qualification research	Modernisation of existing and construction of new facilities (together with the Bund), innovative pilot projects (BLK), forecasting of needs for teaching personnel	
Further education :	Innovative pilot projects (BLK)	Innovative pilot projects (BLK)	Forecasting educational needs : co-operation with autonomous bodies providing further education
Educational system as a whole :	Overall educational planning (BLK), overall educational budgeting (BLK), planning for the different levels of the educational system (BLK)	Overall educational planning (BLK), overall educational budgeting (BLK), planning for the different levels of the educational system (BLK), co-ordination of structures and curricula (KMK)	Local educational planning (with the exception of tertiary education)

Based on Klaus Hüfner's : "Educational Planning in Federal Countries", OECD, Paris, 1978 (mimeographed), p. 20.

II. ISSUES OF MAIN CONCERN IN FEDERAL COUNTRIES WITH SPECIAL REFERENCE TO GERMANY (8)

This section presents some basic problems of educational policy planning in federal states. It will begin with an examination of the role of information and communication in the planning process and then turn to the part played by financing in this process. It will end by drawing some tentative conclusions which might provide a basis for further discussion.

1. The Role of Information and Communication in Educational Planning

This issue is of strategic importance because information and communication integrate the political-administrative, legal-integrative, economic-financial and educational planning aspects of the system. The higher the structural complexity of a social system, the more important is the task of integration and co-ordination through the exchange of information. The system needs a mutual exchange of information between its various parts in order to promote internal and external co-ordination. Information and communication link all the parts to one comprehensive system and, at the same time, relate the total system to its environment. The communication structure whose task is the transfer of information is closely related to the decision-making structure of the system. Thus, communication's function is to enhance the decision-making capacity of the system.

The different educational systems in the 11 Länder present problems of co-ordinating official Länder statistics and standardising an overall scheme at the level of the Bund. (The process of aggregation and disaggregation depends on this "comparability".). During the 1950s the notion of educational planning was still unknown. However, in 1950 the KMK asked the Federal Office of Statistics to participate with the Länder offices of statistics in the process of co-ordination. This process then took place at two levels : within the Länder between the ministries of culture and the Länder offices of statistics, and at the nation-wide level between the Federal Office of Statistics and the KMK. This helped - at least partly - the function of evaluation, for example when the KMK wanted to know in 1959 to what extent its decisions of 1955 had been implemented towards more uniformity in the education systems of the Länder. All in all, however, the influence of the KMK upon the content of statistical questionnaires was rather limited during that period. Within the Länder

---

8. This Part is taken from K. Hüfner's paper : "Educational Planning in Federal Countries", op. cit.

administrations there were no experts on educational statistics or economics. The function of educational statistics remained primarily a routine matter of documentation on past performance.

The situation changed dramatically in the 1960s. The KMK-Bedarfsfeststellung of 1963 required new types of data as an information base for the political debate on educational needs (9). The KMK decided to set up a permanent working group which continued to up-date and improve its information base for quantitative programming activities in educational planning. This, in turn, led to corresponding improvements of educational statistics at the Länder as well as at the national level. At the same time, a number of newly founded institutes for educational research asked for specific data about the performance of the educational system and also started creating their own official information systems. In addition to that, OECD's work on new classification schemes for educational planning began.

The reaction of the offices for statistics to this new situation led to changes in their programmes as well as methodological and technical innovations. In addition the rapid expansion of institutes for planning and research (in the late 1960s each Land had its own planning department within the education administration) required more and more disaggregated data and an extended publication of statistics.

At the KMK level a Commission for Statistics, Prognosis and Economics of Education started its work in 1976. It was to integrate the function of the former working group for educational needs and school statistics and to co-ordinate the development of data banks in the school administrations of the 11 Länder. This KMK "Data Commission" works together with the BLK, the BMBW and the statistical offices at both levels.

For higher education statistics the progress in collecting and improving nation-wide data was remarkable. The most decisive change took place in 1966/67 when the collection and processing of individualised student flow statistics started. It was no accident that this new idea was first realised in the field of higher education. The preconditions were extremely favourable :

a) individualised questionnaires had already been in use for sometime ;
b) the administrations in institutions of higher education did the work themselves and had a keen interest both in the results and in making data gathering more efficient ;

---

9. KMK : Bedarfsfeststellung 1961 bis 1970, Klett, Stuttgart, 1963, p. 94.

c) Because of the long existence of the <u>Wissenschaftsrat</u> the need for nation-wide data was more pronounced in higher education than in the school sector ; and
d) the relatively high degree of autonomy of the universities did not encroach upon the cultural sovereignty of the <u>Länder</u> who themselves were highly interested in a unified data base for higher education.

From a technical point of view the construction of educational data banks was thought to be a great step forward and led to a general optimism among educational planners, administrators and policy-makers. Data technicians were proclaiming that with the introduction of new information technologies all information problems for purposes of educational planning, statistics and administration could be solved. But the "politico-social" problems of such an innovation became quickly visible : the sudden acceleration of change with respect to content, methods and techniques suddenly jeopardized the co-ordination capacities of the different offices of statistics at the different levels. In order to produce national statistics the Federal Office of Statistics needed the information from all Länder. Even where all Länder agreed to collaborate, which did not happen in all cases, the rate of change in content and techniques differed from Land to Land so that the "most backward" Land determined the date of publication of the nation-wide statistics. Until today, time-lags of 3-4 years can be observed. In order to receive a minimum of information as quickly as possible the statistical publication programmes were greatly shortened. In other words : the planning and administration of statistics in federal countries is a task which is at least as complex and difficult as educational planning itself.

It is doubtful whether the present "crisis" situation can be resolved by introducing a comprehensive information system at the Bund level because of the existing differences in educational planning, administration and statistics. In addition, different information is needed for different education planning purposes. This implies that the demand for more or less aggregated information differs too according to the planning level. There is need for "routine" as well as "innovative" information about the various parts of the educational system. In order to fulfil this task a consensus about a common concept of educational planning theory and practice would be necessary - which, in the case of Germany, does not yet exist.

2. Competence in the Field of Educational Finance

During the 1950s the KMK activities concentrated upon the material reconstruction of the German school system. The construction of school buildings had to be realized by the Länder without the financial help of the Bund. In October, 1958, the Federal Parliament (Deutscher Bundestag) decided to set up a commission with representatives of the Bund and Länder in order to suggest alternative plans for the financing of education either exclusively by the Bund, or exclusively by the Länder, or by some cooperative system between the two. The constitutional provisions, however, were supposed to remain unchanged. The lack of school buildings and the shortage of teachers, both at the school and at the university levels, were supposed to be given high priority. The attempt, like many similar ones later on, did not produce any immediate changes. This type of administrative enquiry, however, has to be seen as part of the general background discussion against which specific forms of co-operation between the Bund and the Länder did evolve, though limited in scope and duration.

In 1962 the KMK decided to work out a Bedarfsfeststellung (estimates of the manpower requirements for education, science and research) for the period 1961-1970 (10). Two main arguments were advanced to justify this type of official forecasting (in defence against anticipated charges of "creeping socialism" and "undue state intervention"). One was related to OECD activities in the economics of education and argued that Germany should not lag behind the efforts of the other nations of the Atlantic Community to improve and expand their educational systems. The other argument referred to the bargaining process between the Bund and the Länder over the distribution of the public tax income and the future allocation of public resources. In fact, it was hoped that the cultural tasks of the Länder and municipalities would eventually receive the same weight as the federal expenditures for defence and social affairs. The requirements plan asked for an increase of yearly educational expenditures from about 9 to 20 billion German marks during the period 1961-1970.

Based upon the Bedarfsfeststellung of 1963, the Länder ministers/senators for cultural affairs declared in March 1964 that a re-orientation of German educational policy after a phase of re-construction was of the utmost importance. New guidelines of educational policy had to take into account the process of (Western) European integration as well as "similar reform trends in other modern industrial societies". In the same year, the KMK called for an "integrated concept of educational planning" and asked for new and integrated forms of co-operation between the Bund, the Länder, and the communities and all responsible cultural organizations in Germany.

The continued expansion of secondary and higher education during the 1960s had put a growing strain on the financial resources of the Länder. The recommendations of the Troeger Commission which took into account these developments led in 1964 to some constitutional amendments and

---

10. Ibid.

the introduction of some Gemeinschaftsaufgaben : science, (higher) education, and educational planning.

Table 2 shows to-day's distribution of competence in the field of educational finance. The distribution between the Bund and the Länder refers mainly to innovation pilot projects (50:50) in primary, secondary, and tertiary education, to the modernization and construction of facilities in tertiary education (50:50), and to student support schemes in secondary and tertiary education (65:35). Teachers' salaries in primary, secondary, and tertiary education are borne by the Länder (100 per cent). The Gemeinden have to pay the non-teaching staff (100 per cent) in primary and secondary education. Careful consideration is needed with respect to the distribution of financial competence between the Länder and Gemeinden since there are - for historical, geographical and other reasons - quite a number of differences within the 11 Länder which cannot be elaborated and explained here.

3. Concluding remarks

"Educational planning" as a legal function is a relatively new concept. It is closely related to the notion of "preparing a decision". In Germany, the notion of educational planning did not appear in official documents before 1963. In 1969 educational planning was "legalized" with the introduction of the Gemeinschaftsaufgabe, "educational planning". Compared to other federal countries - Australia, Canada and the United States - educational planning in Germany is much more legally standardized and formalized. In the three other federal states educational planning seems to be much more related to the financing of educational programmes following the political decision-making processes rather than a technocratic rationalized process contributing to policy making.

In Germany the distribution of competence in educational law making, administration and finance is rather closely interlinked and clearly defined. What is missing is the functional and institutional integration of "educational planning" which still has the following problems :

- the use of a still rather underdeveloped theoretical concept of educational planning ;
- the side-by-side existence of a Bund-Länder organ (BLK) and a Länder organ (KMK) with overlapping competencies ;
- the still unclear parliamentary control mechanisms of KMK and BLK decisions which do not guarantee broad participatory decisions on issues of education ; and
- ad hoc relationships between educational research, policy and planning which question the possible existence of independent and eventually helpful

Table 2
Federal Republic of Germany
THE DISTRIBUTION OF COMPETENCE IN THE FIELD OF EDUCATIONAL FINANCE

Part of the Educational System \ Level	Bund	Länder	Gemeinden (Community level)	Institutions/ Organisations
Elementary education :		Contributions (up to 25 %) for staff and other expenditures, for investments	Kindergarten, staff and other expenditures, investments	Parents' contributions
Primary education :	Innovation pilot projects (50 %); students' support schemes (65 %); establishment of industrial training divisions beyond the firm level	Teachers (100 %); contributions for : construction of school facilities, teaching and learning material, student support schemes (35 %), innovation pilot projects (50 %). Contributions for private schools, for school buses	Non-teaching staff (100 %), construction and maintenance of school facilities, teaching and learning material, school buses	
Lower secondary education :				
Higher secondary education :				
Tertiary education :	Modernization of existing and construction of new facilities (50 %) innovation pilot projects (50 %), student support schemes (65 %), support of the construction of student dormitories	Modernization of existing and construction of new facilities (50 %) innovation pilot projects (50 %), student support schemes (35 %), professors and other staff (100 %), maintenance of institutions (100 %), support of the construction of the student dormitories		Fees, Payments for research contracts
Further education :	Own institutions, Innovation pilot projects (BLK), further education beyond the firm level	Own institutions (e.g. further teacher training 100 %)	Peoples' High Schools (Evening Schools) : other expenditures, investments	Fees

156

advisory bodies, which are especially important in federal states.

The implications for education of the Bund's foreign policy competence remains too a controversial issue between the Bund and the Länder. This includes not only representation in international organisations and the composition of national delegations at international conferences but also the so-called transformation of international treaties. According to the Lindau arrangement of 1957 the Bund is supposed to conclude treaties on educational matters only after the Länder have agreed on them. Such consultations also take place in Canada and in Switzerland, though without any established pattern. In Switzerland and the USA the legal application of such treaties is undertaken by the federal governments without further reference to the internal distribution of competence ; in Canada, on the other hand, the implementation is determined by internal competence alone.

In Australia, Canada, and the United States the federal governments have a general "spending power" independent from their law-making competence in education. In the USA as well as in Canada there is already a long tradition of federal financial involvement in education. How the situation can be improved by the introduction of general revenue sharing and more general support programmes is still an open question. The Canadian solution, in which the provinces can choose between specific federal support schemes or a general revenue sharing arrangement would be an interesting case for further study.

The study of the German case gives some idea of the complexities involved in "co-operative educational federalism" and the kinds of adjustment that will be required. Further comparative work on the functional and structural aspects of educational law making, administration, and finance will be important for the future of educational planning. The role of information and communication in this context might be a helpful starting point for better understanding and improving the situation.

Chapter 5

EDUCATIONAL PLANNING IN COUNTRIES WITH UNIFIED SYSTEMS OF GOVERNMENT

A. FRANCE

Since the Commissariat Général au Plan was set up in 1946, there has been a continual process of change in both planning methods and the content of plans to facilitate the adjustment to an evolving economic and social context. As the instruments used by planners were improved and, more generally speaking, a better understanding of the social and economic mechanisms of development was acquired, it was gradually possible to broaden the range of factors taken into account and get a clearer picture of their interactions.

Although the whole range of social structures benefited from this development, as evidenced by the prominence of social policies in successive plans, educational planning took pride of place. First this was because education was regarded as a key to economic and social development and a guarantee of social progress and expansion. Subsequently it is because education seems, at the end of the 1970s, to be at the centre of a number of social contradictions. It is the point at which the aspirations of young people seeking a place in the working and social world to match their level of training come into contact with the demands of employers expressing constraints of a different order.

Two main objectives are pursued : first, to show how educational planning has evolved during the last 20 years in France ; second, to present and discuss the process of integration of educational planning within the overall socio-economic planning of the country. At the end an attempt is made to assess education planning on the basis of the experience acquired and policy priorities for the future.

I. OVERVIEW OF EDUCATIONAL PLANNING IN FRANCE (1)

Introduction

Before the appearance of the Sixth Plan, society as a whole shared the view that it was to be the "reducer of uncertainty". The questions always raised by educational planning were highlighted in discussions held at the Ministry of National Education by statements such as this : "The notion of a plan in education is neither a clear notion nor a distinct one ; for it is not simply a question of planning collective investment or establishing a 'bricks and mortar' plan."

The word planning is itself ambiguous ; at times it has an edifying and voluntarist flavour (we desire the good of society and the good of the individual, don't we ?) ; with a plan, events and uncertainty can be expelled, and time can be "regularised" ; the plan creates an awareness of certain collective needs and an awareness that these are legitimate ; it crystallizes deep-rooted psychological propensities ; it creates an autonomous demand which is expressed in a more or less anarchic fashion, and this can upset the best laid plans and programmes ; the plan itself can create disorder. (2)

This means that any description of educational planning in France involves many risks and, in particular, the risk that one may be unaware of or misinterpret facts or decisions taken 30 years ago, in a context which was very different from that of to-day, and with aims which now appear ambiguous and difficult to grasp.

Nonetheless, an attempt to describe or indeed explain French educational planning is valuable, since it forms part of general planning. Because of this, various procedures and methodologies have been used and objectives have been defined which may be compared to similar exercises in other countries.

But it should also be emphasised that the Ministry of National Education and, after that, the Ministry of Education, had their own internal planning system which had specific objectives and employed procedures which were different from those used in the context of the National Plan.

Like planning systems in other OECD countries, French planning has undergone various changes : at first it

---

1. This Part is based on the French National Report, OECD, Paris, 1979 (mimeographed).
2. Guy Thuillier, "Planning in education", in Droit Social, No. 12, December, 1969.

emphasised quantitative phenomena, specially the "explosion" in the numbers of pupils, then it moved towards a search for qualitative solutions to educational problems.

This observation is true both of national planning and of planning within the Ministry of Education. It suggests three lines for discussion :

Until the Seventh Plan, French planning had developed an increasing concern for thoroughness, setting ambitious educational objectives and studying minutely the conditions under which resources could be used.

The current organisation and aims of planning have led to a thorough review of planning processes and methods, as the Seventh Plan shows.

New concerns have arisen from the crisis, particularly regarding the relationship between training and jobs, the resources allocated to education and the establishment of educational and vocational guidance.

1. A Look at the Past

A review of past French planning and educational planning in particular requires a broad outline of the characteristic features of the procedures used, the working methods employed and the objectives pursued.

Planning activity in France grew out of the need to reconstruct the country's economic infrastructure, which was severely damaged by the Second World War. The terminology employed in planning was indicative ; the first three Plans were called "Reconstruction, équipment, and modernisation plans", and then, from the 1960s on, the expression "economic and social development plan" was used. This change in terminology reflects the change of purpose in French planning, within which educational planning occupied an important place.

It may seem paradoxical to make a distinction between national planning and educational planning, and it is true that the latter is well and truly part of the former in France. It should, however, be said that educational planning in the past has assumed two forms, though these sometimes complement each other : one has been linked to the five-year exercise carried out for the main sectors of national life, the other is specific to educational administration, and closer to ongoing programming than to comprehensive planning, which includes the economic and social aspects, in an attempt to demonstrate their interactions and to exercise some control over them.

Until the Fourth Plan, educational planning had been concerned primarily with problems of a quantitative nature : room had to be found each year for more and more children.

With the Fourth Plan, but particularly with the Fifth and Sixth Plans, educational planning activities began to extend beyond school, university, and sports facilities.

In 1952, when the Second Plan was being formulated (1952-56), education became an item in national planning for the first time. A joint commission was established, chaired by a State adviser and consisting entirely of civil servants from the Commissariat Général au Plan and the Ministry of National Education. This Commission, which was purely administrative, had 25 members : the directors from the central administration of the Ministry of National Education together with some representatives from other Ministries (Interior, and Finance).

A Commission with the same structure but more members was set up for the preparation of the Third Plan (1957-61).

Since at central level the statistical apparatus for education was virtually non-existent, the Commission for the preparation of the Second Plan carried out surveys among school inspectors and Préfets (administrators of Départements). The main concern was to gauge as accurately as possible the size of the population explosion which had affected primary education since 1950.

This information, which was collected at Département level, was used centrally to construct a projection of the numbers of pupils in each level of education. At that time, school attendance was compulsory from 6 to 14 years of age, and secondary education would be affected by the population explosion during the period in which the Third Plan was to be implemented.

For the preparation of the Second Plan, the Commission, divided into four groups, had set itself the task of analysing the consequences of this population increase for the facilities which would have to be provided for school age children.

Four topics had been chosen for the Second Plan :

- an inventory of facilities required ;
- the administrative and financial procedures to be followed so that requirements could be met ;
- financing the facilities ;
- technology and construction costs of the facilities.

These topics indicate the main concern at this period : the planning of facilities. This remained the case under the Third and even under the Fourth and Fifth Plans, because the numbers of children of school age were very large.

But the discussions of the commissions entrusted with preparing the national plans became more wide-ranging as these plans were implemented.

For the Third Plan (1957-61), forecasts of enrolments for the decade 1955-1965 were made in the light of two alternatives :

- the traditional approach which retained an entrance examination to the first year of secondary education (Class 6) ;
- a new approach by which the entrance examination to Class 6 would be abolished.

To explain the use of these assumptions, it should be emphasised that a reform of the educational system was being considered at that time (known as the Billeres Reform, from the name of the Minister of National Education at that time).

In addition to this statistical forecasting, the preparations for the Third Plan included a projection of facilities needed for the period 1957-1961 and the financing plan which would follow from this projection, but, above all, a projection of the number of teachers required for the period from 1956 to 1963-64.

The problem then was the shortage of teachers due to the growing numbers of children who would be coming into the educational system.

However, an "administrative" consequence of these discussions on the problems of facilities was the reorganisation of the central administration of the Ministry of National Education. The section responsible for the problems of school, university and sports facilities was raised to the rank of Directorate in 1956.

With the Fourth Plan (1962-65), which was in fact the third plan for education, important changes occurred during the preparation stage.

The preparatory Commission no longer consisted of civil servants only ; its 32 members - 26 of whom were appointed - included representatives from workers' organisations (6 trade unions were represented), trade organisations, the universities, local government, and departments other than that of National Education. The ex officio members were three directors from the Ministry of National Education and three directors from the Ministry of Finance.

As usual, the Commission set up working parties which were entrusted with providing material for its discussions.

Another innovation should be mentioned here : for the first time the Education Commission was anxious to link its forecasting activity with that of the Manpower Commission. Specific requests concerning forecasts of manpower requirements for 1975 were formulated. Although the work was not completed at the time, because of the lack of sufficient statistical data on jobs, the fact that this concern was expressed should be noted.

The topics already referred to were retained when the Fourth Plan was being prepared : forecasts of number of pupils and teachers required (at the time there were not enough teachers), forecasts of facilities required for primary, secondary and higher education, construction procedures and techniques, financial procedures and administrative resources to be employed.

This preparatory work for the Fourth Plan was occasioned by the new law passed on 31 December 1959, extending compulsory schooling to the age of 16, and thereby increasing the facility requirements for the first and second stages of secondary education.

This concern predominates again in the preparation of the Fifth Plan (1966-1970), which was done in 1964 and 1965. At the time, a reform had just been implemented (1963), the Fouchet Reform, which made compulsory the creation of a network of secondary modern schools (CES), and secondary general schools (CEG). One of the objectives of the Fifth Plan was to assist with the implementation of this reform. It was at this point that planning within the Ministry itself appeared for the first time, with the designation and establishment of the "carte scolaire" (School District Map).

The composition of the Commission was similar to that of the Fourth Plan, though this time there were more representatives on it from trade union and employers' organisations, universities and the civil service.

The tendency to take employment problems into consideration was even stronger in the Fifth Plan. The chairman of the sub-committee responsible for forecasting numbers of school and university students was the chairman of the Manpower Commission for the Fifth Plan himself : Mr. J. Fourastie. The planners hoped in this way to show the interaction between education and employment.

The work undertaken at that time led to an explicit comparison of manpower requirements, assessed by level of skill, to projected number of pupils.

The traditional topics, facilities and teacher requirements were still valid. It was during this period that the Ministry for National Education made an unprecedented effort to provide facilities and the teacher recruitment competitions were opened up to the increasing number of students graduating from the universities, particularly in the literary disciplines.

The preparatory work for the Fifth Plan revealed two difficulties, however, as the chairman observed in his introduction to the Commission's report :

"One new difficulty relating to methods has arisen because of the need to prepare the plan in two successive stages, each approved by a vote in Parliament. First the broad outline for an equipment programme had to be quickly drawn up and costed to indicate the "options" decreed by the Government and adopted by Parliament at the end of 1964. Then, when it had assessed requirements in the light of forecasts of numbers and unit costs, the Commission had the wisdom to define the absolute minimum requirements, while at the same time sketching in broad lines programmes which were more costly but responding better to the real needs of national growth and independence. After that, and despite the fact that their "budget" was fixed at more than 20 per cent below the absolute minimum, they had to prepare a plan and for this plan to establish priorities among the different categories of investment, maintain a reasonable level of consistency in the work of the different sectors, be content with only the most vital or desirable schemes and, in short, take responsibility for defining and accepting the solutions that were least harmful.

A second difficulty, which was no doubt inevitable, arose from the semi-permanent "reform" situation in which the national education structures had existed for two years." (3)

The Fifth Plan was also an opportunity to refine the social indicators which could be used in the field of education and which, even in the Fourth Plan, the Commission for School, University, and Sports Facilities had tried to envisage. Although a mere statement of aims, objectives and activities gives only a general idea of the discussions, these different approaches to educational problems are of interest here. Two aims had been defined and, by a process of deductive reasoning, gradually developed into projects which might lead to their attainment.

<u>The first aim</u>, was economic : education should be the mainspring of expansion. Two objectives and their indicators stem from this statement : to train at every level the managerial staff and technologists required for the life of the nation ; the indicator should measure the level at which educational services are being maintained at a given time ; provide more theoretical knowledge and technical capacities for the pupils ; the indicator should measure what compulsory schooling was achieving.

---

3. General report of the Commission on School, University, and Sports Facilities in the Fifth Plan. p. XI. (Chairman, Mr. Claude Lasry, State adviser).

The means to be used for the attainment of these aims were construction programmes for technical colleges (CET), which have since become vocational high schools (LEP) and the construction of university institutes of technology (IUT).

The material obstacles to education such as financing and siting, then had to be overcome.

Finally, selection and guidance were to make it possible to have a mixture of pupils and enable those who were experiencing difficulties to catch up.

The second aim was social : education must become democratic.

The means which were to be employed to achieve this second aim were, in particular, the establishment of a common base in the first stage of secondary education (this was why the secondary modern schools had been established), and an effort to adapt the school system to the actual needs and aptitudes of the pupils.

With the preparation of the Sixth Plan (1971-75), planning methods and structures reached a sort of "apogée". The title of the Commission (School, University, and Sports Facilities) was changed to "Education Commission" and the Commission became much bigger.

In fact there were 97 appointed members and 12 ex officio members with a chairman assisted by a rapporteur général and accompanied by a group of 42 chairmen and rapporteurs de groupe.

The structure of the Education Commission was fairly similar to the structures previously described : one-third of the members were representatives from professional, trade union and family organisations. The other two-thirds were mainly central government representatives with some university personnel, directors of businesses, and local government representatives. The central government representatives included members of the Ministry of National Education and of the central administration, as well as representatives from the local levels of the administration and 16 members from other departments.

The size of the Education Commission for the Sixth Plan permitted the number of internal groups for the 1985 forecasts - teaching equipment, administrative means, economic and financial studies, information and guidance, decentralisation, educational research, etc., to increase and be added to the traditional groups : forecasting number of pupils, facilities, construction costs, etc.

Another new element in this planning effort was the discussion of quality. The people responsible for the preparation of the Plan discussed the value of this educational system, whose trends, and even whose functioning, they were supposed to predict.

It was particularly at this period that the members of the Commission discussed whether it was good or harmful for pupils to repeat a year. It should also be noted that the lines established by the Fouchet Reform were not questioned when the Plan was being formulated.

With the Sixth Plan again, discussions on continuous training appeared for the first time.

This new way of looking at planning was reflected in the opening lines of the chapter in the Plan devoted to education : "The two basic objectives of the Sixth Plan in the field of education will be to make a contribution to greater equality of opportunity and a better preparation for working life."

The attainment of these objectives cannot be separated from the search for greater efficiency within the educational system. The struggle against failure, the renewal of pedagogy and the improvement of administrative organisation should do more than just improve the internal yield of education by making better use of its considerable resources. These things also increase the benefits of education for the individual and society. (4)

Using a grid analysis identical to that described in the account of the Fifth Plan, it is possible to show aims, objectives, and projects.

First aim : Education has a vocational role.

Four objectives followed from this :

- when they leave the educational system, all pupils will have a vocational training certificate ;
- a balance will be established between openings and training as to numbers of pupils and the content of their training ;
- priority is to be given to the efficiency of the educational system in its teaching and financial aspects ;
- the opening out of the educational system onto society is essential.

Various projects were to ensure that the objectives described here would be achieved :

---

4. Sixth Economic and Social Development Plan, Journal Officiel No. 1371, Imprimerie des Journaux Officiels, Paris, 1971, page 70.

- a re-thinking of the structures of the educational system and in particular the distribution of financing ;
- the establishment of information agencies ;
- the establishment of agencies for school and vocational guidance ;
- the establishment of further education ;
- the provision for teachers of information and assistance in organising their teaching ;
- the encouragement of a renewal of teaching (methods and content) ;
- teacher training ;
- adapting curricula to active life ;
- encouragement of participatory management in the education system ;
- making possible the multiple use of facilities.

<u>Second aim</u> : Education has a cultural and social role.

Three objectives stemmed from this :

- opening out the educational system onto society, an objective which had already been stated in relation to the first aim ;
- improvements in the cultural quality of teaching and the achievement of efficient general education until the end of compulsory school attendance ;
- to play a role of social equalisation with, in particular, action aimed at achieving equality of the sexes, reducing regional disparities, and adapting teaching to the needs of the socially and physically disadvantaged.

Some projects were to be given priority :

- the development of special education, the extension of nursery schools and further education.

In parallel with this quinquennial exercise, the Ministry of Education set up an internal planning system which has continued to develop since 1963.

In 1963 two circulars, dated 3 May and 28 September, defined the general principles of the teaching reform, and their implementation led to the fixing of geographical sectors for the first stage of secondary education :

- the rural sectors (about 6 000 inhabitants) with a population of schoolchildren at the first secondary stage of 400 to 450 adolescents, justifying the establishment of a general education school ;
- mixed sectors (about 10 000 inhabitants) with a school age population at first secondary stage of about 600 adolescents, justifying the establishment of a secondary modern school.

Once a school map of the areas of low and moderate density had been fixed, the Department, with a circular dated 5 January 1965, set out to define the school map for the second stage of secondary education, to establish the first-stage sectors in the densely populated urban areas, and to deal with the practical organisation of these sectors and districts.

Adjustments were made and this new structure was given a statutory basis with the Decree of 11 June 1971. It should be noted that the school map represents a pioneering approach to planning which was later followed by the Ministry of Health with their creation of the hospital map.

Method of fixing the school map

The method for the establishment of the school map involves three basic steps : division into sectors and districts ; calculation of the number of children for whom school places have to be provided ; forecasting of facilities.

Division into sectors and districts

The national territory is divided into school sectors and districts. The sector is the catchment area for a first-stage secondary education establishment, and the district the catchment area for one or several second-stage establishments. Attendance at the establishment in the main town in the sector or district is compulsory, save where derogations are allowed.

Calculation of numbers of children

The geographic division established in this way provided a stable basis for the calculation of the number of pupils to be admitted in each sector or district within the time specified by the school map (1971 for the first map and 1978 for the revised map).

This calculation was made from demographic projections which took account of earlier changes, particularly in regard to population growth and migration.

Adjustments were made to these gross school population figures in the form of deductions for factors such as maladjusted children and private education, or additions for children repeating a class. In this way the number of pupils to be admitted to State secondary schools was obtained for each sector and district.

For the second stage of secondary education, coefficients corresponding to the main types of education (long general second stage, long industrial second stage, etc.) were calculated from work already done on the Plan.

Forecasts of facilities

On the basis of anticipated numbers of pupils and existing school facilities, the forecasts of facilities needed for a given period were made by sector and district.

For the first stage of secondary education, industrialised building systems led to the definition of four types of establishment :

- standard 400 secondary general,
- standard 600 secondary modern,
- standard 900 secondary modern, and
- standard 1 200 secondary modern.

This type of standardization meant that the facilities could not be adjusted exactly to the school populations ; this explains why the number of places forecast was always higher than the school population at Département and educational district level.

At second-stage secondary education level, standardization was less advanced because of the variety of education offered ; nonetheless there were standard structures for technical education establishments (multiples of 108) ; the general education high schools were standardised on the basis of 200, 400, or 800 pupils, with some latitude for exceptions.

Revision of the school map

Since the first School Map prepared from 1964 to 1967 was no longer consistent with the new demographic data and the options of the Sixth Plan, it was decided, by a circular dated 15 November 1971, to revise the whole School Map.

The technical directives in this Revision Circular referred mainly to the method of calculating school populations.

The demographic base was constituted from projections made by the statistical service on data supplied by the National Institute of Statistics and Economic Research (INSEE) from the 1968 census, taking account of a population change coefficient. This concerned the numbers in the 11, 12, 13 and 14 age-groups (first cycle) and the 15, 16 and 17 age-groups (second cycle) at the 1978 horizon, presented by sector and by district.

Calculation of the weighted 1978 State school first-cycle school population

From the numbers in the 11 to 14 year age groups, the number of pupils needing special education was calculated. The maximum proportion was fixed at 8 per cent, and responsibility for 5 per cent of this may be assumed by the Ministry of National Education though this is a long-term objective. The number of pupils who may be educated in private schools was also estimated. Given the limited reliability of the statistics in this area, forecasting difficulties, and the wide diversity of situations, the external services were left to judge for themselves, and made forecasts on their own responsibility. It was however indicated, to help them with their calculations, that because the growth rate of private education had been much lower than that of State education over the previous decade on a national scale, a proportion equivalent to the current percentage of children in private education (corrected, if necessary, according to any changes in this branch of education which could be predicted) could be applied for 1978.

To the result obtained was added a weighting proportion, the ceiling for which was fixed at 10 per cent, to take account of children who repeated a class.

Calculation of the weighted 1978 State second-cycle school population

No deductions were made for special education, since this type of education was practically non-existent at second-cycle level.

The same position was adopted for private education as for first-cycle secondary education.

From the gross school population, pupils admitted to establishments which were the responsibility of the Ministry of Agriculture had to be subtracted. The necessary information was obtained by the inspectors from each regional directorate of agriculture.

Second degree second-cycle schooling, unlike first-cycle schooling, has two specific features :

- it is not compulsory ;
- it is diversified (several training channels are offered to the pupils at the end of Class 3).

The proportion of pupils who would stay on for second-cycle secondary education therefore had to be determined.

The Fifth Plan had determined the proportion which would go on to the second cycle ; of 100 pupils completing

Class 3, 35 would go on to the long second cycle and 40 to the short second cycle.

The Sixth Plan was less precise in this area. The Education Commission's report used two proportions of pupils who would go on to Class 2 in the long second cycle, 42 per cent and 45 per cent, and gave forecasts of numbers relating to the long second cycle and the short second cycle (public + private).

The figure retained for the long second cycle was 42 per cent, and a percentage of 48 per cent for the short second cycle was deduced from the preceding items.

To divide all the pupils between the different types of education, the Plan's voluntarist assumptions were applied ; namely :

- 60 per cent general baccalaureat /= 'A' level/ and 40 per cent technical baccalaureat and technician certificates, divided into half for the industrial and half for the tertiary sector ;
- 50 per cent in the industrial sector and 50 per cent in the tertiary sector for the First-cycle certificates.

Finally the following distribution was arrived at :

LONG SECOND CYCLE

Overall proportion	Type of schooling	Mean partial proportions	Brackets (3)
42 %	A, C, and D Bacc.	47 %	42 to 52 %
	E Bacc. (1), Tech. Bacc., and Tech. Cert. in industrial sector	23 %	21 to 25 %
	B Bacc. (2), Tech. Bacc., and Tech. Cert. in tertiary sector	30 %	27 to 33 %
		100 %	The total must be equal to 100 %

---

1. The E Baccalaureat represents 3 per cent within the partial proportion of 23 per cent.
2. The B Baccalaureat represents 10 per cent in the partial proportion of 30 per cent.
3. The brackets make it possible to adapt the national standards to local situations or educational policies which may operate at district or Département level.

SHORT SECOND CYCLE

Overall proportion	Type of schooling	Mean partial proportions	Brackets (3)
48 %	First-cycle cert. and vocational aptitude cert. in industrial sector (in proportion of 35 per cent and 65 per cent)	60 %	55 to 65 %
	First-cycle cert. and VAC in tertiary sector (55 per cent and 45 per cent approx.)	40 %	35 to 45 %
		100 %	The total must be equal to 100 %

3. The brackets make it possible to adapt the national standards to local situations or educational policies which may operate at district or Département level.

No proportions were fixed as to numbers preparing for the Certificate of Primary Schooling. The numbers from these sections were included in the over-all proportion used for the short second cycle.

From the requirements determined in this fashion, it was possible through revision of the School Map to adjust forecasts of facilities required at the horizon selected.

Special maps

Alongside the general School Map there were special maps, in particular the map of special educational establishments (ENP) and the special education sections and the map of vocational specialisation.

The vocational specialisation map was an attempt to plan technical and vocational education.

Within the framework of total numbers of pupils equivalent to the percentages fixed for economic and industrial education, for each occupational or vocational specialisation the numbers of pupils had to be determined as a function of the manpower requirements in each occupation. From this, the geographic distribution of the equivalent occupational sections was deduced.

With the help of consultative trade committees, numerical objectives were determined by school district and by specialisation and the inspectors established, within the limits set in this fashion, a draft school map for the types of training under consideration, coordinated at national level.

The maps of the trade specialisations were revised from year to year as a function of the changes in the economic situation.

Adjustment of the first-cycle school map

Within the context of political action in favour of the declining rural areas which was taken by the Government from 1975 on, it was decided to retain some small schools, closure of which might have been envisaged in the revised 1971 School Map.

A new type of small school, the modular teaching unit, with about 120 pupils, was provided for and could be set up, most often in the form of two modular teaching units (240 pupils), in rural areas with a low density of population.

Because there was a desire to ensure better services for these areas in the way of special education, it was also envisaged that small sections (64 or 48 pupils) might be established there.

It was against this background that the circular dated 18 November 1975 fixed the changes in the first-cycle secondary School Map.

Another type of planning within the Ministry of Education was the general action programme (PGA).

In was defined in Article 2 of the Order dated 5 July 1974 on the organisation of the central administration of the Ministry of Education :

"The Director-General for Planning and Co-ordination will, with the participation of the other directorates and services and with a contribution from the Inspectorates General defined in Article 1, establish the Ministry's action programme.

This programme will, on the basis of the objectives approved by the Minister, bring together and describe all the projects which contribute to the implementation of educational policy ; it will be multi-annual and revised each year ; it will constitute a new common reference position for the formulation of the Ministry's budget and the execution of projects arising from the different directorates and services as well as those from establishments placed under the authority or supervision of the Ministry of Education."

This document is a tool for the inclusive coordination of educational policy which, because of its nature ("rolling and reviewable"), should serve as a reference point for the projects of the Ministry's directorates and the budget allocated to them.

In this sense, the general action programme established in April 1975 for the period 1976-1979 included 24 programmes covering all the activities of the Ministry of Education with the exception of those relating to facilities and buildings.

The method employed would call for co-operation between the Ministry's directorates and services so that the content of each of the programmes could be fixed according to the resources which could be allocated to them.

At the same time as the content of the programmes was being determined, the Ministry's services were looking for ways of establishing a demographic and financial "framework" which would make it possible to assess the total resources to be allocated to the projects under consideration.

The demographic "framework" was established on the basis of information supplied by the Computer and Statistical Research Service, which had gradually been given more resources by the Ministry of Education as it became aware, in the 1960s, of the importance of quantitative data for ensuring reliable forecasts of changes in the educational system.

The objective was to provide a forecast of numbers of pupils at the different levels of education for the years during which the general action programmes were being carried out. By extrapolation of the trends observed in the past, estimates were supplied on transfers of pupils from one level of education to the next, on the percentages of pupils who repeated a year, etc.

In this way a matrix of flows of pupils in the educational system was established. It was based not on apparent flows, that is, on variations in the "stocks" of pupils observed in the system, but on real flows, that is to say on the schools that the pupils reaching a given level in year n came from.

The financial "framework" also tried to translate into budgetary terms the forecasts of changes in resources which might be expected in the period under consideration. Observation of budgetary variations over the previous period, corrected by forecasts of variations in certain costs (staff in particular) would make it possible to determine the general composition of future budgets in broad lines.

The next operation then consisted of determining the unavoidable items which made up the Ministry's expenditure, in order to assess their cost. Expenditure on staff, certain operating and maintenance charges, expenditure related to the implementation of legislative provisions, etc., were treated as unavoidable expenditure.

It was therefore out of the remaining resources available, consisting of the difference between budget forecasts and unavoidable expenditure, that the projects in the general action programme were to be financed.

Careful planning was then required to show the stages year by year in the implementation of the internal plans.

The value of such a procedure resided entirely in the contribution made by this study and the planning proposal which emerged from it to the preparation of the budget for the next financial year.

Once this had been recorded in the budget and the financial year had started, keeping track of the general action programme became the main necessity for the pursuit of the work. Because planning was "rolling and reviewable", the extent to which the projects described in the general action programme were being carried out had to be observed with accuracy so that further planning could, if necessary, be corrected.

A review of the extent to which the projects described by the general action programme had been carried out and how this was reflected in the budget, for the year 1976 for example, showed that, for all the projects appearing in the general action programme, about 70 per cent had been recorded in the budget ; this may be relatively satisfactory, but the percentage varied considerably, depending on the projects.

Various elements provide an explanation for this.

Some were due to the difficulties encountered in preparing the forecasts, for example, in regard to the numbers of pupils. The largest deviations, however, were in projects which were often of limited scope but affected in their implementation by conjunctural phenomena as the policy operated in favour of certain areas or certain categories of staff.

In fact, the attempt to achieve very detailed planning of all the projects to be undertaken within the educational apparatus did not make it possible to bring out clearly enough what were the priorities which affected the various projects. It then appeared to be necessary to revise the planning method employed, so as to upgrade the applicability of the general action programme.

At the same time, and this is of particular importance, considerable changes occurred in national planning. Until the Seventh Plan, planning was of a global nature and, for the education sector, covered the various levels of education in regard to the facilities to be provided, the staff to be "mobilised" and the number of pupils to be admitted.

The preparations for the Seventh Plan, which were made at the end of 1975 and during the first half of 1976, questioned this "exhaustive" approach by giving priority to certain projects which were judged to be of over-riding importance, in particular for the implementation of a policy of equal opportunity.

From then on, exhaustive planning within the Ministry was not easily compatible with national planning, which had selected a few "anchor points" for which firm commitments were made as to the allocation of resources. The other projects described in the general action programme were by the same stroke exposed to the hazards of the economic situation.

2. The current state of educational planning in France ; the Seventh Plan (1976-1980) and the Ministry of Education's General Action Programme

The profound structural changes which occurred during the 1970s with the energy crisis, the slowing down of economic growth and other important socio-economic shifts, led to the appearance of a new type of planning, employing new methodologies.

The overall economic strategy of the Seventh Plan is constructed along two lines :

- <u>to pursue the restoration of order</u>, that is to say "avoid altering the conditions for competition as much as possible", make "the greatest possible effort... to ensure that society can control changes in incomes and prices", act in such a way that the "rate of increase of incomes is very close to the rate of the expected increase in prices, for the whole population, with the exception of the most disadvantaged categories" ;

- <u>to achieve consolidation</u>, that is to say "to provide the poorest countries with a guarantee that their resources will increase", reduce inequalities, and balance the development of trade between the different parts of the world by trying to keep to the commitment made "jointly with all the industrialised countries" gradually to devote 0.7 per cent of Gross National Product to state aid for the developing countries", make a vigorous contribution to "advances in European construction", in particular to advances in the Common Agricultural Policy, to achieve, finally, a genuine economic and monetary union and to implement common policies in the fields of the prevention of pollution and improvements in working conditions.

Education has a part in these strategic objectives : in particular, it is implicated in the area of those policies which were intended to help full employment.

The preparation of the Seventh Plan can be broken down into three stages which will be considered here from the point of view of education only.

i) <u>First stage : determination of the objectives</u>

This is the options stage, during which four commissions discussed long-term trends in French economy and society and proposed some lines for action for the period of the Seventh Plan.

The work of these commissions led to the adoption by Parliament of a preliminary policy report in the spring of 1975.

The problems of education were dealt with at this stage only in terms of general objectives ; there was concern mainly with understanding the contribution which the educational system could make to reducing social inequalities and improving employment.

The policy report advocated an educational policy which would "meet the requirements that there should be a reduction in the inequalities of opportunity, in particular through the development of pre-school education, and at the same time deal with the concern that people should be better equipped for to-morrow's society and the jobs it would offer".

It should be said here that the Act dated 11 July 1975, relating to education, had identical objectives ; it recommended the development "of the pupils' potentialities at every level, whether this be a taste for practical work or an aptitude for abstract thought".

ii) <u>Second stage : the choice of policies</u>

During the second stage, which was the preparatory stage of the Plan properly speaking, policies were considered and definite projects were examined which could lead to successful implementation of these policies and which required specific planning. At this stage of the preparation of the Plan, concerted action was extended : in addition to the "horizontal" commissions which come under the auspices of the first-stage commissions, there were also sector commissions, including an Education and Training Commission.

In addition, particular committees attached to some of these commissions were set up ; reference has already been made to the Work and Employment Committee attached to the Development Commission. This Committee set up joint groups with the Education and Training Commission, one to deal with continuous vocational training and the other to deal with comparisons of job requirement forecasts and forecasts of numbers of pupils leaving the different levels in the training systems.

The Education and Training Commission consisted of 36 members, 14 of whom were representatives from trade, trade union, and family organizations ; the other members were representatives from Government departments (4 for Education, 9 for the other Ministries). To this were added prominent and well-qualified persons (university people, industrialists, local government people, etc.). This was a marked change in relation to the preparations for the Sixth Plan ; reference has already been made to the size of that Commission.

The main lines proposed by the Ministry of Education for discussion by the Commission concerned several areas ; only a few of which were retained. These were :

- the development and improvement of pre-primary schooling ;
- the creation of manual and technical courses at all levels in the secondary schools and an optional course in technology at the two final stages ;
- initial and continuous training for teachers, in the light of the provision of supportive teaching, the changes in the content of the curriculum, the policy of reducing the numbers of auxiliaries, and the youth of the teaching profession.

It should be stressed that, for the first time in French educational planning, problems of facilities were not dealt with ; facilities in the educational system appeared to meet over-all requirements mainly because the population had ceased to expand since 1974.

iii) <u>Third stage : the priority action programmes</u>

This is the most important innovation in French planning, which until then had been "exhaustive". Before describing the priority action programme devoted more particularly to educational policy, the ends, methods and organization of these programmes should be explained. The planning document itself explains them : (5)

"The particular features of the period 1976-1980 were a justification for this type of planning. Even if there were to be a general recovery of the Western economies, chance may well disturb the French economy in the years ahead. It is therefore necessary to protect the projects which are essential for the achievement of the objectives of the Plan from these fluctuations. In addition, since the financial constraints have rarely been so severe, one condition for success is to concentrate our efforts on priority areas.

"The priority action programmes are also a product of the experience of earlier plans. As one plan followed another, the limitations of planning which is only concerned with public facilities only gradually became apparent. Planning of this kind does not, in particular, ensure that current expenditure and investment expenditure will keep in line. Now, in order to improve health and the quality of life, it is not enough to build schools, hospitals, and dwellings. The presence of the necessary staff and the co-ordination of all the administrative activities directed towards the same end also have to be assured. For example, an improvement in road safety requires road facilities, police, and preventive action as well as suitable care and hospital services.

"The finalised programmes in the Sixth Plan were an experimental step in this direction. They related to the new towns, to road safety, to the prevention of perinatal mortality, improvements in the workings of the employment market, the protection of the Mediterranean forest, the maintenance of the elderly in their own homes. Since these have been successful, it is felt that the range should be extended."

The document goes on to give details of the objectives of these programmes and states straight away that not all the projects which form part of the economic and social strategy of the Plan will have programmes devoted to them.

On the one hand, some very important projects could not be planned. The clearest example of this is the battle with inflation, one of the main priorities but which cannot

---

5. Seventh Economic and Social Development Plan, 1976-1980. Documentation française, p. 85 <u>et seg</u>.

in toto constitute a programme ; the ways and means of action against inflation have to be adjusted at all times as a function of the economic situation.

On the other hand, the number of projects which the Government can guarantee to carry out during the next five years can only be fairly small. The programmes were selected because of the contribution which they would make to the attainment of the main aims of the Plan which were :

- to strengthen the dynamism of the economy ;
- to guarantee our freedom of decision by balancing our external payments ;
- to ensure full employment ;
- to reduce inequalities ;
- to improve the quality of life ;
- to develop research.

In all, 25 priority action programmes were retained for the 5-year period.

The programmes were to be implemented at national level but other levels, in particular, the regions, the Départements and the communes were given free scope to unite their efforts with those of the nation.

"As regards the choice of national programmes, the Government has taken into account the preferences expressed by the regions in their general policy report and the occasion of consultations on the changes in public investment which would be desirable in the course of the Seventh Plan.

Regional and local initiative programmes, ordered by agreement between the State, the regional public institutions, and the local authorities involved, will be added to the 25 national programmes. In this way more account can be taken of the specific features of some regions or some areas.

When it considers the proposals made by the regions and the local authorities, the State will decide to which decentralised initiative programmes it will contribute.

In order to permit the regional assemblies to give their views in full knowledge of the facts, formulation of the programmes include consultation with all the parties involved (ministries, local authorities, private organisations). The regional and local authorities discuss them and the list is sent to Parliament".

Referring then to questions of cost and the administration of the programmes, the document states :

"In order that these programmes may be implemented whatever the circumstances may be, their cost must not compromise the normal pursuit and development of other government projects. The programmes have therefore been drawn up on the assumption that budgetary expenditure will increase, without relying exclusively on new appropriations.

"The 25 national initiative programmes involve budget appropriations which amount to almost 90 billions of 1975 francs for the whole of the period 1976-1980. In addition, there are 20 billions reserved for the financing of the regional or local initiatives programmes. So 110 billion francs of the general budget will be allocated to the programmes and in addition there will be the appropriations for the additional budget for posts and telecommunications, or a total of more than 200 billions."

Finally, the planning document deals with procedures for administering the programmes :

"In each case one of the Ministers is assigned the responsibility of a programme for ensuring the co-ordination among the Ministries participating in the implementation of the programme.

"Each programme reflects one or more particular objectives and brings together the resources necessary for the attainment of this objective, whether appropriations for facilities, for operating costs, or even, in certain cases, provisions which have no direct budgetary cost (laws or regulations, for example).

"The appropriations equivalent to the financing of the programmes will be listed individually in the budgets of each Ministry and summarised in the annex to the Finance Act relating to implementation of the Plan. This document, which will be prepared with the 1977 Finance Act, will, for each priority action programme, include a reminder of the sums provided for the whole period of the Plan and the sums provided in preceding years since the start of the Plan, as well as the sums provided for in the Finance Act to which it forms an annex. These different sums will be expressed in terms which will make it possible to compare them with each another.

"The annex relating to implementation of the Plan will also include information relating to the results achieved in the execution of the programmes, as these are shown by the indicators. For example, progress in "humanising" the hospitals will be followed up by an indicator giving the annual reduction in the number of beds in large wards.

"The implementation of the priority action programmes will benefit from efforts which have been going on for several years now to modernise public administration. The programmes which are most suitable for this will be accompanied by budget option rationalisation studies or articulated with the programme budgets of the Ministries concerned.

"Each year, when the budget is being prepared and voted on, the programmes will be financed in priority.

"The Ministry of Education is the leader for one programme and is involved in the execution of a further 5 programmes.

"It is the leader for priority action programme No. 13, which is to ensure equality of opportunity through education and culture."

The aims of this programme are explained : (6)

"During the past few years there have been important developments in education and in the Seventh Plan the new requirements in staff and facilities will be lower than before. This will make it possible to give fresh impetus to projects which will contribute the most to reducing handicaps arising from children's social and family environment."

There are four of these projects :

- pre-primary schooling, with the objectives of :
  . providing schooling for 45 per cent of 2-year-olds and for more than 90 per cent of three-year-olds in pre-primary schools in 1980 ;
  . reducing disparities related to geographic situation ;
  . reducing the maximum number of pupils in nursery and infant classes to 35 ;
- the teaching of technology in schools, with the objectives :
  . to give all pupils in the secondary schools a manual and technical education ;
  . to give pupils in Classes 4 and 3 the possibility of more training by organising technological options.
- enriching of cultural life in schools, with the objectives :
  . to double the number of pupils affected by cultural enrichment in schools so as to develop their ability to express themselves by developing their imagination and sensitivity.
- sport in school, for which the objective is :
  . to provide three hours of physical education and sport in school in the first cycle /of secondary education/ and two hours a week in the second cycle, in 1980.

The five other programmes with which the Ministry of Education is concerned are :

---

6. Seventh Economic and Social Development Plan, 1976-1980, op. cit., p. 123.

Programme No. 10 : strengthening public action in favour of employment ;
Programme No. 11 : improving vocational training for the young ;
Programme No. 14 : the new family policy ;
Programme No. 20 : increasing road safety ;
Programme No. 21 : better living conditions in towns.

The administrative consequences of the indications given above can be seen in particular in the establishment of controls or follow-ups on the implementation of the programmes.

It should be said here that responsibility for implementation of the work to be done to achieve the objectives established by the Plan does not fall solely on the central services of the Ministry of Education, but also on the decentralised levels of the Ministry : vice-chancellors, school inspectors, heads of establishments, the Prefectures, the Département and commune authorities, as well as regional public establishments. The central services of the Ministry of Education cannot decide on the details of the action to be undertaken at each point in the country and consequently have transferred responsibility by a wide delegation of powers in a number of the matters which are affected by planning.

It is essential, then, if the objectives are to be achieved in the best possible way, that the various decentralised levels should assess each local situation in the light of the national objectives and, on the basis of these observations, decide on the projects to be undertaken, both qualitatively and quantitatively.

Because so many people are involved in the different projects, however, the establishment of a monitoring system is required so that there can be an "operational" follow-up of the attainment of the objectives of the Plan.

This follow-up, which is based on the preparation of "management charts" or "instrument panels", is aimed at ascertaining how the Plan has succeeded in terms of the projects undertaken, of the resources mobilized and of the extent to which the objectives decided on are being achieved.

For this purpose the "management charts" contain indicators of resources, implementation, and results, so that a genuine evaluation of the projects undertaken is possible.

For example, for project No. 1 in Priority Action Programme No. 13 : - pre-elementary education, the data followed up relate to :

- numbers of children admitted to school for each age group (2, 3, 4, and 5 years) ;

- changes in the percentages of children at school in a given age-group ;
- changes in conditions for admitting pupils ;
- correlative change in the number of classes.

On the basis of these indicators, which will provide "forecast" and "observed" data, the evaluation exercise will concern three stages :

- a comparison between what has been achieved and what was programmed ;
- an analysis of any deviations which may be observed and a search for the causes ;
- any adjustments which may require to be made.

Only through a systematic and continuous evaluation of the results is it possible to attain, in the best possible way, the objectives decided on, within a given framework of resource constraints. This evaluation must be based on the establishment of management charts at the various decision-making levels (school inspectorate, vice-chancellors, central administration).

The compound indicators used by the Commissariat-Général au Plan to follow up the implementation of all the priority action programmes were based on the data taken into account in the management chart of the central administration. The efficiency of a tool of this kind for following up projects undertaken within the educational apparatus depends largely on the quality of the information system.

The Ministry of Education has made particular efforts to ensure that planning is followed up properly ; this is why it has :

- improved its statistical apparatus ;
- experimented with and developed modern management methods, in particular the management charts ;
- set up and year by year improved a programme budget which enables the Ministry to obtain better information on costs ;
- established centralised job monitoring.

At the same time as this was being done within the context of national planning, the planning within the Ministry of Education developed considerably.

The objectives of educational policies, as stated in the Act of 11 July 1975 relating to education, mapped out the main features of the work of the services : national planning took as its share two particularly highlighted sectors : pre-primary education and the teaching of technology in the second cycle of secondary schools.

But other points were also worth developing, in particular the prospect of making better use of the resources allocated to education, because population growth - as in many OECD countries - had started to decelerate.

The Ministry of Education decided on a general action programme, the general features of which would be identical to those described earlier (multi-annual, reviewable annually) and the primary objective of which was to illuminate every-day administrative action by plotting the development of several major policies :

- teacher training, initial and continuous training, with a concern for adjusting it to rapidly changing conditions in the teaching profession ;
- the provision of support teaching for pupils who experienced difficulties with elementary or secondary schooling ;
- the opening out of the school onto life, in particular economic life, with the development of educational experience on the shop floor for pupils and working experience in enterprises for teachers during their initial training, but also in the whole range of social, cultural, and artistic activities, which could constitute potential valuable inputs to the schools ;
- as much decentralization as possible of the management of the educational system and the development of modern management methods at all levels of the administration.

Some items from these main lines of an education policy are implemented each year, and the role of the general action programme is to plan them so that they can be translated into budgetary terms, and followed up subsequently.

Finally, it should be stressed that the general action programme, because it is reviewed so regularly, determines educational policy projects empirically and in this way it is fairly closely linked to the economic situation, and at the same time it establishes aims for the future which can serve as guidelines for the educational system.

The general action programme has neither the ambition of a national plan for education nor the value of being one element of a comprehensive national planning exercise. Its main value resides in the forecasting and co-ordination work which the different services in the Ministry must do in order to prepare it and then carry it out. In this it brings together the different services which give life to the French educational system.

II. THE INTEGRATION OF EDUCATIONAL PLANNING INTO THE NATIONAL PLANNING (7)

1. From the Second to the Fifth Plan

Educational planning started in France with the Second Plan (1951-1955). Its aim was to provide the facilities required at a time when the demographic trend and rising school enrolment rates promised substantial increases in numbers. The object was therefore to programme the construction of educational facilities in the light of the finances available to the Government over the period under consideration.

Subsequent developments meant that these initial aims were widened in several directions. First, it was soon apparent that an approach confined solely to facilities was quite inadequate, so planning was extended to cover forecasts of numbers of teaching staff as from the Third and Fourth Plans. Secondly, the planning tended to change from a passive to an active process. The initial purpose was to forecast what would happen during the period of the Plan, other things remaining equal in the organisation of the education system, and thus simply to ensure the appropriate quantitative expansion. The approach changed in the Fifth Plan when qualitative issues were introduced and the implementation of a number of reforms decided by the Government became one of the main objectives (the introduction of new lower-secondary structures and the University Institutes of Technology - IUT., etc.). Consequently, forecasts of numerical trends no longer took account solely of the so-called spontaneous demand - as calculated by extrapolating past trends - but also of the changes in the usual flows which the public authorities intended to bring about (with varying degrees of success).

Lastly, educational planning was to be integrated with overall planning to a greater extent, an approach initially confined to establishing a link and ensuring the harmonious relationship between expenditure on educational facilities and public investment expenditure as a whole. Aside from this limited area of public finance, no comparison was made between the objectives and means of education policy and those of other government policies. In the preparations for the Fifth Plan, a further step was taken in the sphere of vocational training and qualification by comparing the output expected from the education system and the observable requirements of the economy.

---

7. This Part is based on M. Tuchman's paper : "Educational Planning in the Context of Overall Socio-Economic Planning, Special Reference France", OECD, Paris, 1978 (mimeographed).

Educational planning in France is seen from the outset as planning for one sector among others within the overall planning of the economy. Indeed, there has never been an independent planning process for education, and its development has always been considered alongside the development of other sectors of national economic life. It was considered in terms of a number of fundamental global equilibria that have to be established in the economy as a whole, such as production-consumption, employment, public finance, external finance, etc. But this integration remained largely nominal, apart from access to public funds, since no practical instruments were available to carry it out.

Thus, the first educational plans essentially took the form of an attempt to establish an equilibrium between the demands of families and the funds that could be allocated to the system. This planning was therefore incomplete : first, because the equilibrium sought between the increasing demand by families and the funds available was too limited and objective ; secondly, because it was a quantitative plan and not a qualitative one, despite the emergence of qualitative aspects during the preparation and implementation of the Sixth Plan. Thus, in the words used in the report on the implementation of the Fifth Plan (December 1968), although the stage of "bricks and mortar" planning had been passed, the planners "had yet to arrive at the concept of planning the education function" in such a way as to establish an equilibrium between the educational system and social development in a global quantitative planning process fully integrated with economic development as a whole.

2. The attempt to achieve integration in the Sixth Plan (1971-1976)

The Commission on School, University and Sports Facilities became the Education Commission, thus reflecting a desire to extend its horizons to a point beyond the mere programming of the "collective facilities" provided by the National Ministry of Education and local authorities and to encompass forecasts of the requirements and resources of the "collective education function" (8), irrespective of the bodies participating in it, with greater stress laid on the "qualitative" aspects of teaching problems. At the same time, the introduction by the central administration in March 1970 of a structure known as "management by objectives" gave shape to the concept that the whole range of national educational activities should

---

8. For further details on the concept of collective functions, see "Fonctions collectives et planification", "Notes et Etudes Documentaires", Nos. 3991-3992.

be regarded as a system of actions which could each be graded in relation to the others on the basis of the returns to be expected for a given cost.

Lastly, one further step forward was attempted under the Sixth Plan by linking the development of equality of opportunity and improvement of vocational training with the more general aspirations expressed for economic and social development as a whole : strengthening common interests and improving the competitiveness of the French economy.

This process of continual expansion - at any rate in the expressed aims - indicates one of the essential functions of planning, namely to make it possible to maintain an overall view of the activity of the educational system and the trend in expenditure when the consciously pursued objectives become more complex. As the more pressing problems of accommodation were gradually resolved, attention was focused on more qualitative problems and on the role of education in relation to other sectors of society, thus leading to increasing diversification of the needs expressed and, consequently, to problems of criteria for the allocation of resources and justification. These calculations were more complex than the urgency of accommodating children for this new expenditure.

This was a kind of culminating point for a certain conception of planning in terms of both resources and objectives, but it also marked the beginning of a reappraisal of the methods and aims of the Plan. The Government could no longer rely on a consensus to formulate the National Plan, and so did not want to announce objectives which, if attained, would not be chalked up to its credit and, if not attained, would be counted against it. It preferred to use other forms of consultation by means of direct negotiations with management and labour. In the field of education, the main choices of the Commission gave way to the "Haby reform" (9) in which the options were somewhat different. Lastly, those responsible for the Plan had not realised, in spite of certain warning signs, that the deterioration in the employment situation was going to last a long time.

METHODS OF INTEGRATION

Broadly speaking it can be said that, in the early stages, all the social groups concerned were convinced that what was good for education was good for the economy,

---

9. The reform of the educational system under the Act of 11th July, 1975, which was named after the Minister of Education (1974 to 1978).

i.e. for growth, and all that was required was to organise and channel the work of educating the nation. Then, without abandoning this belief, an attempt was made to optimise the allocation of physical resources of all kinds between the productive economy and the educational system. Lastly, attention was focused on organising education and orienting pupils on the basis of the structure of available or prospective jobs. These three lines of approach were matched by several avenues of research :

> i) the first aimed at integration in the macro-economic models used for planning the level of education ;
> ii) the second sought to explain the interactions between the educational system and economic development ;
> iii) the third is the approach through skilled manpower requirements.

But this integration was also sought by means of the planning process itself and the process of implementing the Plan.

1. The theoretical or methodological bases of integration

Macro-economic models

As in the case of the Sixth Plan, the macro-economic model (FIFI) used for economic projections offered no means of describing the economic and financial conditions for achieving a given social objective (10). However, it was presented in a more indicative way and served to evaluate the consequences of several social policy measures, such as the shorter working week.

Nevertheless, these models are made up of relationships that are valid only for the medium term, i.e. too short a period to avoid "cost" considerations overriding the "benefits" which usually emerge over a longer period in the case of social facilities which are difficult to quantify. An attempt was made to correct the extent to which costs override benefits by means of the studies on the rationalisation of budgetary choices but, owing to the importance of qualitative factors, many aspects of social reality remain beyond reach.

---

10. A "vocational training" variant, i.e. a projection for which a few assumptions were changed in relation to the central projection, had been considered during preparation of the Sixth Plan to assess the effects on productivity of an extension of the vocational training policy, but it produced no significant results.

Social indicators

Moreover, since macro-social accounting remains unrealistic in the absence of any integrated theory of social phenomena, the best solution seemed to be to rely on the co-ordinating machinery for the Plan, with a view to asking each commission to make its selection from a set of indicators prepared in collaboration with the responsible government departments. Several indicators were adopted in the field of education - some relating to the "reduction of inequalities" objective, others to the aim to adapt the educational system to society's actual needs - but the progress hoped for in this field has been curbed by methodological and statistical difficulties.

Rates of return

Two methods of optimisation were considered with a view to optimum planning in terms of general equilibria, namely the two techniques of "rates of return" and programming". Studies on rates of return were slow to get underway in France since they did not start until the end of the 1960s. They were largely ignored by the planners insofar as the method focused on areas that were too limited in scope to be used as a basis for general choices. Moreover, the results obtained are difficult to interpret, especially as the prices and costs are calculated on the basis of "ex-post" data and not "ex-ante" prospects as would logically be required if choices are to be made, particularly during a period when a trend is being reversed.

Optimisation model

In 1965, however, the Commissariat Général du Plan financed studies for the preparation of a model for the optimum allocation of resources between the economy and education (11). Improving on the theoretical analyses of human resources and on the cost-benefit analyses which tried to convert them into figures, these studies aimed to show both the physical relationships and their corollary in terms of value which unite education with other economic activities.

The dynamic character of this work highlights the linkages over time between the different variables and their feedbacks. It can also show how different collective functions of preference and various evaluations may lead to results that are sometimes very different and, sometimes, curiously similar.

---

11. In this connection, see J. Benard : "Un modèle d'affectation optimale des ressources entre l'économie et l'éducation" (CEPREL Bulletin No. 6, July 1966).

Although constructed for planning purposes - or at least as a planning aid - and financed under the Plan, this model was not used for the preparation and development of the Sixth Plan. While never made explicit, the reasons would seem partly attributable to its own weaknesses : no account taken of the reciprocal effects of education and income distribution ; inflexibility which leaves no room for substitution between factors of production, levels of education, or teaching methods ; lack of data on the possible acquisition of knowledge, especially occupational expertise, through channels outside the educational system ; and the adoption of a logic restricted to economic efficiency. Furthermore, the basic data were no doubt inadequate at this time. However, the main reasons why this model was not used for the Sixth Plan would seem to be that it was hard to handle and difficult to interpret the results and apply them to political and social reality. The work would certainly have been pursued if the manpower requirements approach had not been preferred.

The manpower requirements approach

As from the introduction of the Fifth Plan, when there was still a shortage of qualified manpower, the breakdown of school enrolment rates by educational structures had been compared with the requirements for qualified manpower as defined by the Manpower Commission. This approach was to be refined under the Sixth Plan - to provide recruitment requirements by occupation under some 40 headings - and then adopted in an updated and expanded form in the studies for the Seventh Plan. As the relevant methodology has already been described in a number of publications, we shall merely recall the forms adopted for the Seventh Plan, the main results and the reservations to which it gave rise.

The method used for the Seventh Plan consisted of a comparison between two magnitudes :

- the potential supply of jobs in 1981 ; and
- the population available in the same year.

The supply of jobs obviously depends on the economic situation, both the general situation and the particular situation for each type of activity, so the data are derived for 1981 from the calculations based on the macro-economic models for the Plan. These data are classified under nine headings, i.e. by four levels of training (engineers and managerial personnel, technicians, skilled manual and clerical workers, unskilled workers) for both the industry and services sectors, while the ninth covers the agricultural sector as a whole. The forecasts of the potential supply of jobs in 1981 were worked out for each of two balanced sets of calculations based on two assumptions

with respect to international economic conditions : one
tending to be optimistic and predicting an incipient return to normal after the difficulties of 1974-1975 and the
other pessimistic in that such difficulties persist.

The population available in 1981 is calculated on the
basis of non-economic factors which are mainly of a demographic nature. Taking the working population in 1975 and
allowing primarily for people leaving the labour force and
deaths, a "residual" population is obtained for 1981. This
is then adjusted to take account of the results of occupational mobility, net external migration and persons coming
onto the labour market from the education system. A comparison of the two terms, i.e. "potential job supply" and
"population available" indicates any manpower surpluses
of shortages to be expected.

This global approach was supplemented at two levels :

- a similar method was used at regional level whereby the national economic forecasting model was
  replaced by a regional development simulation
  model (SDR) ;
- sectoral analyses were undertaken, primarily on
  the basis of the conclusions of specialised forecasting groups for the different sectors composed
  of employers' representatives.

These data as a whole made it possible to establish
a forecast that is not too distorted by the methodological
shortcomings or difficulties involved in the somewhat mechanical comparison of projections of available population
and forecasts of job supply. To sum up, the conclusions
were as follows :

- a more or less balanced situation between the supply
  of jobs and available population in the case of
  engineers, middle-level management in the services
  sector, skilled and unskilled manual and clerical
  workers ;
- a large surplus of technicians in industry ;
- a large surplus of vacancies for top management
  in the services sector.

On the basis of these results, steps might have been taken
to establish orientations for the training system and to
propose the changes that seemed necessary, notably to reduce the output from the types of training which lead to
technicians' jobs in industry and to increase enrolments
in those providing access to senior managerial jobs in the
services sector.

However, the approach whereby output from the training
system is strictly geared to what are assumed to be the
"requirements of the economy" was not adopted as such
during the preparation of the Seventh Plan. An approach

of this kind is in fact based on a number of ideas which are rarely made explicit. First, job content would depend primarily on technological constraints and would as it were be imposed on enterprises. Secondly, access to a job would mainly depend on the content of the initial training and the compatibility of such training with the requirements of the work to be done. The studies carried out in recent years have called into question such presuppositions. It has in fact been found that requirements for a given type of job vary from firm to firm and that personnel management, or even production management, policies show quite a wide variation that the initial training and its appropriateness for the job is not the only criterion used by enterprises, since an employer's view of "qualification" for a job might, for example, include occupational experience, so that no "qualification" acquired in initial training could be regarded as meeting the requirements for such a job.

This discrepancy between the two concepts of "qualification" - one associated with a job and the other with a type of training - clearly showed that it was impossible to define equivalences at all levels between jobs and initial training. This would also explain - other than by the inadequacy of a particular kind of training for a particular job - a rather disturbing development : while young people have a considerably higher level of training than their elders, the proportion of unskilled jobs to which they have access is tending to increase. In order to explain this development, it is necessary to replace the concept of integration into working life by that of progress in a career.

Accordingly, educational planning can no longer be confined to regulating the flows leaving the educational system in terms of the requirements of the economy which are assumed to be immutable. However, the possibility of an imbalance between the potential supply of jobs and the available population calls for the implementation of a diversified policy involving initial training but also continuing training and measures providing incentives for enterprises.

Thus, the report of the technical group concerned with employment-training forecasting under the Seventh Plan concluded, in particular, that it was necessary to find broader descriptions of the jobs offered, pointing out that "flexibility, the capacity of job and employment structures to adjust must not be assumed to be zero".

Moreover, this new approach to the relationships between jobs and types of training has the advantage of offering a way out of the impasse in which educational planning might well find itself. The fact is that the aim of education is not solely to provide the economic system with the qualified manpower required, since the development and self-fulfillment of individuals are also aims which cannot be overlooked and which partly explain the "social demand" for education.

Since there is no absolute economic constraint on the definition of jobs and no close relationship between the type of initial training and the pursuit of an activity, it is not therefore necessary to draw any clear-cut inferences for the educational system from data such as the predicted surplus of industrial technicians or the continued existence - incidentally, with no increase - of a substantial number of unskilled jobs.

Under the Seventh Plan, stress has therefore been laid on the need to reduce the number of pupils leaving the educational system with no occupational training and an inadequate level of general education. This is to be done by developing technological training in secondary colleges in particular, although the "requirements of the economy" i.e. the trend in the pattern of development of enterprises, has suggested that the economy will be offering an approximately equivalent number of vacancies for unskilled jobs by 1981.

2. Integration through planning preparation procedures

The preparation of educational planning, like that of social planning in general, follows diverse and complex paths. In practice, it involves a large number of groups and institutions whose motivations and strategies are both diverse and changeable while, at the discretion of the public authorities, many variable regulations also govern the operation of the educational system.

However, we shall try to bring out the salient features and then describe the forms adopted during the preparation of the Seventh Plan, although no decision has yet been taken on the bases for the Eighth Plan.

a) The agencies and people involved in planning

One of the main features in this sector was initially the uneven confrontation between the Ministry of Education and the Commissariat Général du Plan. Over the last few years a number of somewhat peripheral areas of responsibility have been shifted from the Ministry of Education to the Ministry for Cultural Affairs, the Secretariat of State for Youth and Sport, the General Secretariat for Vocational Training and even to the Ministry of Labour, while a Ministry for the Universities has been set up for higher education. Nevertheless, the Ministry of Education's role is still decisive within the scope of the resources available to it, since the Commissariat du Plan must rely more on its capacity to present and clarify certain problems than on its influence on policy, notwithstanding the fact that it comes under the Prime Minister. The activities of the other government departments are confined to limited areas of responsibility.

The Ministry of Education

The Ministry prepares and manages the country's educational policy. After various administrative reforms, a Directorate has been made responsible for pluri-annual administrative planning, co-ordination between the various other directorates and between the Ministry of Education and the Ministry for the Universities, and also for liaison with the Commissariat Général du Plan. This Directorate incorporates the various internal planning bodies that the Ministry was required to set up at the request of the Commissariat du Plan and the Commissions, it also no doubt intended to prevent an outside body from assuming too much influence and to avoid losing the initiative and powers associated with the development of this function. More particularly, the Directorate is responsible for drawing up the budget for the Ministry's programme and the general action programme.

The principal physical and financial data ought to have been set out in the budget for the programmes and classified according to the structure of the objectives assigned to the Ministry to serve as a basis for annual budgetary procedures. This was not done for two reasons : firstly, because it was not possible to identify a pattern of objectives corresponding to these programme structures - the resources were simply classified according to the different categories of education - and, secondly, because the conventional heading and chapter layout was retained for the discussion of the budget.

The General Action Programme employs the technique of rolling plans which can be revised each year. It differentiates between accommodation measures and measures designed to improve the educational system. At present it has no external financial limiting framework within which it can define and programme any new measures envisaged. Various methods have been used to estimate this financial framework, including the macro-economic data provided by the Plan, but the results are too varied. The General Action Programme therefore confines itself to providing a mechanical forecast of the progression of costs over the next four years, but since the programme is essentially descriptive, it cannot clarify the situation for the responsible authorities, particularly as regards the redistribution of resources within the educational system. After being discontinued for a period, the programme was resumed this year but clearly still depends on external clarification which can at present only be provided in the context of the public finance studies and inter-sectoral arbitrage under the Plan. It nevertheless remains a possible means of enabling the Ministry itself to give practical shape to the choices of the Plan, and may also serve the planners as a frame of reference for their analyses.

It should also be noted that the two Ministries (Education and Universities) are jointly served by the Information and Statistical Studies Service (SEIS), which centralises at national level all general information collected on the school population. This includes personnel, equipment, facilities, the allocation of expenditure, /cost of education per pupil in each category of studies, economic accounting data (12) on education, etc./. It also provides the statistical data required by all Directorates. It accordingly provides the main basic studies for medium- and long-term projections of numbers of pupils and teachers and, in the context of models developed in collaboration with the Directorates concerned, it sets out the normative assumptions consistent with the establishment of educational policy.

The other ministries play a more marginal, more subtle and perhaps more tactical role according to whether they consider it to be in their interest to channel their project through the Plan. None have developed planning or programming machinery. Mention should be made of the General Secretariat for Vocational Training which is responsible for co-ordinating all continuing vocational training schemes, no matter what administration is in charge of such schemes.

The Commissariat Général au Plan

Only the Commissariat Général au Plan is in a position to size up the educational effort in relation to the economic and social policy to be undertaken by the public authorities in the medium and long term. While not itself a research body or a forecasting institute in the strict sense, it is at the centre of all these studies and accordingly has the macro-economic and macro-social instruments which enable it to take an overall - if not integrated - view of social policies in terms of the economic choices or constraints throughout the period covered by the Plan.

It has the necessary "powers" to convene the various administrative departments and research bodies to compare their work in a particular field, to co-ordinate their

---

12. Global information is therefore available on the expenditure that the operation of the French educational system represents for the aggregates of each economic sector in the National Accounts and the cost of education can be determined by major type of establishment.

research, or to request documentation in the context of a working group operating under its responsibility.

As it is not bogged down in problems of management, it can also ensure that innovations are encouraged, especially when they have interministerial implications. Furthermore, it still provides a meeting point for all the groups and agencies involved even if it is no longer the place where all the compromises are reached. Lastly, in certain circumstances it can serve as an ally to the Ministry of Education which may be afraid of being isolated in the course of some types of arbitrage.

Machinery for concerted action under the Seventh Plan

While the Commissariat Général au Plan is essentially responsible for official planning in France, it is assisted by a number of commissions which are renewed every five years and meet very frequently during the period of the preparation of the Plan. Up until the Seventh Plan, educational planning went to a Commission whose field of responsibilities was gradually extended. It was first responsible for school and university facilities (Fifth Plan), then all educational problems irrespective of whether they came within the province of the Ministry of Education and finally, under the Seventh Plan, the Education Commission covered all aspects of education and training. The reason for widening the Commission's responsibilities to include problems of continuing training certainly owed something to the view that it is through the impact of continuing training that changes could be brought about in the practices (methods and content) of what seemed to be the monolithic character of the National Ministry of Education. At the same time, two joint groups were set up under the Education Commission and the Employment Commission : the first to deal with problems of continuing vocational training and the second to compare forecasts of output from the training system with forecasts of the employment situation. Provision was also made for dialogue with other commissions, more particularly the Development Commission, which was the central body for the preparation of the Plan. Having been previously concerned exclusively with economic matters as the "Commission for General Economic Affairs and Finance", this Commission was later assigned overall responsibility for both economic and social matters with the aim of providing a less fragmented view of medium-term development.

Some difficulties were experienced with the operation of this machinery and it did not come up to initial expectations. Membership of the Commission was limited to some 30 persons on a tripartite basis - representatives of the administration, management and labour, and individual members (13). This meant that it could not extend the scope of its activities, which continued to be confined to internal problems relating to the operation and resources of the system. Moreover, although the Ministry of Education supplied the Commission with sound documentation, the Ministry was completing its reform of the educational system at about the same time and did not therefore find it advisable for any matters connected to this project to be taken up by the Commission and thus run the risk of being called into question at the very time that discussions and initial steps to implement the reform were being undertaken elsewhere. At the same time the Commission had to confine itself to dealing with peripheral problems without always having the means of tackling them. There were a number of tacit and tactical agreements, however, notably on primary education, insofar as the Ministry sought the backing of the Commission to obtain the resources for its reform. This aim is reflected, moreover, in the content of the priority action programmes adopted.

It proved impossible, moreover, to make effective use of the contacts with the Employment Commission because the results of the comparisons between forecasts of output from the educational system and forecasts of the employment situation were late in arriving and difficult to interpret. Therefore they were not really incorporated in the analyses of the Education Commission. Consisting for the most part of teachers - no matter how they were labelled - the Commission took cover behind the traditional view that it was detrimental in the long term to subordinate the development of the educational system to the requirements formulated by enterprises, although it did not make clear the practical consequences of such a policy, because this might have divided its ranks. It seems that this point of view was shared by the representatives of the Ministry of Education.

On the other hand, the Employment Commission was not indifferent to the problems made apparent by the comparison between output from the education system and the employment situation and recommended a policy of job qualifications and improved working conditions designed to take account of the widening discrepancy between the aspirations of young people and the jobs offered. Having made these reservations, it can be argued that, despite the limited time available to it, the Education and Training Commission had a positive effect in that it chose to make concrete proposals which could be implemented quickly.

---

13. The representatives included eight from the administration, five from the business world or employers' associations, five from workers' organisations, three from teachers' unions and two from parents' associations, while seven were appointed on a personal basis. Under one heading or another, teachers were in the majority.

b) The content of the Plan

Text of the Plan

The Plan is primarily a set of policies, courses of action, reforms and modifications for the development process, all set out in a report which does not take up every proposal made by the Commissions. Like the other commissions, the Education and Training Commission of the Seventh Plan published its own report on completion of its work, setting out its investigations, analyses, projections and its proposals with respect to the policy orientations adopted. Unlike the Plan, this report does not commit the Government but, together with the reports by the other commissions, is nevertheless an essential product of the planning process, inseparable but different from the Plan itself. The Plan is in fact the outcome of concerted analyses of the issues at stake and the statement of a political commitment by the public authorities.

The text of the Seventh Plan essentially states the view that the increase in economic resources must be coupled with qualitative objectives, including objectives with respect to means.

As far as education was concerned, the aim of the Plan, as it was stated in Part I, was selective and only two priority orientations were adopted : the first was designed to modify the systems of initial and continuing training with a view to facilitating the integration of young people into working life, the reintegration of the registered unemployed and the preparation of workers for change. The second reaffirmed that the major orientation of educational policy during the Seventh Plan should be to promote equality of opportunity for all children. In this connection, it recommended the development of pre-primary education in which the quality of accommodation facilities should be improved, and it stressed the importance of extra tuition in primary and lower-secondary education.

It also recommended the introduction of manual and technical training for all pupils in lower-secondary education.

Programming methods

Programming methods have developed and have made their contribution to the quest for more effective means of integrating social and economic objectives. Drawing on its experience of the conditions governing the preparation and implementation of previous Plans, the Government adopted a different approach to the programming of public measures under the Seventh Plan. Trends in the structure of public expenditure between 1975 and 1980 are given by way of illustration in the test of the Plan itself and, for the first time, breakdowns of both investment and operating expenditure are shown. The Seventh Plan also includes a set of limited but well-defined commitments under priority action programmes (PAP), presented in Part I.

Priority action programmes are designed to answer the need for an approach that is both selective and coherent :

" i) the approach is selective because the Plan defines only a limited number of priority action programmes to be implemented on the basis of a firm commitment by the Government (...). The total funds to be allocated to them may not be more than 5 to 20 per cent of the civil budgetary expenditure covered by the programming (...).
ii) the approach is coherent because data are required to show that these programmes can be assigned a place within the context of the general orientations relating to the sectors concerned..." (14).

Procedure for drawing up priority action programmes

Along the same lines as the "finalised programmes" under the Sixth Plan, the PAPs define the actions to be pursued to achieve given objectives. Both the objectives and the resources to be used to achieve them - no matter what kind of resources - are announced together with the results expected and then obtained, so that a better balance can be established between objectives and resources. Furthermore, the fact that the PAPs are prepared by the administration means that an attempt is made to integrate social policy at interministerial level. However, it should be noted that, while this procedure has the advantage of involving and committing the administrations, it no doubt leaves them with a decisive role in the supervision of programming.

The Commissioner for the Plan and the Ministers concerned were jointly responsible for the development of these programmes in terms of the type of actions planned and the amount and structure of financing. This work was carried out within the specified time by means of administrative working groups which, in each case, assembled representatives of the ministries concerned, the Ministry for the Budget and the Commissariat Général au Plan (notably the financial and sectoral services concerned).

---

14. The Prime Minister's directives to the Commissioner for the Plan.

c) **Implementation of the Plan**

In a field such as education, the problem involved in implementing the Plan is to ensure that responsibility for the options is effectively assumed by the ministries concerned and by the Department of Finance and, more indirectly, that they have been taken into account by the social groups. The different groups do not have identical objectives and attitudes, so the apparent - and partial - consensus sought in preparing the Plan does not mean that the groups will act in unison when it is being implemented. Procedures are used to prevent too wide a disparity between the objectives of the Plan and the annual budgetary arbitrage influenced by short-term demand management requirements : an annual meeting of the commissions, an annual implementing report annexed to the Finance Act, regular information provided to Parliament and the Economic Social Council.

A new mechanism has also been provided by the introduction of a Central Planning Council (15) which must deliberate on the implementation of the Plan twice a year : the first time to assess the progress of the PAPs before the main lines of the budget for the coming year have been laid down ; the second time, after the annual meetings of the commissions to take note of the annual implementing report (prior to publication) submitted to them by the Commissioner for the Plan.

Furthermore, the regular publication of indicators should make it possible to follow the development of the principal magnitudes showing the implementation of the Plan's social objectives. They include some new social and ecological indicators introduced for the purpose of monitoring the implementation of objectives concerned with the improvement of living conditions. These indicators are also used to keep track of the progress made in carrying out priority action programmes and the relevant information is published quarterly.

The PAPs constitute the "hard core" of the Plan and their implementation is monitored by an interministerial steering group under the responsibility of the ministry principally concerned with the PAP in question. The Government has undertaken a commitment to implement the PAPs but their financing calls for a new and thoroughgoing integration of the annual budgetary procedure with the objectives and resources of the Seventh Plan. In particular, the financing calls in part for the reallocation of

---

15. This Council, chaired by the President of the Republic himself, has as standing members : the Prime Minister and the Commissioner for the Plan, the Ministers of the Economy, Budget and Labour, while other Ministers take part in certain meetings, depending on the agenda.

existing appropriations to priority actions and only in part to funds for new measures. A substantial proportion of these appropriations therefore correspond to the redeployment of public expenditure among different ministries or within the same ministerial department.

The budgetary procedure adopted has in fact meant that the ministries give priority to the PAPs, thus ensuring that they are financed while at the same time curbing the growth of budgetary expenditure. Implementation of the PAPs may nonetheless be compromised by the unduly large volume of funds redeployed or by a discrepancy between the objectives pursued and the resources employed. In practice, the priority accorded to programmes depends on the level of resources allocated to the ministry's other tasks. If such tasks are called into question for the reallocation of funds, the order of priorities may be changed. In these circumstances, "monitoring" the implementation of the PAPs becomes essential and cannot be separated from the discussion of the ministry's overall budgetary resources. So far as the presentation of Finance Acts is concerned, the main effect of the new procedure is that the appropriations required for each PAP are entered chapter by chapter in the annual budget of each ministry.

AN ASSESSMENT OF THE SITUATION AND PROSPECTS

A reappraisal of planning

It is not very easy to make an assessment of educational planning ; broadly speaking it shares the destiny of planning in general, benefiting from its advances and suffering from its setbacks. Basically, the record can be divided into three phases :

- the first was characterised by the importance attached to the Plan and is accompanied by political, and to some extent social mobilisation which continues, though losing momentum, up until the Fifth Plan ; the methods used were largely empirical ;

- the second, after 1968, which corresponded to the preparation of the Sixth Plan based on the firm belief in growth as a remedy for social tensions, carries the desire for exhaustiveness, innovations and consistency to its maximum. New and relatively sophisticated methods and instruments began to be used, but the social foundations of the project were appearing more ambiguous. The Plan sought to base its function and interventions on its "technical and scientific" ability to forecast the future and perceive the changes needed ;
- the economic crisis brought down this edifice, already weakened by the crumbling away of the

foundations of the earlier political consensus, in as much as the instruments used were incapable of answering the essential questions : what future, what growth, what sharing of incomes, what new equilibria ? In particular, what role could education play in re-establishing these equilibria : should it be used as a factor contributing to the competitiveness of enterprises, or as a compensation for social disadvantage ?

An assessment of educational planning

After twenty years of educational planning, it is temptating to make a rapid assessment. While the accommodation of pupils has been systematically ensured, none of the ultimate objectives entrusted to the educational system have yet been achieved in a manner satisfactory to the different social groups concerned, despite the efforts made by the country over a period of some fifteen years. The transmission of knowledge is criticised as to its form and content, access to education is still unevenly spread, and the democratisation of higher education remains very relative. Adapting training to jobs is now a matter of national interest.

This assessment would seem to condemn planning, the more so since the Plan is tending to disappear from the political foreground. It would seem, however, that this judgement must be qualified. Apart from the fact that it has helped greatly to organise the very substantial growth of school enrolment, planning has had other results which, while less important, should nevertheless be mentioned. In the first place, as has already been said, the Ministry of Education has responded (or retorted) by taking responsibility for this effort. Secondly the determination to carry on with planning has been accompanied by an appreciable research effort concerning the functioning of the educational system and the training-qualifications-employment relationship and its determining factors. This was the reason, for example, behind the creation of the Centre d'Etudes et de Recherches sur les Qualifications (CEREQ). In addition, the fact that planning in France involves consultations, has meant that all the social groups have been better informed concerning the problems posed by the development of the educational system. In some cases, they have been brought in to help define certain objectives.

However, the limitations are undeniable. Some of these are technical or scientific, with the result that the manpower requirements approach is not directly operational, owing to the lack of an adequate analysis of skills, a better understanding of labour market functions and, at another level, a satisfactory job nomenclature. Macro-economic models cannot take account of the effects of a rise in the level of education. Arbitrage between the different collective functions cannot be "scientifically" justified.

There are also political limitations. In some cases political decision-makers have been unwilling to justify choices which could only be political, while in others they have preferred to define their policies in "technocratic and political" terms, and have therefore resorted to bilateral and secret negotiations. A number of difficult decisions have been systematically postponed. They have been encouraged in this by the general disappearance of any basis for a consensus, this phenomenon being particularly acute as regards education and training issues which have crystallised political differences. It has not always been possible to detect any strategy emerging from these successive and sometimes contradictory choices.

New problems

The change in the economic and social context is going to have a big influence on the educational system. In the next few years, the educational system will be faced with a double constraint which represents a break with past trends.

In the first place, the labour market will remain depressed for a long time to come, while employers, who are in a dominant position, will tend for a period which could last for some time yet to make an increasingly meticulous selection among job applicants in general, and young people in search of their (first) employment in particular. The time has gone when an expanding economy gave rise to quantifiable and foreseeable requirements for skilled labour, making it possible to envisage setting up vocational training schemes which simply matched those requirements, even if the training process has to be completed in the firm. The numbers of school-leavers appearing on the labour market every year, the foreseeable rate of job creation during the coming period, the fragmentation of the labour market, and the diversity of occupational situations make it necessary to rethink both initial vocational training schemes and the transition from training to employment. This is all the more necessary in that, in this context, those without qualifications and who have not acquired vocational training will continue to be the least privileged, the most vulnerable and also the most difficult to train for other jobs.

Secondly, there will be increasing pressure to restrict the share of public expenditure devoted to education, particularly since the generations commencing their secondary education will be less numerous (16), and the acquisition of qualifications will be discredited if it no

---

16. After reaching 850 000 in 1973, the number of births had fallen to a little over 740 000 in 1975.

longer guarantees employment. However, if France's position in the new world economic order is considered to depend on the degree of development of its technology and its capacity to innovate and export, it has to be accepted that educational spending must be maintained, even if it does have to be better organised, more effective, and more consistent with the necessities of economic development.

A hand to mouth policy will not produce solutions to these problems, which will force us to make adjustments to our educational system extending over several years. The Ministry of Education has set up programming services, which may in fact be under-utilised, but the difficulties that the Ministry encounters in using them, both within the Ministry and outside, is indicative of their limitations. In the absence of contextual details and data on the frame of reference, this can at worst be described as blind planning which perpetually reiterates the same targets or fixes them without any regard for economic and social equilibria and, at best, as an exercise in rolling programming. In addition, their habitual interlocutors - the teachers - often share, if not the same points of views, at least the same interests. It may well be that the Ministry, reduced to a defensive position, may not be able to bring about these adjustments, and it remains to be seen to what extent, by what means and on what basis planning can develop.

The role of planning

If planning is understood to mean framing or preparing the ground for a strategy in response to foreseeable changes, it can no longer be considered from a partial or sectoral standpoint. The educational system reflects the contradictions in our society and is interrelated with the other elements of our society.

There is not at present any process or institution in France, other than the Plan and the Commissariat au Plan, capable of trying to locate the choices open to education in relation to global options.

Other factors to be taken into account include the vastness of the educational system and the disadvantages of organising it in too centralised a manner. These are beginning to be appreciated more clearly at a time when more flexibility is required of the system, and when it is no longer possible to shelter behind central regulations and norms. Different social groups and certain social institutions or forces are beginning to take an active interest in the forms of decentralisation and autonomy that might be introduced, while at the same time the Government is transferring to local education authority level some of its powers with regard to capital expenditure. It thus becomes possible to outline a new type of planning which would be done on two levels :

- at national level, data on frames of reference and guidelines would be established ;
- at local level the regulation and taking into account of the environment.

This distinction would give rise to a new breakdown of responsibilities between the Plan, the ministries and the regional bodies concerned.

The Plan

We shall not enumerate the functions that the Plan has to fulfil in France. Suffice it to say that it has to avoid two dangers. It must not be content to be a sounding board for the projects of the ministries, or of any one of them, and it must avoid establishing attractive plans which have no political base. In both cases, however much goodwill it may be able to mobilise and however high the quality of the work, its impact will be slight. The only use it will serve will reside in the amount of information made available in this connection. The Plan must provide more essential indications for preparing and conducting a policy.

A long-term perspective

A long-term perspective has two advantages. It allows the place and shape of the educational system to be defined in the framework of a prospective study on ways of life. Indeed, thinking which is confined to the function of education may well come to nothing because of the number and complexity of the interrelationships between the educational system and society as a whole.

More directly, it must look at the trend of demand for education, and must reveal the main distortions which already exist in present trends as regards those leaving the educational system on the one hand, and job vacancies on the other.

Data on the frame of reference

Effective educational policy in the medium term requires knowledge of certain data on the frame of reference which, in the present state of affairs, only the Plan can provide :

- financial data ;
- population facts and figures (including internal mobility) ;
- forecasts concerning occupational structures during the period covered by the Plan.

Inter-sectoral policies or programmes

It is also the framework of the Plan which can serve to demonstrate the interdependent relations on which the realism of a political orientation depends. If, for example, it is considered that a reappraisal of the value of manual work should be an objective for the coming years, it is necessary to follow up all the consequences with regard to the orientation of education, the income hierarchy and working conditions. Similarly, if the Government wishes to have a policy for a target group such as young people, it must be able to rearrange the component parts of this group's environment, and therefore consider the place of the school with reference to other activities. Mention may also be made here of continuous training which can be seen as part of an industrial conversion policy. However, to broaden the debate, one can try to determine the place of continuous training in a society in which people must prepare themselves for changes of all kinds, just as they prepare for retirement.

The priorities of the Eighth Plan

As regards education, a feature of the Eighth Plan will probably be its concern to develop vocational education and to improve the links between this education and the economic world. If this is the approach, it would appear that action should be pursued along four main lines :

- redefining vocational training on the basis of key skills. The work of the Plan could serve as abbasis for updating the school map, at least as far as vocational training is concerned ;
- diversifying new courses, some of which must be organised in such a way as to enable young people who have left comprehensive school and have acquired occupational skills as part of their job, to turn these to account by means of supplementary training within the educational system. Proficiency would have to be certified by means of diplomas obtained via the system of capitalisable credit units and recognised by both labour and management. These diplomas would make it possible to return subsequently to the various levels of traditional higher education, if necessary by means of refresher courses ;
- the introduction of various formulae for making the transition between training and employment has developed in the last few years for reasons arising mainly from the economic situation. It may be asked whether the development of polyvalent training courses, and the widening split between schools and enterprises do not justify persisting with these formulae which would supplement initial training and help bridge the gap between the educational system and enterprises ;

- by adaptation, higher education should be able to overcome its crisis situation. Because they are not sufficiently independent, the universities are unable to identify the educational, research and development missions that they could fulfil if they were capable of building up links with their environment. Ill at ease and poorly equipped to perceive the needs of their environment, they take refuge behind the central authority which they themselves challenge. They are the institutions which are in most urgent need of (flexible) solutions which will enable them to take responsibility for local requirements. In this way they could produce projects with which all sides (teachers, students, economic decision-makers) would be able to identify.

It seems that this planning would have to be selective, therefore. However, it must be accepted that this selectivity can only serve a purpose if it is the result of global analysis - implicit or explicit.

Priority must also be given to two other questions : the training of school teachers and the redeployment of resources that must take place to allow for the spreading of demographic effects over a period of time. The two problems are linked since, in view of the age pyramid of the teaching profession, recruiting would be almost nil as a result of the decline in enrolment. However, this demographic trend can also lead to improved teaching standards if the educational system is capable of redeploying. Although both these issues contain interministerial aspects, they seem really to come under the internal planning of the Ministry of Education. They could also be dealt with as part of the Plan, however, if the Government so wished.

Planning methods

No significant improvement can be expected in the main planning instruments. Changes in methods will come about much more from the realisation that the educational system is cumbersome and inert when organised from the centre.

Particularly in adapting education to jobs, a more pragmatic approach will be adopted and a distinction made between two levels :

- the main guidelines will be defined at national level. For this purpose information will be collected which will allow an assessment to be made of the nature and scale of the adjustments needed to facilitate the transition between training and employment. Three types of analysis will be used :

retrospective analyses, sectoral studies and a global comparison under nine headings between job forecasts and school leavers, using the new instruments available (17). An attempt will thus be made to establish a chart showing, as far as possible, trades which are expanding and those which are diminishing and also training which has future employment potential and training which involves risks ;
- regional planning of education will consist of "managing" the margins for adjustment which exist inside the educational system - by starting or stopping courses, and its periphery providing supplementary or transitional training - all this within the framework of nationally defined guidelines.

This management is the responsibility of several decentralised parties, namely the local education authorities and the Préfets who take action or decide not to on the basis of consultations or discussions with local bodies.

These decision-makers need information which can only be supplied by transposing to regional level the customary problems of matching supply and demand. The intention is to reduce the gap by means of continuous analysis which should take the place of the forecasts made at regular intervals. The statistical system to be set up will therefore have to combine data available at long intervals, such as population censuses, with data which can be provided annually.

*
* *

Can the Plan still obtain the approval of the various social groups concerned - at least as far as education is concerned ? Does the Government intend to use the Plan to adapt the educational system to the new economic and social context ? These are the two conditions which must be satisfied if educational planning is to recover its effectiveness. They will have to be based on a global long-term analysis of national medium-term guidelines and regionalised regulation.

---

17. Observatory of entries in working life : Répertoire Français des Emplois.

B. JAPAN

Japan's educational development has been guided by two main ideals : to ensure equal educational opportunity to all the population and to provide well-balanced educational conditions throughout the country. Following these ideals, the fundamental policies have been formulated in full cognisance of the changes and progress of the times and with a careful consideration of the future course of development. Under these policies, the various concrete plans have been made and carried out for every field of education with due attention to the relations between them and the priority of each.

Such plans have been worked out for every field of education and have encompassed a wide range of activities, including plans for class organisation, designation of the number of educational personnel and educational facilities at the primary and secondary levels ; they further affect the total size, geographical location, and organisation of specific fields of study of institutions of higher education, and in fact determine the whole structure of higher education with the aim of greater flexibility and higher mobility in higher education and post-secondary education.

This report presents the whole arrangement for formulation of fundamental policies and preparation and implementation of concrete plans in consideration of their mutual relationship within the framework of the policies, in so doing, dealing with the "Educational Planning" of Japan.

I. EDUCATIONAL PROGRESS IN POST-WAR JAPAN

After the war, Japan's educational system experienced a drastic change. The new school system consisted of the 6-year elementary school, 3-year lower secondary school, 3-year upper secondary school and 4-year university or college. This new system of school education was institutionalised in conformity with the spirit of the new Japanese Constitution and with the purport of the Fundamental Education Law which prescribes the basic principles of education. One of the principles in this law is the idea of equal educational opportunity for all. It states that every Japanese must be given equal opportunity to receive education according to his ability, and that there must not be any discrimination in education on the basis of race, sex, social status, economic condition or origin. Japan's post-war education has been disseminated and enhanced in keeping with this ideal so that every citizen may have full access to education.

To take compulsory education as an example, prior to the war the length of compulsory education was 6 years and education was offered only at the elementary school level ; in the post-war days, 3-year education conducted at lower secondary school was added to the elementary school education. As a result, the length of compulsory education was extended from 6 to 9 years.

Post-secondary education before the war was provided by many different types of school and the number of those who proceeded to institutions of higher education was limited, but after the war the school system was simplified so as to provide post-compulsory education through upper secondary schools and universities or colleges, and the doors of universities or colleges were opened widely to all graduates from upper secondary schools.

In order to cope with the later changes in social and economic conditions and to fulfil the nation's needs, a new school system comprising junior colleges, technical colleges and special training schools was established with the above-stated post-war educational system as its foundation.

Such expansion of the educational system has brought successful dissemination of Japan's school education. In 1909, the school attendance ratio in compulsory education had already reached 98 per cent, and during the post-war days in which the length of compulsory education was extended to 9 years, the school attendance ratio reached approximately 100 per cent. The ratio of those who proceed to upper secondary school or technical college after completion of compulsory education has increased remarkably from 43 to 94 per cent during the 30 years since the war. Further, the ratio of children going to kindergarten was less than 10 per cent just after the war's end, but it has now increased up to 65 per cent. Of all elementary school children, the number who have received pre-elementary education at either kindergarten or nursery school is about 90 per cent.

The ratio of those who are enrolled at university, college or junior college after finishing upper secondary education has now reached 39 per cent. Looking at the distribution of total enrolment at institutions of higher education, it can be seen that the enrolment at national institutions is 21 per cent, the enrolment at public institutions 3 per cent and the enrolment at private institutions is 76 per cent. Japan's higher education has expanded rapidly in recent years, and a number of new universities have been created. These include Tsukuba University, the University of Technology and Science and the University of Education whose aim is to provide the training for both would-be teachers and in-service training for teachers.

Approximately 90 per cent of the total enrolment at junior colleges consists of females. This shows that this type of institution of higher education plays an important role in women's education in Japan.

In addition to universities, colleges, junior colleges and upper secondary schools, there are also special training schools and miscellaneous schools. The latter two types of school have been playing an increasing part in providing education and training for the nation. The number of students of those schools is about 410 000 and 780 000 respectively. Special training schools offer three different courses classified according to their entrance requirements. In particular, the courses provided for graduates from upper secondary school (a special training school offering such courses is called a Special Training College) are part of the higher education system. The total enrolment in such courses is about 310 000. These courses are in this way making contributions to the development of greater diversity and flexibility of higher education in Japan. Adding the number of those who proceed to these courses to those who enter other institutions of higher education, the ratio of those who go on to some form of higher education amounts to about 50 per cent of all the graduates from upper secondary school. The miscellaneous schools conduct education that is in nature similar to other types of school education and provide a variety of educational activities to accommodate the educational needs in different sectors of society.

In regard to out-of-school education, the Social Education Law was enacted in 1949 and the Sports Promotion Law in 1961. Under the provisions of these laws, efforts have been made in promoting and improving various activities in the fields of social education, physical education and sports.

The recent changes in social and economic conditions have led to the higher standard of living and the increase in free time of the nation. In order to meet the demands arising from such circumstances, efforts have been made in developing and improving social education facilities, such as citizens' public halls, libraries and museums, and also physical education and sports facilities including athletic grounds, gymnasiums and swimming pools. At the same time, social education services in the form of youth classes, women's classes, family education classes, classes for the aged and university extension courses have been strengthened and so have served to encourage physical education and sports with a view to increasing the nation's physical fitness.

In financial terms, the ratio of the total educational expenditure to the total national income, which is the sum total of the expenses for all the national, public and private schools, local governments' expenditure for social education, and national and local governments' expenditure for educational administration, increased from 6.0 per cent in 1955 to 7.8 per cent in 1976.

II. PRESENT STATE OF THE EDUCATION SYSTEM AND EDUCATIONAL PLANNING

a) Introduction

As the national body responsible for educational administration, the Ministry of Education (also frequently referred to by its Japanese name of "Monbusho") promotes and disseminates school education, social education, science and culture. At the local level, boards of education are established within local public bodies at prefectural and municipal levels. The board of education system started with the idea introduced after the war of local self-government and democratisation of educational administration. It is responsible for promotion and dissemination of school education, social education, science and culture in the area within its jurisdiction.

Private schools up to upper secondary school level fall under the jurisdiction of the prefectural governor's office. The governor grants permission for the establishment of private upper secondary schools and provides financial assistance for such schools and guidance and advice for their operation.

The Ministry decides national standards of minimum requirements for education including those for school curricula, class organisation, fixed number of educational personnel and educational facilities, and also provides guidance, advice and assistance to the relevant authorities of the local public bodies. The Ministry issues, as necessary, notifications and circular notices to educational authorities and organises regular meetings of the superintendents, who supervise the business executed by the Secretariat of the board in conformity with the policies adopted by the board and the chiefs of departments of the secretariat, who are in charge of the actual educational operations, for the purpose of maintaining close relations between the Ministry and the local public bodies.

In financing education, the national government applies a variety of policies. The government itself establishes educational institutions including national universities or colleges and expands and improves them. At the same time it extends financial assistance to institutions of higher education established and operated by local government or private bodies, and to local public bodies as well.

Financial assistance from the national government to the local public body is classified roughly into contributions and subsidies which are granted for specific purposes and tax equalisation grants. The contributions and subsidies are provided for these items : compulsory education teachers' salaries, provision of facilities, the establishment of new upper secondary schools and the expansion of existing ones. These are funded by the national government. They cover about one- to two-thirds of the total expenses required for each of these items.

In addition, tax equalisation grants are provided by the national government for the local public bodies. The grants, which include the amount designated for education, are designed to ensure a certain level of revenue to the local public bodies regardless of their different volumes of tax revenues and also provide independence of the local public bodies in terms of financing.

The local public bodies, with the contribution, subsidies, tax equalisation grants from the national government and their own financial resources, establish and operate elementary, lower and upper secondary schools. They also take measures to promote social education, physical education and sports in their respective areas.

From the above description, it can be said that in every aspect of educational administration and finance, the national government takes the lead while the local public bodies enjoy freedom and independence, which makes it possible for the national government and the local public bodies to establish and maintain smooth and effective communication and co-operation with each other.

At the national level, plans are formulated and implemented for every field of education with due consideration of the social and economic trends and the nation's needs. In formulation of the plans, the recommendations and reports submitted by various councils and co-operators' conferences, which are the Minister's advisory bodies, often make a valuable contribution.

The most representative of those councils is the Central Council for Education. The Council, as an advisory body to the Minister, conducts studies and holds deliberation on policies of fundamental importance to education, science and culture and submits to the Minister recommendations or reports on matters which the Minister refers to the Council. In 1971, the Council submitted to the Minister the recommendation entitled "On the Basic Guidelines for the Development of an Integrated Educational System Suited for Contemporary Society". This recommendation offers propositions on school education in the long-term perspective and addresses the question "What should school education be like in future ?". In addition to this Council, there are others closely related to departments or divisions of the Ministry. These councils conduct studies and deliberate on the matters for which the departments or divisions have responsibility. They, too, make recommendations and reports on various policies to be followed in the future, making contributions to policy-making by the departments or divisions of the Ministry.

At the local level, the local public authorities usually formulate the long-term, overall plans for local community development. The policies of educational planning and a long-term educational development plan are integrated into the community development plan in the effort to promote such policies and plans under a well-prepared programme.

b) Schools for Compulsory Education

In Japan, the guardians of children have an obligation to send their children from age 6 to 15 to the 6-year elementary school and the 3-year lower secondary school in accordance with the provisions of the Japanese Constitution, the Fundamental Education Law and the School Education Law.

On the one hand, the State imposes this obligation upon the guardians and, on the other, makes it obligatory for the municipalities to establish elementary and lower secondary schools and for the prefectural authorities to establish schools for the blind and the deaf and other special schools. The State provides contributions and subsidies, amounting to over 50 per cent of the total budget of the Ministry, for educational personnel salaries and allowances, school facilities, teaching materials and school equipment and apparatus. This is conducted under the provisions of the pertinent laws and for the purpose of maintaining and elevating the national educational standards.

Under this system, the State has been applying planned measures for educational improvement to reduce the pupil/class ratio in order to increase efficiency in teaching and learning and to fix the number of educational personnel to be placed at each school. The Law Concerning Class Organisation and the Standard of Fixed Number of Educational Personnel of Schools for Compulsory Education, which was enacted in 1958, aims at establishing standards of appropriate class size in schools for compulsory education and ensuring an appropriate placement of educational personnel at such schools, thereby helping maintain and elevate the level of compulsory education. Under the provisions of the law, the standard maximum number of children in each class is decided along with the number of classes in each school. This provides the basis for deciding the standard maximum number of educational personnel to be employed by each prefecture. Before the law was promulgated, there were many extremely large classes, but in 1959 the standard maximum number of children in one class was set at 50 under this law. The number was reduced gradually to 45 in 1964. At present, a plan of reducing the number to 40 is being studied. The standard fixed number of educational personnel is decided on the basis of the number of classes to be formed, and one half of the total amount of their salary is defrayed out of the National Treasury in accordance with the provisions of the Law for the National Treasury's Share in the Expenses for Compulsory Education ; the other half is paid out of the tax equalisation grants. In other words the financial resources are secured from the State for the salary of educational personnel up to the standard fixed number.

In regard to school facilities, teaching materials and equipment and apparatus, financial assistance has been extended by the State under the provisions of the Law for the National Treasury's Share in the Expenses for Compulsory Education School Facilities and the Law for the National Treasury's Share in the Expenses for Compulsory Education. As regards teaching materials and school equipment and apparatus, a plan under which 160 000 million Yen should be invested over 10 years started in 1967 and another plan in 1978 investing 460 000 million Yen over 10 years in an effort to enhance these areas.

As stated above, Japan has been making, under well-defined plans, efforts to provide better educational conditions through appropriate placement of educational personnel and the enhancement and improvement of school facilities, teaching materials and school equipment and apparatus for the purpose of maintaining and raising the level of education.

c) <u>Upper Secondary School</u>

In Japan, the elementary and lower secondary schools were institutionalised after the war as schools for compulsory education. Consequently, there has been a remarkable increase in the number of upper secondary schools as the educational institutions succeeding the lower secondary schools. In 1979, those who proceeded to upper secondary schools or technical colleges amounted to 94 per cent of all graduates from lower secondary schools. From the fact that an increasing number of graduates has entered upper secondary school or college, it is believed that the percentage will be higher in the future.

The public upper secondary schools are established by the prefectural authorities and also by the municipal authorities of cities, towns or villages with a population of more than 100 000. The private upper secondary schools are established by juridical educational persons subject to authorisation by the governors of prefectures. There are about 5 000 upper secondary schools throughout the country. Of these 76 per cent are public and 24 per cent private.

In 1961, the Law Concerning the Establishment of Public Upper Secondary Schools and the Standard of Appropriate Placement and Fixed Number of Educational Personnel was passed. The law prescribes the standard for the maximum number of students in each class of upper secondary school and the fixed number of the educational personnel to be employed by the prefectural authorities. The financial resources to pay salaries and allowances of the educational personnel and other expenses are guaranteed by the tax equalisation grants.

For private upper secondary schools, a financial measure was taken in 1970 which aims at ensuring financial resources under the tax equalisation grants system to the prefectural authorities so as to extend financial assistance to juridical educational persons in relation to the operating expenses of the schools. In 1975, the subsidies were first granted out of the National Treasury to the prefectural authorities to contribute to the operating expenses of private upper secondary schools.

The ratio of those who go on to upper secondary schools varies in different prefectures, the highest being 98 per cent and the lowest 86.5 per cent. In recent years, the areas around the large cities have become densely populated, and the establishment of new upper secondary schools and the expansion of the existing ones have become an important problem as the population of the corresponding school age increases. These prefectures have worked out plans for establishing new upper secondary schools and expanding the existing ones which are to be completed in several years. The national authorities have secured the budgetary appropriation on the basis of the information and data from the prefectural authorities and have been granting the subsidies in the amount corresponding to one third of the expenses for the construction of new schools and the expansion of existing ones. In the case of prefectures in which the ratio of the applicants for admission to upper secondary school is lower, efforts are also being made in working out and executing the plan to enable many more of the applicants to be admitted to upper secondary schools.

d) Higher Education

As of 1978, the ratio of those who proceeded to institutions of higher education, mainly universities and junior colleges, had reached 39 per cent. Japan's higher education developed rapidly after World War II, and in the course of development, measures have been taken for an increase in the number of students in the courses of natural science and technology so that the demands derived from the charges in social and industrial structure and employment conditions might be met. In the meantime, so rapid was the expansion of higher education that an imbalance of geographical location of the institutions and the number of professional courses offered by the institutions has appeared, along with the problem of the level of higher education in terms of its quality.

In order to improve such conditions and solve the problems of higher education today, more attention must be paid to a well-balanced development of education and well-defined plans formulated and implemented in the field of higher education.

To that end, a committee on higher education was established in 1972 as an advisory body to the Ministry of Education, Science and Culture. The committee has since been studying a plan for improving and enhancing higher education.

In 1976, the committee submitted to the Minister its report entitled "The Planned Improvement and Enhancement of Higher Education". In the report, an 11-year plan for higher education development is envisaged with 1986 as its target year. The 5-year period of 1976-1980 is set as the initial period, and the report presents the course of action to be followed and the programmes to be carried out in an effort to improve and enhance higher education during that period. The report can be summed up by these two points :

1. It should be recognised that higher education is now provided not only by universities, junior colleges and technical colleges but also by other institutions to which the graduates from upper secondary schools are admitted, including the University of the Air (Higher education courses via broadcasting), university correspondence courses and special training schools. It is necessary, therefore, that positive steps be taken so that higher education can be organised in its totality with greater flexibility and mobility, well co-ordinated vertically and horizontally. It is also suggested that the graduates from junior colleges or technical colleges be guaranteed an opportunity to enter a higher scholastic year of university, that a flexible method of learning offered by the University of the Air be studied and developed, and that the institutions of higher education be further made available to the community by means of re-admission of working adults and adult university extension courses.
2. It is suggested that expansion of the number of universities and junior colleges be permitted as a rule only in cases where it is considered necessary for reducing geographical differences, for

rectifying the disparity of professional courses to be offered and for conducting training of personnel under a well defined plan. It also suggests that the aim of the improvement and expansion of an institution be clarified with reference to the characteristics of the area in which the institution is located, that the concentration of institutions in big cities be restricted, that expansion and improvement of the institutions in local districts be encouraged and finally that the practice of private universities' and junior colleges' admission of students in numbers exceeding the specified limits for incoming students be corrected.

Japan's higher education policies are now being carried out in line with the suggestions made in the report. For example, the demand for medical care has become greater in recent years. In order to meet the demand, it has become necessary to conduct the planned training of medical doctors. A programme to enable every prefecture to have a medical college has been conducted since 1973. Under this plan, 16 medical colleges and departments of medical science of universities have so far been established by the national government.

At the same time, subsidies have been granted to private universities and junior colleges (which account for 70 per cent of all institutions of higher education) since 1970 to be applied to their operating expenses. This is an effort made by the government to raise the quality of the education provided by these institutions. In 1975, the Law for Subsidies for Private School Promotion was enacted so that the effort might be intensified. In addition, it has been decided that the establishment of new private universities or junior colleges should not be authorised until 1981 except in cases of special necessity in order that the subsidies may be made more effective, the quality of those institutions raised and their expansion restricted.

The institutions of higher education will have to provide places for lifelong education as the need for post-secondary education is more generally felt by the people. An effort is thus being made to inaugurate the University of the Air which will offer higher education by means of mass media such as radio and TV and serve as the most important institution of lifelong higher education. Much is expected of this University of the Air.

As regards the programmes for the latter period of 1981-1986, studies are being made by the committee on higher education planning which was established by the University Establishment Council. The committee prepared its interim report in June 1979. What is presented in the report is generally a follow-up of the fundamental course indicated by the plan formulated for the initial period and, for further study of the report, the organisations and the individuals concerned will be called upon to advance their views and comments.

e) <u>Kindergarten Education</u>

After the war, kindergarten was recognised as an educational institution and developed rapidly. The Ministry of Education has attached importance to pre-school education, and in view of the social needs for this level of education, it formulated a 7-year development plan for kindergarten education and has carried it out since 1964 in an effort to enhance and improve the kindergartens. Under this plan, 3 500 kindergartens were established and the proportion of children going to kindergarten increased 20 per cent.

In 1971, the Central Council for Education pointed out in its recommendations to the Minister, the necessity for adopting an effective promotional policy in regard to kindergarten education. Following the recommendations, the Ministry set in 1971 the main principles of a kindergarten education promotion plan which presented the fundamental course of action to be followed in promoting kindergarten education for a period of ten years after 1971. Under the plan, all children of 4 and 5 years of age who wish to enter kindergarten will be enrolled by 1982. (In the plan no reference is made to measures for nursery schools since these schools fall under the jurisdiction of the Ministry of Health and Welfare). The plan is now under way and in order that kindergarten education is developed in line with the plan, the State has been subsidising public and private kindergartens to provide for their facilities. In this way, the establishment and expansion of kindergartens are in progress under a well-defined plan.

f) <u>Special Training School Education</u>

In 1975, the School Education Law was partly amended to provide for the establishment of a new educational institution called the "special training school". Before the special training school was institutionalised by this law, Japan's school education was provided by a stream of schools starting with kindergarten and ending with university and other educational institutions called miscellaneous schools. At the miscellaneous schools, education is conducted with the aim of meeting the community's and the individual's need for knowledge and skills required for work and daily life. Of the miscellaneous schools, the ones conducting education on a particular scale and at an appropriate level have been institutionalised as special training schools so that they may benefit from the promotional measures taken by the government. The schools are classified into three categories according to the entrance requirements : the first offering upper secondary level courses for lower secondary school graduates (upper secondary special training school), the second offering professional courses (Special Training College) and the third offering general education courses for youth and adults, for which there are no entrance requirements. Of these schools, much is expected of the first and the second categories in particular because of the role they play as institutions of upper secondary and higher education in the broad sense of those levels of education.

As of 1978, there were 2 253 special training schools throughout the country with a total enrollment of 407 000. In 1977, a co-operators' conference was set up with the aim of studying what the special training schools should be like in the future, conducting research and studying developmental measures for the schools. In 1979, the conference prepared its report on "the immediate steps to be taken for promotion of the special training school education". In the report, it is suggested that an effort be made to develop the special training schools in such a way as to provide diversified learning opportunities to enable students to select according to their needs. It is necessary from the viewpoint of more flexible and diversified organisation of education as a whole that these schools serve as part of the upper secondary or higher education system to meet the needs of the community in an appropriate manner and make further contributions to lifelong education. The conference made seven propositions regarding the immediate steps to be taken for promotion of special training schools, which include :

i) expansion and improvement of educational programmes and teaching methods,
ii) improvement of teacher quality by means of in-service training and other training programmes,
iii) betterment of students' learning conditions, such as establishment of scholarship systems,
iv) establishment of the practice of sound school management by expanding and increasing the forms of financial assistance to the schools, and
v) establishment and maintenance of contact between the schools and other educational institutions.

g) Social Education

In 1949, the Social Education Law was enacted to encourage social education and extend assistance to it with due respect to the independence of this education, which includes all the organised educational activities for youth and adults other than those conducted on the basis of school curricula. Under the provisions of the law, the Ministry of Education has undertaken the advancement of measures for encouraging and assisting the various types of social education services, to plan the establishment and improvement of places for learning activities such as citizens' public halls, museums and libraries and to train and recruit leaders in the field of social education. Since social conditions have undergone changes as the result of the progress of industrialisation and internationalisation of society, the birth of an information-intensive society, the increase in population in the upper age brackets, the concentration of population in urban areas, the increase in the proportion of nuclear families, the elevation of the level of the nation's educational career and so forth, there is a greater necessity for studying what social education should be like in the future.

In 1971, the Social Education Council submitted to the Minister of Education a recommendation entitled "On Social Education in a Rapidly Changing Society". In the recommendation, reference was made to the role of social education in the future, and propositions were made on the following matters as the fundamental courses of action to be followed in the field of education : reorganisation of social education from the viewpoint of lifelong education, elevation of the level of the programmes and methods of social education and diversification of these programmes and methods, promotion of organisations' and volunteers' activities, expansion and improvement of facilities, and effective organisation of the leader training programmes in the field of education.

Following the recommendation, the Ministry has now been extending financial assistance for the promotion of various learning services organised by local public bodies and encouraging organisations' and volunteers' activities at the local level. In addition, the Ministry established standards for facilities such as citizens' public halls, libraries and museums, and for their management in its effort to enhance and improve those facilities ; at the same time, the Ministry has been trying to train social education leaders and improve their quality.

III. EDUCATIONAL PLANNING IN THE OVERALL NATIONAL DEVELOPMENT PLANNING

In recent years, educational planning has been considered an important component of national overall economic plans and national land development plans. This does not mean that a comprehensive plan covering every aspect of education has been formulated, but it means that the future course of action to be followed in education has been identified within the framework of the overall national development plans.

a) Economic Plans and Educational Planning

Since 1949, when the first national economic plan was formulated, more than 10 economic plans have been made. It was in the 1957 Economic Plan that educational planning was first considered as an integral part of economic planning. In the subsequent plans, the necessity of training scientific and technical personnel was pointed out as being in keeping with the structural changes in Japan's economy as it was supported by technical innovation which entered the stage of high rates of growth. The plans attached importance to the role of education as an agent for developing ability, so that efforts were made to integrate education into the plans.

In very recent years, economic plans began to deal not only with aspects of economic development but also with the development of a welfare society, which opened the way for education to become the component of economic planning.

Under the 7-year Economic and Social Development Plan completed in August 1979, the materialisation of a Japanese-style welfare society had been considered as one of the fundamentals for the management of the economy. It had also indicated that education should be upgraded on grounds that it should meet, in an appropriate manner, the needs of society, due to changes in social and employment structure and further ensure educational and learning opportunities to the people of Japan for fulfilment of their evolving educational and learning needs. As regards social overhead capital, it pointed out that selection of the areas for investment and determination of priorities was required to better meet the nation's need for higher quality and wider variety of education and to contribute to well-balanced national land development. The plan further indicated that expansion and improvement of educational facilities should be given a higher priority in compliance with the demands of the nation. The ratio of the investment in educational facilities to the total amount of public investment for the period planned increased as compared with that under the preceding plan, reaching 8.7 per cent under the new plan.

b) National Land Development Plan and Educational Planning

In 1977, the Third National Overall Land Development Plan was formulated. The primary aims of the plan are to provide the environment necessary for the harmony of man and nature, with a sense of security, health and culture. However, this must be pursued with a due consideration for the limited Japanese land area and natural resources and for preservation of the characteristics of the locality and its historical and traditional culture. The purpose of the plan is to restrict the concentration of population and industries in big cities, and at the same time to promote the development of different regions through appropriate, geographical location of the institutions of higher education such as universities, of the high-level, functions of medical care, of the cultural functions, and of the central administrative functions. The plan has also set as priority targets in education the establishment and improvement of the educational facilities relevant to the lives of the Japanese people, which include kindergartens, elementary, lower and upper secondary schools ; restriction of the establishment of new institutions of higher education such as universities in the existing cities and towns of large urban areas ; encouragement of the relocation of institutions of higher education away from densely located areas ; establishment and expansion of universities characteristic to their locality ; and the establishment and expansion of citizens' public halls, sports facilities, and libraries, etc. which adequately meet the needs peculiar to the area in which they are or will be located.

IV. FUTURE TASKS

In recent years, the viewpoint of lifelong education has been attracting greater attention in Japan. Fulfilment of the goal of lifelong education is a new task that cannot be ignored in the planning of education. The task is to identify the various educational needs which emerge in the course of one's life and to review the various educational functions of the present society so as to remodel them to meet the existing needs. The Central Council for Education is now studying lifelong education as an important subject for Japan's future education. The Council prepared an interim report in June 1979. In the report, the significance of lifelong education is defined, the present state of education in Japan is referred to and, as a matter of urgency in lifelong education, provision of the fundamental conditions for education is emphasized, including effective relations and co-operation among the functions of school education, social education and family education. A new concept of school education to cultivate childrens' and students' abilities required for their lifelong learning is noted along with diversified and flexible higher education, the expansion and betterment of special training schools and the expansion and improvement of social education. Further study will be made by the Council, and it is expected that the Council's recommendations will provide an important guideline by which Japan's educational administration will be implemented under an appropriate and well-prepared plan to meet the needs of the times.

C. NORWAY

I. INTRODUCTION

In Norwegian public administration, planning is not a clearly defined administrative function. It is sometimes associated with the work of specific agencies formally responsible for planning functions (18). However, it is quite clear that work of a similar nature takes place in many parts of public administration not specifically designed as planning units. At the same time, the kind of functions covered by specific planning units in different ministries vary considerably.

As a consequence, a description of planning in Norwegian public administration, and also particularly educational planning, must go beyond the work programmes of units specifically designed as planning agencies. We shall have to look for the performance of functions which may be described as the <u>systematic organisation and structuring of information for political decisions over a substantial period of time</u>. Although rather vague and not easily distinguishable from other administrative functions, such a definition of planning may still be helpful in locating its distribution within public administration. It should be noted that while the political bargaining process preceding final decisions is excluded from our definition, it does include the systematic definition of problem areas to clarify various policy options, although not necessarily leading to one specific suggestion. Thus defined, many planning activities do not necessarily lead to the preparation of specific plans or programmes.

It should be mentioned that even in <u>professional</u> terms, planning is not an easily identifiable field in Norway. Previously, economists were extensively used for specifically defined planning functions. This is still to some extent the case, although professionals from a variety of disciplines have gradually been brought into the field of planning. There is an increasing consensus in most parts of Norwegian administration, that the proper performance of planning functions is typically an interdisciplinary task that cannot be entrusted to any specific profession.

The lack of a special category of personnel specialised in "planning", and the general rejection of the idea that planning should be regarded as a specific profession,

---

18. In such cases, planning functions are often combined with others, e.g. in agencies for "research and planning", "planning and development", etc.

thus makes specific staff qualifications unsuited for the identification of planning functions within the Norwegian public administration.

For education in particular, the recruitment basis for most administrative functions in the schools and at the level of local government is teacher training and experience (19). At the central level, the ministries have traditionally been staffed with a high proportion of lawyers, mixed with specialists from the sector concerned. This pattern is gradually yielding to a much wider recruitment basis in terms of professional background and experience.

Over the last decade, some noticeable <u>changes</u> have occurred <u>in the conception of planning</u> in Norwegian administration. They can possibly be summarised as follows :

- Planning is seen more as an integrated part of a political/administrative process. As a consequence, there is more emphasis on interplay with practitioners, other administrative staff and politicians, and less on the development of exclusive "planning techniques".
- There has been a shift from primarily emphasizing programming and control functions in planning, towards efforts to broaden the information basis for policy decisions and analysing the consequences of alternative policies.
- Typically, sectorial planning activities increasingly cross the traditional sectorial borders bringing a much wider set of data and concerns into sectorial decision-making. This leads to mutual overlap between sectorial planning activities and more extensive inter-sectorial collaboration.
- Increasingly, planning activities draw upon research findings, initiate research and establish broader contacts with the research community. Correspondingly, international experience is increasingly used as supplementary data for national planning activities.
- The tendency towards more genuine interdisciplinarity in planning has loosened the links with specific professional disciplines, and reduced the dependence of planning activities on specific professional methods, approaches and value biases. Planning problems are viewed more in the perspective of those directly concerned by the policies in question, and less from the narrow standpoint of specific fields of research.

---

19. Institutions of higher education are to some extent an exception here.

Such tendencies have occurred at different times and with different strength in the various sectors of public administration. There is thus a wide scope for further developments in such directions, and we may still be only at the beginning of a more fundamental change in the conception of public planning. The paradigm of "scientific management", implanted in public administration from outdated forms of industrial organisation, may still survive in parts of public administration for a long time.

II. AN OVERVIEW OF EDUCATIONAL PLANNING IN NORWAY

In recent years a number of distinct features have marked the development of educational planning in Norway. To some extent, similar developments can be found in other European countries, and in the thinking on educational planning within such international organisations as the OECD and UNESCO. In Norway, however, the changes in planning theory and practice may have gone somewhat further in such directions than in most of the neighbouring countries.

The changes are characterised by the following features :

- a widening of the scope beyond what would normally be thought of as "educational matters" ;
- a broadening of the conceptual framework to include elements of all the social sciences, without any particular relationship to a specific discipline ;
- a profound change in the conception of planning as an administrative function, with far-reaching consequences for its relationships to other political/administrative functions.

The extended scope of educational planning

The widening of scope has partly been directed inwards towards the interior of the "black boxes" of the traditional approaches to educational planning. But there has also been a parallel expansion towards external phenomena beyond the limits of the educational system, whatever system definition one would like to use. We shall sketch the former development first :

Traditionally, educational planning in Norway was an exercise in figures : Numbers of pupils at various levels and in various sectors of the system, and their transitions between levels and sectors. Numbers of teachers with various qualifications attached to those pupil numbers. Other resource inputs in various sectors and the transformation of total resource input into budgetary figures. The main emphasis was on internal consistency control within the system as a whole, and increased predictability of future events.

It may be regarded as a continuation of the same line when efforts gradually turned to similar phenomena at the micro level. Yet the increasingly detailed studies of combinations of resource inputs in concrete school situations, based on extensive cost models, gradually turned away from the emphasis on controlling the future towards stressing the notion of choice. Focusing on the substitutability of input variables made it easier to link in with available pedagogical insights on ends/means-relationships in concrete educational situations. At the same time, it meant a move away from the notion that education primarily aims at the production of a specific set of predefined products, towards a fuller realisation of the multiplicity of educational aims, and not least those which cannot easily be expressed in cognitive terms. A logical consequence of this was the realisation that in education, qualities associated with the process itself are not only important, but sometimes more essential than the final products.

Parallel to this came an increasing concern with organisational structures. Firstly, the size, localisation and distribution of educational facilities. Secondly, the possibilities for institutional integration of such facilities and the new requirements caused by such institutional integration. A more complicated step, although a logical consequence of the former, is an integration of subjects and disciplines within the institutions, breaking the traditional monopolies of the various scientific disciplines and professional groups in defining the "proper" structure of knowledge.

Furthermore, traditional ideas about school organisation had to be looked into. Are we drifting into a situation in which schools copy, in the most undesirable way, structures found in established industrial and bureaucratic organisations ? Are false ideas about "professionalisation" pushing us towards a form of specialisation and compartmentalised expertise within and around the schools, which make sure that no essential decision about a child will be taken by anyone who knows more than a fraction of the child in question ? Are the "general practitioners" of the system, the ordinary teachers, being relegated to the bottom position within a professional pecking order, devoid of any other function than providing a little warmth to the children, and identifying problems for specialist decisions ?

Quite logically, the whole question of decision-making structures within education tends to come to the foreground. What scenarios can be developed for future decision-making structures ? What are the present trends ?

What would we like to see happen ? Should the real power rest with central government politicians and officials, or with an unofficial, but perhaps even more rigid, authority structure of expertise ? Should schools primarily be run by ordinary teachers ? But what about local authorities ? Parents ? Pupils ? What are the consequences of various forms of power sharing for the variety of educational objectives which we tend to put forward in educational pep-talks ?

Thus educational planning in this sense has moved into both the intricacies of pedagogical thinking as well as organisational theories relevant to both educational and other institutions, and the problems of decision-making procedures common to democratic theory in the variety of fields.

The expansion <u>beyond</u> the system of education does not stop at the traditional concern for a mysteriously developing "social demand" for education, or an equally mysterious set of "manpower needs".

The role of education in a policy for social equality necessarily calls for education to be viewed as a sub-system of a much wider societal system, in which any attempt to attribute "causal" responsibility to any particular sub-system must be looked upon with suspicion. The question of educational contributions to social mobility may be of some interest, but is largely irrelevant to the level of inequality in society as a whole. This is much more a question of how education can provide weak groups in society with the means to improve their own relative situation, not by sending a few more of their members to the top of an existing social structure, but by changing that structure itself. Furthermore, the whole issue of equality is as much a question of control over the criteria according to which equality is being measured. Conventional standards of achievement and performance needs re-examination, and possibly reinterpretation in terms of values different from those predominant within a traditional power structure.

When facing such issues, educational planning inevitably penetrates such fields as economic policy, social policy and cultural policy, and has to face such issues as e.g. geographical mobility, professional mobility and social mobility, as well as basic questions relating to formal and informal incentive systems, human preferences and value conflicts.

As the essential nexus between education and work, we have had to look critically at work organisation and the definition of jobs, not only as they are, but as they ought to be. If the aim is to provide satisfactory jobs for everyone who wants it, what would have to characterise such jobs ? It may be a matter of their location, qualification and performance criteria, the possibilities they offer for personal development, social contact and control over one's own work situation, flexibility of working time, etc. Rejecting the idea that the task of education is to adapt individuals to given work situations, we shall have to train people for the kind of work-life we would like see developing in the future - probably the best means of advancing towards such objectives.

An extended concept of education beyond the limits of formal institutions brings educational planning into the enormous complex of learning activities taking place within the family, at work and in leisure time, through informal learning situations and opportunities created by the mass media. Conditions and values controlling such learning situations become essential planning variables and bring especially the field of cultural policies and planning into focus. It is no accident that such new developments in educational planning run parallel to a series of new approaches to cultural policy, based on a wide and more pluralistic definition of culture, and more emphasis on culture as a process in which everyone is involved, as contrasted to the more traditional concept of culture as a set of professional products.

Correspondingly, in the field of research policy, an extended research concept is emerging. A clear recognition of the intrinsic interdependence between the validity and the relevance of research puts more emphasis on research as a process of learning and development in broad social contexts, instead of solely on the highly specialised production of research "products". This provides new opportunities for more basic planning efforts concerned with the interrelationship between education and research, both regarding the use of research as a pedagogical tool, and the more fundamental question of alternative knowledge structures.

This interpenetration of educational planning with planning undertaken in other traditional sectors of public policy, which seems to gain growing momentum in the Norwegian context, is based upon a series of political and institutional preconditions, some of which I shall return to later on. At this stage, I shall only mention the tendency to break away from traditional bureaucratic structures within central government administration. Increasingly, inter-sectorial problems are handled through horizontal collaboration between the different sectors, within ministries as well as between them, without the traditional reference to superior, and usually over-loaded, co-ordinating bodies.

The most recent example of this nature is provided by the preparation for the government's long-term programme 1978-81. In the preparatory stage, more than twenty inter-ministerial bodies have been created, each dealing with a specific inter-sectorial problem. Planning personnel all over government administration are involved in such activities, extending far beyond their own formal sectorial responsibilities. Typical groups for involvement by educational planners deal with such subjects as : "Combining work and education", "Suitable employment for all", "Particular problems of underprivileged groups", "Client producing societal processes", "Local community problems", etc.

It goes without saying that the increasing involvement of educational planning in sectors other than education, as traditionally defined, also implies a reciprocal involvement by planners from other sectors in educational matters. Economic and social planners cannot neglect educational factors, nor can those involved in cultural planning or research policy. Yet, the level of sophistication achieved within educational planning, which in many respects far exceeds that of e.g. traditional economic planning, has put the former in a position to contribute importantly to this general development in planning theory and practice within the central government.

Expanding the conceptual framework of educational planning

Already the sketchy description above of the increasing scope of educational planning in Norway makes it obvious that a major extension is needed in the number of variables brought into the formal and informal planning models applied, as compared to more conventional planning approaches. It is interesting to note, however, that this would also be the case, and nearly to the same extent, if a more comprehensive planning approach had been applied solely to the educational sector as conventionally defined. The extension beyond such sectorial limits does not, in fact, add major new requirements in terms of conceptual tools. It rather serves to provide a more generalised context for the application of such tools within the educational sector as such.

It should also be fairly self-evident that no single scientific discipline can provide an adequate conceptual apparatus for such a comprehensive approach to planning issues. Typically, we have moved from an emphasis upon economic theory and techniques towards much more extensive use of sociological approaches. Increasingly elements of pedagogical theory and organisation theory have been adopted, as well as aspects of psychological thinking. Some modern orientations within political science have proved increasingly useful, as have certain theories and procedures within social anthropology. More traditional auxiliary disciplines such as social geography and technology still have something to offer, and we have tentatively played around with elements of systems analysis and futurology, admittedly with increasing doubts about their usefulness. Statistics keeps, of course, its position as a basic tool, and demography offers some useful insights.

It is interesting to note that as the approaches to planning become more comprehensive, many of the established research models and techniques within the traditional disciplines become less appropriate, and even directly useless. Examples can be found from many disciplines, and I shall only mention a few.

Traditional manpower forecasting tends to become relatively uninteresting, not because we are not concerned with the interplay between education and work, but because the most essential features of the problem escape available analytical techniques.

In view of the multiplicity of objectives, and the systematic interdependence between a wide set of variables, most of the techniques offered by economists and systems analysts for identifying "optimal" solutions have only limited value. This certainly applies to the PPBS-approach, with its unrealistic assumptions about the possibility of identifying programmes with one-dimensional goal structures, and its emphasis on largely irrelevant effectivity measures. The same applies, of course, to related ideas about "management by objectives", etc.

Cost models are extensively used, also as a simulation device relating to concrete decisions. More elaborate techniques of cost-benefit analysis have not, however, proved useful in most cases ; partly due to the difficulties of benefit identification, and the implicit value-judgements built into the techniques of weighing. More fundamentally, the neglect of process qualities in favour of "delivered products" often makes such forms of analysis more misleading than useful.

We have found work on social indicators useful to illustrate the multiplicity of decision consequences, far beyond any stated objectives. Most of the work done, however, suffers from the same bias towards final products as the cost-benefit analysis, and implicit and explicit attempts on weighing indicators face the same fundamental problems as those connected with cost-benefit analysis.

We can make only very limited use of human capital models and of more specific educational "production functions". In general, the consistent bias of economic theory towards economic values, as defined by market mechanisms, makes its contributions to a more comprehensive form of planning relatively limited. The stringent econometric training of Norwegian economists still make them valuable partners in planning activities, and it may still be worthwhile exploring the possibilities of expanding economic theory to cope with new sets of problems. Yet, at the present stage the main problem appears to be to break away from the narrowness of traditional economic models for planning.

Sociological theories on professional and institutional roles have proved very useful, and theories on inter-human relationships, bordering on social psychology, e.g. in the field of guidance theory and client relationships, play an important role for our thinking. As indicated above, we have more problems with the sociological tradition of defining societal equality primarily in terms of individual differences and mobility. It appears that a more historically oriented form of sociology could have more to offer in this context. Furthermore, the question of predominance of specific group values, defining "legitimate" criteria for equality, appears to escape many of the more empirical approaches by sociologists.

In political science and organisational theory, we have found many elements of modern decision-making theory essential for the understanding of key issues in educational planning. However, we cannot use theories implicitly based on perfect harmony models, nor on absolute conflict models. Incidentally, theories drawn from peace and conflict research have provided valuable insights in this context.

Differential psychology and testing theory have less to offer when selection according to given criteria is not a prime objective of a planning operation. When questions are raised about the implicit values built into discipline-based curricula, and about the "objectivity" of the traditional power-hierarchy within the individual disciplines, many current approaches to curriculum work become less relevant. The notion that one can establish globally, or even nationally, valid criteria for performance within different subjects becomes dubious and tends to reduce our interest in comparative exercises in this field. We try instead to draw more upon experience from clinical psychology and developmental psychology, especially the regrettably rare theories which bring peer interaction into focus.

Systems analysis theory may serve as a valuable reminder of the lack of subsystem autonomy. Yet, most formal techniques in this field disregard the fact that individual humans are in themselves partly autonomous and dynamic systems, influencing their environment as well as being formed by it. Biologically oriented systems analysis tries to take this into account, yet the predominant orientation in this field has not succeeded till now. Quite apart from this, our general experience is that substance knowledge in a field provides a better basis for an approach to more general planning issues than the detailed knowledge of specific generalised techniques.

We have been rather reluctant to make extensive use of future forecasting. Seeing planning as an important element in a change process, we find more or less camouflaged trend prolongations of limited interest. Largely, consensus seeking techniques of the delphi-kind appears to have strong built-in elitist biases, though we follow with some interest experiments in future choice exercises for ordinary individuals. Scenario writing has been tentatively used by us, though we are fully aware of the nearly unlimited manipulatory possibilities implied in such techniques, which basically rest upon rather doubtful assumptions about complementarity or alternativity between social phenomena. However, we still have some confidence in the use of alternative future scenarios as a pedagogical tool.

As indicated by this extremely sketchy summary, we have grown increasingly sceptical about highly formalised planning models and techniques. When we use models, we try to make them simple enough for everyone concerned to master not only their use, but also as far as possible their implications. A "client" shall have the full opportunity to take part in a discussion not only on the outcome of a model operation, but on the shape of the model itself and its appropriateness to the problem at hand.

Though still drawing extensively on more conventional national and international research, we make extensive use of relatively uncontrolled practical experiments, in which a variety of variables change at the same time. Various forms of action research also prove useful in identifying problems and initiating open-ended processes, the outcome of which will be determined by the "clients" themselves. We have moved a certain distance away from the notion that research is something which can only be performed in universities and other specialised research institutions.

We do not make extensive use of formal evaluation techniques, although we try to establish fairly extensive systems of more "open-ended" feed-back from various experiments and reforms.

An essential element in our concept of planning is that the extensive informal system of information, feeding information back to decision makers through the political system in the widest possible sense, should not be substituted for by highly structured, internal information systems based on the value premises of the various professional groups involved. Even more formal evaluation exercises should thus use criteria close to those applied and understood within the informal information system. We think it essential that all those concerned should be in a position to evaluate on their own premises the more formal evaluation criteria used.

It goes without saying that this excludes most of the formal measures of "efficiency" often applied in planning contexts. It also excludes the notion that any genuine form of "accountability" can be based on specific professional value premises.

Educational planning as a political/administrative function

Most of the developments and assessments indicated above stem from a definition of the planning function which in the Norwegian context has emerged most clearly in the educational sector, but which seems gradually to spread also to other sectors.

At the level of central government, we would not like planning to fall into the traditional bureaucratic pattern of exclusive responsibilities. An agency "responsible" for planning should thus not monopolise something called the planning function, but should assist in the performance of such a function within all parts of the organisation. Decisions as to what is the "right" kind of planning rest with the operational units, and cannot be over-ruled by the planning unit, which systematically refrains from appealing conflicts on such issues to the superior co-ordinating body (in this case the Minister). The specific task of a planning unit can thus be described as initiating and feeding intellectual input into processes within other units, the outcome of which will be determined by the "clients".

Interestingly enough, 10 years of experience with such horizontal operations within still basically hierarchical government structures have proved to function surprisingly well. This is for instance indicated by the fact that other units still invite the planning unit to undertake more work than it can possibly accomplish.

The planning unit is a key contact point within the Ministry for relations to other ministries and to external research. However, even in this case, the unit's task is primarily to engage the rest of the Ministry in such contacts, establishing the widest possible network of relationships for the Ministry as a whole.

Basically, this approach to planning becomes a pedagogical function, aiming at the continuous stimulation of learning processes within the organisation as a whole. Increasingly, as indicated above, such learning processes are also developing externally, across the traditional governmental sectors.

Parallel to those developments at the central level runs a systematic decentralisation of decisions to political bodies at the local levels, to institutions and to different groups within institutions. The key function of central government in this context is not so much to give directions as to regulate the relative influence of the various groups involved, and gradually to develop genuine planning functions within each of these groups. This clearly increases the need for informative instruments by central government, as well as the need for measures which may build up the strength of the weakest partners in the educational power game. Recently, the move has been towards strengthening the position of local government, individual teachers and students. The approach is largely experimental, and probably no one sees the final outcome of the change processes initiated this way.

This attempt to stimulate the learning capability of the system as a whole is not based on the assumption that an educational system can realistically be described by a harmony model. There are genuine conflicts of interest which cannot be solved simply by talking together around a table. Conflicts often block development, and the process of learning to handle such problems is in many cases a slow one. Planning activities at various levels may sometimes help to identify feasible compromises, but may also create new imbalances. Central planning activities have an important information function in this context, and are thus not only directed towards an internal learning process within the central ministry, but towards the total educational system, as well as other systems surrounding it.

We are certainly only in an early stage of the development of a comprehensive approach to educational planning, based on the notion that planning is primarily a pedagogical instrument. We know the general rules of the game, that our task is not to solve other people's problems for them, but to assist them in finding their own solutions, and that this applies to educational decision makers at all levels, from ministers of education to individual pupils and parents. The practical application of such rules are, of course, fraught with difficulties in a country where social and geographical inequality still exist, hierarchical organisation patterns still prevail, and with new aspiring centres of technocratic and meritocratic power constantly emerging. Till now, however, it has proved an extremely rewarding experience, pointing towards planning procedures that may open up for far-reaching developments in many fields, and a development of planning theory away from its traditional close association with specific professional values and the notion of centralised, hierarchical organisations.

III. ORGANISATION AND STRUCTURE OF EDUCATIONAL PLANNING

Planning activities can be found at all levels within the educational system, from the individual pupil and student to the background work for the government's long-term plan. In the following, we shall try to indicate some important planning activities, reflecting at the same time the actual - not necessarily the formal - structure of decision-making within education in Norway.

The school level

Important decisions are taken by pupils, students and parents in terms of educational choices at various levels, and ways of adapting to school requirements, in curricular as well as other respects. Often, elements of long-term planning of individual goal attainment and careers underlie such decisions. They are often guided by counselling services offered at various stages within or connected to the schools, although our guidance principles do not permit "societal" concerns to overrule individual preferences. In spite of the fairly extensive availability of formal counselling services, research evidence indicates that the predominant influence on actual choices comes from informal guidance through the family peer groups, mass media, etc.

The individual teacher has considerable freedom of choice in terms of methods of teaching, materials to be used and the progression of teaching within his subjects. In planning such activities, he is supposed to include the pupils, especially at the higher levels, and to some extent also the parents. He has to co-ordinate his activities with other teachers dealing with the same class. When team teaching is the predominant form, such planning activities must be undertaken in common by the team.

Formal bodies more or less involved in such planning operations are the pupils' councils at the class level and their representatives, meetings of parents, the teachers' council, the principal and other administrative officials, and the general collaboration committee for the school, consisting of representatives of teachers, parents and pupils.

The school as a unit must plan for accommodation of pupils in the years ahead, their organisation in groups, the allocation of teachers to various tasks and the time schedule, social and extra-curricular activities, the use of available resources beyond minimum requirements for ordinary teaching tasks, etc.

Of special importance is the question of resource allocation. In the upper level of compulsory education, ordinary teaching in full class requires for instance 30 "hours" of teaching per week. The school has, however, 47 1/2 teacher "hours" at disposal for each class. The rest, nearly 60 per cent above the necessary minimum, can be used for remedial teaching, for splitting up the classes in smaller units, for two teachers operating simultaneously in the class, and in a variety of other ways. Planning the utilisation of available resources in terms of teacher time is thus an essential element of school administration.

It should also be mentioned that each school has at its disposal one full week of teacher time per year, which can be used for planning purposes, developmental tasks, internal retraining, etc. This, too, has to be planned far in advance.

Planning also includes the supply of voluntary subjects in the upper stages of compulsory education, including options to spend part of the time in a work situation outside school. In upper secondary and higher education the planning of courses to be offered, including possible new ones, is time-consuming and must be done well ahead of actual implementation, including as it does also questions of facilities, new staff and possibly curricular development.

The prime responsibility for such planning tasks rests with the principal and other administrative officials, in collaboration with the teachers' council and the general collaboration committee. Initiatives may come from many sources, but the concrete planning work rests mainly with the institutional administration.

The local authorities

The political body responsible for compulsory education in Norway is the commune. The communal council is an elected body with its own administration, responsible for a variety of functions. Budget-wise, educational tasks claim on the average about 20 per cent of the budget of a commune. There are about 450 communes in Norway, ranging in size from about 1 000 to nearly 500 000 inhabitants, the average being about 10 000.

The commune's school board is composed of representatives from various political parties in proportion to their strength, as reflected in the composition of the elected commune council. Among its prime planning tasks is the location, design and construction of school buildings, the recruitment of teachers with an appropriate mix of skills, the allocation of teaching resources beyond the minimum requirements set by central government rules, and of other resources such as equipment, materials, etc. Furthermore, the school board plans and organises the transport of school children, and where necessary, their accommodation. It develops and runs the commune's teacher support centre and plans in-service training activities for the teachers within the commune. Planning the institutional and individual treatment of handicapped children is also one of its functions. Local development work and school experiments are planned, often in collaboration with national advisory bodies.

The school board has its own administration and often a wide variety of sub-committees as instruments for such planning tasks. They are performed within the limits set by central authorities in certain areas, such as minimum requirements for school buildings, nationally negotiated salaries and working conditions for teachers, centrally prepared curriculum guidelines, centrally regulated teaching hours, arrangements for the sharing of financial responsibilities with the central government, etc.

The school board is in most respects subordinate to the commune council, which determines budget limits and discusses other important issues relating to the local school system along with other local problems. Plans for the development of the local school system have to be co-ordinated with more general plans for the development of the commune, its population structure, communications, economic development, land use, social services, cultural activities, etc. Local school planning at the commune level is thus closely related to other sectorial planning. In particular, the development of facilities for sports, libraries and the performing arts are closely co-ordinated with the planning of school facilities. Transportation schemes for pupils often constitute an essential element in the planning of the local transportation system, etc.

Norwegian upper secondary education is the responsibility of the county, a political body at the intermediate level structured roughly as a commune. There are nineteen counties in all, ranging from about 100 000 to about 500 000 inhabitants, averaging about 200 000. The county school board is composed of representatives of political parties in the same proportion as the elected county council.

The county school board has full responsibility for planning the upper secondary system, including the localisation and dimensioning of school units, the construction of school buildings, the theoretical and practical courses to be offered, and staff to be recruited. By and large, the planning functions of the county school board run parallel to the functions of the school board of the commune. The counties also have financial responsibilities shared with central government. The educational plans developed by the communes are intergrated parts of the more general county plans. They are communicated to central government, but the educational development plans do not depend on the central government's approval.

The county school board have their own administration, which forms a part of the general county administration. A variety of permanent or ad hoc sub-committees deal with various planning issues related to upper secondary education.

The central government level

The responsibilities of the central government for educational matters vary somewhat for the different parts of the educational system. A common task for all central planning activities, however, is to contribute to the continuous development and revision of legal, financial and informative policy instruments available to the central government, initiation and support of experimentation and innovation, and the provision of relevant information to the system as a whole.

The role of the central government in relation to <u>primary and secondary education</u> is sufficiently similar to be dealt with simultaneously : Central government planning in this area follows closely the development in pupil numbers and pupil flows, the provision of teachers and other resources, and the institutional cost structure as it relates to the type and size of institution. Alternative models for resource allocation and distribution according to types of institutions, local communities and geographical areas are closely examined.

Current organisational structures are under constant review, including the organisation of teaching itself. A multitude of experiments with alternative organisational forms are encouraged and studied.

The functioning of the system in relation to the various geographical areas, different types of local community, pupils from different social backgrounds, the two sexes, ethnographic and cultural minorities, etc. are closely followed, and new means of achieving central policy goals in these areas are closely watched.

The decision-making structure within the education system, as well as the more informal power structure underlying it, has been subject to major changes in recent years. The consequences of such changes are examined as a basis for possible future policy initiatives.

The forms of financing and their effects on a variety of policy goals are studied, and alternative uses of financial instruments examined. Resource standards are continuously evaluated and the implications of changes in the salary structures for school personnel and their working conditions are worked out.

Teacher demand and supply are examined under a variety of alternative assumptions, bringing out the implications of alternative future policies. Special measures related to geographical areas or types of institutions with problems of teacher recruitment have been subject to extensive studies.

A general framework and indicative guidelines for curricula in the different parts of the system have been developed, and are subject to regular revision at intervals. Continuous developmental work is undertaken, accompanied by extensive experimental activities, centrally initiated or generated at the local or institutional level.

Interaction between the school system and other sectors is extensively studied. As examples may be mentioned a variety of interactions between the school system and work-life, relations between the school and its local community, interaction between the school and social services, interplay between education and cultural activities, the school as an agent for general, local and regional development, the role of education in general youth policies, education and employment, etc.

Central planning activities draw heavily on extensive programmes of experimentation and developmental work, as well as on research activities and experience from other countries. The aim is not only to provide a better basis for central decision-making, but at least as much to provide the educational system as a whole, and the general public, with background material for educationally relevant decision-making at all levels of the system. As an example might be mentioned the central collection, structuring and dissemination of information on school building, as a support activity for decisions taken at the local level.

In performing such planning tasks the ministry can rely on <u>advisory councils</u> with their own permanent staff, such as the Council for Compulsory Education, the Council for Continued Education (the upper secondary level) and the Council for Innovation in Schools. Within the ministry, a small planning department is responsible for overall planning tasks in relation to the education system, as well as to other parts of the ministry. In addition, the operational departments also have a significant planning capacity, often used in collaboration with the planning department.

Extensive use is also made of <u>ad hoc committees</u> and commissions, studying specific problems and making proposals for future actions. Such committees have their own ad hoc secretariat facilities, but they are also often assisted by the more permanent bodies mentioned. The committees are usually composed of representatives from various interest groups, as well as independent experts. Occasionally, a significant proportion of the members are politicians, often drawn from parliament. In terms of major reform politics, ad hoc committees are probably the most important planning instruments in Norwegian public administration.

Due to the extensive decentralisation of planning and other political/administrative tasks to local authorities, the central Ministry of Education and its affiliated advisory bodies have a relatively limited permanent staff, about 300 in all. It should be remembered that the staff does not only handle educational policy matters, but is also responsible for cultural policy, research policy, youth policy and ecclesiastical affairs.

Due to an extensive practice of external consultation, planning activities of non-governmental organisations may play an important role in the total policy-making process. Particularly important in the field of education are the teachers' unions, the trade unions, the employers association and various professional associations. Historically, the research councils have played a certain role in educational planning, particularly the councils for science and technology and for agricultural research. In this context, the councils may be said to act partly as pressure groups for their specific educational interests, mostly related to higher education.

In the field of higher education, most of the planning tasks mentioned above do also apply. In addition, the ministry has the direct responsibility for planning the location and planning of the total higher education system, including the establishment of new institutions and new fields of study. Resource allocation between institutions is an essential part of central higher education policy, including the allocation of staff resources. Regional considerations come strongly into the picture, as well as the interplay between higher education and research. Organisational structures and the forms of institutional collaboration are important elements.

Manpower considerations, based on forecasts of assumed manpower needs, have not played a dominant role in higher education planning in Norway. In certain fields, however, concern for the labour market situation within specific professions does influence the provision of institutional facilities and conflict with the demand for places by aspiring students.

There is no general advisory body for higher education affiliated to the ministry, although the establishment of such a body is under discussion. Specialised advisory bodies exist in the fields of teacher training, social works training and a few others. In addition, a conference of university principals often acts in an advisory function to the government, and has developed a certain planning capacity.

The trend in recent years has been towards moving more and more decisions on higher education policy from the ministry to the institutions. This is particularly the case for internal resource allocation, planning for building and equipment and developmental work. The responsibility for curricula has always rested with the institutions. Within the ministry, the main emphasis of its planning work is on the budgetary framework, overall design, institutional localisation and general structural issues.

As to adult education, most of its extensive activities (20) are entrusted to voluntary organisations, often affiliated to political or ideal organisations of a countrywide coverage, such as political parties, religious organisations, sports organisations, cultural associations, etc. Although most of the activities are financed by central and local government, the organisations have full freedom in planning their own activities. Within the ministry, and to some extent also in the counties and the communes, planning activities are mainly concerned with ensuring that adult education activities are oriented towards groups with special needs, such as those with little initial education, women, and people in outlying areas. The present organisational structure of adult education in Norway, with its relatively limited basis in the regular educational institutions, seems to serve many of the purposes of adult education rather well. It does, however, limit the availability to the central government of policy instruments aimed at pursuing specific policy objectives.

Overall educational planning activities, as well as extensive support activities to planning undertaken in other parts of the ministry, rests with the ministry's Department of Research and Planning. Its planning priorities and its mode of operation may be said to have an important impact on educational planning activities in general, as described in detail in the previous section II.

Beyond the Ministry of Education, the Ministry of Finance has a general responsibility for overall planning in Norway, specifically in the preparation of the government's 4-year plans. Education has traditionally played an important part in such overall planning since the early 1950s, and regular and close forms of collaboration have been developed between the planning department of the Ministry of Education and the corresponding department in the Ministry of Finance.

Correspondingly, the Ministry of Environment has general responsibility at the central level for regional and local planning. The planning department of the Ministry of Education actively participate with the advisory body for the Ministry of Environment in their general planning responsibilities.

In recent years, problems relating to full employment, and youth employment in particular, has led to the establishment of a specific body for collaboration between the ministries of education, manpower and social affairs, with its secretariat located in the planning department of the Ministry of Education. This body has taken a number of

---

20. One in four adult Norwegians take part in at least one adult education course annually.

initiatives relating to the "youth guarantee" which ensures all youngsters below 20 years of age the right to education or work. It also systematically works through other issues generated by the interface between school and work-life.

An essential background for planning activities in all fields is the work of the Central Bureau of Statistics, which draws together most public statistical work in Norway. The development of educational statistics, as well as statistics in the cultural field, is subject to close and continuous collaboration between the bureau and the department of planning in the Ministry of Education.

Finally, it should be mentioned that the special committee on educational affairs within Parliament has some administrative capacity, permitting an independent role in the planning of essential policy decisions in this field.

IV. SOME AREAS OF SPECIAL CONCERN

As indicated above, Norwegian planning activities in the field of education take place in a large number of central and local settings, and cover an extremely wide spectrum of concerns. In the following, we shall only mention a few of the main current issues, with a certain focus on central planning activities.

In <u>compulsory education</u> a major issue in recent years has been the integration of handicapped children into regular educational institutions. Planning the integration of individual children has engaged parents, teachers and fellow pupils at the school level, as well as the local support centre and the local school board. The notion that such integration may require more change in the school environment than in the pupil himself, calls for rather complex strategies. At the central level, the corresponding planning issues are related to the forms of financial transfers, and the arrangements whereby additional resources follow the handicapped child into whatever institution is found to be most suitable for him. In addition, changes in general regulations, teacher training arrangements, etc. have needed careful examination.

In more general terms, the questions related to differentiated teaching of classes of mixed ability following the abolishment of formal streaming, have called for extensive changes in the approach to planning at the classroom and school level. The changes are followed centrally with the aim of developing appropriate teaching materials, teacher training and formal regulations.

Major changes are being discussed in the financial relationships between central government and local government aiming at more decentralisation in the allocation of public resources. In the school sector a variety of systems for financial transfers are being studied in order to estimate their impact on various policy goals, in particular the current system of positive discrimination according to geographical criteria and school size. This is a field of close collaboration between the planning department in the Ministry of Education and the Ministries of Finance and Local Government.

Work experience as an optional subject for pupils in the upper stages of a compulsory system has developed through a series of local experiments. On the basis of experience gained, such options are now generalised for all schools. This requires extensive local planning activities in order to obtain possibilities for practice in real work situations and ensuring genuine educational value of such work experience, as well as the active utilisation within schools of the experience gained by many of the pupils. At the central level, the forms of such options have to be brought within a common general framework, problems have to be sorted out with the teacher organisations, the trade unions and the employer's association, evaluation problems must be considered, etc. At the same time, this way of utilising educational resources in work life must be seen in relation to the use of work experience in post-compulsory education as well as the need to provide work for unemployed youth.

In upper secondary education, extensive planning efforts, both at the central and local level, go into the implementation of the principle of the right to three years education at this level for everyone. The expansion of facilities should at the same time satisfy the actual demand for the variety of courses offered, without getting out of touch with expected employment possibilities in the long run. At the same time, the educational content of both theoretical and practical streams are under continuous revision, bringing together specialised vocational courses in broader fields of vocational preparation, and integrating elements of vocational training with more theoretical directions. This requires extensive developmental work at the central level combined with a multitude of local experiments and major efforts to adapt the new structures in individual schools.

The "youth guarantee" requires close and continuous collaboration between educational and manpower authorities, both at the central and local level, in order to keep track of their movement between school and work. Centrally, the main efforts are on detailed statistical information, broken down geographically, forms of financial support for appropriate local solutions and corresponding modifications of existing regulations. Locally it is often a matter of finding concrete solutions to individual cases, requiring flexibility and innovative thinking.

As a means of opening up access to education at the post-compulsory and higher levels, and also as a step on the road to a more extensive system of recurrent education, emphasis is put on work experience as a criterion for access. Actual admission practices are examined, and alternative practices and their consequences are tried out.

In <u>higher education</u>, the gradual development of a system of regional colleges with close links with county authorities has been pursued for a number of years. Regional boards gradually take over the planning of the further development of this institutional system, but the individual institutions are eagerly planning their own futures, while central authorities try to find a proper framework for the general developments in this field. Pressures from institutions and political and professional organisations call for extensive examination of proposals for the expansion of various sectors within higher education. Structural changes in the economy are often behind such pressures, as well as strongly organised professional interests. Proposed expansion and structural changes must be examined in order to maintain an overall comprehensive policy for the development of higher education.

Although there is no reason to believe that "over-education" is a typical phenomenon in Norwegian higher education, there is continuous need to examine the way in which grades and certificates are being used to reinforce professional monopolies in various fields. A programme is being developed in order to control the use of formal competence requirements in various parts of professional life, in order to avoid a too rigid and meritocratically oriented division of functions. The role of the school as a prime supply mechanism for social positions is being modified, a process which requires careful long-term planning and strategy development.

In the field of <u>adult education</u>, a main problem is the development of policy instruments which can secure a socially desirable distribution of the resources available, while at the same time maintaining the present autonomy of the various adult education organisations. The main effort goes into modifying and refining the system of financial support to the organisations.

A general problem, relevant to the whole field of education, is the decision-making structure within the system. In formal terms, recent trends have been towards decentralisation of decisions, although more to the individual institutions than to the local authorities. This in itself creates problems, as well as the informal power structure represented by teacher organisations and local power groups. The functioning of the total system in such terms has been examined, and various major alternatives for future development have been studied in order to predict their consequences for the running of the system as a whole. Legal, financial and informative instruments are studied in this context and their effects on various objectives are evaluated.

Finally it should be mentioned that the main directions of research efforts in the field of education are under continuous debate, and attempts are made to outline a general strategy for the further development of this field. Special emphasis is put on moving research closer to practice, and on obtaining a wider distribution of research activities beyond the limits of the traditional research institutions. Inter-disciplinary approaches are encouraged, as well as unorthodox combinations of research, experimentation and developmental work. Research activities are increasingly seen in the light of the general development of professional competence within the system as a whole.

The main concerns of educational planning are changing over time, partly dictated by new emerging needs, and partly by new policy priorities. In principle, planning activities should identify problems which have not yet become acute at the policy level, and prepare the ground for a rational and balanced handling of such problems. They should gradually increase the general understanding within the educational system as a whole of how the system functions, and how it relates to the world beyond education. They must be seen as part of a general learning process, not only aiming at central decision makers, but at those responsible for decisions at all levels within the system. Only in such terms can the effect of the total planning efforts be judged in the long run.

Part Three

THE FUTURE OF EDUCATIONAL
       POLICY/PLANNING

Chapter 6

LONG-RANGE EDUCATIONAL POLICY PLANNING PERSPECTIVES IN OECD COUNTRIES : A REVIEW OF ISSUES AND POLICY PROPOSALS

by

J. Tinbergen and G. Psacharopoulos

I. INTRODUCTION

Educational systems throughout the world are at present in a state of flux. This is especially true in advanced industrial countries where the combination of high social demand for education, youth unemployment and budgetary restrictions have produced much uncertainty about basic factors which affect the development of educational systems. There certainly does not exist a consensus on how to plan an educational system and for what purpose (1).

The aim of this paper is to discuss a set of key factors that are likely to affect the development of education systems in OECD countries in the decades to come. It is our belief that knowledge - even in an imperfect way - of the likely movement of factors affecting school systems will help educational policy planning discussions for adaptation and change. Our discussion therefore is only an attempt to identify the main forces likely to determine the process of education in OECD countries in the medium term and up to the end of this century. To that end we also attempt to indicate the new kind of research needed to supplement the insufficient knowledge at our disposal. The report is not the final word in this respect. It is only meant to provide a broad picture of likely developments

---

1. For excellent within-single-country discussions, however, see Dutch Ministry of Education and Science, Contours of a Future Education System in the Netherlands, 1975, and Danish Ministry of Education, U-90 : Danish Educational Planning and Policy in a Social Context at the end of the 20th Century, 1978.

and a framework for which more country specific analyses could be prepared.

The future of education, at least in the medium term, depends on the reactions of all involved in it to the challenges of the recent past and on the sensitivity of those responsible for policy specific action.

This is an extremely complex and dynamic social process. Understanding it involves the contribution of a variety of disciplines beyond education per se. Analyses based on sociology, psychology, economics, demography, politics and administration will be indispensable. In this respect, the present report may appear to be unbalanced, relying more on economic thinking. This does not only reflect the authors' background but also an implicit purpose of the report. The reader, however, should not lose sight of the interdisciplinarity involved. The education process is a part of a much more general social process where all relationships are in a state of continuous transformation. The associated educational changes reflect, therefore, the many interdependencies between the educational system and the rest of society. As an example of the educational "problématique" today one may cite what the Club of Rome has called the "problematique of the predicament of mankind (2)". The existing educational systems were structured many centuries ago to meet past societal needs. But how adequate are these systems today to respond to new demands stemming from our evolving societies ? The real question might be more profound than, for example, whether to have comprehensive schools or not.

Synopsis of the main argument

Given the complexity of educational planning one must first attempt a disaggregation for analytical purposes. The procedure which has been adopted in this report is to discuss the four basic elements of the following two-by-two matrix :

Educational Demand Side	Educational Supply Side
Individuals or Families	Private schools (including industries)
Productive system - private - public	Public schools

---

2. See, for instance, D.H. Meadows, D.L. Meadows et al., The Limits to Growth, New York, 1972, Universe Books, p. 10.

The Government's regulative role is manifested both on the educational demand side through, for example, its educational policies and hiring for the civil service, and on the educational supply side by determining the number of available public school places and controlling the expansion of the private school sector.

The recent experience of educational systems in the OECD countries as well as throughout the world has been that of crisis. This phenomenon is attributed mostly to :

a) unfavourable macro-economic conditions and the resulting financial squeeze
b) demographic developments seriously affecting the school-entering cohorts
c) changing attitudes and increasing scepticism towards education as a whole.

The immediate future is likely to be dominated by these recent trends, unless of course a drastically changed political will disrupts this trend.

In the more distant future, however, the eventual state of educational systems in OECD countries will be the result of the interplay between the individual demand for education and the Government's decision on how much of the demand to accommodate and how. The manpower dimension of demand is a factor affecting both pupils' and the Governments' decisions.

Although the manpower factor is important, it would be myopic to attempt at any time to equate, quantitatively and qualitatively, educational supply to manpower demand. It is not very far-fetched to suppose that societies of the future might accept as entirely meaningful the concept of an educated (rather than 'over-educated') taxi-driver or agricultural worker. Education as a value in itself might be increasingly accepted for the emerging and growing group of the retired population. The old notion of everyone getting as much education (quantitatively and qualitatively) as he or she likes is still alive, although it creates budgetary problems. It also raises the issue of the political acceptability of reallocating scarce public resources to social services or alternatively the political acceptability of expanding the private school sector to resolve financial problems. It is evident that budgetary constraints will ultimately determine the nature of equilibrium between educational supply and demand. It remains to be seen, however, what the exact nature of this equilibrium will be. Will the "regulators" of the educational systems accept the idea of an "educated taxi-driver" or will they continue to fear that increased education will alter his attitudes and make him aspire to a different occupation, thus creating pressure on the labour market or increasing the level of graduate unemployment ?

On the other hand, would graduates be convinced that societies are not obliged any more to guarantee to all a fixed occupation corresponding to the education they have received ? The possible de-linking between education and work might be one of the main elements of the "problématique" on both sides of society and their respective educational policies in the future.

Given the present state of our knowledge it is very difficult to formulate specific predictions about the final result of the interplay between the many factors and actors involved in the change process discussed in this paper. Perhaps the only firm conclusion which could be formulated is that the eventual outcome will depend heavily upon the political will of the Government.

On a more speculative basis, however, it is possible to formulate a series of probable future tendencies as working hypotheses around which discussion of the future could be organised. Thus one may anticipate a gradual institutional change from learning in schools towards learning within the firm, especially regarding the provision of vocational skills. This probable development should be welcomed on the grounds of technological adaptation and on the grounds that it represents a shift of finance from the individual and family towards the employing firm.

A related institutional change one may anticipate is in the content of the curriculum. Future curricula at all educational levels might very well be more concerned with "learning why" than "learning how".

Examination of several cohort demographic projections reveals the upswings and downswings an educational system can go through ; hence the need for planning for flexibility and adaptation. OECD countries in the last quarter of this century are not likely to share a common demographic trend. There exist substantial differences between countries and over time within countries. However, all trends generally indicate decreased enrolments relative to the boom period of the sixties, at least in the medium term.

Examination of labour force participation ratios of selected population groups leads to a rather confident prediction of a dramatic increase in the number of women in the labour market. This links to the provision of schooling that caters for traditionally female occupations and raises issues about the education of children of working mothers.

Aggregate enrolment projections indicate negative or modest post-secondary increases in Europe and North America and moderate increases in Japan, Australia and New Zealand. The enrolment time trends within individual countries exhibit swings according to the changing size of demographic cohorts.

The extent to which educated population groups will find themselves in the labour force and the effort they will make to do so, depends upon the supply elasticity. Although very divergent estimates are found in the literature, the increased participation of married women seems to be a firm prediction. Turning to the capacity of the state school systems in Member countries, one may predict that it will get tighter, at least in the medium term. A large part of the increased cost of schooling might have to be shifted, one way or another, to the student and his family or the employer of educated labour.

It is extremely difficult to make a firm prediction on whether ability limitations can determine the capacity or degree of expansion of a school system. The reason for this is the high correlation between ability (as currently measured) and socio-economic status.

One should be less confident about the future evolution of the demand for educated manpower relative to the supply. One clear trend we have been able to detect is the rise of the tertiary production sector and the concomitant rise in demand for complex professional services. It might be that the service industries can act as a buffer absorbing an increased academically trained output. This trend, however, puts the onus once more on the curriculum to turn out flexible men and women who will work in changing careers throughout their working life.

The race between education (supply) and technology (demand) has been such as to more or less maintain a substantial income advantage of the more educated in the recent past. The future will very much depend upon the willingness of the Government to increase the number of places in prestigious schools.

It is reasonable to assume that the future demand for teachers will follow that of anticipated enrolments. However, one should underline the difficulties inherent in correctly projecting the demand for teacher <u>numbers</u>, let alone the fact that schools of the future might need teachers of different <u>quality</u>. For instance there is a relationship between the quality of new teachers and the instructional "software" needed by the silicon chip pedagogic technology of the years to come.

It is also difficult to make predictions about the outcome of interplay between supply and demand. In terms of prices one can hypothesise cobweb oscillations around a never reached market equilibrium point. One way of dampening these oscillations might be through an information and signalling system to be used in educational planning.

Given the conditions of uncertainty described earlier, one might be slightly optimistic regarding the future level of unemployment. Youth unemployment is expected to be taken care of by demographic developments in the medium term. It is difficult to share the view that the future level of unemployment will be a multiple of its present size. It is more likely that the very concept of "unemployment" will change by the end of the century through reduced work time, increased leisure time and labour absorption in "software" industries.

Section VI outlines six research areas in educational planning. Some of the research headings sound familiar, although changes in emphasis and content are advocated. Thus two largely _normative_ research topics are proposed to discover or establish a consensus on the expectations in various groups, first for the education system, then for society in general. Once these values or normative weights are obtained, they can become input for more technocratic, _positive_, analyses or specific links in the educational planning process.

We anticipate and advocate a shift in research emphasis from manpower requirements towards understanding the individual demand for education processes. When the expected labour market conditions, as seen from the students' viewpoint, are matched with actual market conditions obtained by employee surveys, these two elements can form the backbone of an information-communication network. We put great faith in experiments with an advance warning system in Member countries, and would welcome more of them. Such an information system can clear up and even prevent the development of dynamic cobwebs and graduate unemployment due to lagging supply response frictions.

Research in these new areas, however, will have to be different from the "ongoing" kind. We lament the several years lead-time between the conception of a research project and the use of its results in practice. Speed should be the characteristic of the new research in educational planning.

Additional research areas refer to the changing content of the curriculum and childhood education. Future formal educational programmes might have to be of the _general_ rather than narrow vocational type, the latter type being relegated to the firms.

II. FROM THE RECENT PAST TO THE NEAR FUTURE

It is only reasonable to assume that medium-term developments in education will be affected by conditions prevailing in the recent past. Therefore, our initial task is to identify the most important recent trends and factors which still affect education in order to understand future developments, say, to the middle of this decade.

The Inertia Factor

One could summarise what has been happening in education in the recent past by a single word : "Crisis" (3). The euphoria of the sixties has been followed by increasing disenchantment in the seventies.

Perhaps one can identify four major factors in the educational crisis we are presently experiencing : demographic, economic, psychological and political. These have presently combined and reinforced each other to produce a result nobody could have predicted in the early sixties.

The demographic decline following the post-World War II baby boom contributed to the fall in enrolments in all levels of education. It is normal for established educational institutions and their staff to attempt to maintain their relative position after a fall in the demand for places, but this contradiction between actual demand and the intended supply might be only a minor element of the crisis.

This trend was reinforced by the economic recession that hit virtually all countries in the early seventies. It meant less money from all sources, public and private, flowing into the educational system. Comparative statistics on the share of the Gross National Product or the budget designated for education might underestimate the extent of the actual cuts involved because economic growth in real terms has been minimal if not negative.

In the midst of this situation the two main actors involved (the public at large and the Government) started changing their perception of the value of education in modern society. Students and their families, perhaps for the first time, realised that more education does not necessarily lead to a good job. Widespread youth unemployment challenged the idea of a link between education and work. At the same time an opposite trend developed, especially among the élite, of attempting to accumulate as many prestigious diplomas as possible and pass highly selective examinations so as to stand out from the crowd and move up in the labour market queue.

The elements of this crisis of course contributed to reshaping not only the value system of individuals but also the political will of the Government towards education. After the early sixties bonanza of "education for human resource development" (4) or for the "satisfaction of social

---

3. See T. Husén, *The School in Question : A Comparative Study of the School and its Future in Western Societies*, Oxford University Press, 1979, Chapter 1.
4. Compare the proliferation of publications on this theme, especially by the OECD.

demand" (5) they had second thoughts which resulted in extreme budget cuts (6). In view of these conditions, it is very unlikely that the situation will change in the medium term. According to OECD's Interfutures, economic growth will not be spectacular in the years to come. Demographically, the number of students who are in school level x have already determined those who will be in school x+1 tomorrow. For these reasons, and because inertia is a basic characteristic of both human nature and social systems, it will probably take a considerable amount of time for people's value systems to change in relation to education.

The Political Will of the Government

Yet one need not be equally pessimistic about near future developments in education when one considers the "degree of freedom" that still exists, in the form of the Government's political will. It is not inconceivable that politicians will act to reverse the recently observed trends in education. This would of course require both their political will and the support of the electorate, and even then it could still run into the financial constraint.

When considering the possibility of fast changes in political attitudes, one should not be misled by the apparent stability in the political structure of OECD countries. This is due to the virtually unchanging relative importance of the political parties in the Member countries. It is, however, a misleading stability because changes often do not occur in the number of seats in parliaments but within political parties themselves. Their programmes already reflect some of the changed needs of society, though by no means all of them.

Education can be viewed both as a lead and as a lag variable in a continuously changing social system. In the planning literature it is education's lead role that is often stressed (e.g. the by now familiar slogan : education _for_ economic development). However, a comprehensive planning process has also to consider education's lag role, for instance how it is affected by non-education socio-economic developments. To put it differently, education is a policy instrument, but at the same time this instrument is influenced by changes of the social system. Because of the simultaneities involved it is very difficult, if not impossible, to make a distinction between exogenous and endogenous variables in the perpetuum mobile of the education and society nexus.

---

5. Cf. the report of the Robbins committee in England.
6. At those currently experienced in the United Kingdom.

Our task in the following sections will be to attempt to identify the several factors affecting the educational system and also trace the people's reaction to the underlying changes. To facilitate this task several "working assumptions" about the future have been formulated. Although these assumptions are based on an expert public opinion poll conducted in the United States (7) and presented in some detail in Appendix A, they seem to be shared by people of other OECD countries. This may need to be carefully tested however. According to the survey the following developments can be expected :

- population stability
- less sex discrimination
- faster technological change
- more women entering the labour force
- increased mid-career job changing
- decreased enrolment in traditional post-secondary institutions
- increased adult participation in part-time higher education schemes
- increased financial competition between post-secondary institutions
- increased investments of employers in the training of their employees
- increased willingness to sacrifice monetary pay for extra leisure time.

These working assumptions, which may vary in degree from country to country, provided an information base for our perspective analysis, though this information is also used to test the validity of the assumptions.

III. THE DEMAND FOR EDUCATION

At the outset we would like to distinguish between the two main sources of demand for education. These are :

a) the _individual_ demand for education i.e. education as a _valuable_ acquisition leading to a multiplicity of social goods, including employment. This is manifested in the demand for school places by the students and their families. It is sometimes called "_social_ demand" for education (8) ;

---

7. See R. Glover, Alternative Scenarios of the American Future, 1980-2000, Future Directions for a Learning Society, The College Board, New York, 1979.
8. For a more precise definition see K. Härnqvist, Individual Demand for Education : Analytical Report, Vol. I, OECD, Paris, 1978.

b) the <u>manpower</u>-related demand for education, or the <u>production system's</u> demand for certain skills, reflected in school graduation requirements and corresponding output (9).

It is hard to draw a sharp distinction between these two sources of demand for education because there exists considerable overlap, as shown in Figure 1. Labour market conditions certainly affect pupils' decisions for further education but this is not the only factor. There are other factors, such as psychological, sociological or cultural, which also influence pupils' educational plans (10).

Because of the simultaneous existence of these two sources of educational demand it is hard to determine educational supply without explicitly considering the political element involved. For educational supply decisions, whether public or private, are decisions made on the basis of the manifest demand but with due consideration of political and economic constraints.

A. Individual Demand

The process of education is characterised by a number of features common to all countries. First of all, a distinction between formal and informal education is customary and useful. Formal or "organised" education is not only the task of schools but also of some business departments that have the explicit task of preparing their employees for a concrete job function. Informal education takes place outside these institutions, in the environment of the family, in the environment of the dwelling, around the school and, later, around the job location. The line between formal and informal education is somewhat blurred when provided on the job. On-the-job training is formalized in some countries more than others, and in some industries more than others.

Secondly, part of formal education is compulsory. This part has grown from nothing in the early nineteenth century to ten years in some countries today. Some societies are stricter than others in controlling the legal requirements. The rural areas are sometimes a tacit exception.

---

9. It should be noted that several other social systems of a society such as the "cultural", "religious", etc. exert demands on the education system for specific services. These demands, however, have not been explicitly considered here.
10. See Härnqvist, <u>op. cit</u>.

Figure 1 **THE OVERLAP BETWEEN INDIVIDUAL AND MANPOWER DEMAND FOR EDUCATION**

Educational qualifications voluntarily obtained by the individuals as a result of social demand

Educational requirements of the economy for the completion of output targets

INDIVIDUAL DEMAND

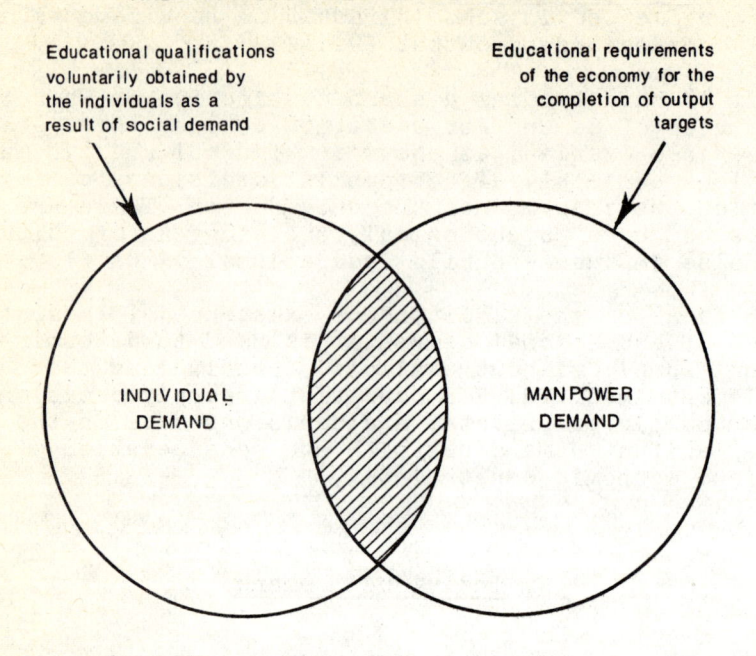

MANPOWER DEMAND

Thirdly, there is a historically documented parallel between societal development and the evolution of education. It is only natural that there exists such parallelism. Schools from the start have had the task of preparing students for their future tasks as citizens. This does not mean necessarily that there is a complete parallel as schools often do have additional aims not strictly related to societal "tasks". Moreover, the tasks may be interpreted as having both production and consumption aspects, including the use of leisure. Partly as a natural phenomenon and partly as a traditional one, there is task differentiation between the sexes as well as recent attempts to eliminate them.

Fourthly, informal education depends on the environment provided by the family, whether this is of the conventional household, the extended or the "nuclear" kind. Child psychologists point out the importance to children of affection and stability in the family (11). Recently these elements have been affected by the desire of women

---

11. See J.A.B. Sanders-Woudstra, <u>Kinderpsychiatrie in Perspectief</u>, Rotterdam University, 1976.

to participate in the (paid) labour force, by the increased divorce rate and by experiments with living in communes. The consequences of these developments on the future structure of societies are hardly known with any precision ; much remains to be investigated.

Fifthly, educational tasks, in line with society as a whole, have become increasingly complicated. Whereas, until a few decades ago, the educational system was characterized by rigidity and aversion to change, the last few decades have shown a widespread inclination to doubt the appropriateness of traditional education and to set up alternative systems of education. Even if there is presently too much desire for experiment, the need for research in education is real possibly with opposed objectives : both the proponents for great changes and the adversaries want a more solid base for their policies.

Sixthly, it is usual and also analytically useful, to distinguish three main sectors of education, sometimes called primary, secondary and tertiary. The division lines are not always drawn in a uniform way : finer subdivisions are preferable in many respects so that terms such as elementary and extended elementary are often used. Whatever subdivision is made, corresponding "levels of education attained" are distinguished and the attainment is acquired by passing a given examination. Although dropouts of course attain a lower instructional level, the education they receive up to that point also has a given social value.

Finally, it is useful to make a distinction between quantitative changes and qualitative changes in a given organisational structure of education. The latter stands for a change in curriculum or a change in the conditions for passing a given examination. In this report the main emphasis will be on quantitative changes ; it is impossible, however, to ignore qualitative changes. Although the latter are more difficult to deal with, their importance demands some attention.

Apart from the features common to all educational systems in OECD countries, one may observe three tendencies which could be used to differentiate the orientation of educational systems :

The emphasis laid on vocational education as distinct from general education, as seen in Germany, a stronger emphasis on non-cognitive performance, especially physical exercise, as seen in Britain and the United States, heavy emphasis on intellectual (cognitive) performance, as seen in France.

Demographic Factors

The natural starting point in examining quantitatively the individual demand for education is demography, as cohort sizes set the upper limit of potential demand for school places of all types. In order to make an estimate of the future demand for education or levels of educational attainment, the following information is needed for each population cohort involved :

1. the size of the cohort at a given point of time ;
2. the enrolment propensity of the cohort towards various types of education processes ; and, possibly
3. the numbers passing examinations relevant to the educational level attained.

Variable 1 is meant to summarise the purely demographic aspects. Each cohort starts with a number of newly-born children and this number depends on a variety of important factors, the study of which is shared by demographers, sociologists and psychologists. Some of these factors will be discussed in the later part of this section. In addition, the size of the cohort is reduced by death rates at various ages.

Variable 2, enrolment in various types of educational institutions, depends, to a large extent, on the socio-economic status (SES) of the family head, innate capabilities, the motivation to learn and the private cost of the course followed. Enrolment, looked at from the side of the families involved, is also called the "social demand" for the type of education at stake and will be discussed at more length later in this section.

Variable 3, the passing of examinations, essentially depends on the same factors, although with different weights, in view of the strong administrative component.

Analysing the flows involved one can assess their combined effect on the new generation in terms of a given educational attainment.

Turning now to the demographic factors at play, some figures may illustrate the expectations of demographers (cf. Tables 1 and 2). From these tables it is clear that, in contrast to the developing countries, OECD countries are expected to show only moderate population increases. According to these estimates the European Community of the Nine is expected to be close to stable, which may enable us to apply some techniques of analysis valid only for stationary populations without making a large error. This situation is expected in the United States circa 2025 if a fertility rate of 1.7 is assumed, as compared with 1.8

in 1975 (cf. Table 3) (12). Of course unexpected circumstances and strong positive policy measures can intervene and invalidate these estimates in the long run.

Table 1

ACTUAL POPULATION IN 1950 AND 1975
AND PROJECTED POPULATION IN THE YEAR 2000
BY MAJOR REGION

In millions

Year	World Low	World High	Western Europe Low	Western Europe High	EEC(9)
1950	2 700		351		215
1975	4 120		404		259
2000	5 800	6 400	440	450	260 (1)

1. Average of low and high estimates.
Source : EEC, The Courier, No. 57, September-October, 1979.

Table 2

POPULATION IN 1975 AND ESTIMATED POPULATION IN 2000,
FOUR GROUPS OF DEVELOPED COUNTRIES

In millions

Year	North America	Japan	EEC(9)	Other Western Europe
1975	237	112	259	147
2000	275	133	265	164

Source : Interfutures, OECD, Paris, 1979, Table 2 (Scenario not specified).

---

12. As estimated by the Commission on Population Growth and the American Future.

Table 3

TOTAL POPULATION AND PERCENTAGE THEREOF IN SELECTED COHORTS RELEVANT TO EDUCATION IN THE USA, 1976 TO 2050

Total in millions, cohorts in per cent

Year	Total Population	5-13 years	14-17 years	18-24 years
1976	215	15.3	7.9	13.1
2000	246	11.8	5.6	9.0
2025	252	9.9	4.6	8.1
2050	231	9.6	4.5	8.0

Source : US Commission on Population Growth and the American Future, quoted in T.J. Espenshade, "Zero Population Growth and the Economics of Developed Nations", Population and Development Review 4, 1978, pp. 645-680.

It seems appropriate to cite a Commission statement accompanying these figures : "We have looked for, and not found, any convincing economic argument for continued population growth. The health of our country does not depend on it, not does the vitality of business, nor the welfare of the average person" (Espenshade, loc. cit., p. 646).

This conclusion is in line with the findings of two studies which have shown, for a group of developed as well as for a group of developing countries, that the average efficiency of a country can be explained satisfactorily by its endowment with physical as well as human capital, whereas production increases do not contribute significantly to the country's level of efficiency (13). Tables 4 and 5 present related statistics for the United Kingdom and Canada. The comparison of these two countries is illustrative of country differences in the future evolution of cohorts relevant to education and hence demonstrates the difficulty of making general predictions. The relative population stability in the United Kingdom is associated with mild reductions, if not stability, in the future cohort structure. The rapid population growth in Canada on the other hand is associated with drastic reductions in the percentage of education-age persons in the future.

---

13. J. Tinbergen "Some Remarks on Slow Growth", in Reflections on Economic Development and Social Change, Essays in Honour of Professor V.K.R.V. Rao, 1979, pp. 15-27, and J. Tinbergen "Is Growth a Precondition for Efficiency ?", 1979.

Table 4

TOTAL POPULATION AND PERCENT IN SELECTED COHORTS
RELEVANT TO EDUCATION IN THE UNITED KINGDOM,
1978 TO 2011

Year	Total Population (10^6)	5-9	10-14	15-19	20-24
1978	55.9	7.5	8.2	7.9	7.2
1981	55.7	6.6	7.9	8.4	7.7
1991	56.7	6.9	5.6	6.5	7.9
2001	57.5	7.7	6.6	5.6	6.4
2011	57.7	6.2	6.6	7.4	7.6

Source : Based on UK, Central Statistic Office, Annual Abstract of Statistics 1979, p. 21.

Table 5

TOTAL POPULATION AND PERCENT IN SELECTED COHORTS
RELEVANT TO EDUCATION IN CANADA, 1976 TO 2031

Year	Total Population (10^6)	6-13 years	14-17 years	18-24 years
1976	23	14.4	8.2	13.5
1986	26	11.3	5.7	12.2
1996	29	11.6	5.6	9.3
2011	32	9.7	4.9	9.5
2031	34	9.3	4.7	8.8

Source : Z. Zsigmond, G. Picot, W. Clark and M.S. Devereaux, Out of the Labour Force, Statistics Canada, Ottawa, 1978, p. 86.

As for the psychological factors which may affect the birth rate, some light may be thrown on this problem by a comparative study of the countries involved. There is a striking difference e.g. between Germany, where birth figures are very low, and the other larger OECD countries, where they are higher. There seems, therefore, to be scope here for inquiries about these differences and their causes, along the lines of current demographic work (14).

---

14. See Hervé Le Bras, Child and Family : Demographic Developments in the OECD Countries, OECD/CERI, Paris, 1979.

The Evolution of Enrolments

Not all of the increased population will find its way into specific educational institutions.

Table 6 shows the percentage distribution of enrolments by major OECD country area and educational level at three points in time : 1970, 1980 and 2000. The projections indicate a possible relative stagnation of higher education in Europe and North America, and a faster rise in Australia, New Zealand and Japan. These trends can be seen more easily in Table 7 which shows the anticipated rate of growth of enrolments.

Table 6

THE PERCENTAGE DISTRIBUTION OF ENROLMENTS
BY LEVEL OF EDUCATION AND REGION, 1970, 1980 AND 2000

Region	Year	Primary	Secondary	Higher
North America	1970	50.3	35.3	14.3
	1980	44.9	34.0	21.1
	2000	45.3	33.6	21.1
Europe	1970	60.0	34.1	5.9
	1980	51.3	40.4	8.4
	2000	51.0	40.2	8.9
Japan	1970	47.7	43.2	9.0
	1980	48.0	40.6	11.4
	2000	41.9	43.5	14.7
Australia and New Zealand	1970	58.7	35.1	6.2
	1980	54.6	35.5	9.9
	2000	51.0	36.6	12.4

Source : Unesco, Tendances et projections des effectifs scolaires par degré d'enseignement et par âge, 1978, Table V.

Again, these aggregate figures hide individual country differences. Thus university enrolment in the United Kingdom is expected to have stabilised at a higher level relative to the 1970s and oscillate around just over half a million (See Table 8). The same pattern is expected to be observed in Canada where enrolments at all levels will initially rise and then decline because of changes in the demographic structure of the population (See Table 9).

Table 7

THE RATE OF GROWTH OF ENROLMENTS BY LEVEL
OF EDUCATION, REGION AND SEX, 1980-1985

Average annual rate of growth

Region	Sex	Primary	Secondary	Higher
North America	M+F	1.0	- 1.4	- .6
	F	1.0	- 1.4	- .2
Europe	M+F	.2	.1	1.3
	F	.3	.1	1.4
Japan	M+F	.9	2.7	3.1
	F	.9	2.7	3.5
Australia and New Zealand	M+F	2.4	1.5	2.0
	F	2.4	1.6	2.4

Source : Unesco, Tendances, op. cit., Table VI.

Table 8

THE OVER-TIME EVOLUTION OF HIGHER EDUCATION
STUDENTS IN GREAT BRITAIN, 1961-1966

Year	Students enrolled (000)
1961	179
1971	446
1981	546
1991	592
1996	520

Note : Figures refer to the "central projection".
Source : Department of Education and Science, Higher Education into the 1990s : A Discussion Document, London, February 1978, Table 5.

Table 9

THE EVOLUTION OF POST-SECONDARY ENROLMENT
IN CANADA, 1971-1986

Index, 1971 = 100

Year	Non-university	University	Total post-secondary
1971	100	100	100
1976	132	117	122
1981	132	119	123
1986	112	110	111

Source : Zsigmond et al., Op. cit., p. 127.

However, all forecasts agree on the following point : The percentage of women in higher education in developed countries is expected to keep rising from a 38 per cent in 1965, and reach the 45 per cent mark by 1985 (15) :

When these flows (i.e. enrolments) are translated into stocks, one can arrive at predictions of the educational structure of the population as a whole. Figures available for the United States given in Table 10 may illustrate the official view in that country.

Table 10

PERSONS 25 YEARS AND OVER AND THEIR EDUCATIONAL
ATTAINMENT, USA 1950, 1976 AND 1990

Percentage

Year	Total (millions)	Elementary School Less than 5 years	5-7 years	8 years	High School 1-3 years	4 years	Colleges 1-3 years	4 and more years
1950	87.5	10.9	15.9	20.2	16.9	20.2	7.2	6.0
1976	118.8	3.9	7.1	9.7	15.3	36.3	13.0	14.7
1990(1)	150.2	1.8	3.7	5.8	14.5	39.3	14.8	20.1
1990(2)	150.2	1.8	3.7	5.9	14.9	40.4	14.7	18.4

(1) Assuming lower rates of termination than indicated by the trends from 1957/9 to 1969/70.
(2) Assuming higher rates of termination than the trends mentioned under, in "Tendances", op. cit., p. 43, Unesco.
Source : Statistical Abstract of the US, 1977, p. 137, Table 220.

---

15. UNESCO, Tendances, op. cit., p. 43.

Educational Finance Capacity

The finance capacity of both individuals and Governments are extremely important factors affecting individual demand. This social demand for education might fluctuate in the coming decades according to the funds available to sustain a higher level of "educational production".

Public educational financing as it now operates in most OECD countries has several disadvantages which may have an adverse effect on future educational growth. As has been shown, under existing public educational financing low-income groups subsidize largely high-income groups (16). This places low-income groups at a disadvantage which under conditions of low or zero income growth may prevent them from continuing education beyond the compulsory level. It is therefore evident that a change in the public system of educational financing may have a decisive effect by encouraging low-income pupils, particularly those with high school performance, to continue their studies.

Public educational financing suffers also from the fact that it is based on taxes. The level, therefore, of the funds made available to education depends entirely upon the political will of Governments rather than on the will of the consumer. Problems may be eased, however, by further growth of incomes. If the demand for less material and more spiritual satisfaction increased as a possible and desirable reaction to present-day materialism, more private means for education may be one of the forms this new life style may take.

Under present conditions the public finance capacity of formal school systems might become increasingly limited. Table 11 shows only modest increases in educational expenditure in advanced and developing countries between 1965 and 1973, which may be attributed to the reluctance of governments to increase educational spending. The pressure on state budgets might continue pari passu with increases in the social demand for education. One might envisage the end result of this interplay as being a gradual shift of the cost burden to the direct beneficiaries of education, i.e. the student and his family under conditions of positive discrimination in favour of the less well-off.

Mental Ability

Sociologists and geneticists have given ample attention to the relationships essential to answer the question whether

---

16. See G. Psacharopoulos, "The perverse effects of public subsidisation of education, or, how equitable is free education?" in Comparative Education Review, Vol. 21, No. 1, February 1977.

Table 11

PUBLIC EXPENDITURE ON EDUCATION AS PERCENTAGE
OF GNP OR THE STATE BUDGET, BY REGION, 1965 AND 1973

Region	Education expenditure			
	As percent of GNP		As percent of Budget	
	1965	1973	1965	1973
More developed	5.2	5.8	15.2	16.3
Less developed	3.0	3.7	13.1	14.9
World	4.9	5.5	15.0	16.2

Source : Unesco, A Summary Statistical Review, Paris, 1977, p. 45.

more people can be educated and attain higher levels of education (17). The usual "path analysis" included as factors determining a person's educational attainment the IQ and SES of parents, childhood IQ and several other variables. So far these analyses are only beginning and require extension in several directions ; this is illustrated by the relatively divergent coefficients and the rather low portion of the variance explained (see Appendix, Table B-1).

Clearly, no matter how "ability" is measured, it is closely related to socio-economic status (SES). For example, in the United States, college students are distributed as follows by ability and SES categories :

---

17. Bowles, S. and H. Gintis, Schooling in Capitalist America : Educational Reform and the Contradictions of Economic Life, Basic Books, New York, 1976.
Bulcock, J.W., H. Fägerlind and J. Emanuelsson, Education and Socioeconomic Career, Institute for the Study of International Problems in Education, No. 6, Stockholms Universitet, 1974.
Dronkers, J. and U. de Jong, "Jencks and Fägerlind in a Dutch Way", Social Science Information, Vol. 18, 4/5, 1979, pp. 761-8.
Jencks, C. et al., Inequality : A reassessment of the Effect of Family and Schooling in America, Harper, New York/London, 1972.
Psacharopoulos, G. and J. Tinbergen, "On the Explanation of Schooling, Occupation and Earnings : Some Alternative Path Analyses", in De Economist, Vol. 126, 1978, pp. 505-520.

Table 12

THE DISTRIBUTION OF COLLEGE STUDENTS
BY ABILITY AND SOCIOECONOMIC STATUS, USA

Ability or SES category	Percent distribution of college students	
	Ability	SES
1. Low	9	16
2.	19	32
3.	28	
4. High	44	52
Total	100	100

Source : C.A. Anderson, M.J. Bowman and V. Tinto, Where Colleges Are and Who Attends, McGraw-Hill for the Carnegie Commission, New York, 1972, p. 146.

The SES stratification is even more remarkable when one standardises for ability and generates the within-ability-groups SES college student distribution, as shown in Table 13.

Table 13

COLLEGE DISTRIBUTION AS PERCENT OF
SECONDARY SCHOOL GRADUATES, BY ABILITY,
DESTINATION AND SOCIO-ECONOMIC GROUP

USA (per cent)

SES	Ability quarter			
	1 (Low)	2	3	4 (High)
1. Low	8	17	24	50
2.	13	27	40	60
3. High	28	47	63	79

Note : The overall ability - SES mean is 39 per cent.
Source : C.A. Anderson et al., op. cit., p. 142.

The transition probabilities between secondary school and college are, therefore, a sharply rising function of socio-economic status. What are the likely future developments in this nexus ? On the basis of past experience it is not unreasonable to expect that the last quarter of this century will be marked by a dramatic decrease in the disparity of numbers as shown in Table 13. More "low ability" (i.e. as currently measured) students may attend institutions of higher learning and more offspring of less well-to-do families may enrol in all forms of post-secondary education, due to relatively increasing family mean incomes and educational attainment (factors determining SES).

To the extent that this hypothesis is correct, the increased participation of lower SES groups will have more impact on the future development of school systems in Member countries than the ability dimension. In the first place, the very concept of limited "ability pool" (18) is suspect. To a large extent "ability" might be subject to formal teaching and also being informally influenced by the environment. Therefore, it is difficult to predict any adverse internal efficiency effects from the increased participation of "low ability" groups in institutions of higher learning.

The increased educational participation of low SES groups, however, might have effects beyond the familiar arguments for equalisation of opportunities. This trend would certainly be consistent with the new cultural needs in Member countries, as expressed by the electorate. Educational institutions might once more have to adapt their curriculum to the different vocabulary, motivation and informal stock of knowledge of their new raw input. This is a matter of maintaining their _internal_ efficiency as educational institutions in an area where the argument might be shifted from ability to socio-economic background and environment. It is also reasonable to anticipate _external_ efficiency effects of the increased participation of lower SES groups. These might take the form of the human capital notion of "worker effect", where, other things being equal, more educated low SES employees would now make a greater contribution to the social product. It is anticipated that a great part of the increased participation would be female and not necessarily persons who contemplate a professional career. To the extent that this proposition is true it would have the effect of upgrading consumer choice, creating a more informed electorate and, most important, giving a boost to the quality of "household production" (19).

---

18. See L. Robbins, Higher Education Report, HMSO, London, 1963.
19. For a collection of papers and a review of the many aspects of household production and consumption and
(Continued on next page)

Finally, there are a couple of related considerations : one is that not only parents' innate qualities are relevant, but also those of grandparents. The other is that not only cognitive, but also non-cognitive qualities are relevant for a person's socio-economic status and occupation. The possibilities of raising educational attainment are not only dependent on the kind of schooling currently provided, but also on what <u>new types</u> of schools can be added to those presently in existence. Some further comparative research on the effects of differing school systems in the OECD countries seems appropriate.

A famous aspect of the divergencies in opinions on the complex problem of intelligence is Goldberger's attack on Burt, who maintained that 80 per cent of IQ variance is innate (20). It has now been proved beyond doubt that this result was based on faked statistics (21).

Changing Value Systems

The future of education in OECD countries is likely to be significantly influenced by changes in the value systems of the coming generations. There are considerable deviations - sometimes very outspoken - between the present and past generations. These are viewed with concern by representatives of older cohorts, but others look at them with hope. Moreover, there are considerable differences in value systems between individuals of the same age. Examples of value systems considered with concern - if not alarm - are those of drug-addiction and the corresponding criminality and terrorism. The numbers of these - not to be identified with each other - are small, but the effects of their activities are not. If not with alarm, then at least with some uneasiness, an increased indifference towards the quality of work is observed. Increasing numbers of errors in performance, ranging from typographical to aeronautical, are typical of our times. A whole group of such attitudes may be brought under a heading like "lack of motivation" or "alienation". In part of this area remedies can even be identified, such as more participatory forms of business organisation. But many of these attitudes, sometimes strange, sometimes downright destructive, remain unexplained.

(Note 19 continued)
the relationship of education to it, see T.W. Schultz, <u>The Economics of the Family</u>, National Bureau of Economic Research, New York, 1974.
    20. A. Goldberger, "Twin Models : A Skeptical View", in P. Taubman (ed.), <u>Kinometrics</u>, North-Holland, Amsterdam, 1977, where further quotations are given.
    21. See L.J. Kamin, The Science and Politics of IQ, Penguin, London, 1974.

Deviations of value systems of younger generations giving rise to hope are attitudes showing concern for the environment and for the risks of nuclear energy.

Due to changes in value systems, education is likely to be increasingly perceived by the new generations as a value in itself, i.e. less and less for strictly vocational purposes. The behaviour of the education "consumers" is already changing in this way. The end result of this trend will be increased individual consumption of higher education and particularly of non-vocational, liberal arts subjects. The demand of the third-age group is also likely to move in this direction (22).

B. The Demand for Educated Manpower

We now turn to the second category of demand – the demand for education for manpower purposes, as related to the production system of the economy. Thus the subject of this section is to discuss the future evolution of the demand for manpower with different levels of educational attainment, with a view to assessing its impact upon the supply of education.

Demand for labour is exerted by "the organisers of production", taken in the widest sense of these terms. The organisers may be private firms or public authorities. Production includes not only the manufacturing of material goods, but also the provision of services. In the production process factors of production (natural resources, labour and capital goods) are combined in order to obtain goods or services as outputs. The latter are subject to demand from consumers and investors, both private and public. It is in this sense that the demand for various types of labour is a "derived" demand.

This demand depends upon a host of factors such as the level and composition of output, its rate of growth, the technology by which it is produced, the market organisation, the degree of substitution between the different inputs in production and the institutional framework. In what follows we discuss the likely evolution of such factors in the future and the way they might affect educational systems in Member countries.

---

22. For the possible existence of a saturation level of enrolments, see Appendix "C".

The level and composition of output

Future demand for goods and services depends to a large extent on the size and distribution of total incomes. Some key relevant figures in this respect are presented in Table 14.

Table 14

GROSS DOMESTIC PRODUCT BY COUNTRY GROUP, 1975 AND 2000

In billion $ of 1970

Country Group	1975	2000 Scenario A	B2	C	D(3)
OECD	2 357	6 885	5 556	4 154	5 388
Eastern Europe	608	2 058	1 962	1 700	1 962
Developing countries	816	3 955	3 481	3 002	3 432
World	3 802	12 970	11 057	8 984	10 836

Source : OECD, Interfutures, Table 21.

As observed in the demographic section above, the rate of population growth of European Western countries, is assumed to be close to zero ; that for the USA and Japan is not expected to be much above zero between 1990 and 2000 either. Productivity, however, is expected to be rising around 3 per cent per annum in EEC, 6 per cent in Japan and 1.5 per cent in the USA (23). One may interpret this as a growth in the availability of finished products, with less input of material natural resources. There will be a necessity to save on purely material inputs as a consequence of their increasing scarcity. This is true mainly for exhaustible resources, such as oil, some ores and some energy sources other than oil.

The link between the demand for goods and services and the demand for labour with different educational attainment is not a rigid one. Yet, there exist considerable differences in the composition of the labour force used by different industrial sectors. Some examples will be

---

23. OECD, Interfutures, op. cit., Table 45.

found in Table 15 for the Netherlands (24) and in Table 16 for the United States (25). Both tables illustrate that as demand changes towards other kinds of products, there is likely to be a shift in the demand for labour with different levels of education. Regarding total demand for goods and services we have to keep in mind that part of the production is for export. The structure of exports in turn, depends on competitiveness and on trade policies. Under fairly general conditions it can be shown that optimal welfare will be approached if impediments to trade are minimised. At present Western governments are not behaving as if they believed this although there is some evidence of a desire for a more free international trade, at least among the OECD countries (26).

Table 15

COMPOSITION OF THE DUTCH LABOUR FORCE,
BY MAJOR ECONOMIC SECTOR AND EDUCATIONAL LEVEL, 1975

In thousands

Economic Sector	Education			
	Primary	Secondary	Tertiary	Total
Primary	477	522	1	1 000
Secondary	417	538	45	1 000
Tertiary	265	567	168	1 000

Note : The tertiary educational sector includes only those with university training.
See Table D-1 in the Appendix.

---

24. For a disaggregation of this table, see Appendix Table D-1. See also Table D-2 for the growth of graduates in the labour force in other countries.
25. These figures are available for a small number of countries only (at least in published form).
26. See for example "Manpower and Employment Measures for Positive Adjustment", OECD, Paris, June 1979 (mimeo).

Table 16

COMPOSITION OF THE AMERICAN LABOUR FORCE
BY MAJOR ECONOMIC SECTOR AND EDUCATIONAL LEVEL, 1970
(EXPERIENCED CIVILIAN LABOUR FORCE, 16 YEARS AND OVER)

In thousands

Economic Sector	Primary[a]	Secondary[b]	Tertiary[c]	Total
Primary	391	559	50	1 000
Secondary	234	697	69	1 000
Tertiary	136	704	160	1 000

(Education)

a) 8 years elementary school or less
b) 1 to 3 years college or less
c) 4 years college or more.

Although the differences in educational systems between the USA and the Netherlands prevent an exact comparability, the general features of the two tables are rather similar (27).

As a consequence of rising per capita income one must anticipate a shift in demand from the primary and secondary economic sectors to the tertiary sector (services). This tendency, already emphasised in 1949 by Jean Fourastié reflects itself in the labour force distribution shifts between 1963 and 1976 shown in Table 17.

Table 17

PERCENTAGE OF LABOUR FORCE EMPLOYED
BY MAJOR ECONOMIC SECTOR, 1963 AND 1976.
SOME REGIONS AND OECD COUNTRIES

Region or Country	1963 Agr.	1963 Ind.	1963 Other	1976 Agr.	1976 Ind.	1976 Other
OECD :						
Europe	23.5	38.8	37.7	16.1	37.3	46.6
North America	7.3	33.0	59.7	4.0	29.0	67.0
Japan	26.0	31.7	42.3	12.2	35.8	52.0
France	19.8	39.6	40.6	10.8	38.1	51.1
Germany	11.9	47.9	40.2	7.1	49.1	43.8
Italy	27.2	41.0	31.8	15.5	43.5	41.1
United Kingdom	4.4	46.4	49.2	2.7	40.0	57.3

Source : OECD Labour Force Statistics, 1965-1976, Paris, 1978.

---

27. Also, compare the high percentage of graduate labour employed by the public sector in Member countries, see Appendix Table D-3.

For a projection up to the year 2000, at least two sources of shifts have to be taken into account. First, a further rise in income will change the composition of demand for goods and services. Second, the demand for manpower with different levels of education by economic sector will also change, depending on the relative prices of the various types of labour and on other factors, such as changes in technological possibilities and the general effort to increase productivity. Some of these factors are discussed below.

The future key role of the tertiary sector

Many economic factors exist that are likely to affect future developments in education. In the nascent educational planning field of just 15 years ago the prime mover was the anticipated (or planned) rate of economic growth. The moderate rate of economic growth anticipated in Member countries makes one look for other possible developments that will shape the kind and quantity of education to be demanded by employers or supplied by the State. One such major factor is the composition of future output rather than its size.

We know that every society has undergone such transformation pari passu with economic development. Thus one of the major symptoms or concomitants of development has been the relative decline of the agricultural share in the composition of gross national product and the corresponding rise in manufacturing.

In recent years, however, another major structural composition of output is being detected in highly advanced countries, namely the rise of the services sector, in some cases at the expense of manufacturing.

There exist several explanations of this phenomenon. As life becomes more complex, a variety of new professions have developed to deal with such things as highly specialised consultancy services, information, communications and management. Labour-saving technical change in manufacturing has released a considerable amount of manpower. On the other hand, rising real per capita incomes have been increasingly allocated to the consumption of service industry products. For example, within a four-year period (1972-1976) about one-half million jobs were lost in the U.K. manufacturing industries while another one million jobs were created in the service industries (28). These industries account today for about 60 per cent of total employment in the United Kingdom and a further substantial

---

28. See P. Sadler, "Do the service industries hold the answer to unemployment", The Times, 22 May, 1978.

rise is predicted in the next decade (see Figure 2). This phenomenon can be explained in terms of a high income elasticity of demand for services, in exactly the same way as the shift towards manufacturing took place in the earlier stages of economic development.

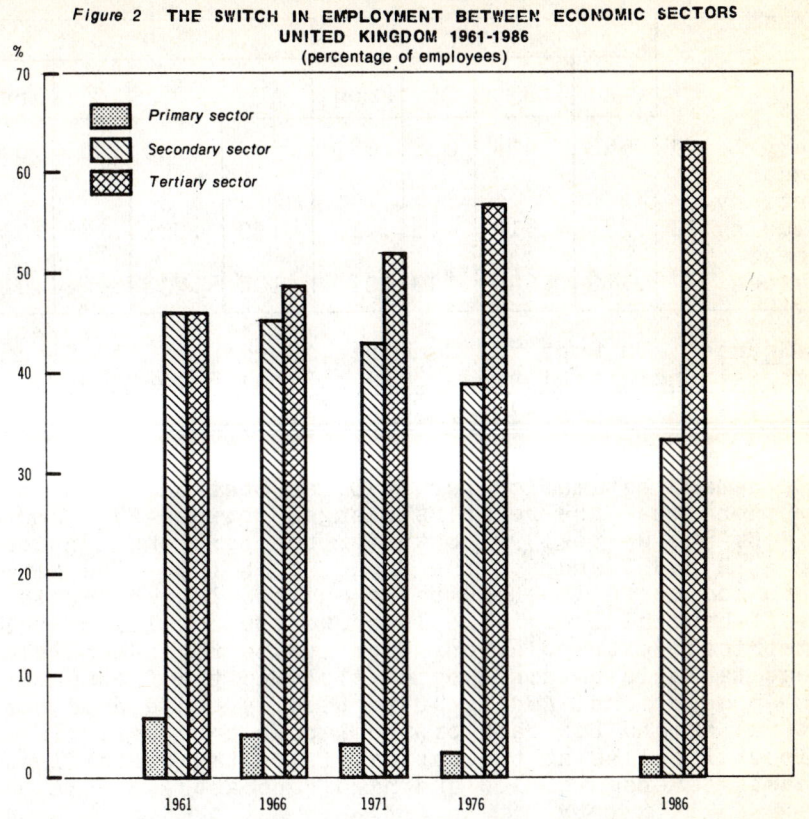

Figure 2 THE SWITCH IN EMPLOYMENT BETWEEN ECONOMIC SECTORS
UNITED KINGDOM 1961-1986
(percentage of employees)

- Primary sector
- Secondary sector
- Tertiary sector

Source : C. Leicester, «Recruitment in the '80's : Reading the market and reducing the risks», *Personnel Management*, Vol. 10, No. 4, April 1978.

Another illustration of the shifts in demand for labour of the three educational levels A, B, C by the three economic sectors I, II, III has been estimated for the United States in 1970. Educational level A is up to 8 years of elementary school, level B is up to 3 years of college and C is more than 3 years of college. Economic sector I is the one known as primary (agriculture and mining). III is business services except advertising, which is, among the Census data available for 1960 as well as 1970, closest to research services. II stands for all other activities, i.e. all secondary and tertiary activities excluding III. In Table 18 the three figures on each line show the portions of the labour force with educational levels A, B and C. The figure under the heading Freq. shows the portion of the total experienced labour force employed by the economic sector considered. In 1960 figures refer to persons over 14, in 1970 over 16 years of age, male and female.

Table 18

LABOUR FORCE ACCORDING TO EDUCATIONAL LEVELS
A, B AND C, IN ECONOMIC SECTORS I, II, III,
USA 1960 AND 1970

	1960				1970			
	A	B	C	Freq.	A	B	C	Freq.
Primary I	.568	.404	.028	.080	.391	.559	.050	.046
Secondary + Tertiary excluding Business Services II	.288	.614	.098	.910	.170	.701	.129	.939
Business Services III	.170	.690	.140	.010	.108	.731	.161	.015

Source : US Dept. of Commerce, Bureau of the Census, Industrial Characteristics, 1960 : Final Report PC(2)-7F, Table 21 ; 1970 : PC(2)-7B, Table 3.

A demand estimation for 1990 has been based on the assumptions that the relative changes between 1960 and 1970 will continue up to 1990, both for the portions mentioned under A, B and C and for the frequencies (29). The former have to add up to 1 horizontally and the latter vertically. The left-hand side of Table 19 shows the results of this "geometrical" extrapolation. From it the right-hand side of that table is obtained by multiplying the frequencies by the proportions. Adding up vertically these products the total demand for each of the labour categories is obtained. The line at the bottom yields the official supply forecasts (average of low and high forecasts).

The following features of this table contain interesting suggestions, for what they are worth :

a) The demand pattern of all three economic sectors will shift towards more educated labour.
b) A shortage of people with a B level of education is to be expected.
c) A considerable surplus of the A group, but a relatively small surplus of the C-group may be expected, and
d) Demand for research will more than double.

---

29. This implies the assumption that substitution elasticities between 1960 and 1970 have also been extrapolated, in a way to be revealed by further analysis.

Table 19

LEFT-HAND SIDE : EXTRAPOLATION OF FIGURES
OF TABLE 18 FOR 1990 (FOR METHOD SEE TEXT).
RIGHT-HAND SIDE : DEMAND FOR LABOUR
OF TYPES A, B AND C, AS PORTION OF TOTAL LABOUR FORCE

	1990 Extrapolation				1990 Demand		
	A	B	C	Freq.	A	B	C
I	.130	.756	.114	.014	.002	.011	.002
II	.051	.763	.186	.953	.049	.727	.177
III	.040	.762	.198	.032	.001	.024	.006
				Total Demand	.052	.762	.185
				Supply	.114	.694	.193

Sources : cf. Table 3.18 for Supply ; <u>Stat. Abstract USA 1977</u>, p. 137.

The service industries and education

The increased supply of education in the 1960s has certainly fed the explosion of service professions. But this would not have happened unless there existed a corresponding demand. Looking at British data (Table 20), the specific area where employment has grown most in the last ten years is what the statistical office describes as "financial, business, professional and scientific services". This narrow sub-sector alone now accounts for over one-fifth of total employment in the United Kingdom. To the extent that this trend will continue, it will make demands for graduates of the upper levels of the school system.

Table 20

THE RISE OF EMPLOYMENT IN A SERVICE SUB-SECTOR
IN THE UNITED KINGDOM 1968-1977

Year	Total employment (10^6)	Employment in financial, professional and scientific services (10^6)	Professional and related services as per cent of total employment
1968	22.7	3.6	15.9
1977	22.7	4.8	21.1

Source : Based on Central Statistical Office <u>Statistical Abstract 1979</u>, p. 154.

The exact nature of the skills to be demanded, however, is still uncertain. What one could reasonably anticipate is a further explosion in the sub-sector of information services. The introduction of the "silicon chip" is still at the early stages of the invention-innovation-adaptation process. To put it in technical jargon, the industry's operating point is still high on a rapidly falling average cost curve. Full exploitation of the underlying returns to scale is likely to lead to further price reductions of information storage and retrieval systems.

This development is a two-edged sword. On the one hand employment will be lost among traditional professions as clerks and accountants. On the other hand employment will be gained as the consumption of the new "information" product increases.

Nobody could claim it is possible to forecast what will be the exact outcome of these two opposite forces. But if we extrapolate the experience from the introduction and full adaptation of past innovation, one could formulate the following hypotheses about future trends :

a) it is unlikely that widespread technological unemployment will be experienced in OECD countries by the end of the century ;
b) the educational system might have to contribute towards this by forming flexible, adaptable men and women.

The race between education and technology

Technology has been subject to continuous change and has profoundly affected the economies of most countries. Western societies have gone through enormous transformations as a consequence of such inventions as the steam engine, electricity, the development of nuclear power and chemical knowledge. The immediate impact on society was, in many cases, dramatic. Traditional or simpler processes of production were abandoned and led to unemployment among artisans and workers, sometimes creating serious upheavals. Looked at from a longer time perspective, it is observed that new employment was created by increasing demand and by shortening working hours (see later section). Increasing demand was partly due, again, to the lower prices of mechanically produced goods and partly to the increased buying power of incomes.

At present, much attention is given, as observed by the new wave of technological change, to the computerised sectors of production, i.e. the "silicon chip". Reductions in employment are anticipated in banking, insurance and administrative sub-sectors. In order to estimate the changes to be expected, information is needed about the new demand for the products of minicomputers in their various fields of potential application. Clearly, there is a need for large-scale market research ; and possibly something can be learned from the impact of introducing the previous generations of computers.

As already stated, the sector composition of OECD economies will have to adapt to these new possibilities. The sectors to be chosen as part of an optimal structural policy must be those in which OECD countries show the highest comparative advantage. It is our view that an optimal policy should be characterised by free entrance to markets. Alongside markets for goods and services for individuals a demand for public goods is created by community decisions ; in principle by decisions of governments and in the last resort by parliament.

An optimal market policy requires competition and avoidance of monopolistic situations. This is not only true for product markets, but also for factor markets, hence labour markets. There is reason to believe that the markets for some of the professions and for top managers are not free from monopolistic elements. One example is the existence of restrictive practices via study barriers in some of the medical professions (30).

For example, how much of the income differentials shown in Table 21 are compensatory (say, because of longer working hours or training costs) and how much is pure rent ?

Table 21

PROFESSIONAL EARNINGS AS A MULTIPLE OF
PER CAPITA INCOME, SELECTED OECD COUNTRIES

Country	Doctor	Dentist	Professor	Lawyer	Civil Servant
United States	4.2	2.8	2.1	2.4	4.1
United Kingdom	4.3	3.3	3.8	3.2	8.9
Canada	2.9	2.1	2.0	2.6	4.1
France	4.8	5.5	2.9	n.a.	3.7
Germany	2.6	1.9	4.1	2.9	6.7
Denmark	3.0	n.a.	2.3	2.6	2.6
Norway	2.2	2.4	2.1	2.2	2.2
Sweden	4.2	2.2	2.4	3.9	2.6

Source : T. Scitovsky, "An international comparison of the trend of professional incomes", American Economic Review, March 1966, pp. 35, 38-40.

30. For the disputed nature of such restrictive practices, see G. Psacharopoulos, Earnings and Education in OECD Countries, OECD, Paris 1975, Chapter 5.

A common feature of both market forces and public policies is a rather short time horizon (31), which implies a serious neglect of the longer-term interests of the very people involved. This is a topic already analysed by Pigou. Part of this neglect is seen in the need for more research than presently undertaken by both the private and the public sector. Even so, with increasing affluence, we observe a relative rise in the demand for public goods as distinct from private goods.

It seems important to be aware that these developments in technology, education and public goods will have significant long-term consequences for the incomes of third level educated groups. Of the three variables mentioned, education acts as an equaliser of incomes, whereas technology and demand for public goods act as disequalisers. Estimates by Keller (32) for the Dutch economy show, however, that the trend in education is likely to "win the race" with the disequalisers. This is of considerable importance for the societal role of education policies as dealt with in the introductory section.

Substitution possibilities

Similarly to the substitution possibilities on the supply side of labour markets there is a clear possibility for substitution on the demand side, especially in the longer run, which is the main concern of this report. Economists are accustomed to deal with these problems by using the concept of substitution elasticities derived from production functions.

In the early period of research on substitution possibilities between factors of production, substitution between capital and labour was the main issue at stake. Essentially this is the basis for judging the consequences of mechanisation. In the first case studies, a substitution elasticity of -1 was found, meaning that a relative price change of labour-to-capital by x per cent would lead to a relative shift in demand by $-x$ per cent. With the aid of more complicated functions a lower figure of some -.6 was found for the United States (33).

---

31. Deutsch, K.W., "Gesellschaftspolitische Aspekte der Oekologie", IIVG Reprint 1979-1, Wissenschaftszentrum, Berlin, 1979.
32. Keller, W.J., "Effects of education, technology and public expenditures on the distribution of income", Institute for Fiscal Studies, Discussion Paper Series 7901/P, Erasmus University, Rotterdam, 1979.
33. J. Tinbergen, "Changing Factor Shares and the Translog Production Function", in : Greenfield, H.I. et al., Theory for Economic Efficiency : Essays in Honor of Abba P. Lerner, MIT Press, Cambridge, (Ma.), 1976.

Recently, for obvious reasons, the substitution of energy by other factors was intensively studied (34).

The subject of substitution between various types of labour was taken up by Dougherty, Psacharopoulos and Hinchliffe, Ullman and others, the result being estimates ranging from -0.6 to -9.0 (see Table D-4 in the Appendix). An attempt was made to re-interpret the existing material and to explain some of the more divergent results (35). Further estimates were added, based on translog production functions in which two or three types of labour were introduced (36). Part of the diversity in substitution elasticities can be ascribed to the varying number of labour types assumed to exist on the production side. The specification of a large number of labour types means that higher substitution possibilities are likely to be found. This may explain Dougherty's high elasticity estimates. The results also depend on the additional demand factors included in the analysis. If only two labour types are distinguished, values of the substitution elasticity around -1 or -2 are often found. Even so, the results found require research : several of the existing estimates are, in our opinion, too unreliable.

The demand for teachers

Part of the demand for individuals with a higher level of education is the demand for teachers at all levels. The relationship with demand for goods and services, on which the preceding sections were based, is a more indirect one here, comparable with the demand for investment goods ; hence the use of the phrase "derived" demand. This implies that an increase in the demand for an educated labour force has to be preceded by an increase in "teaching the teachers". Planning for teacher colleges and similar institutions, is more urgent than planning for the directly productive labour force. Also, an acceleration or deceleration of general development requires adjustments which imply temporary disturbances in the relative composition of the various levels of educational activity. The characteristics of these adjustments and disturbances have been

---

34. Berndt, E.R. and D.O. Wood, "Engineering and Econometric Interpretations of Energy-Capital Complementarity", in The American Economic Review, Vol. 69, 1979, pp. 342-354. See also Jan R. Magnus, "Substitution between Energy and Non-Energy Inputs in the Netherlands 1950-1976", International Economic Review, Vol. 20, No. 2, 1979, pp. 465-484.
35. Tinbergen, J., Income Distribution, North Holland, Amsterdam, 1975.
36. Tinbergen, J., "Changing Factor Shares and the Translog Production Function", in : H.I. Greenfield et al., (eds), Theory for Economic Efficiency, Essays in Honor of Abba P. Lerner, MIT Press, Cambridge, Ma., 1979.

formalised in a simplified but instructive way (37). The adjustment may imply a work load deviating from normal and hence unemployment for part of the teachers. The same applies, of course, if changes in age groups occur, such as the reduction - to about half of its size - of an annual cohort of age 15-20 in Germany between 1982 and 1992.

One might think that teachers are the case par excellence for making manpower demand projections. However, the demand for teachers does not only depend on the level of enrolments in given schools. Even if enrolments were correctly predicted, the teacher-student ratio may change in the future, say, because of an upgrading of quality or an educational innovation. What have been the past developments in this respect ?

To start with, there have not been dramatic developments in the teacher-student ratios, except, perhaps, at the tertiary level (see Table 22).

Table 22

STUDENT/TEACHER RATIOS BY LEVEL OF EDUCATION AND REGION, 1960-1975

Region	Year	Primary	Secondary	Higher
North America	1960	28	25	13
	1970	24	19	15
	1975	22	18	16
Europe	1960	24	16	15
	1970	22	15	13
	1975	21	14	11
Oceania	1960	32	23	16
	1970	28	19	15
	1975	25	17	14

Source : Unesco, A Summary, op. cit., p. 33.

---

37. Tinbergen, J., "Die Unterrichtsplanung im Rahmen der allgemeinen Wirtschaftsplanung", in : E. Boettcher (ed.), Gedenkschrift für Mackenroth, J.C.B. Mohr (Paul Siebeck), Tübingen, 1963, Chapter 14.

But there have been changes regarding the distribution of teachers by educational level, that for higher education growing in all countries (see Table 23).

Table 23

THE DISTRIBUTION OF TEACHERS BY EDUCATIONAL LEVEL AND REGION, 1960-1975

Region	Year	Primary	Secondary	Higher
North America	1960	56	29	15
	1970	44	36	20
	1975	40	38	22
Europe	1960	66	27	6
	1970	57	33	10
	1975	49	39	13
Oceania	1960	63	31	6
	1970	53	39	8
	1975	48	41	11

Source : Unesco, A Summary, op. cit., p. 31.

It is not unreasonable to assume that these trends will continue and to anticipate an increase of the share of female teachers in the total teaching force of OECD countries. Similarly, one could anticipate an increase in the number of specialised kindergarten teachers.

On the other hand, it is difficult to predict the number of Ph. Ds (most of whom will be university teachers) even in a specific country framework. This is demonstrated by the divergent forecasts in the United States (see Figure 3). What should be emphasised however is that the future teacher problem is likely to be one of quality rather than quantity. Thus far, teachers have learned traditional pedagogic techniques and specialised subjects. Tomorrow's world, however, is going to be very different and the onus will be on teachers to turn out flexible people. Curricula of teacher training programmes might have to be drastically revised.

In addition to the aspects discussed so far, another component of the problem of how many teachers to train is the question of the extent to which the intensity and hence the quality of the learning process can be enhanced by a smaller student-teacher ratio. Some attempts to improve the quality of teaching, such as the methods used in Montessori or in Dalton schools, have been partly successful, but require an increased work-load for teachers. Research in these areas is incomplete but may contribute to a simultaneous solution of two problems : enhancing teaching quality and reducing the threat of unemployment for teachers.

A solution to this problem might be found in the introduction of micro-electronics in schools and colleges. Firm plans for micro-electronics development programmes in schools and colleges are already being considered in several OECD countries as for example recently in the United Kingdom (38). Such programmes cover curriculum development, arrangements for teacher training and the development and standardisation of software.

The reduction of hours worked

The demand for certain types of labour will also be influenced by the expected reduction in working hours likely to result from various societal pressures. Reduction in working hours has been a continual phenomenon since the beginning of industrialisation. Over longer periods an average reduction by one-half of one per cent per annum has been observed, meaning a reduction by 40 per cent over a century. A special pressure for reduction of working time is building up because of the unsatisfactory level of unemployment since the early seventies. Moreover, the desire of women to raise their participation rate has led to an increase in the demand for part-time jobs.

Reduction in working time over an individual's entire life may take very diverse forms. Let us briefly discuss them :

1. Early retirement seems to be appropriate for those who have physically hard work conditions ; it exists in mining and a few other industries. However, for a number of other jobs, as the consequence of improved general health, later retirement is being recommended.
2. Longer holidays have become a general phenomenon in European countries and can be recommended on various counts.
3. Shorter working weeks or days are widely discussed and can take different forms in different production processes.

For fully continuous production processes, the switch from four to five shifts is already taking place. For

---

38. The Times, London, 6 February 1980.

continuous processes stopping during the weekend, an increase in shifts has also been proposed. Proposals have even been made to abolish the simultaneous weekly holidays altogether. These met with the difficulty that members of one family may get different free weekends - clearly a social disadvantage.

Activities now performed in one shift may switch towards a second shift or even a part-time character. This could have the additional advantage of overhead cost reduction, important to reduce prices.

Finally, activities with heavy daily fluctuations (like transportation, communications and postal services) seem to be a natural ground for the introduction of part-time jobs.

Quite a few problems prevent easy application of the measures listed. First, an increase in shifts may require the presence of foremen and supervisors not always available. Quick training courses may be an answer, but the experience needed for these jobs may not always be obtained at short notice. Secondly, the question of remuneration often constitutes a stumbling block. International competition may set a clear limit here, especially in countries already having a high level of labour costs.

From the preceding remarks it is evident that changes in the organisation of work may imply changes in demand for foremen and supervisors. The changes considered are urgent enough, however, to justify increased research activity in this area.

One can assess the future scale of changes in leisure time by reference to Figure 4. It is our belief that a great part of the new free time will be used for non-formal educational activities of all kinds, thus putting pressure on the development of new "leisure type" courses (39).

---

39. Reference is made here to the extensive OECD work on recurrent education.

Figure 3 **THE TIME TREND AND ALTERNATIVE FORECASTS OF THE NUMBER OF DOCTORATES, UNITED STATES**

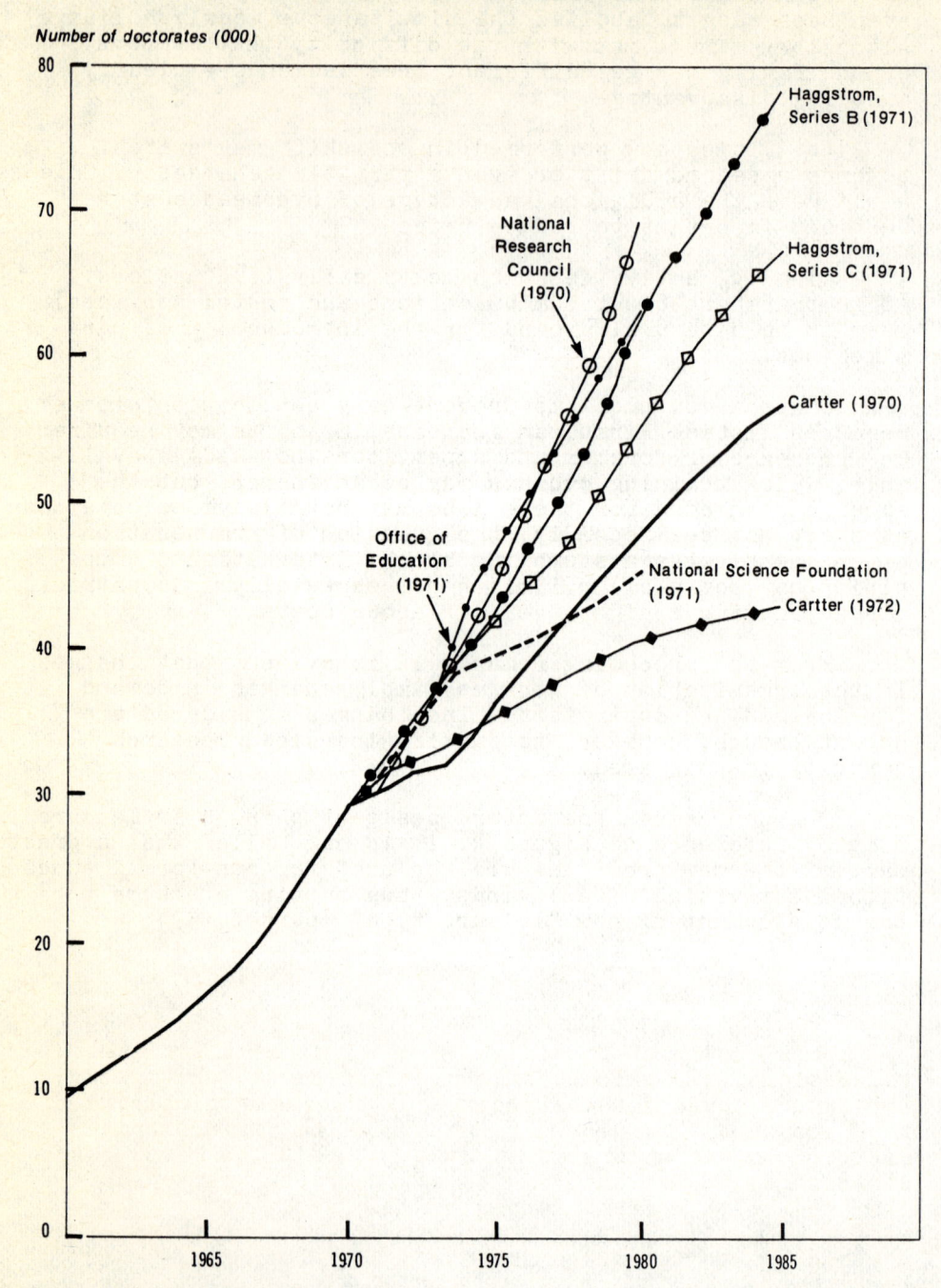

Source : A.M. Cartter, «The academic labour market», in M.S. Gordon, ed., *Higher Education and the Labour Market*, Mc Graw-Hill, New York, 1974, p. 297.

Figure 4 **THE TIME USE OF THE AVERAGE FRENCHMAN IN 1800, 1900 AND 2000**

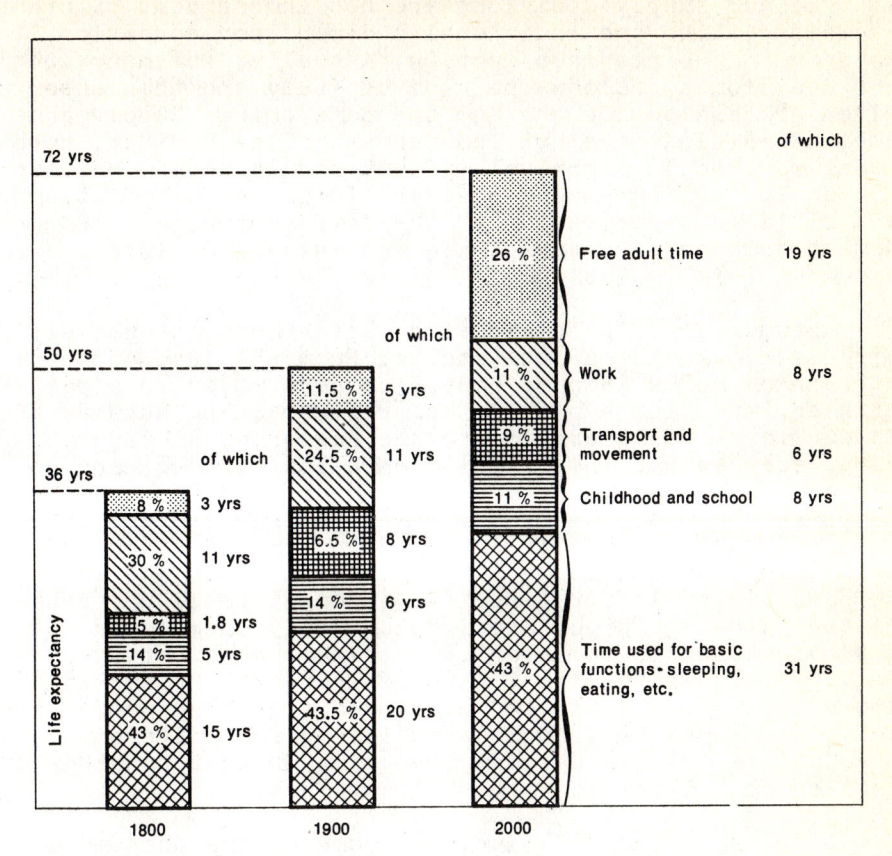

	1800	1900	2000
Life expectancy	36 yrs	50 yrs	72 yrs

1800: 8% - 3 yrs; 30% - 11 yrs; 5% - 1.8 yrs; 14% - 5 yrs; 43% - 15 yrs

1900: of which 11.5% - 5 yrs; 24.5% - 11 yrs; 6.5% - 8 yrs; 14% - 6 yrs; 43.5% - 20 yrs

2000: of which
- 26% Free adult time — 19 yrs
- 11% Work — 8 yrs
- 9% Transport and movement — 6 yrs
- 11% Childhood and school — 8 yrs
- 43% Time used for basic functions - sleeping, eating, etc. — 31 yrs

Source : EEC, *The Courier* no. 57, September-October 1979, p. 31.

IV. THE SUPPLY OF EDUCATED MANPOWER

When education is linked to economic manpower considerations, two main questions arise. First, what will be the future educational structure of the "economically active" population ? Secondly, what will be the economic needs of educated manpower in the future ? The first issue corresponds to the supply side of the labour market and is examined below under the headings of labour force participation and labour supply elasticities. The second issue corresponds to the demand side of the labour market and, as discussed in the previous section, is linked to the changing composition of output and elasticities of substitution.

Labour force participation

Labour supply decisions are not independent of other decisions, like the individual's demand for education covered in the previous section. Actually, for many people the decision to follow one kind of study and then enter a given profession are one and the same thing. Supply and demand decisions are not independent of each other, both being moulded in a gradual (if not simultaneous) process. For analytical purposes, however, it is useful to attempt an initial categorisation of the different supply and demand components before these are integrated into a "reduced form" solution.

Labour force participation varies most intensively with age, sex and marital status. From the 19th century pattern of child labour, societies have moved to a pattern with an important number of cohorts remaining outside the labour force. This applies to the age group subject to compulsory education, to children below that age and to age groups beyond retirement age, hence roughly to those under 15 and over 65. Of the remaining age groups, 15-64, a considerable number is involved in some education process ; and housewives, strangely, are not considered to be part of the labour force (40). Some 5 to 10 per cent of the 15-64 age group are involuntarily unemployed and a tiny portion is voluntarily outside the labour force. This part is increasing for those in recurrent education. Among those involuntarily unemployed a growing number are unfit for work. Retirement age differs for different occupations and discussions are going on as to whether an earlier or a later retirement is preferable.

Tables 24 and 25 illustrate some of the phenomena described and some of the expectations of OECD's "Interfutures" report.

Table 24

PERCENTAGE OF POPULATION IN VARIOUS AGE
GROUPS : DEVELOPED COUNTRIES

Age Group	1975	1980	1985	1990	1995	2000
0- 4	8.2	8.3	8.3	8.1	7.7	7.5
5-14	16.8	15.6	15.5	15.7	15.6	15.1
15-64	64.5	65.0	65.4	64.9	64.7	65.0
65	10.5	11.1	10.8	11.3	12.0	12.4

Source : OECD Interfutures, op. cit., Table 26.

40. According to recent estimates, the value of work of a housewife with children is £ 130-150 per week. See J. Slaughter, "The Price of an Ordinary Woman", The Observer, 24 February 1980.

Table 25

ACTIVE CIVIL POPULATION, AS PER CENT OF
AGE GROUP 15-64 : SELECTED OECD COUNTRIES

Country	1975	1990	2000
United States	67.2	67.1	67.9
Japan	70.6	69.0	70.0
France	65.8	63.7	65.6
Germany	65.4	65.4	64.1
Italy	53.7	53.0	53.5
United Kingdom	72.5	71.0	74.0
Average	64.4	63.2	64.3

Source : Interfutures, op. cit., Table 29.

These aggregate labour force statistics, however, hide sex and marital differences that are likely to have important implications for educational planning. Thus, Table 26 shows that in the United States, huge reductions are anticipated in the labour supply of 16-24-year-old males by 1990, and a dramatic increase of 35-44-year-old females. What this might mean for schools and their output is a shift from the present "youth unemployment" problem to a future "children's education" problem. The reason is that the increase in female participation will mainly be among married women (41).

More or less the same picture is anticipated in the United Kingdom where the labour force participation rate of 35-44 married women has risen from 24 per cent in 1951 to 68 per cent in 1977.

This important aspect of labour force participation by sex cannot be properly discussed without mentioning the practice of not including in the labour force the activities of housewives. This practice is the consequence of several factors.

---

41. For a non-technical explanation of this phenomenon, see J. Mincer, "Labour Force Participation", International Encyclopedia of the Social Sciences, Vol. 8, 1968.

Table 26

LABOUR FORCE PARTICIPATION AND ANTICIPATED LABOUR FORCE CHANGES, USA, 1975-1990

Percentage

Sex and age	Labour force participation 1975	Labour force change 1975-1990
Males	77.3	16.5
16-24	72.9	-11.0
25-34	94.2	32.1
35-44	94.8	59.2
45-64	84.8	1.1
65 +	20.8	- 2.9
Females	45.7	31.4
16-24	57.3	2.0
25-34	54.3	54.6
35-44	55.6	79.9
45-64	50.2	12.8
65 +	7.8	21.1

Source : U.S. Department of Labor, Employment and Training Report of the President, 1977, p. 253.

For example, the large anticipated reductions in the German labour force (see Table 27) might be nominal rather than real when working wives are taken into account. The most important factor is probably that most housewives are not paid for their work. Another may be that their work is considered as part of the consumption rather than the production process. Great doubts can be expressed with regard to the latter argument, especially when the education of children is given the importance it deserves. In a period where the education process shows shortcomings sometimes of a serious degree - often because of the absence of both parents during working time - there is need for a serious debate, based on reliable information and free from doctinaire views.

It is hardly possible to deal with this all-important issue in this report in the necessary interdisciplinary way it deserves. But as economists we would like to stress the following points. First, we want to reiterate the emphasis on the importance of bringing up the young generation. Secondly, we want to state that socially non-optimal choices are made by a considerable number of women partly because housewives are not paid in accordance with the

Table 27

NET ADDITIONS TO THE LABOUR FORCE
AT THE END OF EACH DECADE, GERMANY

Per cent

Year	Net addition
1980	+ 22
1990	− 2
2000	− 33

Note : Estimated as the difference between entries to working life and retirements and on the assumption that current fertility trends are maintained.

Source : H. Wander, "Demographic aspects of the active population", Council of Europe, Strasbourg, document SEM/PS(76)2.

social importance of their work. Thirdly, we want to make it clear that payment in accordance with this work's importance is not easy to organise. The questions arising here are :

a) who has to pay ? and
b) should not the payment depend on the quality of the work done ?

Answers to (a) vary between payment by the husband and payment by the community as proposed by A. Ehrenfest (42). In the authors' opinion payment should indeed depend on the quality, if only approximately. But that statement leads us to a fourth aspect : are there possibilities to exert some quality control ? In most societies only criminal neglect of the child's interests are dealt with by the community. Can this supervision be refined ? One other instrument already partly used is to prepare prospective educators - both parents - by home economics courses extended to include educational aspects and to introduce examinations and diplomas. Emotions on all sides will be evoked by these observations. Yet we feel that youth behaviour has developed into such disastrous directions that the problems mentioned - and several more - must be urgently tackled.

---

42. See A. Ehrenfest, "Het Plan Ehrenfest", Haagse Post, 26 May, 1979, pp. 32-38.

Labour supply elasticities

One factor that is likely to determine the supply of labour by educational level is its price. The relationship between the change in wages and change in the amount of labour supplied is summarised by the concept of elasticity of supply.

A particularly careful piece of research on this question has been conducted by Freeman (43), who studied the markets for various occupations requiring a college education in the United States. The price elasticity of the annual flow of new engineering students could be estimated with considerable precision and was found to be close to unity. A similar figure can be derived from material collected by Dougherty and used by one of us (44). The elasticity varies from 0.54 to 2.64, depending on the method used. Dresch finds a figure equal to 2.1 (45). The latter three figures apply to all university-educated ; Dougherty's refer to the stock, but Dresch's to new entrants, as in Freeman's study.

It seems worthwhile to discuss the relationship between flow and stock elasticities. The annual flow is a very small portion of the stock because a working life is normally about forty years long. Therefore, the stock elasticity is one where a distributed time lag applies, extending over a very long period. The two kinds of supply elasticities are only identical if the price change is average over some forty years. Short-term effects are much smaller.

An additional estimate has been made by Ullman Chiswick (46). She finds a mainly negative elasticity for the stock of educated labour (in her case non-production workers), varying from 1.25 to +.17. The attempts at estimating the supply elasticity mentioned so far may be supplemented by Evans' opinion that it is negligible (47).

---

43. A. Freeman, The Over-Educated American, Academic Press, New York, 1976.
44. C.R.S. Dougherty, "Substitution and the Structure of the Labour Force", The Economic Journal 82, 1972, p. 170, and J. Tinbergen (1975), op. cit., p. 96.
45. S.P. Dresch quoted in J. Tinbergen, op. cit.
46. C. Ullman-Chiswick, (1972) "The Growth of Professional Occupations in the American Labour Force 1900-1963", (Unpubl. thesis Columbia Univ. World Bank Summary). An updated version is in press.
47. Evans, quoted by Espenshade, "Zero Population Growth and the Economies of Developed Nations", in Population and Development Review, Vol. IV, 1978.

As earlier recalled, one of the most important areas of labour supply response is that of married women. Table 28 shows that the probability of labour force participation of this group increases with the level of education and decreases with the number of children. Evidence of this kind links labour force supply policies with policies for children.

Table 28

THE PROBABILITY OF WORKING BY NUMBER OF PRE-SCHOOL CHILDREN AND YEARS OF SCHOOLING : USA

Number of children under 6	Years of schooling		
	8	12	16
0	.30	.47	.66
1	.09	.18	.32
2	.01	.04	.09

Table 29

TRANSITIONS BETWEEN OCCUPATIONAL SECTORS IN THE UNITED KINGDOM 1970-71, IN PER CENT OF TOTAL WORK FORCE

Occupations in 1971	Occupations in 1970				
	Farms & mines	Blue collar	Personal services	Other white collar	Total
Farms, mines	3.11	0.05	0.01	0.02	3.19
Blue collar	0.09	44.58	0.21	0.50	45.38
Pers. services	0.01	0.27	11.20	0.23	11.71
Other white collar	0.02	0.56	0.23	38.91	39.72
Total	3.23	45.46	11.65	39.66	100

Source : Jonathan Gershuny, <u>After Industrial Society, The Emerging Self-Service Economy</u> ? Macmillan, London, 1978, p. 63.

The concept can be applied to single persons, but also to the occupations of parents and those of their children. It is especially in this sense that we propose to consider it. A low occupational mobility then results in the phenomenon that society's structure narrows the choice of occupations and hence education types open to an individual. Society in many countries is compartmentalised by differences in SES (socio-economic status). These compartments, according to some authors, are virtually watertight (48) : there is a tendency for children to stay in the socio-economic group of their parents, regardless of the options to which their innate capabilities would entitle them. One cause might be discrimination by those who advise parents on the further education of their children, and another might be the education system itself, in what is encouraged or discouraged by teachers and curricula.

For example, the drive towards increased fertility in Western societies will have as an indirect impact the withdrawal of a number of women from the labour force. However, the increased educational level of women will tend to counterbalance this trend so that the eventual net result is unclear.

Occupational mobility

By the term occupational mobility we mean the speed of transition from one occupation to another. An example is provided by Table 29, albeit for a very short period. The other democracies alluded to are also Anglo-Saxon and Northern European countries. In Latin societies - whether American or European - social stratification is more pronounced than in Anglo-Saxon or Germanic societies.

A number of studies in occupational mobility have been made in various countries. Continuation and extension of such studies is desirable. Some facts point to a reduction of stratification. One is that the percentage of the population considered to be an élite - for instance, the main professional group - is increasing. Thus, the percentage of professional, technical and kindred workers in the United States labour force has increased from 4.2 to 15.2 per cent thus far in this century and keeps rising (49).

---

48. S. Boroles and H. Gintis, Schooling in Capitalist America, Basic Books, New York, 1976.
49. U.S. Bureau of the Census, Historical Statistics, Colonial Times to 1970, p. 139 and US Department of Labor, Employment and Training Report of the President, Washington D.C., 1977, p. A-15.

Another factor is that income differentials of such groups to average incomes are diminishing. For example, in the United States the relative earning advantage of college over secondary educated labour dropped by 15 per cent in the 1949 to 1971 period (50). Also, of top executives in America 45 per cent were reported to originate from "wealthy" families in 1900, only 8 per cent in 1976 (51). Moreover, their compensations remained equal in real terms between 1952 and 1976, whereas average real income went up by some 30 per cent (52).

Similar reductions have been observed in other countries, especially following the higher education explosion of the late sixties.

But no matter how we measure the underlying variables, schooling relates positively to occupational mobility. For example in the United Kingdom, the "social distance" travelled from father's to son's occupation relates to small differences in educational attainment (see Table 30) (53).

Table 30

INTERGENERATIONAL SOCIAL MOBILITY
AND LEVEL OF SCHOOLING, UNITED KINGDOM

Mobility category	Mean years of schooling
None	9.9
Upward	11.0
High upward	11.7

Source : G. Psacharopoulos, "Family background, education and achievement", British Journal of Sociology, Vol. 28, No. 3, September 1977, p. 330.

---

50. G. Psacharopoulos, Earnings and Education in OECD Countries, OECD, Paris, 1975, p. 168.
51. F.D. Sturdivent and L.D. Adler, "Executive Origins : Still A Grayflannel World ?", Harvard Business Review, 1976, Nov/Dec., p. 125 ff.
52. C.G. Burck, "A Group Profile of the Fortune 500 Chief Executives", in Fortune, May 1976, p. 173 ff.
53. See also G. Psacharopoulos and J. Tinbergen, "On the explanation of schooling, occupation and earnings : Some alternative path analyses", in De Economist, Vol. 126, 1978, No. 4.

It remains an open question whether in an education-saturated society of the future, schooling will continue to have the same impact on mobility. Although the top professional class will keep growing, the bottom occupations will be fed by immigrants, the children of whom will strive for higher levels of education in a competitive society. The eventual "distance" travelled by such minority groups will depend upon Government policies towards the education of immigrant children.

The educational level of the labour force

The end result of the interaction of the various components discussed above is a continuous change in the structure of the labour force by educational level. As an example, the case of the Netherlands is presented in Table 31.

Table 31

ACTUAL AND PROJECTED LABOUR FORCE
IN THE NETHERLANDS ACCORDING TO THE LEVEL
OF EDUCATIONAL ATTAINMENT

Percentage

Year	Elementary	Extended Elementary	Secondary	Tertiary (of which univ.)
1960	56	39		5
1975	33	40	16	10 (3)
1990	19	67		14 (7)

Sources : Central Bureau of Statistics, Pocket Year Book 1977, pp. 102/3. Central Planning Bureau, Occasional Papers, No. 11, Table 5. (The number of those with university education is taken from Parliamentary Document, 13323, 1975).

These figures are based on the assumption of a zero price elasticity of supply (54), of a continuation of the shift observed in the period 1960-1970 from vocational to

---

54. Perhaps this is the most realistic assumption to make in view of the divergent estimates of labour supply elasticities, which are the net result of the interaction between income and substitution effects.

general education, increased participation of women (which used to be low) and a decreasing average duration of university education (which in the Netherlands was quite long until the sixties). The figures refer to full-time schooling only.

These figures are mere projections in the sense that they do not incorporate assumptions about the possible need for a change in government policies based on the need perceived for a correspondence between education and the general process of social change referred to earlier. Possible social policies could be directed towards lessening social tensions and alienation. Policies which were sufficient in this respect around the "fifties" and the "sixties" may not be satisfactory any more in the "eighties" or "nineties". Present day inequalities in living conditions are less than half a century ago (55), but are still felt to be unacceptable by a majority of the population of most industrialised countries. "Insufficiently thorough political debate on the kind of society we want in the year 2000" is being suggested by Ekström (56) even for a country like Sweden. Education policy has been recognised to have the potentialities of an "equaliser", but several attempts made so far to find an operational solution in this respect have been rather unsuccessful. Furthermore, new developments in preferences may make different approaches more promising. Changes in motivation for schooling, the growing awareness of the danger of pollution, the reluctance to use some types of energy and the shrinking of plant and animal gene reserves (57), require a reorientation in several policy aims, including those of education. Some of these problems will be taken up again in a later section.

V. MATCHING SUPPLY AND DEMAND

The supply of educated manpower is not always a straight function of the demand for education. This is especially true in countries with very developed public educational systems which exercise a direct control on the supply side. Thus in setting educational supply targets governments have to take into account not only the two sources of demand, discussed previously, but also such factors as their budgetary constraints and the political pressure from various organised groups which may demand either the restriction of the supply of a specific type

---

55. See J. Tinbergen, Income Distribution : Analysis and Policies, North Holland, Amsterdam, 1975.
56. S. Ekström, Sweden in a New International Economic Order, Secretariat for Future Studies, Stockholm, 1979.
57. N. Myers, The Sinking Ark, Pergamon Press, Oxford, 1979.

of qualified manpower or the contrary. Future educational supply, therefore, will depend, as it has in the past, not only on the demand and supply factors discussed in the last two sections, but also on governments' political decisions affecting all levels of education and particularly upper secondary and higher. The final result in each country will depend on the extent to which governments control the educational system. Thus given the demand conditions for education (from the point of view of individuals and the productive system) we will have different development scenarios according to government policies. Figure 5 shows two such scenarios based on two hypotheses : an expansionary government policy resulting in Scenario 2 and a restrictive government policy resulting in Scenario 1.

Past government policies were expansionary and there were points like C' that have been observed. This trend might now be reversing (58).

A. Symptoms likely to be observed

But there are some problem areas not covered above that result from the interplay of supply and demand. Such areas, which are bound to affect private and government decisions, are the level of unemployment and the relative earnings of graduates. To put it in terms of the race between supply and demand, we would like to know where the intersection points, such as A, B, C, in Figure 5 will lie in the future, and whether the years to come will be associated with a permanent rise of unemployment for school graduates.

The future level of unemployment

It is commonplace to state that demand for and supply of manpower do not match. This is true regarding total numbers, but also for a considerable number of groups, either characterised by level of education or defined by other criteria. What is socially most undesirable is the unemployment of young people which has increased more than unemployment as a whole. Thus in the European Community, unemployment of those below 25 years of age between 1969 and 1977 grew from 400 000 to 2 million, or 24 per cent to 37 per cent of the respective age groups, whereas these cohorts represented only 17 per cent of the total labour force.

---

58. For a documentation of this point see : J.P. Smith and F. Welch, "The Overeducated American ? A Review Article", The Rand Corporation, Santa Monica, California, November 1978, p-6253.

An important reason for this uneven burden on young people is the unavoidable fact that by definition a school leaver has no work experience, and his theoretical knowledge, obtained from schooling, by necessity lags behind the requirements of the world of work.

Since the cohorts in question are likely to increase in size until 1983, more attention to the problem of youth unemployment is urgent. Measures so far taken by the European Commission and many governments are of an order of magnitude incommensurate with the size of the problem. However, many economists and demographers expect the youth employment problem to diminish towards the last decade of this century as the age composition of the population shifts.

There is another factor whose development is likely to cause changes in education. This is the future <u>overall</u> level of unemployment in Member countries. According to British estimates, the level of unemployment by the last decade of this century will be about three times its present level (see Table 32).

Table 32

UNEMPLOYMENT STATISTICS, UNITED KINGDOM, 1976-1991

Year	Total unemployed (in millions)	Male unemployment rate (per cent)
1976	1.3	6.1
1986	2.9	14.6
1991	3.4	16.5

<u>Sources</u> : C. Leicester, "Keeping the jobless in touch with work", <u>The Times</u>, 15 May 1978 and C. Leicester, "Unemployment rates by age and sex", Institute of Manpower Studies, University of Sussex, Paper GN 113, September 1978 (mimeo).

This predicted dramatic rise in the level of unemployment cannot be accepted at face value and has already generated a great deal of controversy. Demands for a world-wide "operation employment" are frequently expressed. Let us here accept as a possible scenario that unemployment will substantially rise in OECD countries by the end of the century. If this is the case, it has implications for the development of the school system.

In the first place, unemployment means a reduction of the social and private cost of education (because of

Figure 5 **THE FUTURE EVOLUTION OF THE MARKET FOR EDUCATED LABOUR**

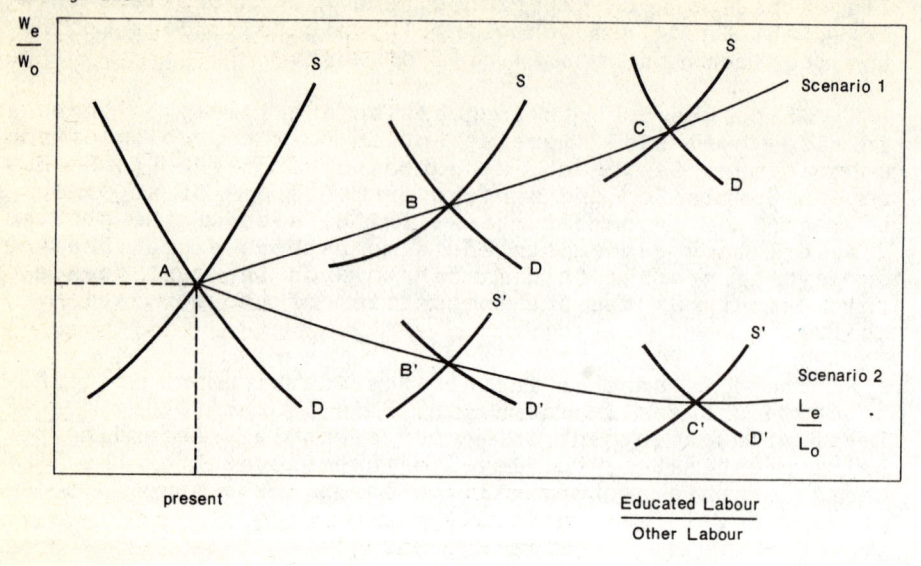

the near zero foregone earnings), especially at the post-secondary level. This is likely to set two forces in motion : a higher social demand for schooling and a more abundant state provision of educational facilities "to train or retrain the unemployed". Such developments and schemes already exist in Member countries, and it is reasonable to anticipate that their importance will grow <u>pari passu</u> with the rise of unemployment.

Secondly, the alleged rise in unemployment might help to shake educationists out of the inertia in which they have been operating for years. With the excuse of a lack of a comprehensive learning theory, schools at all levels continue to offer traditional curricula, transmitting knowledge by more or less the same methods during the last fifty years or more. Of course there are exceptions (e.g. the open university) but these exceptions are a long way from the general modus operandi. If the end product (i.e. the graduate) does not fit the world of work, educationists will be increasingly motivated to go back to the drawing board and devise more "relevant" or flexible curricula. In our opinion, curriculum relevance of the future will be tantamount to <u>flexibility</u> by means of the provision of <u>general</u> knowledge.

It is also realistic to anticipate widespread use of "distance learning systems" such as television-telephone hook-ups. The technical innovation part of this development is already in existence (e.g. the British "Prestel" system) and the system can be simply adapted to teaching at a distance. This kind of teaching is especially suitable for adults (hence for the unemployed or those changing careers) and also for women who have household commitments.

Areas of unsatisfied social demand for places

Apart from the serious problem of age groups just mentioned, there are structural disequilibria of other types. There are industrial, vocational and geographical groups in which supply is larger, and other groups in which supply is smaller than demand. In other words, industrial, vocational and geographical mobility falls short of what is needed to minimize unemployment. It is self-evident that in a period of recession the number of individuals seeking employment exceeds the number of vacancies. Sub-groups of those looking in vain for employment need particular attention, for example the sub-group which has received training in activities with shrinking perspectives or one which is denied training as a consequence of monopolistic (restrictive) practices.

An example of the first category - the one with shrinking perspectives - is people trained for occupations in industries no longer competitive in the world market. This is the situation in some industries where developing countries have increasingly become competitive, such as parts of the garment and textile industries, those of leather and leather products, and some woodworking industries. In some developed countries the tendency to protect these industries has grown in order to safeguard employment, but from a work point of view this is ill-advised (59). Retraining for jobs in activities with a more promising future is preferable, as has been recently shown (60).

With regard to the second category - that of restrictive practices in education - it is widely believed that in some medical faculties the number of students is limited in order to affect favourably the incomes earned in these professions. Similar practices are attributed to other faculties, or sub-faculties. If correct, this is objectionable and independent investigations are needed to check these accusations.

---

59. Balassa, B., "The New Protectionism and the International Economy", Journal of World Trade Law, Vol. 12, 1979, pp. 409-436.
60. J. Tinbergen, "Enkele opmerkingen over herstructurering" Econ.-Stat. Berichten, Vol. 64, 1979, pp. 364-366.

Areas of likely skill shortages

We now turn to the opposite phenomenon of established cases of skill shortages. In the Netherlands, a lack of skilled construction workers prevails which has been publicised already for a year or so in advertisements placed by construction firms. The shortage is confirmed by a retraining programme adopted in the city of Rotterdam, where skilled metal workers will be retrained for construction work (61).

Another likely shortage is in the printing trade, where, in the Netherlands, an apprentice regulation exists and the places available for apprentices are partly unfilled. We are less well informed about other countries but have the impression that the Netherlands compares unfavourably with some other countries in the motivation to work. More serious inquiries are therefore desirable with a view to further investigating the situation in Member countries and identifying the necessary remedies.

A third category of likely shortages is one not so much of skill in the usual sense, but of willingness to accept dirty or otherwise unattractive work. This lack of willingness is one of the reasons why migrant workers have been "imported" by employers ; and in a way it is an old phenomenon, reminding us of slavery in the Americas and related phenomena of a more remote past. From a worldwide point of view we want to repeat that labour migration of the type discussed is generally undesirable and that the best solution is a much more intensive co-operation between developed and developing countries.

A last category of possible shortages is that of highly qualified people earning high incomes. Their high incomes, insofar as they are not attributable to monopolistic markets, are an indication of their scarcity. The possibility exists that this scarcity is due to innate capabilities possessed only by a limited number of individuals. Opinions on this issue among those who have studied the problem differ considerably. More evidence is desirable on the possibility or impossibility of further reducing income differences by giving access to education to groups so far deprived of it. The eventual decision, however, depends upon the political will of the Government.

The relative salary position of graduates

The earning power of university graduates in Member countries has substantially declined in the seventies. This relative decline should clear out some cobwebs in the

---

61. The initiative was taken mid-1979 by alderman J.C. van der Ploeg.

market for college trained people. The reason is that there exists a lagged asymmetry between supply and demand for educated manpower. Whereas demand from the point of view of the employers is a function of current wages, the supply of academically trained people today is a function of the salaries observed in the market four or five years ago. Extrapolating what has happened in the past, it is reasonable to anticipate a continuous oscillation around an equilibrium supply and demand intersection point that might never be reached in practice. What this means is we shall alternate between shortages and surpluses as well as between higher and lower salaries in different professions.

In the long run, this is not such a terrible situation. Actually, it is very healthy from the point of view of a market feedback and a supply response of the individual. However, any inherent non-clearing market friction is equivalent to a social efficiency loss and should be minimised in the short run. An information-signalling system sponsored by a Government planning agency seems to be essential in this respect, a theme to be elaborated below.

B. Future Policy Action

Public policy in matters of education constitutes an important component of public policy as a whole. The amount of public money spent on education is enough to illustrate this.

The aims of education policies can be classed as direct and indirect. Among the direct aims are :

   i) setting of standards for compulsory education,
  ii) providing education in order to meet individual demand,
 iii) meeting manpower demands,
  iv) influencing individual demand where this is deemed necessary to match manpower demand.

Such corrections may be needed concerning public policies, in cases where some social groups have to be protected against short-sightedness which may damage their own longer-term interests. In fact, compulsory education up to a certain age is a case in point in that it might be viewed as a "merit good". But there are other dimensions of education where myopia also makes people do things they might later regret.

The most important indirect aim of education policy is its contribution to an optimal "general policy", i.e. a policy aiming at maximum social welfare. Therefore, this optimum depends on a particular society's social welfare objectives. A concrete example may be a reduction in inequalities in income and the efforts made to obtain income (62). Another example is the undertaking of research into problems of greater urgency for society's future than is reflected in the spontaneous volume of research undertaken at the initiative of existing private and public institutions. Examples can be found in the last section of this chapter. A final example is the degree of decentralisation in education policies : should decisions be made at the local, or at higher levels, and if so, at what level ?

One very general heading under which both education policy as a whole and the particular aim of matching supply with wish and demand can be offered, is the encouragement of recurrent education. In a way, recurrent education is the return to a more natural life programme, usual in older forms of economic activity as well. Its main characteristic is starting with simple jobs and gradually proceeding to higher levels until the level most appropriate to each individual is reached. Increasingly, as we move to a more complicated production process, we find people participating in refresher or re-orientation courses, in order to keep abreast of social development in all senses. The idea of recurrent education is linked in particular to lengthening re-orientation courses to periods of up to some years. This alternation of theory (school) and practice (production in the widest sense) is especially suited to occupations requiring practical experience or maturity, as for instance theologists, psychologists, medical doctors and agogists of all sorts. Another aspect is that for everybody, whatever their future occupation may be, some personal experience in other "spheres of life" is desirable ; this has led many policy advisers to the idea of instituting two years or so of "social service" as part of everybody's education.

It seems appropriate to end the preceding arguments in favour of recurrent education with one argument against it for some classes of "final occupation", namely those for which it is known that the peak in productivity occurs at an early age. This is not only true for heavy physical work, but also for intellectual work with an important mathematical component (natural scientists, engineers, computer programmers, etc.).

Signalling to influence private behaviour

Turning now to more modest and more specific policies to adjust differences between supply and demand, information

---

62. G. Psacharopoulos, "Economies of Education : An Assessment of Recent Methodological Advances and Empirical Results", in Social Science Information, No. 314, 1977, "Result No. 8".

policies for the process of education must be mentioned. Precisely because education processes take considerable time, it is possible to warn both potential suppliers and potential demanders of some type of labour ahead of time of possible discrepancies giving them time to take measures in favour of equalising supply and demand. Information of this type already exists ; secondary school leavers are provided with information about the demand for alternative third level jobs open to them. This will have an impact especially on those whose endowment with intellect or other capabilities makes them hesitant about exactly what job to aim at.

Not only should the potential future suppliers be more systematically informed about the cohorts in each pipe-line, but, also, future employers. The lack of skilled workers of some types may be forecast on the basis of figures about the flows of students to the corresponding vocational schools a few years before it comes into effect.

Alternatively, the choice made at the end of a lower vocational school may be followed. Thus, in the Netherlands, the outflow from lower vocational schools, after rising between 1968 and 1973, fell slightly between 1973 and 1974 and steeply from 1974 to 1975 ; from 34.8 to 24.3 thousands of students. On the other hand, the percentage choosing to continue at the mid-level vocational schools went on rising. The same was true of the outflow from general extended elementary education and of the percentage choosing to continue to mid-level vocational schools. So it could be seen from 1974 and 1975 figures that the numbers passing the final exam of the lower vocational schools in 1976 were abnormally low (39.1 as compared with 40.9 five years earlier).

Lags in policy implementation

The normal Government policy procedures are characterised by long time lags relative to individual action. This is a drawback of bureaucracy only too well known. It is conceivable to shorten established procedures, though this sometimes depends on personalities in the government machine. Another approach is to start procedures at earlier stages in the process, and the length of education processes may make this possible. Making available the results in record time would also help. The decline of employment in a number of labour-intensive industries, for instance, could have been predicted long ago. Government or private medium-term reconnaissance studies on the 3 to 5-year prospects of a number of industries should be given more attention, in simple language, in newspapers or directly in educational governing bodies. The performance of governments and businesses in encouraging or implementing "new combinations" (to use Schumpeter's characterisation of entrepreneurs) has been very disappointing. Few private firms have shown vision here, and few governments have set out a clear pattern of restructuring the industrial system of their economies.

Institutional changes

Perhaps this is the appropriate point at which to start contemplating future institutional changes and the way these changes are likely to affect education. Predicting institutional changes must be based on circumstantial evidence or "hunch", as there exist no statistical time series data for a technocratic projection.

Thus, taking up institutional distinction made earlier, one may anticipate a shift of emphasis from training in formal schools to training within the firm. There are several factors that point in this direction. First, there is the inability of the formal school system to keep pace with recent technological developments. Firms have a stronger incentive to respond more effectively and faster to the need for training their personnel according to the latest technological demands (63). Second, training on the job shifts a great part of the social cost of training from the individual and the taxpayer to the eventual user. Given recent trends in tax finance capabilities of state-provided education systems, it is likely that this shift of the burden towards the firm would be welcomed by the politicians in power.

To the extent that this institutional change is real, it might have at least two further major implications for education. First, the curricula of formal schools might change towards the provision of general skills in preference to specific capabilities. This is because the latter would have been relegated to the firm. Second, one may anticipate a fall in the total uninterrupted length of formal training in advanced Member countries and a corresponding rise in the later-in-life education component. In spite of the intense lifelong education research activity and literature during the last ten years, lifelong education has not developed much in practice (64). Perhaps one of the reasons for this is that the present institutional arrangements are such that it is extremely difficult for the 40-year old to go back to school. But if we are correct

---

63. See also Stanley D. Nollen, "Paid Educational Leave : New Element in Firm-Level Manpower Policy ?", IRRA 39th Annual Proceedings, 1978, pp. 274-283.

64. e.g., see OECD/CERI, Equal Educational Opportunity : A Statement of the Problem with Special Reference to Recurrent Education, Paris, 1970.

in our hypothesis of a shift from formal schools to training on the job, lifelong education would increase although it might be radically different in form from what is advocated today. Namely, it would be provided on the job rather than in formal educational institutions. This would make attendance by adults easier.

Turning to another area, one cannot anticipate sweeping changes in the compulsory school leaving age. Practically all Member countries by the end of the century will have instituted the 16th year as the end of compulsory education. This has implications for the demand (and hence, supply) of teachers, a theme already elaborated above.

Increased attention might have to be given to the quantity and quality of children and this would be reflected in higher enrolments in nursery schools in all Member countries (65). Thus, we anticipate an increased emphasis on extended schooling towards early childhood in the same way, though perhaps more dramatically, as the 1960s saw the expansion of education into early adult life with the universities (66).

Given these circumstances, it is not unreasonable to anticipate rapid institutional changes in the hiring practices of both the private and the public sector. Perhaps less emphasis will be given to certificates and more to the content of education received, as evidenced by the curriculum of the school from which the potential employee has graduated. Dropouts might be rewarded to the extent that they have some general skills that facilitate on-the-job trainability. Actually, dropping out is likely to be encouraged so as to relieve the state financial burden. Selection procedures might take the form of an initial working-learning period within the firm.

Another area within which to anticipate vast institutional changes is that of the content and quality of state-provided formal schooling. As already mentioned, curricula might be redesigned along general rather than vocational lines. Also, teaching methods might radically alter to employ computerised, self-teaching technology. This technology is already developed and dropping in price. Radical changes are expected in library systems and vast substitutions of computer "hardware" for teachers. To the extent that these expected developments materialise, they will affect the demand for teachers on the one hand, and the rapidly expanding service industries providing and maintaining the necessary teaching "software" on the other.

---

65. See *Caring for Young Children*, OECD/CERI, Paris, 1982.

66. For a discussion of these two different kinds of educational policies, see G. Psacharopoulos, "The Economics of Social Services for Children", in *ibidem*.

New cultural needs

Culture, like society, is continuously changing. The last decades have shown a number of changes, especially in the realm of sub-culture of migrant workers. These decades have also witnessed intensive discussions on the need for cultural changes occasioned by the "new scarcities" : threatening scarcities in the fields of energy and of a healthy living environment (67). Alongside these more dramatic aspects of Western culture it has gradually become clear that the affluence brought by technological development has raised the consumption of various goods beyond healthy levels. Thus, not only the consumption of the "old enemies" such as alcoholic beverages and tobacco products has risen to unhealthy levels but also some "new enemies" are at work ("drugs" for short) and some goods considered innocent - meat and sugar, for example - have in fact become enemies. From a broader point of view, affluence has also raised the consumption of "nonsense" goods.

We cannot possibly go into details concerning the impact that the elements listed above are likely to have on the demand for education. But a few examples can be mentioned, if we bear in mind that there is a difference between what is likely and what is normative. Education facilities for migrant workers and their families are insufficient in many countries and to the extent that the migratory movement will continue, such facilities need to increase. A new type of teacher might accordingly be demanded.

Some of the new subcultures have changed the motivation for schooling. The extent to which these changes on the supply side will evoke reactions on the demand side is difficult to estimate. It is somewhat similar to the opposite phenomenon of an excess of requirements on the demand side. In a number of sectors in several countries educational attainments are required beyond what is needed for a proper performance on the job. Sometimes, both on the supply and on the demand side, an element of prestige seems to be involved. As a healthy reaction to such situations, proposals are under discussion in the Netherlands to reduce the length of university training. The Dutch situation is far from representative, however, as the average length of university education is long compared to other countries.

However, one must be extremely careful on the interpretation of statistics on "educational inflation". The statistics typically come from job descriptions as provided by employers. These statistics do not tell (and

---

67. N. Myers, op. cit., 1979.

cannot tell) whether a more than minimally educated typist would in fact perform better (i.e. be more productive) in her job.

VI. ON FUTURE POLICIES AND RESEARCH

In this last section we try to pull together the threads and discuss some general policy lines that are likely to be highly debated in OECD countries in the years to come. We also give an account of the research needed to support the relevant policy decisions.

A. Future General Policy Lines

The spirit of this report has been that increased attention will be given to the individual demand versus the manpower aspect of educational provision. Government decisions in this respect will have to be based on information on what people want. Also, individuals must be kept informed about likely changes in labour market conditions. Thus, "information provision" might be a new policy line of the future (68).

To the extent that this general policy will be adopted, it will necessarily increase the burden on the state finance capacity. Another main point in this report has been that the extra resources required by future educational expression might have to be sought in the private sector. For example, it might be the case that in view of finance difficulties many countries would take a more relaxed view towards the private educational sector and work-linked learning.

In view of the above trends, what one might see in the near future is a more open policy towards types of schooling and/or faculties that do not adhere to the traditional "vocational schooling for work relevance" view. To the extent that more weight is placed on individual preferences and private finance, increased enrolments are to be expected in "software faculties" such as the social sciences, humanities and liberal arts. We predict an increased emphasis on a more general curriculum, both at the secondary and at the higher education levels.

---

68. For an elaboration of the kind of information needed, see G. Psacharopoulos, ed. Information : An Essential Factor in Educational Planning and Policy, Unesco, Paris, 1980.

All this will demand flexibility, not only from the point of view of the recipient of education but also of the providers of education.

In our changing world no student is expected any more to follow a fixed lifetime career. Also, teachers will have to be flexible in adapting to changing circumstances, both in terms of what they teach and the demand for their services following the silicon chip revolution. Teachers will have a key role to play in maintaining the vitality of the educational enterprise under conditions of contraction and/or changing curriculum demands. A policy of school-based in-service training here might be the equivalent of learning on the job at the employer's expense, a trend we predict in terms of upgrading other professions.

B. A framework for research

At several points in this report we identified and made remarks on gaps in our knowledge regarding particular links in the educational planning process. We also made passing suggestions on areas where further research is needed. The research referred to was mostly of the traditional, technocratic type. However, quite new kinds of research might be needed in the future because of the changing social context and the substantial contribution education could make in this respect.

The purpose of this final section is to suggest briefly a cluster of fundamental research areas that, in our opinion, should be put high on the research agenda of Member countries. In doing so we have tried to move away from existing research lists, even recent ones, including our own (69).

We have done this for two main reasons : first, there already exists a plethora of published and unpublished results on particular bits of the educational planning process in a variety of social settings. We see little point in suggesting repetition of old-style, old-methodology research studies in Member countries (70). In most cases, one could comfortably predict the empirical outcome of such studies before they are carried out.

---

69. See G. Psacharopoulos, "Economics of education : An assessment of recent methodological advances and empirical results", in Social Science Information, No. 3/4, 1977. 1977.
70. See G. Psacharopoulos, "Academic work and policy formation", UNESCO Prospects, Vol. IX, No. 4, 1979.

Our solid motive for setting aside traditional educational research is that the rate of change of our society is accelerating. Under these conditions, the results of research embedded in tradition (if not sheer inertia) are likely to be obsolete before one reads the computer printout, let alone the published research document (71).

Research area No. 1 : Normative social values

Increased understanding is needed on the kind of society desired in the future. This is not only to reduce social conflicts, but also because of the several "limits to growth" determined by ecological factors and by the risks involved in adopting alternative forms and volumes of energy. Related to social problems is research into the non-cognitive factors required for many jobs and, in addition, research on desirable and possible occupational mobility. Related to the "limits to growth" are a great number of highly urgent research sub-projects. How many of these should be carried out in the coming decades and which part of the labour force should be devoted to them ? How are these activities to be financed ? Finally, part of research on the future structure of society must be on home activities, regarding especially women and children.

The usual approach in economics is to explain personal behaviour by axiomatically assuming that each individual strives for maximum welfare, and then to assume the task of the government is to maximise social welfare, as measured by the "general interest" of the people it represents. Today, there already exists a trend in dealing more scientifically and more quantitatively with these various problems than in the past. Research along these lines has already begun, but is still in its infancy (72). In principle, two methods are available to arrive at the relevant information : observation of actual behaviour and collection of opinions (73).

---

71. Note that the lags involved in today's research are approximately as follows : conceptualisation to funding : one year. Funding to survey completion : another year. Survey completion to statistical analysis and report writing : yet another year. Report completion to publication : another year, at least. This makes a total of four years before the user of the research results (e.g. the policy maker) is even aware of their existence. Digestion time could continue for several years thereafter.

72. This kind of research is conducted in the United National Research Institute for Social Development (UNRISD) in Geneva and the Arbeitsgemeinschaft für Lebensniveauenvergleiche in Vienna.

73. See J. Tinbergen, Income Distribution : Analysis and Policies, North-Holland, 1975, B.M.S. van Praag, "The
(Continued on next page)

For quite some time welfare, then often called utility, was assumed by economists to depend mainly on the quantities of goods consumed and the quantity of labour performed. Now, however, the number of factors recognised to be relevant has rapidly increased under the impact of criticism formulated by sociologists, labour psychologists and representatives of other disciplines. Thus, the type of labour performed, the training effort made, its relationship to other individuals or groups ("reference groups"), state of health, family life and the like have become the subject of enquiries. Among relationships to others, those of closest colleagues on the job and people living in the neighbourhood are of particular relevance. The areas of research involved are expanding rapidly and integrating into multi-disciplinary research. Attempts at integration are now under way which bring together the disciplines mentioned by education experts, and even geneticists. This integration is sought because of the important problem : what are the limits of expansion in education ? To what extent are these limits dependent on the role played by heredity or "innateness" or some other personality traits ?

Research area No. 2 : The social demand for education, revisited

This sounds like a familiar research topic, yet we would like to give it a new twist and propose new areas of enquiry. First, consider the transformation over time already taking place regarding the content of "social demand" analyses. Initially, these analyses were of the demographic, transition-proportions type (74). A given cohort was followed through time and given mobility probabilities were applied to the base matrix so as to arrive at future school enrolments.

Today, social demand for education analyses are of the behaviouristic psychological attitude type. It is this research direction we would like to encourage in the sense of discovering what people expect from the educational system, how the demand for given levels of education is generated and what factors are likely to influence it. Knowledge of these factors will facilitate educational planning on two fronts : adaptation and change.

The focus of social demand research should be pupils and students at decision points on the school ladder. Thus,

---

(Note 73 continued)
perception of welfare inequality", in European Economic Review, 1977, p. 181 ff. ; and S. Levy and L. Guttman, "On the multivariate structure of well-being", in Social Indicators Research, 1975, p. 361, ff.
    74. See R. Stone, "Input-output and demographic accounting", in Minerva, Vol. 4, Spring 1966.

pupils in the last year of compulsory schooling should be sampled in order to see what factors go into the non-continuation or the pursuit of secondary education of different kinds (e.g. vocational versus general). Similarly, secondary school students should be sampled regarding their attitudes and motivations for further study, especially regarding their choice of discipline.

We place great emphasis on the curriculum choice by different socio-economic groups, as we consider it central to future discussions on the "match" between education and work or the "transition" problem.

Social demand studies will increasingly generate expected labour market outcomes, as perceived by the students. Knowledge of the expected parameters can be used in a policy geared to influence them, as outlined below.

The social demand for education area is linked to research area No. 1 above, in the following sense. From the first kind of research one obtains the social consensus regarding _group_ preferences. The second kind of research pays tribute to the considerable _individual_ differences in preferences between students and their families within a given country. Only a holistic approach to this problem (i.e. taking into account group and individual preferences) can lead to an educational policy that is likely to succeed.

Social demand will be determined partly by changing value systems ; hence the need for research on changed motivation for choosing between continuing with education and joining the labour force.

Research area No. 3 : The curriculum content

We mean by this the curriculum content by individual year of education and not only level. Old discussions in curriculum research emphasised its "relevance" or "non-relevance". As a rule, the relevance factor referred to the individual's job function in subsequent employment.

After so many years of research on the subject, we can now legitimately ask : "Relevance for what ?" An increasing number of people in Member countries do not wish to acquire "relevant" education as seen through the myopic eyes of an allergic-to-change, committee-overloaded civil servant. What some people want is education for its own sake, say a degree in Indian philosophy or liberal studies. Are these areas completely irrelevant to social needs ? We do not think so. Whereas in less developed countries one might be excused for taking a manpower view of educational provision, this is not where OECD Member countries are heading. As we stated earlier in this report, we expect an ever-increasing separation between education and employment. Educational planners are called to observe and cater for this trend, otherwise they will soon be swimming in unfamiliar waters.

Even if we take an educational manpower view, the future calls for extreme curriculum flexibility to changing economic needs. What the economy of the future will require is flexible, adaptable men and women easy to train on the job. What the curriculum of the future should teach is how to <u>think</u> about things rather than how to <u>do</u> things.

Research area No. 4 : Educational finance

If people, as we predict, will increasingly want education for its own sake and of the general kind, this will raise (and has already raised) finance problems. Even rich Member countries will not be able in the long run to foot the educational bill by public funds. An increasing burden of educational finance will fall on the individual student and his family and the firms that use educated labour.

This trend is likely to have both desirable and undesirable consequences. For example, one of the desirable consequences might be increased internal and external educational efficiency, since the discrepancy between private and social costs of education will narrow. The most evident undesirable consequence (according to our value judgment) will be on social equity. It is the educational planner's task to try to reap the benefits from the social-to-private finance shift while minimising the costs.

The agenda of old-fashioned research topics such as educational loans or vouchers might have to be reopened. A brand new area of research, however, would be how to shift part of the finance burden to the employers of educated labour. This would maintain the following social symmetry. This might be an extreme example, but we feel it illustrates the point we wish to make. Piano lessons financed mainly by the student and his family ; learning how to repair integrated circuits financed mainly by a multinational electronics company ; and the state would be the go-between to finance corrective potential distortions.

Research area No. 5 : Information and signalling

Labour market research of the traditional type will certainly continue. There is too much inertia for it to be stopped, but the content of such research will be different. Fewer academics and practitioners will be interested in embarking on research projects involving five-year delays such as those described above.

The collection and processing of information will be faster thanks not only to the silicon chip but also to the research design that would be geared to immediate dissemination and application of the generated results.

Let us take a specific example. No policy maker will be able to afford even a 2-years tracer study. The results of it will already be obsolete by the time the computer output is produced. If we are correct in anticipating lagged responses and cobwebs in the market for educated labour, then tracer studies of the future will be of the "mini-type" (75), i.e. the current situation will be polled and the results disseminated to those who contemplate study in given subjects in a matter of days (not years), the information being delivered to their homes by a communication system already in existence (such as the British "Prestel" television-telephone hook-up).

The generated and nearly instantly transmitted signal will not only refer to the relative salary type. Job conditions, location and length of unemployment of particular outputs of the school system can also be assessed and advertised.

Knowledge of the current chances and state of the market will contribute towards changed decisions on the part of prospective students and their families. Such signalling and information transmission can make the difference between a successful and an unsuccessful educational policy. Once more, the necessary hardware exists and is rapidly dropping in price. Where research is needed is on the necessary "software" to accompany it.

The results of social demand studies and mini-tracer surveys are essential ingredients. But they have to be combined in an intelligent way and delivered to the educational consumer (or, investor, if you wish) in a record time. Speed will be one of the characteristics of successful future research. The world moves too fast for old-fashioned, leisurely research procedures to survive.

Research area No. 6 : Childhood education

As we predict shifts from manpower to social demand research, from vocational to general curriculum, and from public to private (including employer) educational finance, so one may also anticipate a shift of attention from post-compulsory levels to pre-school education. Research will increasingly concentrate on the formation of the raw input before it enters the school pipeline.

---

75. For a description of such study see G. Psacharopoulos, "Questionnaire Surveys in Educational Planning", Comparative Education, No. 2, London, 1980.

Existing research across disciplinary boundaries already indicates the importance of children's pre-school environment and informal education (76).

Economically speaking, children are at the same time consumer durables and investment capital. Early life experiences may instil various stereotypes and hence completely precondition behaviour during a lifetime. It is our opinion that educational planners should shift their attention from what strictly goes on in schools towards the quality of the ultimate factor : input to the system. Although research has begun on this front, the area ahead is completely uncharted. Part of this research will be on the extension and improvement of the path analyses made by geneticists and educationists, including research on the "production function" of learning and on what limits there are to the "learnability" of certain qualifications needed by society.

---

76. See OECD/CERI, Caring for Young Children, op. cit.

Appendices

Appendix A

RESULTS OF AN EXPERT OPINION POLL

Those participating in the poll were about 1 500 U.S. policy-makers, educators and scholars who, by virtue of their positions, are capable of influencing the future direction of society. This Appendix illustrates a few results from this poll that bear directly to some of the scenarios or theses we put forward in this chapter (1).

The results are in terms of the percentage (2) of those who thought a particular circumstance is more likely to prevail in the future, e.g. when asked on future population growth, the poll gave the following result.

		Per cent
Population growth :	− decrease	34
	0 stable	30
	+ increase	36

which means that a relative stability is expected.

Action to compensate discrimination against women:	− decrease	21
	0 no change	25
	+ increase	52

which means that an increasing number of women will occupy roles traditionally performed by men. This has repercussions both within the schools and at the work place.

Impact of scientific knowledge on the rate of technological change :	− decrease	4
	0 no change	15
	+ increase	78

---

1. See R. Glover, <u>Alternative Scenarios of the American Future, 1980-2000, Future Directions for a Learning Society</u>, The College Board, New York, 1979.
2. The percentages do not always add up to 100 because of the "non-opinion" category.

which means a yet greater uncertainty on the nature of skills to be provided by schools and an even greater uncertainty regarding employer demands for educated labour.

Per cent

Percentage of women
entering the work force :
- decrease   1
- 0 no change   5
- + increase   93

which means a difficult transition period for women, family and society as a whole because of the inevitable sex-career conflict and the possibility of highly qualified women replacing marginal men.

Frequency of mid-career
job change :
- decrease   3
- 0 no change   9
- + increase   88

which means less preparation in schools for specific occupational roles and a shift towards liberal arts and general education for the provision of transferable knowledge and skills.

Opportunities for job sharing
work schedules and reduced
work weeks :
- decrease   1
- 0 no change   6
- + increase   93

which means a further boost for women entering the labour force.

Enrolment in post-secondary
education :
- decrease   64
- 0 no change   11
- + increase   23

which means there will be a decline in the number of traditional university students and the creation of problems for many institutions of higher education some of which will be forced to close or re-evaluate their purpose.

Enrolment of adult part-time
learners in post-secondary
education :
- decrease   2
- 0 no change   4
- + increase   93

which means a substitution of part-time for full-time learning especially by those who are unemployed, women and employed workers contemplating a career change.

Per cent

<u>Competition among post-secondary institutions for students and financial resources</u> :

- − decrease   1
- 0 no change   4
- + increase   94

which means higher efficiency and quality standard of the raw input (student selection) and output (instruction).

<u>Investment of employers in human capital through continuing education and training of their employees</u> :

- − decrease   3
- 0 no change   11
- + increase   83

which means increased adult learning and specialisation later in life either in formal institutions or at the work place.

<u>The willingness to sacrifice higher pay for more leisure time</u> :

- − decrease   10
- 0 no change   36
- + increase   51

which means the effective supply of labour will be less, other things equal.

These general expectations about future social trends can become more specific by reference to the supply side and demand side of the market for educated labour and degrees.

Appendix B

Table B-1

THE DETERMINANTS OF SOCIAL SUCCESS
(USA, MALES, AGED 25-34)

	Zero order correlation	Path coefficient	% of variance explained
I. Dependent variable : <u>years of schooling</u>			
Early intelligence	0.54	0.405	16.40
Siblings, number of	-0.35	-0.148	2.19
Father's education	0.41	0.161	2.59
Father's occupation	0.43	0.199	3.96
II. Dependent variable : <u>occupation</u>			
A. Family variables : direct effect			
Siblings	-0.28	-0.04	0.16
Father's education	0.34	0.04	0.16
Father's occupation	0.39	0.12	1.44
B. Family variables : effects via education			
Siblings		-0.074	0.55
Father's education		0.081	0.65
Father's occupation		0.100	1.00
C. <u>Early intelligence</u>	0.41		
via education		0.200	4.00
Joint with family via education			2.72
Net of education via later intelligence		0.082	0.67
D. <u>Education</u>	0.64		
Total direct effects		0.502[a]	(25.00)[a]
Effects net of B and C			14.54
Joint with direct family effects			8.20
Joint with later intelligence			5.90
III. Dependent variable : <u>earnings</u>			
E. Occupation	0.39		
Total direct effect[b]		0.26	6.76[b]
F. Later intelligence	0.31		
Total direct effect		0.13	1.69
G. Education	0.35		
Total direct effect		0.09	0.81
H. Other			
Joint occupation with later intelligence			3.04
Joint occupation with education			3.28
Joint education with intelligence			1.38
Father's education		0.03	0.90

a) Includes effects of family and early intelligence via education.
b) Includes effects of intelligence, family background and education operating via occupation.
<u>Source</u> : C.A. Anderson, M.J. Bowman, and V. Tinto, <u>Where Colleges are and who Attends</u>, McGraw-Hill for the Carnegie Commission, p. 146.

Appendix C

ESTIMATING THE SATURATION LEVEL OF ENROLMENTS

Part of the research needed for analysing the future of education is an attempt to find out whether limits can be ascertained to the levels of enrolment to be expected. As an illustration the results of two first attempts we made will be discussed here.

A simple method of estimating the level at which enrolments x become asymptotic, consists of assuming the time pattern of the difference between x and observed levels of enrolments y_t at time t satisfies the equation.

$$x - y_t = e^{-ut + v}$$

where u and v are constants and time is the period between the initial period (in the case of France 1959-60) and the other years for which data are given (See Table C-1).

In the case of France enrolments figures are available for ages up to 24 years in 1959-60, 1966-67 and 1970-71, as shown in Table C-1.

Table C-1

ENROLMENT FOR FOUR AGE COHORTS, FRANCE

(%)

Age Group	1959-60	1966-67	1970-71
13 - 16	65.7	74.9	83.4
17	28.1	39.8	45.5
18 - 20	10.9	20.5	22.7
21 - 24	3.2	7.0	9.5

Source : INSEE, Annuaire statistique de la France, various years.

These figures indicate an increase, although at a decreasing rate, and graphical representation suggests that each of the enrolment figures is tending towards an assymptotic level, which by 1990 may have been reached. One may speak of a phenomenon of saturation. This tendency to saturation is not shown, however, by Maddison's figures since 1950 over three decades (1). Using the method described above the asymptotic levels of enrolments for the above cohorts in France are as shown in Table C-2.

Table C-2

PREDICTED SATURATION LEVEL OF ENROLMENT
PERCENTAGES FOR FOUR AGE GROUPS, FRANCE

Age Group	Asymptotic Enrolment (%)
13 - 16	100*
17	60
18 - 20	30
21 - 24	16

* A figure > 100 was found, and replaced by 100.

The result suggests that extended primary education becomes general, that enrolment in the highest grade of secondary schools will tend to 60 per cent ; enrolment for courses aiming at a bachelor's degree to 30 per cent and for a master's degree 16 per cent. Enrolment does not imply attaining these degrees, of course.

An alternative method to find out whether some sort of saturation of the percentage of total population able to attain third-level education is to be expected may be based on a cross-section study among advanced countries. The OECD Educational Statistics Yearbook provides figures of the nature just discussed for 15 countries ; those for Canada and Sweden do not include non-university third-level education and are therefore left out of our analysis. Assuming as an important determinant of x the total years of tertiary education per capita y GNP per capita, we find a correlation coefficient of .818 between these two variables. In order to introduce the possibility of a curvilinear relationship between x and y, a term in y^2 was

---

1. Maddison A., "Long-run Dynamics of Productivity Growth", Banca Nazionale del Lavoro Quarterly Review, Vol. 128, 1979, pp. 3-43.

added. The regression coefficient for y^2 becomes positive and R rises to .856. Inspection of the figures for individual countries makes it likely that the positive coefficient for y^2 is mainly due to the figure for the U.S.A. The conclusion to be drawn from this first cross-section analysis seems to us to be at most that no indication of saturation is suggested by this data set. More sophisticated research, based on a questionnaire, seems desirable.

Appendix D

Table D-1

LABOUR FORCE BY EDUCATIONAL ATTAINMENT AND ECONOMIC SECTOR, THE NETHERLANDS 1975

Economic Sector	Percentage of total labour force	Elementary	Extended elementary General	Extended elementary Vocational	Secondary General	Secondary Vocational	Semi high	High	Total
Agriculture, fisheries	6.4	47.7	3.4	46.6	0	1.1	1.1	0	100
Mining, manufacturing, utilities	24.6	42.4	9.1	32.3	-3.0	8.1	4.1	1	100
Trade, horeca*, repair	19.8	37.0	16	30	4	9	3	1	100
Transports, warehouses, communications	6.7	42	16	25	4	9	3	1	100
Banking, insurance, business, services	10.6	15	28	14	11	18	8	6	100
Administration (public authorities)	6.2	17	43.4		25.5		7.9	6.2	100
Education	5.9	10.7	9.7		14.1		49.0	16.5	100
Medical, veterinary	4.9	15.6	27.6		36.7		9.6	10.5	100
Social, cultural services	4.6	31.9	30.9		22.1		13.1	2.0	100
Research institutions	0.9	15.2	26.7		21.0		17.7	19.4	100
Total labour force	100.0	33	12	28	4	12	7	3	100

* Horeca : hotels, restaurants, cafés.

Sources : Central Bureau of Statistics, Pocket Yearbook 1977, p. 102/3
H. de Groot, "Werkgelegenheid in de kwartaire sector", Ec.-Stat-Berichten 63(1978) p. 816 ff.

Table D-2

THE INCREASING SUPPLY OF GRADUATES
IN THE LABOUR FORCE

Country	Percentage of graduates (year)	
United Kingdom	3.0 (1966)	6.0 (1971)
Germany	2.9 (1961)	7.5 (1976)
France	2.7 (1962)	6.1 (1975)
Netherlands, men	5.0 (1960)	9.8 (1973)
Netherlands, women	4.1 (1960)	9.3 (1973)
Canada, Ontario	8.3 (1961)	16.7 (1974)
United States	12.6 (1969)	15.5 (1974)

Source : OECD, "Medium-term employment prospects for higher education graduates", 28 December 1979, (mimeo) p.4.

Table D-3

THE PERCENTAGE OF GRADUATES EMPLOYED
BY THE PUBLIC SECTOR

Country	Public Sector Share
Germany	60
Netherlands	66
Denmark	80
Sweden	75
France	44
United Kingdom	60
United States	37
Italy	66

Source : OECD, "Medium Term Employment Prospects for Higher Education Graduates", 28 December 1979, (mimeo) pp. 8-9.

Table D-4

ESTIMATES OF THE ELASTICITY OF SUBSTITUTION BETWEEN
HIGHLY TRAINED AND OTHER LABOUR, VARIOUS AUTHORS

Author	Nature of study	Elasticity estimate
OECD	Cross section 22 countries	-1
Dougherty	Cross section 22 US states	-3.3 to -9.0
Bowles	Cross section 12 countries	-4.8
Psacharopoulos and Hinchliffe	Cross section 18 countries	-2.2
Dresch	Time series USA 1956-68	-3.82
Fallon and Layard	Cross sections 22 countries	-0.61 -3.54
Berndt and Christensen	Time series USA 1929-68	-4.9 to -6.1
Freeman	Time series	-2.3
Ullman	Time series USA 1900-63	-1.5

Source : J. Tinbergen, "Substitution of academically trained by other labour", Weltwirtschaftliches Archiv, Vol. 111, No. 3, 1975, p. 469.

Note : Original sources are as follows :

OECD, Occupational and Educational Structures of the Labour Force and Levels of Economic Development, Paris, 1971, p. 81.

C.R.S. Dougherty, "Estimates of Labor Aggregation Functions", The Journal of Political Economy, Vol. 80, Chicago, III, 1972, pp. 1101 sqq.

Samuel Bowles, "Planning Educational Systems for Economic Growth", Harvard Economic Studies, Vol. 133, Cambridge, Mass., 1969 ; George Psacharopoulos and Keith Hinchliffe, "Further Evidence on the Elasticity of Substitution among Different Types of Educated Labor", The Journal of Political Economy, Vol. 80, 1972, pp. 786 sqq.

Stephen P. Dresch, "Demography, Technology and Higher Education : Toward a Formal Model of Educational Adaptation", The Journal of Political Economy, Vol. 83, 1975.

Ernst R. Berndt and Laurits R. Christensen, The Specification of Technology in American Manufacturing, Discussion Paper 73-17, University of British Columbia, October 1973. Idem, "Testing for the Existence of a Consistent Aggregate Index of Labor Inputs", The American Economic Review, Vol. 64, Menasha, Wisc., 1974, pp. 391 sqq.

R.B. Freeman, The Market for College-Trained Manpower, Cambridge, Mass., 1971, estimates by Tinbergen.

P.R. Fallon and P.R.G. Layard, "Capital Skill Complementarity, Income Distribution and Output Accounting", Journal of Political Economy, Vol. 83, 1975.

C. Ullman, "The Growth of Professional Occupations in the American Labor Force : 1900-1963", World Bank summary of unpubl. thesis, Columbia University, 1972.

Chapter 7

<u>AN AGENDA FOR THE FUTURE : A FRAMEWORK</u>
<u>FOR EDUCATIONAL POLICY PLANNING</u>

by
G. Williams

I. THE BACKGROUND TO EDUCATIONAL PLANNING IN THE 1980s

At the beginning of the 1980s it is salutary to remind ourselves that in 1971 the OECD held a conference on <u>Educational Growth</u> which concluded that expansion would continue in the 70s although at a slower rate. A sentence from the concluding chapter of the report illustrates its main conclusions. "The generalization of secondary education which has now been largely achieved will give rise to an increasing demand for higher education in the 1970s, and one of the major problems of policy will be how to respond both to it and to an expected expansion of education for adults" (OECD, 1971, p. 136).* In fact, the period of rapid expansion came to a halt in many countries sometime between 1970 and 1975, and the last few years of the decade have been increasingly difficult ones for education. The causes of this change of fortune are many and not easy to disentangle.

In the first place the optimistic expectations of the 1960s about the contribution of education to economic growth and the creation of a more equal society were not fulfilled. Studies of the utilisation of qualified manpower showed little relationship between expenditure on education and economic growth (e.g., OECD, 1970). Indeed, by the early 1970s there were beginning to be doubts about the social desirability of economic growth itself. Other studies in the OECD and elsewhere indicated that although one of the main aims of expansion had been a reduction of inequality, the outcome was a pattern of social class

---

* See references at the end of this chapter.

participation in post-compulsory education very similar to that which existed at the beginning of the 1960s, and in addition there was no evidence that incomes or occupational structures were becoming any more equal as a result of educational expansion (Jencks, 1971 ; Halsey et al., 1980).

A less theoretical disappointment for many graduates was the emergence of unemployment amongst people with high educational qualifications and the narrowing of earnings differentials between highly educated and less well educated workers. It is likely also that the organised political militancy of students of the late 1960s and early 1970s favoured opponents of educational expansion. Such considerations undoubtedly moderated the demand for post-compulsory education and encouraged policy makers to question the value of the apparently limitless demands of educational systems for additional resources.

The growing interest in various forms of recurrent and continuing education has so far been backed in only a very few countries by any substantial political commitment.

However, there can be no doubt that the fundamental causes of the problems facing education at the beginning of the 1980s are the reductions in rates of economic growth brought about largely by the massive rises in the price of oil and other raw materials and, possibly even more important, the decline in birth rates which began in the mid-1960s.

One effect of slow economic growth is that few jobs are created and, given the high degree of job security enjoyed by many members of the labour force, unemployment tends to be borne disproportionately by young people entering the labour force. The effects of this on the demand for education are complex. On the one hand there is little doubt that in most countries unemployment is lowest amongst young people with the best educational qualifications.* However, there is also an incentive for able young people to leave school early in order to take jobs that may be available rather than risk an even worse employment situation some years later. Finally, the existence of large numbers of school and college leavers can, on a superficial analysis, be diagnosed as resulting from a failure of the education system to prepare them adequately for the world of work. For any individual this may well be true. The reason he does not get a particular job is often that he is not believed by the employer to have an appropriate educational background.

---

* Italy may be an exception.

Another problem is that slow economic growth appears to be having a particularly damaging effect on the public sector, possibly because of the mildly progressive taxation system in OECD countries. A high proportion of educationally qualified young people, in the past, have entered public sector employment ; now they are likely to find their prospects particularly adversely affected by reductions in rates of economic growth.*

The effects of declining birth rates are more direct. The most direct is that fewer births mean fewer entrants to nursery schools three years later, primary schools six years later, secondary schools eleven or twelve years later and higher education eighteen to twenty years later. There is, of course, no obvious reason why this should be a problem. It might be assumed that when there are fewer pupils, each pupil will be able to have more classroom space and more teacher attention. There are in fact three separate effects that need to be distinguished. The first consists of the state of there being fewer pupils in one period compared with another ; the second is the change from expansion to contraction or slower growth ; the third is political and financial : it is difficult to secure additional resources for education if there is no obvious pressure of student numbers.

Intrinsic problems of smaller numbers arise from the smaller size of educational establishments and systems. This causes difficulties in maintaining curricular alternatives and diversity of educational opportunities even when resources are not unduly limited.

Possibly the most serious effect of a change in growth rates is on the teaching profession. With any given career structure there is a certain pattern of career prospects associated with any given long-term rate of growth. It is intuitively obvious that the higher the rate of growth, the better the career prospects. However, if growth slows down or becomes negative, career prospects do not merely decline to the appropriate new equilibrium level but become worse for some years. Such problems are intrinsic in any hierarchical career structure.

Another implication is that the average age of teachers rises. From some points of view this may be advantageous. There is, for example, a larger proportion of experienced teachers. However, to the extent that new ideas are brought into the educational system by new recruits,

---

* It should be noted that the point being made here is in terms of long-term secular changes in growth rates. In short-term cyclical fluctuations there tends to be greater stability of employment in the public than in the private sector with short-term deficits by governments financed by borrowing.

a reduction in the numbers of new teachers can result in a less positive attitude to innovation. It is certainly the case that as career prospects worsen it is more difficult for people from other occupations to enter teaching in mid-career. This can result in the educational system becoming more and more isolated from the world of work. A specific social problem that may arise is that job opportunities are reduced for part-time teachers and for married women wishing to return. Such problems result directly from a reduction in the growth rate of student numbers and are not caused by the accompanying financial stringency though they are, of course, exacerbated by it.

A further effect that was insufficiently realised when education systems were growing rapidly is that a buoyant demand for teachers has a stimulating effect on the general labour market for qualified manpower. In the 1960s up to 40 per cent of the output of the higher education system of OECD member countries was absorbed into employment in education. This effectively set a floor to the job expectations of graduates and meant that the "worst" job a graduate could expect was teaching. This intensified the impression of shortage of qualified manpower elsewhere and made employers more likely to hoard such manpower for fear of losing qualified workers and being unable to replace them. The situation was reversed when the educational system offered fewer opportunities for qualified manpower. With such manpower more readily available, other employers had less incentive to employ more than their immediate needs.

Within education slow growth has other damaging effects. It becomes harder to justify the replacement of specialist teachers who leave. An overall surplus of teachers can coexist with a shortage of specialists in some subjects. Indeed, it is specialist teachers of subjects in demand elsewhere in the economy who are most likely to have opportunities of leaving teaching. Unless resources are made available for their replacement over and above the apparent overall need for new teachers, the profession may well come to consist more and more of specialists in subjects which have less and less economic and social relevance.

Somewhat similar problems are caused by the non-replacement of school buildings. It is difficult to justify the provision of new educational buildings at a time of spare capacity particularly as capital programmes are relatively easily reduced in a time of expenditure restraint. Educational innovations often need to be embodied in new buildings and major new items of capital equipment. Nearly all change is facilitated if it is accompanied by purpose-built accommodation and equipment. Less directly, a situation in which new buildings and new equipment are appearing from time to time helps to create favourable psychological attitudes to change. Slow growth and limited resources for new buildings have the effect, therefore, of hindering innovation and generally encouraging inflexibility.

The problems discussed so far have begun to appear in OECD countries during the 1970s and were for the most part not foreseen by educational planners and policy makers at the beginning of the decade. In examining the development of national educational planning during the 1980s and the types of resource re-allocation that will be needed, it is necessary first to consider the extent to which current trends are likely to continue. The two most prominent of these are the slow rates of economic growth with their associated stringency in public expenditure and the declining school age populations. To what extent do these trends appear likely to continue into the 1980s ? The answer is not quite clear cut. The causes of economic growth are still not clearly understood and just as the secular decline in economic growth in the West was not foreseen at the beginning of the 1970s, so it is not inconceivable that the technological changes brought about by the micro-processor revolution and other science-based industries will bring about not the massive unemployment which many people fear, but renewed economic growth based upon technical change similar to that which has occurred in other periods of rapid technological change. Such renewed economic growth would certainly be technologically based and would make substantial new demands on systems of education and training.

If this hope appears a little optimistic in the present climate, another possibility is that economies may adapt to slow rates of growth caused by limitations of natural resources by expanding labour-intensive service activities, particularly in the public sector. The practical and political problems of achieving such a solution appear at the moment to be insurmountable. It would require considerably greater flexibility in relative earnings levels and a willingness of individual groups of workers to sacrifice their own immediate economic interests for the general long term good that does not appear to be much in evidence at present and is particularly difficult to achieve in a period of slow growth. However, political changes do occur and it is not impossible that by the mid-1980s labour-intensive public sector activities will come to be seen as a solution to high rates of unemployment if slow economic growth continues.

The continuation of the decline in school age population is also not certain.* The number of births is currently on an upward trend in many OECD countries. The

---

* Although of course the babies already born will be having an impact on various parts of the educational system during the rest of the present century.

number of women of childbearing age is growing, reflecting the rising birth cohorts of the late 1950s and early 1960s. There are some signs that this rise in the childbearing population has since 1978 been accompanied by a rise in fertility rates. If this trend continues it will have substantial effects on the primary school population within five or six years and on teacher training needs much earlier than that.

In brief, while it is prudent for educational planners to prepare for the 1980s in the expectation that financial stringency and slow population growth will continue, allowance should also be made for the possibility that one or both of these constraints might disappear as unexpectedly as it appeared. Certainly the fundamental dilemma of educational planners in the early 1980s will be to encourage changes in the content and structures of educational systems that will help them to regain their political popularity, and to do this in an environment in which there are few additional resources. Essential changes will have to come about largely at the expense of existing activities and the vested interests which they represent. At the same time, however, planners must watch carefully for changes in the economic and political climate.

How are education systems to maintain their vigour and to continue to adapt in a positive functional way in a climate conditioned by severe resource limitations and major uncertainties ? An agenda for a national educational planning group during the next ten years might consist of the following seven questions :

a) What political priorities should be accorded to and within education in the light of changing social and individual needs ?
b) How feasible, and how desirable according to alternative social cost-effectiveness criteria, are policies to attract new kinds of students ?
c) What steps are needed to increase the acceptability of necessary changes in the teaching profession, bearing in mind that some at least of the necessary developments will be detrimental to the interests of existing teachers ? In particular, what steps can be taken to ensure that the potential benefits of falling school rolls in bringing about improved pupil-teacher ratios and space per student are not squandered through defensive actions by teachers to protect their existing position ?
d) What scope is there for increasing the flexibility of use of educational buildings and other capital equipment and how great a resource saving can this make in practice when falling school age populations are resulting in widespread excess capacity ?
e) How can mechanisms of educational finance be adapted so as to promote greater flexibility of a kind that will enable educational systems to

respond to changing circumstances without damage to the essential fabric of equitable and efficient public provision of education ?
f) What kind of mechanisms can be developed for planning qualitative change ? Despite the deficiencies of quantitative forecasts widely accepted methodologies have been developed for charting the progress of many quantitative educational indicators. Few operational criteria have been developed for determining resource allocation in respect of the major qualitative aspects of education : curricula, institutional arrangements, management structures and so on. It is at present almost impossible to predict with any degree of reliability the resource implications of educational development other than changes in the scale of provision.
g) While accepting the necessity of making estimates of likely future developments as a basis for policy decisions about the allocation of resources in spite of the inevitable uncertainty of such predictions, what strategies can be adopted by planners to ensure that the waste of resources resulting from "incorrect" forecasts is minimised ?

Each of these topics provides a substantial research agenda for planners and subject for detailed discussion by policy makers. In the remainder of this chapter this agenda is discussed briefly in the light of existing knowledge and what appears to be the general political climate in many OECD countries.

II. OBJECTIVES AND PRIORITIES

One of the most delicate problems for a national educational planner is to maintain the right balance between being a propagandist for education against other claimants on national resources and being a technician, attempting to find some "objective" basis for determining appropriate educational expenditures. During the period of rapid expansion this dilemma remained beneath the surface. The threefold belief in economic growth, in greater social equality and that education made a major contribution to both meant that the broad paths of educational advance were clear. Although in retrospect it seems likely that the main impetus for the great expansion of the 1960s was a response to _private_ demand from individuals seeking personal advancement, there did not appear to be any conflict between private and social objectives either in promoting the claims of education against other economic activities or in distributing resources between different educational activities. The role of the planner was essentially that of expressing _strategic_ objectives in operational terms and of devising methods of encouraging the educational system as a whole to move in the direction of broadly agreed major policy objectives.

In the United Kingdom an example of such a model is the planning of higher education since the publication of the Robbins Report (1962). The Robbins Committee, reacting to the rapidly growing demand for university places in the early 1960s, proposed a broad policy objective that "courses of higher education should be available for all who are qualified by ability and attainment to pursue them and who wish to do so". The government of the day and all successive British governments (at least until 1979) accepted the objective. The planning problem was to convert the objective into operational terms. This involved, first, a precise definition of the terms "higher education", "ability", "attainment", "wish to enter higher education", and, second, a quantification of the various categories during a specific planning period. The exercise was repeated periodically to take account of changes in underlying parameters such as the size of the relevant age group and the "willingness" of young people to obtain the necessary qualifications and to enter higher education. This approach was also used in many other OECD countries, for example, Germany, Sweden, Australia, Ireland and France. It was also widely used to plan the provision of facilities in primary and secondary education where the main motivating force was not the voluntary "demand" for these branches of education but the imperatives of demographic pressures.

The provision of places in teacher training follows a somewhat different version of the model in that the "social demand" or "individual demand" criterion was replaced by a manpower criterion that sufficient teachers should be trained to meet the predicted needs of pupils in primary and secondary schools. In this case also the broad objective of meeting manpower needs required "operationalizing" by expressing "needs" in quantitative terms : so many teachers per thousand pupils between the ages of six and eleven, and so on.

The main debate about the establishment of priorities for educational planning up until the mid-1970s was largely about the relative merits of "private demand" and "manpower needs" as a starting point for planning educational provision. In very broad terms it may be said that with a few exceptions such as the training of teachers and doctors, and to some extent engineers, most OECD countries adopted the social demand approach[*], while in the centrally planned economies of Eastern Europe manpower needs

---

[*] French indicative economic planning which encompassed broad categories of manpower needs was, to some extent, an exception.

has been the point of departure, and elaborate procedures have been established for quantifying needs for engineers, scientists, literature graduates and so on (see Fulton et al., 1980).

The increasing doubts about the economic and social value of education have reduced the validity of such "technocratic models" of educational planning. National planning groups are seen as being among the pressure groups out of whose interactions policy emerges. In other words planning, and the research on which it is based, become inputs into the policy process rather than the means by which previously agreed political objectives are prepared for implementation.

According to this analysis it is incorrect to try to make any clear distinction between planning and the establishment of strategic policy priorities. Part of the educational planner's role is to be an advocate for the educational system against other public and private sector claimants on resources. The proper extent of such advocacy and which forms are considered acceptable and which are efficacious are matters for debate. Different groups of planners may have different responsibilities. For example, planners in national ministries of education appear to have a clear-cut responsibility to present the case for education with as much skill as they can, leaving others to make the case for the health service, defence, the private sector and so on. Conversely, others, possibly in national ministries of finance, have a greater obligation to consider the merits of education in relation to other activities.

In the 1980s one of the aims of educational planners should be to try to have restored some sense of perspective in the priority accorded to education. While the great expectations of the 1960s about the economic and social benefits to be derived from educational expansion are now seen to have been naive, the pessimism and cynicism of the late 1970s is equally ingenuous. Just as it was simplistic to believe that l'enseignement peut tout, so it is equally simplistic to take the view that l'enseignement ne peut rien. An urgent task in the 1980s should be to make a realistic appraisal of the economic and social roles of education, in particular evaluating the evidence which has recently begun to appear that despite the claims of sociologists such as Jencks (1971) schools do make a difference to what young people know and believe.

There are, of course, difficulties in stimulating a realistic debate about objectives and the political priorities. While in Western democracies it is inevitable, and indeed desirable, that part of the debate should be about fundamental values, and hence in the party political arena, there are dangers about allowing fundamental objectives to be treated as only a matter for party politics. Many of the issues involved are complex ; and in education, possibly even more than most other social activities, policies can have unintended effects that may be diametrically opposed to the original policy aim.

Public debate about educational objectives <u>outside</u> the framework of party politics also has its dangers. It is almost invariably diffuse and dominated by vested interests. The issues are inevitably, and to some extent deliberately, over-simplified. It is now clear from the debates of the 1960s and 1970s that the evidence about the contribution of education to economic growth or to social equality was never clear cut. It is by now beginning to be understood that some kinds of education in some circumstances may take direct contribution to future levels of national income and/or the quality of life while other kinds of education in other circumstances are irrelevant to them. These are complicated issues that simply cannot be reduced to simple conclusions for public debate about the social effects of education in general.

At the same time it is equally undesirable that the discussions about fundamental objectives should be entirely a matter for small groups of experts. Even if experts were capable of adopting a completely neutral view, it is not at all clear that they should do so.

One of the concerns of the 1980s should be to find ways of organising planning activities which encompass widespread public discussion about objectives while ensuring that professional expertise is used to best advantage in developing educational policies which are both efficient and equitable.

International organisations can contribute through comparative studies of general and specific educational policy objectives. National differences in the detail of the main policy criteria in educational provision, although significant, are less important than the similarity of the major issues involved.

III. ATTRACTING NEW CATEGORIES OF STUDENTS

An area of policy likely to attract considerable attention in the 1980s is that of attracting new kinds of students to supplement the impending shortfalls of "traditional" pupils and students, particularly in the various branches of post-compulsory education. However, there are many planning dilemmas. On the one hand, a strong case has been made for a shift of emphasis in educational policy towards various kinds of recurrent education (for example in OECD, 1973) and is by now widely accepted in general terms in most OECD countries. However, there has been little consideration of what should or could be sacrificed within a given educational budget in order to increase the emphasis on the recurrent education of adults. Furthermore, the decline in school age populations has created a network of pressure groups which have vested interests in attracting a new clientele for schools, colleges and universities in order to protect the jobs of people currently employed in such institutions. It is sometimes difficult to determine whether the case being made for a particular form of recurrent education is based upon a genuine need or whether it originates from a group whose members are, quite legitimately, primarily concerned with selling their "product".

Recurrent education programmes are unlikely to be politically persuasive if they are seen to be motivated primarily by self interest of the staff of educational institutions. Any policy to attract priority for new categories of students must start by establishing sound social and economic reasons for re-allocating scarce national resources in this way. There are four categories of reasons why the allocation of resources to attract new types of students may be socially justified even when resources are severely limited.

The first is where individuals or groups are ill-informed about the probable benefits of continuing education. The obvious approach here is the provision of information services. The need for advice and guidance is usually greatest amongst people whose initial education has been poorest. The provision of counselling services for potential adult students can therefore be seen as a policy measure in accordance with the broad social objective of greater equality. However, it is also the case that educational institutions have a vested interest in attracting adult students to whatever courses are currently under-subscribed. The line between counselling and advertising is thus not a clear one. If counselling services are provided, there is a strong case for them to be either a nationally provided service or a professional activity independent of educational institutions.

A second reason for making special efforts to redeploy educational resources in the direction of new categories of students is where there is reason to believe that there is a latent demand which has not become an actual demand because of financial, cultural, institutional, social or other constraints. Lack of finance is the most obvious. Most OECD countries now have a system of scholarships and grants for students in the voluntary stages of initial education. There has also been considerable discussion about the provision of paid educational leave, and in a number of countries legislation has been passed and some provision is being made. There are, however, many doubts about whether systems of student aid which were established in the 1950s and early 1960s are appropriate in the very different conditions of the 1980s. It has, for example, been fairly well established in most countries that there is a tendency for most aid to go to students from families which have least need for it. Similarly, there is accumulating evidence that paid educational leave is most likely to be taken by workers in white collar rather than blue collar jobs. Student aid needs to be carefully focused if it is to make its maximum impact with respect to particular policy objectives.

Non-financial barriers include non-availability of time and geographical distance. Both of these can often be overcome without additional resources by reorganisation of educational provision. There is in some countries a growing interest in what has come to be called flexi-study, of which correspondence education is the best-established example. There is, however, a substantial gap between claiming that flexible modes of study can make educational opportunities available to many otherwise disadvantaged groups at relatively low cost and actually devising specific policies in specific circumstances. The planning function of helping to devise appropriate policies, to predict their likely effects and to evaluate their outcomes in this area alone is considerable.

A third justification for the expansion of recurrent education and training is the growing need in technologically advanced societies for individuals to have opportunities for re-training at various stages in their lives. The development of micro-processor technology appears likely to accentuate this need. The rationale for professional upgrading and re-training is based upon different political criteria from those discussed above. While the provision of information and the removal of barriers to access is concerned mainly with the policy objective of social equality and the non-material quality of life generally, the need to re-train workers to adapt to technological changes springs mainly from efficiency considerations. A workforce that is incapable of making the best use of new technological developments will find it harder and harder to compete for new investment in the capital markets of the world and can rapidly become impoverished. The dilemma for the educational planner is that this criterion for the provision of recurrent education can be very inegalitarian. If economic efficiency is the criterion, a substantial part of the available resources will need to be devoted to re-training and updating people who have already acquired substantial amounts of initial education and training. It is possible to envisage a scenario in which there is a growing gap between the educational "haves" in technologically advanced occupations and the educational "have nots" in relatively unskilled manual occupations. The potential conflicts between recurrent education policies aimed essentially at egalitarian social objectives and those directed towards greater economic efficiency have not been properly explored. If policies on recurrent education are not to have unintended and undesirable effects this is an issue which needs careful examination.

Fourthly, there is likely to be an increasing demand for education for leisure. In a climate of public expenditure restraint this may sometimes be a difficult case to argue. However, a case can be made that the growth of appropriate labour-intensive but otherwise low resource-using leisure industries can alleviate the social problems arising from technological change. Adult education itself is such an industry and there is a good case to be made for it as simply a civilised alternative to unemployment.

One area of education for leisure that could receive political support is preparation for retirement. Most OECD countries have an ageing population together with growing pressures for early retirement. Preparation for retirement should be a major growth point in the educational systems of the 1980s.

IV. THE TEACHING PROFESSION

A problem of the 1980s will be to persuade teachers' organisations to accept changes, many of which will appear to be detrimental to the interests of their members. Many of the ideas for resource reallocation could be readily put into practice if teachers' salary scales and conditions of service were infinitely flexible. If teachers were willing to move from one school to another at reduced levels of pay there would be few problems in maintaining all schools open despite a lack of finance and declining school populations. In this case the entire burden of the adjustment to the reduced school population and the resource reallocation resulting therefrom would be being borne by the teaching profession[*]. This clearly offends against intuitive ideas of fairness and would be almost certainly politically and socially unacceptable in OECD countries. However, the kind of developments which are likely to be essential in the 1980s will almost certainly require some sacrifices by the teaching profession. Already it is becoming apparent that if education budgets are fixed there is a direct trade-off between higher pay and reducing unemployment amongst trained teachers. In such

---

[*] It is thus at the opposite end of the spectrum from proposals put forward by educational pressure groups that all educational budgets should be maintained despite falling and changing patterns of enrolments. In this latter case the whole burden of educational adjustment must be borne by the rest of the community.

circumstances teachers' dissatisfaction with their pay is likely to increase. A disgruntled teaching profession is likely to do little to improve the public and political image of the education service.

Many of the resource problems of the 1980s will be related to the supply, utilisation and career development of teachers. There are several areas in which it is possible to make reasonable estimates of the implications of policies such as early retirement schemes, voluntary redundancies, the effects of financial incentives on the willingness of teachers to move, the effect on overall pupil-teacher ratios of efforts to maintain an appropriate proportion of teachers required to maintain a prescribed curriculum, the cost of schemes for facilitating staff exchanges between industry and education, and so on. However, the estimate of costs and other implications of such schemes is the least difficult part of the planning exercise. The main difficulty is to persuade teachers collectively and individually to accept policies that may not be in their direct interests. Obviously this is a difficult task in which the skills of the diplomat and politician will be at least as important as those of the planner. However, without them resource redeployment is likely to be resisted at every juncture and the educational system is likely to experience a disorderly retreat rather than any re-grouping of forces for selective attacks at points where the chances of victory are greatest.

V. BUILDINGS AND EQUIPMENT

Educational building has been a major concern of the OECD since the early 1960s. In broad terms, the main trend of development over the past two decades has been a period of severe shortage when the overriding consideration was one of providing "roofs over heads", giving way to a period of surplus when the concern is often how to create as few educational and social problems as possible while taking educational buildings out of use. The policy issues associated with the developing surplus of school buildings in many countries have been analysed in a policy paper prepared for the OECD Education Committee by the Steering Committee for Building (OECD 1979 ; referred to below as the Programme on Educational Building).

As with teachers, the problem of excess capacity in educational buildings has several dimensions. There are those which are inherent in a situation where buildings are inadequately utilised and there are those created by the existence of excess capacity in a period of severe resource constraint. Problems would remain even if more resources were available ; they would, however, be easier to deal with.

This distinction is important because as experience shows it is difficult to assess accurately the real extent of surplus. While a growing number of schools are under-utilised in relation to current norms new demands are emerging for qualitative improvements in education, for more spacious accommodation and for more differentiated educational opportunities. Because of these new demands, the question arises as to whether emerging surplus space in schools is in fact surplus. Current expectations as regards quality mean that many buildings are deficient in one way or another. It is virtually impossible to define full utilisation of educational buildings. Where space is inadequate to meet needs, schools can work a two- or even three-shift system in order to use expensive capital investments more intensively. This gives a very much greater degree of utilisation at the cost of some inconvenience for those using the buildings. The use of school premises for adult education activities in the evenings and of universities and colleges as hotels during their vacations are other ways of increasing rates of utilisation. Conversely, if space is plentiful educational activities can readily expand to fill the space available, often bringing educational advantage and increased comfort to pupils and teachers.

Buildings are investments in fixed capital that have already been made and their real current cost is very low. There are, however, two types of costs associated with maintaining the buildings for educational purposes, and they point to different policies. First, there is a real or an imputed rental. If funds have been borrowed to build the school, loan repayments must be made whether or not the building is fully utilised. If the authority owns the building outright there remains the opportunity cost of having a building empty that could have alternative uses. These considerations would encourage an authority to keep a building open as long as it has _any_ educational use.

A second category of costs consists of those which are directly associated with the use of the building, for example, heating, lighting, repairs and maintenance. These _can_ be avoided if the building is closed altogether but do not decline proportionately to the degree of utilisation. Even if there are only a few pupils in a school or classroom, that building must be lit, heated and protected against the ravages of the weather, etc. These considerations give an incentive to withdraw buildings from use well before their rate of utilisation falls to zero. Thus, even from a purely financial viewpoint the rate of utilisation at which closure is the best policy is not unequivocal. When broader social issues are brought into the calculus the solution becomes still less determinate. The decision must be "political" and based on "judgement". The "planner" can define the bounds within which acceptable solutions are likely to lie.

The existence of excess capacity makes it more difficult to justify new building for innovation or in order to improve the quality of education.

Obviously, one type of solution to such dilemmas is to find alternative uses for schools and other educational buildings. There are four categories of alternative use :

  i) alternative uses in public education
  ii) use by private education
  iii) non-educational public sector use
  iv) non-educational private sector use.

Alternative use within the public sector of education is often desirable. Population decline does not affect all branches of education at the same time. Primary school populations start to decline while secondary school populations are still rising. This gives an incentive to use primary school accommodation for secondary school classes. There may also be possibilities of using primary schools for adult education and teaching re-training centres, and so on.

Temporary re-use of primary school facilities for other educational purposes is attractive because the large fall in the birth rate is being followed in several countries by an increase. In the late 1980s there may well be criticism if the educational service has to pay high prices for new buildings after having disposed of capacity only a few years earlier.

Thus, alternative educational uses for surplus buildings is the best strategy in many circumstances. However, although population decline affects different parts of the educational system at different rates at different times, financial stringency affects it all simultaneously. If surplus buildings in primary education are actually "needed" at the secondary level then clearly a saving of resources results from using buildings already in existence[*]. If, however, it is proposed to use the buildings to cater for new categories of students, there are other considerations. If the provision of facilities for certain categories of adults can bring additional recurrent expenditure into the educational service as a whole, then the case for using spare building capacity for this purpose is strengthened. If, on the other hand, the use of surplus buildings for adults means that associated recurrent expenditure must be found from elsewhere in the education budget, then a cost is imposed on the rest of the service which may or may not

---

[*] Provided, of course, that there are not too many associated recurrent costs such as transporting pupils to a school whose geographical location is not convenient.

be greater than leaving the buildings unused or continuing their original use with under-utilised capacity.

Another possibility is to lease buildings for private educational purposes. Obviously this can raise delicate political issues. However, in most OECD countries there is a private sector of education and its existence increases the total resources available for education. As well as primary and secondary schools there are substantial numbers of private establishments providing vocational and recurrent education : colleges for managers, secretaries, bank assistants, hairdressers, motor car mechanics, foreign language training, and so on. If surplus educational buildings are rented to private colleges they will help to increase the total resources for education now. In addition, the public authorities will be able to terminate the lease or to raise the rental to an economic level if the buildings are needed by the public sector later on.

A third alternative is non-educational public sector use. The decline in the school age population in many countries is being accompanied by equally rapid increases in the numbers of retired people. Some unused or under-utilised schools may be able to be converted for retired persons or other social and health services such as day nurseries, community centres, centres for the temporarily homeless, refuges for those suffering from marital problems, and so on.

Such policies are unlikely to succeed unless school buildings are seen as community resources to be devoted to the best possible use in the light of the current needs of the whole community. In practice this is not straightforward. Educational services and other community and social services usually have different administrative and financial arrangements. Administrative changes at a high level or even legislative action may be necessary before buildings can be transferred from, say, the education services to the health services. Nor should the power of bureaucratic rivalries be underestimated. Education administrators are unlikely to yield control of their property willingly. Such an attitude is not entirely selfish. The future is uncertain and there is a good possibility of school populations increasing again by the mid-1980s. It may be difficult to recover the use of buildings which have been transferred to other worthy public activities.

The fourth possible use for unused educational buildings is to sell them. The attraction of such a strategy is that it brings additional resources into education which can be used for capital expenditure on innovations or quality improvements elsewhere. However, there are also disadvantages. The need for school closures will be concentrated in areas where population decline is greatest : in general, those areas which private investors also are likely to find unattractive. There is also the problem that school buildings which are sold cannot be restored to educational use if there is a need for them in the future.

A final problem is that the closure of schools causes considerable inconvenience to pupils and their families who do remain in areas of population decline and is likely to accelerate the stagnation of these areas. This may be particularly serious in rural areas and in inner city areas, in both of which schools can have a far more important social role than simply providing places for pupils. Decisions about closure need to be based on considerations far wider than a simple financial cost-benefit analysis. Otherwise school closure may provoke worse social and economic ills than those it is intended to cure.

VI. FINANCE

The allocation of resources to public education involves a chain of decisions in which taxes are raised from private individuals by central and local government, a proportion of these is allocated to education generally and finally the education budget is allocated amongst various programmes and functions. There are thus three major sets of decisions between those who bear the ultimate costs of education and the expenditure of money on educational services : the proportion of national income to be appropriated by the public sector, the proportion of the public budget to be devoted to education and the allocation of the education amongst all the different claimants in the education service. Obviously none of these is a single decision ; they all involve many different political considerations and technical judgements.*

The response of educational institutions to changing social and economic pressures is influenced by the way in which they receive their funds. An institution which has an independent, secure source of funds, such as are obtained from the ownership of property, can if it wishes, withstand most pressure from planning authorities and must be persuaded rather than coerced into implementing national policy. Although few institutions have absolute financial security some do have considerable freedom of action in deciding how to respond to national plans and policies. For example, all universities in the United Kingdom are private corporations receiving a large part of their funds in the form of a block grant from the government, and it is a strongly held political convention that governments

---

* A theoretical analysis of the flow of funds to the providers of educational services is contained as Appendix 5 of <u>Methods and Statistical Needs for Educational Planning</u>, OECD, 1967.

do not interfere with the internal operation of individual universities.

Such independence has its disadvantages for national planning and policy making : central authorities are unable to ensure that resources are transferred from one educational activity to another in accordance with <u>national</u> economic and social needs. Naturally those activities which are to lose resources will oppose any change vigorously. Indeed, a local authority or educational institution required by central government policy to make a reduction in its expenditure or to transfer resources from one activity to another has some incentives to ensure that any cuts made are concentrated in those areas where they will do the <u>greatest</u> amount of social and economic damage. This will increase the public and political visibility of expenditure reductions, and it may thus become harder for central government to implement its policy of expenditure restraint. The net effect is that resources may not be concentrated in those areas in which they can be used most efficiently in relation to <u>national</u> policies.

Centralised financial control also has its problems. It often results in alienation between teachers and those who are responsible for administering the educational service, and it can result in financial irresponsibility in the lower levels of the bureaucracy. Budgets once allocated must be spent, regardless of efficiency considerations, if the individual spending unit is to be able to justify its claim for a similar or enlarged budget allocation the following year.

Such bureaucratic deficiencies of both centralised and de-centralised systems have led some economists to suggest that greater efficiency would be achieved in the allocation of resources to education if they were linked directly to student choice. The relative merits of subsidisation of institutions versus the subsidisation of individuals has been much debated in the literature on the economics of education. Broadly speaking, the outcome was that those who believed that ultimate decisions about the pattern of educational provision should be determined by the consumers (students and their families) agreed to disagree with those who believe that ultimate decisions about educational provision require the professional judgement of teachers and administrators.

An educational market place in which the survival of schools and colleges depends on their success in attracting students has the potential political advantage of providing apparently objective answers to the politically hazardous question of which institutions should close and which should prosper. Questions that are ultimately unanswerable about the real worth of different institutions are left in the hands of millions of individual consumers taking marginal decisions rather than depending upon single non-marginal judgements of policy-makers who may be swayed by a variety of political considerations.

The general case against politico-bureaucratic decision-making in the provision of public education has been put eloquently by Crewe and Young (1977).

> "The economics of politics emphasises that decisions in the public sector can by no means be guaranteed to be in the public interest - whatever meaning may be given to this very elusive concept. The British system of representative democracy, for example, has elections at intervals of several years, with choice between the packages of policies on a wide range of issues offered by two major parties ... Under these circumstances even a vote maximising politician may have considerable discretion to pursue policies which, taken individually, would not necessarily have the support of the majority of voters.
> "Besides, many important decisions are taken in practice by administrators even less responsive to the preferences of individual citizens ; not only do they have tenure, but their relative monopoly of information is an important source of discretionary power, and the theory suggests that it will be in their interests to use this power to maximise the size of the "bureaucracies" to which they belong.
> "Partly because of the lack of widely available information on policy issues, it is further to be expected that pressure groups will exert an influence on decisions disproportionate to their members. Thus in higher education, teachers and students will have a strong incentive to organise to press for more resources to be allocated to them ; and their relatively small numbers will make the task of organisation easier. By contrast, the far more numerous taxpayers amongst whom the costs of higher education will ultimately be spread have, individually, a lesser incentive to resist such a policy ; the task of organising them is far more difficult, and they generally lack independent information on the true merits of the claims."

Apart from such fundamental disfunctions there are more practical problems of bureaucracy. There are many steps between a national policy decision to deploy educational decisions in a particular way and the actual expenditure on the school where teachers meet pupils. Unless each step is understood there is a high probability that policy outcomes will differ considerably from policy intentions. It has been shown in the first section of this chapter that the outcomes of educational policy during the period of expansion were often very different from the expectations. It may even be that the disappointment of these expectations is one of the main reasons for the present lower political priority accorded to education.

If unintended outcomes can have harmful effects when resources are increasing, they are an even greater danger when resources are severely limited.

VII. PLANNING QUALITATIVE CHANGE

Educational planning in the past has been essentially quantitative. In some respects this is paradoxical, since most educationalists are more concerned with qualitative issues. Possibly one of the main reasons for the unintended outcomes of many educational plans has been their concentration upon the easily quantifiable aspects of an activity whose most important aspects cannot be readily converted into numbers and costs. If it is to be fully effective in the 1980s educational planning should comprise qualitative as well as quantitative aspects.

The term qualitative in this context is not easy to define. Educational planning must continue to be concerned primarily with issues relating to the allocation of resources, and this implies quantitative evaluation. To claim, therefore, that educational planners must be more concerned with the qualitative aspects of education is not to argue for decision-making based simply upon competing value judgements. Methods must be found of bringing matters relating to the content and methods of educational provision into a systematic framework alongside more obviously quantifiable features such as pupil numbers and costs.

Manpower planning is an example. In the past it has been essentially a matter of attempting to estimate the number of employment opportunities available for various categories of qualified manpower. Thus forecasts are made of the "necessary" (or "desirable", or "optimum") output of doctors, teachers, engineers, and so on. Sophisticated methodologies have been developed for relating the apparent needs of employment to the necessary outputs of the educational system and hence the required number of students and expenditure on education. It cannot be claimed that these attempts have been conspicuously successful in OECD countries, and even in Eastern Europe where manpower planning has been much more widely used there is evidence of mismatching between requirements and output. Employers have frequently expressed criticisms, not so much with respect to the _number_ of engineers, scientists and other qualified manpower being produced, but rather about the _quality_ of the output. In such criticisms quality appears to have three distinct meanings. First is a concern about the general _intellectual_ capabilities of school and university leavers ; second is the view that their _range of knowledge_ is not sufficient to prepare them for employment ; and third are complaints about their _attitudes_ to employment. Educational planning should be concerned not only with the numbers of students undertaking various specialist courses but also with the content of those courses, the combinations of courses taken by individual students and the quality of the teaching they receive during their courses.

Similar considerations apply if the basic criterion of educational provision is individual or social demand. Here also, educational plans have consisted mainly of forecasts of the number of places needed to meet various criteria of social or private demand. There has been little concern with the quality of the educational experience of pupils and students. Some of the current reluctance of young people to take advantage of the educational opportunities available to them may stem from the fact that the education they have already experienced does not live up to their legitimate expectations.

Educational improvements in the 1980s are likely to have to be made against a background of little or no quantitative growth in student numbers and resources. Any improvements will have to be achieved largely by redeploying resources within the educational system so that outputs are improved with a given quantity of inputs.

Planning involves the establishment of targets in relation to overall political objectives, the specification of these targets in operational terms (which invariably involves some form of quantification) and the development of appropriate indicators for monitoring progress towards the objective. There certainly exist indicators of the qualitative performance of many educational activities, examination results being the most obvious. There are, however, intrinsic problems in using measures that were intended to assess the performance of individual pupils as indicators of the performance of the institutions and systems to which they belong. The need for qualitative improvement in a period of severely limited resources makes it essential to seek progress in this area.

Two pressing tasks for educational planners are to devise ways of bringing educational objectives other than student numbers and costs into a decision-making framework so that the different objectives can be compared with one another, and to develop indicators of qualitative performance so that progress towards objectives can be monitored. This is a large task but it is not completely intractable. For example, educational researchers are beginning to undertake empirical observation based on analytical models which quantify the effects of different teaching styles and different school environments.

VIII. PROBLEMS OF UNCERTAINTY

An issue whose importance is insufficiently appreciated outside theoretical literature arises from the well-known fact that the future is uncertain. Any attempt at rational decision-making involves a prediction of the probability of various outcomes if a particular policy intervention is made, a prediction of the outcome if that intervention is not made and a comparison of the costs and benefits of each. That such processes are at present carried out in a largely intuitive way by educational planners and policy makers does not lessen their importance, nor the need to make such considerations explicit wherever possible.

In order to understand the apparent perversity of many political and bureaucratic decisions, it is necessary to appreciate that there is an intrinsic asymmetry between the rewards for being right and the penalties for being wrong. In public sector decision-making it is at least as important to guard against the possibility of being wrong as it is to take that course of action which would be best if the outcomes of policy decisions and future constraints on policy were known with certainty.

Uncertainty is of various kinds, but for educational planners the most widespread results from imperfect knowledge of the system. Knowledge of essential relationships within the educational system (for example, how different teaching inputs affect educational outputs) is scanty, and knowledge of the relationships between the educational system and the rest of the socio-economic system (for example, how does a university degree in humanities influence a person's performance in the job market) is even scantier. The unintended effects of educational policies have been mentioned several times in this chapter, and there can be little doubt that disappointment about the outcomes of educational policies in the past helps to account for the relatively low priority devoted to education in the political processes of many OECD countries today.

In general there are two ways of dealing with the problem of uncertainty. The first is to reduce it as much as possible by undertaking research into the key relationships within the educational system and other social systems, while the second is to adopt planning and policy strategies that minimise the ill-effects of "incorrect predictions". Research programmes aimed at reducing such uncertainties through studies of input-output relationships within educational processes should have a high priority. Such research is likely to be more sharply focused if it is located within a systematic planning activity which can indicate where the potential benefits of reducing uncertainty are likely to be greatest. This does not mean that the research needs to be done within national ministries of education, or that the specification of the research programme can ignore well-informed advice from research workers about where progress is most likely to be possible. Any programme of educational policy research must be to some extent a compromise between what is useful and what is feasible.

It would, therefore, be unduly optimistic to expect rapid improvements. The relationships involved are complex and few reliable methodological tools exist. Even in the long term there is no possibility that our understanding of the relationships in social systems will have the degree of precision which would permit the construction of finely tuned educational planning models analogous to the engineering machinery made possible by discoveries in the natural sciences.

A substantial part of the uncertainty inherent in educational planning must, therefore, continue to be treated as inescapable, and various "coping" strategies will have to be adopted. Such strategies include the frequent revision of forecasts, the maintenance of as much freedom of action as possible for as long as possible and the creation of flexible institutional arrangements. These are all essentially empirical palliatives and considerable work needs to be done in the direction of developing criteria for optimising their use : How frequently should forecasts be revised ? What criteria can be established for determining the optimal length of time to delay decisions in specific circumstances ? What kind of flexibility is appropriate in particular cases ?

There is, as has been indicated above, a cost-benefit dimension to many of these considerations. For example, the case against manpower planning is in the last analysis based on uncertainty. The nature of free market economies is such that it is impossible to make forecasts with any reasonable degree of accuracy of the likely employment opportunities for different kinds of specialists for more than a very short period in the future. This is supplemented by uncertainty about how individual young people will develop and what their individual strengths and interests will be when they enter the adult world. The best strategy, therefore, appears to be to provide a general educational background for as long as possible and to delay selection and specific training until the students have entered or are about to enter employment.

There are, however, quite definite costs associated with such a strategy, which can be made clear by considering a somewhat unrealistic example at the other end of the spectrum. If it were possible to ascertain early in a child's life exactly what his intellectual and physical development and adult interests would be, and if it were known for certain what jobs would be available in the economy during the next half century, it would clearly be in the interests of both the child and the economy to prepare him or her for specific jobs from a very early age. Precisely this kind of practice is widespread in selecting young people for training for high level performance in sporting and cultural activities. For most practical purposes, however, the question is not whether to provide all young people with a completely general education till their early twenties or whether to train them for specific jobs from the age of five onwards, but rather at what points the emphasis should shift from broad preparation for a wide range of adult roles to specific preparation for the particular adult roles that particular young people will be filling. The debate about the advantages of specialist versus general education in secondary and higher education can readily be fitted into such an analytical framework. The general solution is that the richer the country is, the more it can afford to extend the period of general education given to its young people ; while the greater the degree of certainty about the potential capabilities and interests of young people and the opportunities likely to be available to them, the more justified it is to provide them with an education and training suitable to their capabilities and interests from an early age. In the context of the 1980s, financial stringency and reduced employment opportunities point in the direction of increased vocationalisation of secondary and higher education, while the likelihood of rapid technological change and increased uncertainty about the value of earlier educational achievement in predicting future performance suggest emphasis on general preparation in a wide range of skills.

A different kind of uncertainty results from the growing, and welcome, trend towards wider participation in educational decision-making. The difficulty is that the wider is public participation and the earlier it takes place in the planning process, the easier it is for vested interests to organise opposition to any change that appears likely to damage their interests. This would not necessarily be harmful if all interest groups were equally powerful, since they would in effect cancel each other out and the outcome would be fairly readily predictable. However, some interest groups are more powerful than others ; but, more important, the general nature of many educational policy decisions is such that the social costs are concentrated while the benefits are diffused. There is thus likely to be organised opposition to almost any change, particularly of the type that is likely to occur in the context of falling enrolments and financial stringency. To the economist the analogy is between the perfect competition model and the oligopolistic competition model. In the former case, where there are large numbers of equally powerless individual consumers and producers, the outcome is, at least in theory, predictable. In the latter case of oligopoly (and/or oligopsony), where there are few producers (or consumers) competing with each other, the outcome is completely unpredictable, depending upon the relative power of the different groups, the degree of information available to them and chance factors such as who establishes a niche in the market first. Economic planning under conditions of oligopoly is an entirely different matter from economic planning where the structure of markets corresponds more closely to the perfect competition model. So educational planning in a world of pressure groups is a far more indeterminate affair than planning in a world of atomistic students and teachers and employers.

IX. A FINAL RECOMMENDATION

In this chapter an attempt has been made to outline a possible programme of work for national educational planners that will help them to define the problems involved in planning the re-allocation of educational resources in the likely circumstances of the 1980s. The environment in which planning will take place is likely to be one of falling numbers of young people, shortage of public funds and rapid technological change. Planners will have to face such problems in a system whose basic structural relationships are little understood. Uncertainty about the outcomes of policy interventions will be intensified by the activities of interest groups which will use whatever political pressure they can exert to divert resources towards their particular areas of concern.

Particular problems will be created by the declining career prospects of teachers and the excess capacity in school buildings. There are likely to be pressures for an increased vocationalisation of education at the upper levels from both students and governments, and this may well conflict with accepted liberal ideas about the fundamental purposes of education. If improvement through innovation is to take place, it will happen for the most part only by redeploying resources from some educational activities to others. This will mean that nearly all planning decisions become politically charged policy decisions, and successful planning will need to be even more closely integrated than previously into the policy-making process.

A concluding recommendation is that some educational planning activities, at least, need to be undertaken in centres of expertise that are independent of government. The case for this is two-fold. On the one hand, the essential complexity of most current social issues gives inordinate power and influence to those with access to detailed information and the ability to process it. Often it is only governments that have such power. Independent centres of technical expertise outside government can help other interests to engage in policy debates on less uninformed terms.

It is not only a matter of redressing the balance with respect to access to complex information. Governmental bodies are often inhibited from public discussion of policy options lest these be taken as reflecting policy commitments that may well be subsequently used to oppose the government by interest groups and opposition political parties. Independent groups of planning advisers need have no such inhibitions. Policy options can be presented for public discussion on the basis of the best available current information with no implication of government commitment. Thus public participation in the planning process can be facilitated while governments retain their freedom of action to respond flexibly to changing circumstances. Informed debate about educational planning strategies can take place amongst all the interest groups while democratically elected governments retain their freedom of action to determine their policy tactics.

REFERENCES

Crewe M.A. and Young A. *Paying by Degrees*, Institute of Economic Affairs, London, 1977.

Fulton O., Gordon A., Williams G. *Manpower Planning for Higher Education Planning*, I.L.O., Geneva, 1980.

Halsey A.H., Heath A.F., Ridge J.M. *Origins and Destinations*, Clarendon Press, 1980.

Jencks C. *Inequality*, Basic Books, 1971.

OECD, 1967. *Methods and Statistical Needs for Educational Planning*.

OECD, 1970. *Occupational and Educational Structures of the Labour Force and Levels of Economic Development*.

OECD, 1971. *Educational Policies for the 1970s*.

OECD, 1973. *Recurrent Education : A Strategy for Lifelong Learning*.

Williams G. "Educational Planning Past, Present and Future", in *Education Policy Bulletin*, Winter 1979.

OECD SALES AGENTS
DÉPOSITAIRES DES PUBLICATIONS DE L'OCDE

ARGENTINA – ARGENTINE
Carlos Hirsch S.R.L., Florida 165, 4° Piso (Galería Guemes)
1333 BUENOS AIRES, Tel. 33.1787.2391 y 30.7122

AUSTRALIA – AUSTRALIE
Australia and New Zealand Book Company Pty. Ltd.,
10 Aquatic Drive, Frenchs Forest, N.S.W. 2086
P.O. Box 459, BROOKVALE, N.S.W. 2100

AUSTRIA – AUTRICHE
OECD Publications and Information Center
4 Simrockstrasse 5300 BONN. Tel. (0228) 21.60.45
Local Agent/Agent local :
Gerold and Co., Graben 31, WIEN 1. Tel. 52.22.35

BELGIUM – BELGIQUE
CCLS – LCLS
19, rue Plantin, 1070 BRUXELLES. Tel. 02.521.04.73

BRAZIL – BRÉSIL
Mestre Jou S.A., Rua Guaipa 518,
Caixa Postal 24090, 05089 SAO PAULO 10. Tel. 261.1920
Rua Senador Dantas 19 s/205-6, RIO DE JANEIRO GB.
Tel. 232.07.32

CANADA
Renouf Publishing Company Limited,
2182 ouest, rue Ste-Catherine,
MONTRÉAL, Qué. H3H 1M7. Tel. (514)937.3519
OTTAWA, Ont. K1P 5A6, 61 Sparks Street

DENMARK – DANEMARK
Munksgaard Export and Subscription Service
35, Nørre Søgade
DK 1370 KØBENHAVN K. Tel. +45.1.12.85.70

FINLAND – FINLANDE
Akateeminen Kirjakauppa
Keskuskatu 1, 00100 HELSINKI 10. Tel. 65.11.22

FRANCE
Bureau des Publications de l'OCDE,
2 rue André-Pascal, 75775 PARIS CEDEX 16. Tel. (1) 524.81.67
Principal correspondant :
13602 AIX-EN-PROVENCE : Librairie de l'Université.
Tel. 26.18.08

GERMANY – ALLEMAGNE
OECD Publications and Information Center
4 Simrockstrasse 5300 BONN Tel. (0228) 21.60.45

GREECE – GRÈCE
Librairie Kauffmann, 28 rue du Stade,
ATHÈNES 132. Tel. 322.21.60

HONG-KONG
Government Information Services,
Publications/Sales Section, Baskerville House,
2/F., 22 Ice House Street

ICELAND – ISLANDE
Snaebjörn Jónsson and Co., h.f.,
Hafnarstraeti 4 and 9, P.O.B. 1131, REYKJAVIK.
Tel. 13133/14281/11936

INDIA – INDE
Oxford Book and Stationery Co. :
NEW DELHI-1, Scindia House. Tel. 45896
CALCUTTA 700016, 17 Park Street. Tel. 240832

INDONESIA – INDONÉSIE
PDIN-LIPI, P.O. Box 3065/JKT, JAKARTA, Tel. 583467

IRELAND – IRLANDE
TDC Publishers – Library Suppliers
12 North Frederick Street, DUBLIN 1 Tel. 744835-749677

ITALY – ITALIE
Libreria Commissionaria Sansoni :
Via Lamarmora 45, 50121 FIRENZE. Tel. 579751/584468
Via Bartolini 29, 20155 MILANO. Tel. 365083
Sub-depositari :
Ugo Tassi
Via A. Farnese 28, 00192 ROMA. Tel. 310590
Editrice e Libreria Herder,
Piazza Montecitorio 120, 00186 ROMA. Tel. 6794628
Costantino Ercolano, Via Generale Orsini 46, 80132 NAPOLI. Tel. 405210
Libreria Hoepli, Via Hoepli 5, 20121 MILANO. Tel. 865446
Libreria Scientifica, Dott. Lucio de Biasio "Aeiou"
Via Meravigli 16, 20123 MILANO Tel. 807679
Libreria Zanichelli
Piazza Galvani 1/A, 40124 Bologna Tel. 237389
Libreria Lattes, Via Garibaldi 3, 10122 TORINO. Tel. 519274
La diffusione delle edizioni OCSE è inoltre assicurata dalle migliori librerie nelle città più importanti.

JAPAN – JAPON
OECD Publications and Information Center,
Landic Akasaka Bldg., 2-3-4 Akasaka,
Minato-ku, TOKYO 107 Tel. 586.2016

KOREA – CORÉE
Pan Korea Book Corporation,
P.O. Box n° 101 Kwangwhamun, SÉOUL. Tel. 72.7369

LEBANON – LIBAN
Documenta Scientifica/Redico,
Edison Building, Bliss Street, P.O. Box 5641, BEIRUT.
Tel. 354429 – 344425

MALAYSIA – MALAISIE
University of Malaya Co-operative Bookshop Ltd.
P.O. Box 1127, Jalan Pantai Baru
KUALA LUMPUR. Tel. 51425, 54058, 54361

THE NETHERLANDS – PAYS-BAS
Staatsuitgeverij, Verzendboekhandel,
Chr. Plantijnstraat 1 Postbus 20014
2500 EA S-GRAVENHAGE. Tel. nr. 070.789911
Voor bestellingen: Tel. 070.789208

NEW ZEALAND – NOUVELLE-ZÉLANDE
Publications Section,
Government Printing Office Bookshops:
AUCKLAND: Retail Bookshop: 25 Rutland Street,
Mail Orders: 85 Beach Road, Private Bag C.P.O.
HAMILTON: Retail Ward Street,
Mail Orders, P.O. Box 857
WELLINGTON: Retail: Mulgrave Street (Head Office),
Cubacade World Trade Centre
Mail Orders: Private Bag
CHRISTCHURCH: Retail: 159 Hereford Street,
Mail Orders: Private Bag
DUNEDIN: Retail: Princes Street
Mail Order: P.O. Box 1104

NORWAY – NORVÈGE
J.G. TANUM A/S Karl Johansgate 43
P.O. Box 1177 Sentrum OSLO 1. Tel. (02) 80.12.60

PAKISTAN
Mirza Book Agency, 65 Shahrah Quaid-E-Azam, LAHORE 3.
Tel. 66839

PHILIPPINES
National Book Store, Inc.
Library Services Division, P.O. Box 1934, MANILA.
Tel. Nos. 49.43.06 to 09, 40.53.45, 49.45.12

PORTUGAL
Livraria Portugal, Rua do Carmo 70-74,
1117 LISBOA CODEX. Tel. 360582/3

SINGAPORE – SINGAPOUR
Information Publications Pte Ltd,
Pei-Fu Industrial Building,
24 New Industrial Road N° 02-06
SINGAPORE 1953, Tel. 2831786, 2831798

SPAIN – ESPAGNE
Mundi-Prensa Libros, S.A.
Castelló 37, Apartado 1223, MADRID-1. Tel. 275.46.55
Libreria Bosch, Ronda Universidad 11, BARCELONA 7.
Tel. 317.53.08, 317.53.58

SWEDEN – SUÈDE
AB CE Fritzes Kungl Hovbokhandel,
Box 16 356, S 103 27 STH, Regeringsgatan 12,
DS STOCKHOLM. Tel. 08/23.89.00
Subscription Agency/Abonnements:
Wennergren-Williams AB,
Box 13004, S104 25 STOCKHOLM.
Tel. 08/54.12.00

SWITZERLAND – SUISSE
OECD Publications and Information Center
4 Simrockstrasse 5300 BONN. Tel. (0228) 21.60.45
Local Agents/Agents locaux
Librairie Payot, 6 rue Grenus, 1211 GENÈVE 11. Tel. 022.31.89.50

TAIWAN – FORMOSE
Good Faith Worldwide Int'l Co., Ltd.
9th floor, No. 118, Sec. 2,
Chung Hsiao E. Road
TAIPEI. Tel. 391.7396/391.7397

THAILAND – THAILANDE
Suksit Siam Co., Ltd., 1715 Rama IV Rd,
Samyan, BANGKOK 5. Tel. 2511630

TURKEY – TURQUIE
Kültur Yayinlari Is-Türk Ltd. Sti.
Atatürk Bulvari No : 77/B
KIZILAY/ANKARA. Tel. 17 02 66
Dolmabahce Cad. No : 29
BESIKTAS/ISTANBUL. Tel. 60 71 88

UNITED KINGDOM – ROYAUME-UNI
H.M. Stationery Office, P.O.B. 276,
LONDON SW8   5DT. Tel. (01) 622.3316, or
49 High Holborn, LONDON WC1V 6 HB (personal callers)
Branches at: EDINBURGH, BIRMINGHAM, BRISTOL,
MANCHESTER, BELFAST.

UNITED STATES OF AMERICA – ÉTATS-UNIS
OECD Publications and Information Center, Suite 1207,
1750 Pennsylvania Ave., N.W. WASHINGTON, D.C.20006 – 4582
Tel. (202) 724.1857

VENEZUELA
Libreria del Este, Avda. F. Miranda 52, Edificio Galipan,
CARACAS 106. Tel. 32.23.01/33.26.04/31.58.38

YUGOSLAVIA – YOUGOSLAVIE
Jugoslovenska Knjiga, Terazije 27, P.O.B. 36, BEOGRAD.
Tel. 621.992

Les commandes provenant de pays où l'OCDE n'a pas encore désigné de dépositaire peuvent être adressées à :
OCDE, Bureau des Publications, 2, rue André-Pascal, 75775 PARIS CEDEX 16.
Orders and inquiries from countries where sales agents have not yet been appointed may be sent to:
OECD, Publications Office, 2, rue André-Pascal, 75775 PARIS CEDEX 16.

66899-10-1983

OECD PUBLICATIONS, 2, rue André-Pascal, 75775 PARIS CEDEX 16 - No. 42581 1983
PRINTED IN FRANCE
(91 83 05 1) ISBN 92-64-12500-0